PUBLIC PLACES
AND
PRIVATE SPACES

PUBLIC PLACES
AND
PRIVATE SPACES

The Psychology of Work, Play,
and Living Environments

ALBERT MEHRABIAN

Basic Books Inc., Publishers

NEW YORK

Library of Congress Cataloging in Publication Data

Mehrabian, Albert.
   Public Places and Private Spaces

   Bibliography:
   Includes indexes.
   1.   Environmental psychology.   2.   Architecture—Psy-
chological aspects.   I.   Title.
BF353.M4   155.9   75-36775
ISBN: 0-465-06776-X

Dedicated to

My Beloved Romantic, Humanist, Altruist,

and Bon Vivant Uncle Amir

Preface

IN THE NEXT few decades, environmental psychology can make an enormous contribution to our lives. Environmental psychologists already know a good deal about what can be done to improve the social and physical settings in which people sleep, eat, work, travel, make love, recover from an illness, get drunk, and otherwise live their lives. But this knowledge is not readily accessible to most people.

Information about environmental psychology is to be found in the various professional journals; however, it is often fragmented, encrusted with statistics, or expressed in specialized language. There are occasional pieces in popular magazines or Sunday supplements, but these usually record the insightful solutions of interior designers or architects to a relatively limited set of environmental factors— converted farmhouses, inflatable plastic homes, or energy-conserving advantages of dome-shaped structures. And then there has been an enormous flood of writing on The Environment. Sometimes the "environmentalists" are talking about the web of natural systems which sustains all life on our planet. All too often, however, they are really talking about pretty green trees, a hatred of the automobile, or an antiquarian interest in animals they've never had to share territory with.

When environmental psychologists talk of environments, they can mean a cocktail party, your apartment building, a park, the clothes on your back, a retirement community, or a kitchen. Anywhere you are, anything within sensory range, constitutes an environment which can be described accurately and succinctly. Certain guidelines have emerged that should enable people to relate the nature of particular environments to their own feelings and behavior—to figure out the different environments in which they find themselves, and to understand why some environments make them feel good or bad, excited or bored, tense or comfortable. I've written this book partly in order to set forth these general guidelines in a compact and orderly way. I hope that readers will also find them practical tools for understanding, and doing something about, the unverbalized though persistent environmental problems which confront us in our daily lives.

I've organized this book into seven main sections. The first section introduces the reader to some of the terms environmental psychologists have devised in order to practice their science. These terms are almost invariably polysyllabic and cold sounding. But they are useful terms, somewhat more sharply defined than *paranoid* or *Capricorn*, and even more descriptive or meaningful. The following six sections deal in concrete detail with increasingly larger environments, beginning with our bodies and ending with the communal environments of which all people are willing or unwilling members.*

Environmental psychology is to a certain extent about manipulation, which has become a very bad-sounding word with connotations of *1984* or at least of petty calculation. But it is well to recall that the Latin root of this word is *manus,* "hand." It is perhaps significant that there are very few English idioms in which the word *hand* has a negative connotation. To give someone a hand, for example, is to approach openly and defenselessly, to offer help, or to applaud. What we can touch with our hands we can in some way control, transform, or truly know. And it is in this positive sense that we are now able to manipulate our environments and as a result manipulate ourselves and other people. Human beings can learn to manipulate their environments in order to make themselves happier, more comfortable, freer, and more productive, and I cannot see anything inhumane or sinister in this.

Several students and colleagues have helped to make this book

---

* For those who wish to explore various topics in greater depth, a list of suggested readings follows each chapter. However, such outside readings are not necessary for comprehension of the text. Suggested readings are cited by giving author name(s) followed by year of publication. References at the end of the book are listed alphabetically by author names.

possible. James A. Russell, one of my students, worked with me on environmental problems over the past several years and I have drawn upon many of our findings. I am grateful to Carol Falender and Herb Reich, who have read and provided useful comments and additions to the various chapters and to Tim Lambert for the drawings. I also owe a very special debt of gratitude to Malcolm Jensen for his editorial assistance.

A.M.

Beverly Hills, California

Contents

Contents

Part Three

RESIDENTIAL ENVIRONMENTS

Part Four

WORK ENVIRONMENTS

Part Five

THERAPEUTIC ENVIRONMENTS

Part Six

PLAY ENVIRONMENTS

Contents

Part Seven

COMMUNAL ENVIRONMENTS

EPILOGUE

PART ONE

BASICS

1

What Is Environmental Psychology?

CONSIDER your living room as an environment. What are some of the elements or variables that determine what kind of room it is? There is furniture of varying styles, colors, and degrees of comfort; all of it can be arranged in many formal or informal ways. There is the color scheme, which can range from dim to very bright and highly saturated. There might be many plants, a profusion of mirrors and paintings, or none at all. There may be a piano, a stereo, or a TV, and any of these could be in use or not. The temperature of this room could be anything from freezing to broiling. The windows might be open, in which case there may or may not be sunlight, a breeze, odors, or traffic noise entering the room. The main view might be the Pacific Ocean, an airshaft, a garden, or a freeway. There might be no one in this room, a few people quietly conversing, or a large party going on.

How can we describe such a room? One way to do it would be to make an immensely long and detailed catalogue of every single item in the room and its spatial relationship to every other item, and then add variables like brightness, humidity, noise level, temperature, odor, and so on. Assuming that this list could be an exhaustive one, it could only be accurate for a given moment in time. The room could be rearranged, tidied up, or a new chair added, and its whole complexion would change. Add a few people, turn on or turn off a few lights, and the catalogue would have to be revised. If one were to try to describe many places in this way, the cataloguing would amount to a labor worthy of Hercules and Sisyphus combined.

But describing this living room, with its immense number of changing features and stimuli, is precisely the sort of task environmental psychologists undertake. And the fact that they can do it—if need be in one word—means that environmental psychologists are doing something that no other kind of psychologist does, namely, to describe environments as wholes.

This is what distinguishes environmental psychology from the other branches of psychology. The various psychological disciplines allow one to predict what effect a single variable or cluster of like variables will have on a particular kind of behavior—fantasy, memory, learning, complex problem-solving, or socializing. These disciplines do not however try to predict the collective effect of all the stimuli in a room upon different people's feelings and behavior. More importantly, they are not equipped to compare a living room with a vest-pocket park and a classroom as whole environments; and they don't predict which people will find these different environments most suitable for studying French, reading a science fiction novel, or taking a nap.

Aside from the necessity for a taxonomy of places, environmental psychologists require a corresponding taxonomy of people. The same environment affects different people in different ways. Some of the reasons for this are the differences in the physiological makeup of individuals; in attitudes toward, and past experiences with, various places; in familiarity and sophistication in dealing with places; and in the ways people cognitively process the information they receive from their surroundings. This is how a very posh restaurant may intimidate some people, be relaxing to others, or even cause boorishness in a few. Clearly, environmental psychologists have been challenged to develop a succinct, comprehensive method to describe differences in individuals' reactions to places, and our approach will include some of the highlights of these differences.

With their tools, environmental psychologists can tell you, for example, whether people who gather to socialize in a given living room will tend to be subdued, stiff, noncommital, or anxious to leave, or whether they will tend to be outgoing, friendly, relaxed, or eager to remain and have a good time. They can make fairly accurate predictions not only about the group as a whole but also about the individuals who comprise it. They can predict whether a particular person, depending on the kind of day he's had, will become either extremely nervous or bored in this room, or will try to make the room a more suitable environment by smoking heavily, drinking too much, moving around a lot, walking to a less crowded part of the room, starting an argument, or suggesting a game of strip poker.

Environmental psychologists can make such evaluations and predictions because they've developed a system for doing so based on massive amounts of data. This system, like a good blackjack system, is built not only upon a huge number of observations but also upon a few simple do-or-don't rules, a handful of crucial assumptions, and a few handy or inspired generalizations.

One of the main generalizations is this: people's reactions to all environments fall into one of two main categories, *approach* or *avoidance*. These categories are broad, of course, and include many different kinds of behavior. An extreme example of approach might be the case of a man, who has accidentally broken his leg in a hiking expedition, trying to make his way back to the nearest town. He is physically moving toward the town and has in fact summoned up his last reserves of strength to do so. An example of extreme avoidance would be the infantryman fleeing the noise, confusion, and terror of combat. He is physically moving away from an intolerable environment and only the application of overwhelming force could prevent him from doing so.

But approach and avoidance mean more than just physically moving toward or away from an environment. These terms are also used to characterize behavior in environments from which a person cannot physically remove himself. If, for example, you place a person all by himself in an unfamiliar environment, he may or may not *explore* it—look around eagerly, stroll about, pick up objects and examine them, and in general try to become intimate with the place. Exploration is a form of approach behavior, and the degree to which a person or laboratory animal explores a new environment can be measured quantitatively. Lack of exploration—as when a person walks into a waiting room in an office building, hospital, or bus station and immediately takes a seat and stares up at the wall, pulls out a book from his briefcase, or goes to sleep—is a form of avoidance behavior, even though the person may have chosen to enter the environment and to remain in it.

Another measure of the degree to which one approaches or avoids an environment is *affiliation*, or one's reaction to other people in the environment. Approach behavior or positive affiliation means that a person attempts to enter into communication with others by establishing eye contact, smiling, nodding, greeting, helping someone with a package, or starting a conversation. Avoidance behavior or negative affiliation is just the opposite: others are ignored, eye contact is avoided, physical distance from people is increased, the body is turned away from them, and conversational attempts are rebuffed.

Performance, or how well one does a particular task, is also a measure of approach or avoidance. Let's say you have someone do one of those jobs experimental psychologists make up: judging the duration of a sound signal, fitting blocks together, solving abstract puzzles, or remembering a list of nonsense syllables. Suppose his score is average. If you then ask him to do a similar task but change the environment so that he scores way above average, this means you have managed to give that environment an improved approach aspect, at least in relation to the task. Conversely, if you change the environment so that he scores considerably below average, then you have given the environment an avoidance aspect that expresses itself as deteriorated performance.

What is an optimum environment for the performance of one task or activity may of course be all wrong for another. A family room with the TV going and the kids playing electronic football may be a suitable environment for rug-hooking or scanning the evening paper, but not for doing your income tax. If you try to do your income tax there, the room will take on a pronounced avoidance aspect, even though it might normally be one in which you take great pleasure. In order to reduce avoidance behavior—making errors in your return or taking twice as long to do it—you'd probably have to change the family room environment by reducing the number and intensity of the stimuli in it. At the very least, the TV would get shut off, the electronic football match would get a change of venue, and sooner or later everybody else would be expelled.

A further generalization about approach or avoidance is that approach behavior, or an environment that causes approach, is usually a positive or desired sort of thing, having to do with movement toward, exploration, friendliness, improved performance, and voiced preference or liking. Conversely, avoidance behavior or an avoidance-causing environment is generally negative, having to do with movement away from, withdrawal, interpersonal coldness, defective performance, and voiced dislike.

There are times of course when we want to produce avoidance behavior and deliberately use an environment in such a way as to make someone uneasy or uncomfortable. We sometimes receive guests we don't really want to entertain in a room that is "cold," make them sit in the least comfortable chairs, or get rid of a houseguest who abhors untidiness by letting the house get messy. But most of the time people create avoidance-causing environments through inadvertence and ignorance: the employer who wants to improve productivity and therefore puts his foot down about the coffee machine, throws the office into an uproar, and costs himself a hundred manhours; the host who wants to give a good party but finds that half his guests leave after an hour; the teacher who wants her students to "get it" but finds that class performance gets worse as the year progresses; the husband or wife who, after looking forward all day to an enjoyable evening, arrives home to bitchiness or weariness. It is fair to say that most people most of the time want to create environments that cause approach behavior but just don't always know how to go about it.

What are some of the factors that lead people to commit themselves inadvertently to the wrong environments? Since we have been lacking an explicit and commonly shared discipline of environmental psychology, people rely on accepted and traditional standards for the designs of their homes, schools, offices, factories, or places of recreation. For example, many living rooms are still furnished much like front parlors or formal sitting rooms, even though few people observe or want the formal "calling" behavior this design elicits. Such traditional standards may have been suited to the times when they were devised, but may be inappropriate for current life styles and changing activity patterns. That is, some of the environmental design failures are due to inappropriate adherence to outmoded standards. But, numerous new settings are created every day by architects and interior designers—professionals who can transcend the constraints of accepted tradition. Why don't such innovations succeed as often as we would like them to? One reason is that the professionals who are even today engaged in the design of our working, living, and recreational spaces operate artistically and intuitively, for the most part, rather than through reliance on well-established psychological realities. An architect may intuitively yet erroneously select a house design which *feels* just right to him, but which may hardly be appropriate for his client who has a different personality or life style. It is not surprising that most of the approaches to design which have achieved fame and influence follow the one-basic-design-for-all formula. Even though such design principles may be suited for some people's personality dispositions or life styles, as we shall see, they can hardly be suited to all.

The many failures in environmental design—whether created by the professional architect or designer or in most cases intuitively selected by the individual himself—can be attributed to simplistic and all-encompassing notions and traditions which fail to draw upon psychological facts to fit persons, their personalities, and their many diverse daily activities, to places. Once a person has inadvertently committed himself to a partially effective living or working space, economic considerations make drastic change difficult. What's more, lacking concrete knowledge of improvements which could result from a more appropriate environment, the individual is hesitant to risk additional expense and effort for elusive gains. And this is why, as in many other realms of life, people continue to live with what is only partially satisfactory, discouraged by the cost, effort, and the risks of drastic experimentation with change.

How, then, can one approach the problem of systematic and efficient design or selection of daily environments? You'll recall I said that the system environmental psychologists have developed contains a number of crucial assumptions. The successful blackjack player, for example, assumes that everybody is operating under the same rules or statistics as himself—he assumes that the house won't cheat. Environmental psychologists make several far-reaching assumptions too.

Perhaps the most controversial of these assumptions has to do with the wellsprings of human behavior. Put bluntly, it is assumed that people's feelings or emotions are what ultimately determine what they do and how they do it. It is also assumed that environments can cause in us feelings of anger, fear, boredom, pleasure, or whatever, and do so regardless of how we think we should feel in such environments; and furthermore, that these feelings will cause us to behave in certain ways, regardless of how we think we should behave. This is not to say that we cannot exercise fairly substantial control over our public behavior. We can, for example, refrain from overt aggression if we are angered. But we cannot usually will our anger to go away, and we cannot entirely mask the countless physiological and behavioral symptoms of anger—everything from increased blood pressure to the tiny verbal and nonverbal signals which invariably accompany a state of anger. Even if one's anger is successfully masked from the untrained or unobservant, there are still gross behavioral differences lurking in the wings. A person who is masking his anger or even denying to himself that he is angry will not behave in ways that are consistent with feelings of pleasure and relaxation. He will not joke and smile, or touch us in an affectionate way.

The second big assumption is that feelings are not mysterious and fuzzy things that must by their very nature elude precise description and quantification. In some cultures, emotions have been considered things that women primarily know about, like preserving raspberries. As a consequence, emotions have sometimes been contrasted with the more "masculine" cognitive abilities or structures like logic, philosophy, analytical methods, mathematical languages, or science. As a result, people have sometimes believed or asserted that feelings are somehow not a fit or manageable subject for scientific examination. But anything that can be manipulated in a fine-tuned way can be described and measured in the same way. If emotions could not be manipulated with some exactitude, our human culture would be entirely devoid of song, poetry, comedy, tragedy, or dance, to say nothing of successful politicians, million-dollar-club salesmen, or great utterances and deeds of profoundly emotional nature—from Leonidas at Thermopylae to the Churchill war speeches to the last Medal-of-Honor performance in Vietnam.

For the moment, then, let me just put the following assumption up front where it can be seen: human emotions are amenable to precise description, quantitative measurement, and statistical analysis. Environmental psychologists working under this assumption have provided a sound descriptive framework for emotions, a framework which will be discussed in some detail in chapter three. This descriptive framework forms one of the crucial elements of the system that has been developed in order to evaluate whole environments and people's reactions to them.

The general framework is organized something like this. A particular environment causes certain emotional reactions in a person. These reactions in turn cause the person to approach or avoid the environment to a greater or lesser degree. By approaching or avoiding the environment in whatever degree, the person introduces some sort of change in it.

I will not stress at this point the effect that people do and can have upon their environments, because most of this book will be devoted to that subject. But I don't want to leave the impression that the system I'm beginning to sketch presupposes a passive or purely reactive role for human beings. Environmental psychologists work with the converse assumption. Human beings have a Promethean gift amounting to genius for deliberately altering their environments, and to deny or minimize this gift is to be ignorant. But this human genius can be more or less informed, more or less disciplined, more or less effective in achieving its goals. And this is what environmental psychology is all about: giving people informed, disciplined, and effective means of coping with what surrounds them.

Suggested Readings

The following are general sources of readings on environmental psychology: Barker (1963), Barker and Schoggen (1973), Brand (1970), Craik (1970), Fiske and Maddi (1961), Friedman and Juhasz (1974), Mehrabian and Russell (1974a), Moos and Insel (1974), Proshansky, Ittelson, and Rivlin (1970), Sommer (1972), Toffler (1970), and Wohlwill and Carson (1972).

2

How Do You Call an Environment?

Scene 1: You have the whole beach to yourself. The sun is warm, but not too hot. The ocean is greenish blue and quiet. The surf rolls in. The sand is clean and white and you can see for miles up and down the coast. The air is fresh and crisp and reminds you of a million seashores. There are a few pale clouds high up. Your transistor radio is playing something gentle and melodious. You stretch back on the blanket, close your eyes, and think vague, warm thoughts.

Scene 2: A mob rushes onto the beach. A helicopter thumps the air overhead. Children scream, dogs run. The sky is full of inky, swirling clouds. Huge waves curl like paws and crash onto the beach. A dozen transistor radios are blaring something loud and different. Huge mounds of kelp pile up on the shore, and flies buzz like bullets past your ears. A fight starts nearby. People are tossing a frisbee back and forth over your blanket. A bedraggled, mud-stained old woman staggers toward your blanket from the left. From the right, a large, well-groomed man in a business suit comes toward you.

HOW WOULD you compare these two beach environments? What happened to change the first into the second? And how would you compare both these environments with, for instance, going to bed with your spouse for the 3,000th night, lunching with old friends in a well-loved restaurant, or doing your Christmas shopping at 6:00 P.M. on the 24th of December?

Environmental psychologists have invented a system to describe and hence compare such varied and dissimilar environments. The keystone of this descriptive system is the concept of *information rate,* or the amount of information contained or perceived in the environment per unit of time. The more information in the form of stimuli that must be processed by the observer, the greater the information rate.

For convenience, I'll refer to the information rate of environments as their *load.* An environment having a high information rate is a *high-load* or *loaded* one. A *low-load* environment is one having a low information rate.

We have developed the following list of descriptive adjective pairs that enable us to rate the load of any given environment: uncertain-certain; varied-redundant; complex-simple; novel-familiar; large scale-small scale; contrasting-similar; dense-sparse; intermittent-continuous; surprising-usual; heterogeneous-homogeneous; crowded-uncrowded; asymmetrical-symmetrical; immediate-distant; moving-still; rare-common; random-patterned; and improbable-probable.

An environment to which one can apply many of the left-hand terms in these adjective pairs has a high load; one that can be described mostly with the right-hand terms is low-load. In other words, environments that are more varied, complex, novel, large scale, contrasting, dense, surprising, heterogeneous, crowded, asymmetrical, moving, rare, random, or improbable have more load.

Let us take one of these adjective pairs, for example, crowded-uncrowded, and see how it works as an environmental descriptor. Twenty-five passengers who have been packed into an elevator will describe it as extremely crowded; the same group scattered about a huge ballroom will describe that place as extremely uncrowded.

Most environments of course include many characteristics which help to determine their respective loads. A man who has ridden the same crowded elevator every morning at 9:20 for ten years, and has shared it mostly with the same bunch of bleary-eyed late risers, will describe his elevator ride as crowded, dense, immediate, moving (high-load descriptors), but also as familiar, probable, and usual (low-load descriptors). If we actually ask him to rate his daily elevator ride on all of the adjective pairs, we will probably get an overall load estimate that is above average for all situations. No matter how many years that man rides that elevator with his cronies, its load is never going to fall to the levels associated with, say, a quiet evening at home and a snooze in his favorite armchair.

At the risk of oversimplification, we might say that environmental load is equivalent to the level of *uncertainty* about what a place is all about or what is happening there.* Alternatively, and for the sake of convenience, we can refer to the load of any environment as a combination of its *novelty* and *complexity*, since each of the descriptors in our list relates to some aspect of these two dimensions.

The novelty of an environment has to do with how well we know it and hence how well we can predict what will happen in it. If a setting is new or unfamiliar, it makes us feel uncertain. We are not sure what it is, what it intends, and how we should react to it. We perceive such an environment to be uncertain, improbable, rare, surprising, or unexpected—it has a high load. Conversely, an environment that is probable, usual, common, or expected will elicit a low level of uncertainty and has a low load.

The complexity of an environment has to do with how many elements, features, or changes it contains. The more elements or changes, the greater the uncertainty and hence the higher the load. Elements that are asymmetrical rather than symmetrical, intermittent rather than continuous, random rather than patterned, in motion rather than at rest, different rather than alike, crowded rather than uncrowded, or close up rather than distant, all have more load.

For example, there is more uncertainty about a moving basketball than a stationary one. Also an utterly blank room containing nothing but basketballs on the floor would be a less complex environment than the same room containing basketballs, ping-pong balls, baseballs, and golf balls. A room containing all these various balls scattered around at random would be a more complex environment than one in which the balls were grouped according to type, spelled out letters, or formed a pattern—one row of golf balls, one row of baseballs, and so on. This is because we feel a greater uncertainty in a random or unpatterned environment and may pay more attention to it in order to discover in it or impose upon it some sort of pattern, regularity, or meaning. When we have succeeded in making a

* To avoid possible confusion due to the common sense meanings of these terms, it is important to clarify the relation between information rate (what we'll be calling load) and uncertainty of situations. The uncertainty we have about the outcome of an event—for instance, whether a basketball will go into the hoop or not—*equals* the amount of information provided by the event after it occurs. Again, as our eyes travel across a painting or a landscape, the uncertainty about what is to come next equals the information provided by what we in fact see next. This is why it is correct to say that a situation has an amount of uncertainty which equals its information—with the two terms simply distinguishing the "before the fact" from the "after the fact," respectively.

complex environment meaningful or patterned, we have not reduced its complexity, but we have made it more familiar or less improbable, and hence have reduced its total load. For example, people often bone up on an opera or play they have not seen before by familiarizing themselves with the plot in the act-by-act summaries provided in the program. They do this because the plot structure represents one of the larger patterns that can give a meaning or form to the events on stage, thereby reducing somewhat the load of a particular performance without in any way reducing its complexity.

People are perhaps the richest single source of uncertainty. This is especially so for strangers, who are unfamiliar and hence to a greater or lesser extent unpredictable or improbable. The more crowded an environment, the heavier its load. If it is crowded with people we don't know, the load is even heavier. People often prefer to go to large parties or the newest in-bars as members of a group, or at least with a companion. Interacting with familiar persons in novel settings helps to reduce the high load and this is the reason why some people don't socialize with strangers at the party or bar until a good deal of time has passed—until the place and its denizens have become more familiar, more predictable.

The factor of distance is also related to the complexity of environmental information. The closer you get to anything, the more you perceive it in detail. A person who is standing thirty feet from you provides less information than someone standing a foot away. In the latter instance, you can smell the person, hear his breathing, accurately gauge his height, weight, and strength in relation to your own, tell if he's wearing a hairpiece, readily determine his mood, or touch him.

In some cases distance may for the sake of convenience be treated as metaphorical distance. That is, if you are extremely close to a person in the sense of depending on him, of being extremely sensitive to minute changes in his mood, or, in short, if you are in love with him, this person will become an extremely complex or high-load stimulus. Anywhere the loved one is, that setting will have a heavy load. Even familiar environments will have an unusually high load, and hence have a different feel. Popular lyrics are written unceasingly about this phenomenon.

Unusual distances can also introduce either complexity or novelty. We are accustomed to viewing environments or environmental features at certain standard distances and in a certain scale. People of northern

European descent sometimes feel vaguely uncertain when talking to people of Mediterranean ancestry, and vice versa; each finds the other standing too close or too far away. We are not accustomed to seeing Campbell's soup cans or comic strip characters three feet high, hence the piquancy of pop art or even of the movie closeup, in which familiar objects become both detailed and huge.

When the factors of novelty and complexity are tallied up, we get a single, reliable measure for any environment, namely, its load. The load of a given environment causes certain emotional reactions in a particular person. These reactions in turn cause the person to approach or avoid the environment.

Let's look back at the two beach scenes using the concept of environmental load. The beach environment in the first scene is not complex. First of all, it is uncrowded. There is only a handful of environmental features: the sun, the salty breeze, the sand, the sea, the sky, a few wispy clouds, some soft and simple music. The scenic vistas are distant ones; the only thing that is close is the music, and that does not seem too close because the volume is down. Perhaps the only way to increase the complexity of this environment would be to peer at the sand very closely, from a distance of about four inches, and attempt to count the grains. There is nothing novel about this environment, assuming for the moment that you have experienced a number of fine, clear summer days at the beach and have been able to find secluded spots when you wanted to. That is, the peaceful beach environment is likely to be a familiar one; you have no reason whatever to expect that the sky will fall, that the sun will go out, or that an automobile or Neptune will charge out of the waves. Thus the low novelty and low complexity of this environment combine to make it one of low load.

Of course, if you had never been to a beach, never seen the ocean, or had never been alone under a broad sky, the unfamiliarity of this environment would be considerably higher. Nevertheless, the low complexity would have an averaging effect on the total load that could be fairly precisely calculated. For very young children the formula is considerably different; the load, even for our tranquil beach environment, is higher. For them, most environments have a fairly high load because things are generally less familiar.

The beach environment in the second scene is loaded. It is complex; there are lots of stimuli, both visual and auditory. Many of the stimuli—the helicopter, the clouds, the children, the dogs, the surf, the frisbee, the flies—are in motion, and hence induce more uncertainty than they would in a state of rest. The environment is crowded, and a number of environmental features are close: the flies are inches away; the frisbee is occasionally close enough for you to notice the direction of spin; the helicopter is a hundred feet up, which is close enough for most people; the people, children, and dogs are on the periphery of your territory, which may not amount to more than a four by seven foot blanket. Even the clouds have the effect of making the sky seem closer. The old crone and the fully dressed man who are moving toward you introduce a strong element of novelty: Who are they? What do they want? Why are they dressed like that? What will they do? In Times Square or on Sunset Strip such persons would still be improbable, but far less so than on a beach, where people usually wear certain outfits, usually do not panhandle, arrest you, shoot you, or serve you with a subpoena.

But how can we predict what effect either of these two environments will have on a given individual? In the first beach environment, one person might fall asleep; another might grow bored unless he had a book to read; another might grow so bored and restless after a few minutes of sunbathing that he'd leap up, dash into the surf, and swim vigorously out toward the horizon. In the second environment, one person might rise in alarm; another might quickly put his things together and walk away; another might start playing with the stray dogs or enter into a conversation with someone on the next blanket; another might join the fight, and someone else might wave an invitation to the old woman.

In order to predict who will feel and do what in these two environments, or in any other environment, we've got to be able to provide a workable description of emotional reactions, and then link specific kinds of emotional reactions to the load of any given environment. And in order to do all this, we've got to move on to the next chapter.

Suggested Readings

The basic mathematical theory bearing on the concept of "information" is given in Attneave (1959), Cherry (1966, chap. 5), and Garner (1962). Mehrabian and Russell (1974b) discussed that theory, its relevance to environmental psychology, and provided experimental data on how to measure the information rate of everyday environments.

3

People and Feelings

CHRISTOPHER AND LINDA SANSUM have been married for five years. They have no children. They are educated and sophisticated, and both have seemingly good jobs.

Linda Sansum pre-tests television commercials. She sets up audience study experiments, interprets the data, and makes recommendations to manufacturers and advertising agencies. Much of her job is performed in a high-load and frequently unpleasant environment. She addresses large groups of people and deals constantly with self-important decision makers or touchy creative types. Linda Sansum dislikes her job and is thinking of quitting even though she makes $22,000 a year.

Christopher Sansum's job is also highly loaded. He is a regional sales manager for a medium-sized educational publisher. He is responsible for the performance of the salesmen in his territory. He must protect them from unreasonable management demands and at the same time encourage them to produce more and more. He must monitor their expense-account statements, which sometimes requires that he question a man's basic honesty and worth. He must maintain good relations with unpredictable and eccentric editors. He must also participate directly in important selling situations in which, for example, an entire state school system is deciding whether to buy his books or somebody else's. Christopher Sansum hates his job but feels he must stay with it until something better turns up.

When Linda and Christopher have both had horrendous days at work, and come home tense and wound up, all they want to do is relax. They have a couple of good stiff drinks right away. Their whole routine can't be interfered with: the stereo goes on—always something like a Mozart horn concerto; they change into familiar old sweaters, pants, and slippers. The seven o'clock news is de rigueur, and they will answer no phone calls during this time. Another drink may be consumed during the news. After the news, they become "human" and will at least talk civilly to each other. They are willing to throw a steak into the pan or call out to the local Chinese restaurant, but won't cook anything more complicated or take any chances with a restaurant they've never been to before. Christopher is especially vehement about maintaining the routine; he likes to have his few drinks, watch TV, and hit the sack at about eleven.

Unfortunately, the working lives of Linda and Christopher Sansum, like those of many active professionals, are stressful. This, as we shall see, explains their environmental preferences when they come home. In addition, Linda and Christopher are different emotional types. They respond somewhat differently to environments having the same pleasantness and load levels. These basic emotional differences will express themselves in seemingly unrelated behavioral realms— sleeping habits, choice of friends, personal tidiness, sexual perform- ance, or the rate at which coffee, alcohol, barbiturates, or cigarettes are consumed.

It is one of the key axioms of our approach that people react to enormously varied environments in terms of a few basic emotional dimensions, and that these basic emotional dimensions can in turn produce enormously varied kinds of behavior. This proposition can be thought of as a kind of input-output system. The *input* or environment end contains literally anything that can be perceived— colors, smells, trees, candlelight, a physical threat, Mondrians, or strippers. The *output* or behavioral-response end includes anything within the human repertory—how you walk, how many drinks you have at a party, whether you express boredom in a given situation by yawning and slouching, whether you take a nap during a flight from Los Angeles to New York, or how well you do on a particular exam.

But the basic emotional dimensions that mediate between the input and output ends, that is between environmental and behavioral diversity, are only three in number. These dimensions are called *arousal- nonarousal, pleasure-displeasure*, and *dominance-submissiveness*.

Arousal means how active, stimulated, excited, frenzied, jittery, wide awake or alert you are. When you are aroused, all sorts of things are happening in your body: your brain puts out a characteristic wave pattern; blood pressure, heart and breathing rates are way up; your muscles are tense; your pupils are dilated; the blood vessels in your skin and extremities contract, so that your skin temperature is lower, you bleed less if cut, and in some cases feel less pain if there is external injury. Your entire bodily system is ready for "fight or flight" —to cope in some vigorous way with an environment demanding extreme approach or avoidance. Conversely, if you are unaroused, you are relaxed, calm, sluggish, dull, sleepy, or inattentive; the parasympathetic nervous system is in control and is producing a slow pulse, muscular relaxation, slow breathing, and so on.

Pleasure means that you are joyful, happy, satisfied, contented, or feel good. Pleasure expresses itself in terms of overt responses that we can instantly recognize in ourselves and in others—smiles, chuckles, meaningful gestures, a warm tone of voice, and positive verbal expressions. Conversely, displeasure means that you are unhappy, annoyed, dissatisfied, melancholic, or feel bad, and the corresponding bodily and verbal expressions are equally clear.

Dominance means that you feel in control—feel influential, unrestricted, important, or in command of the situation. If you feel dominant, you feel free to act in a variety of ways. For example, if you are listening to *La Bohème* in your living room, you will feel free to lounge around in pajamas, fix yourself a drink, light a cigarette, riffle through the libretto, or wave your arms and sing along. If, on the other hand, you are attending a Monday night performance at the Metropolitan Opera, your behavior is greatly circumscribed; there are certain standards of dress and behavior from which a departure will bring painful social disapproval. This is what is meant by feeling submissive; it is a feeling of being awed, guided, circumscribed, or looked after in such a way that one does not or cannot make decisions. You feel submissive at a formal dinner party, bowling alley, Tenderloin bar, Hindu temple, or precinct house if you feel you must abide by its "etiquette" and want to do whatever is right for that particular environment.

The three dimensions of emotional reaction—arousal-nonarousal, pleasure-displeasure, and dominance-submissiveness—form the basic palette from which all feelings are created. Each dimension is independent of the other two. That is, there are environments which can cause radical changes in one feeling dimension without affecting the other two. For example, take anger. When we are angry we are highly aroused, displeased, and have feelings of dominance. In the dominance dimension, we feel that for one reason or another we are free to strike out physically or verbally, that we can control or influence our environment by literally or figuratively blasting it. On the other hand, feelings of fear or anxiety are also high on arousal and displeasure but low on dominance. When we are afraid or anxious we are highly aroused and displeased, but we do not feel free to lash out in one way or another at whatever is causing our arousal and displeasure. Instead, we perceive that we will have no significant or influential effect upon the environment, or that whatever we do will have negative consequences—will cause us to suffer defeat, to be more controlled, or to be more hurt than before.

Indeed, this particular example may be used to explain certain broad-scale social movements. For example, it has been said that the 1950s in America was an anxious time. Many people responded to its uncertainties by trying to conform to acceptable norms, and there were few overtly aggressive or angry responses to arousing and displeasing sociopolitical conditions. In the middle and late 1960s, however, many persons, especially those who perceived themselves to be minority members of society—blacks, homosexuals, blue-collar workers, chicanos, and, to some extent, women—experienced a change in the dominance dimension. Anxiety or fear turned into anger or hostility, and the result was riots, demonstrations, and overt or rhetorical challenges to norms of one sort or another. It might be a fruitful exercise for historians and sociologists to determine what changes in the environment resulted in this shift from high arousal, high displeasure, and submissiveness (anxiety) to high arousal, high displeasure, and dominance (anger). It is clear that most minority groups—including for example the minority that made the American Revolution—at some point undergo such a shift in the dominance dimension. Frantz Fanon, Che Guevara, and other revolutionary theorists throughout the ages have commented upon the "liberating" effects of revolutionary violence. What they are talking about is precisely this shift from a feeling of submissiveness to a feeling of dominance. It gives people a dominant feeling to break a window, to boycott an imperial power's tea or cotton goods, to badger a hated symbol of authority, or to destroy a system. Wise administrators have always sought to reduce the feelings of excessive arousal and dis-pleasure on the part of people for whose behavior they are responsible, and at the same time to increase people's feelings of dominance by giving them a say or access to influence.

Every feeling we have words for—anger, boredom, anxiety, joy, love, contentment, laziness, and so on—may be described as a certain combination of the three dimensions of arousal, pleasure, and dominance. In fact, these common feelings, or even extremely uncommon or complex ones like love-hate or "I don't know what I think," can be statistically correlated to the three dimensions and can thus be expressed as equations.*

The arousal-pleasure-dominance dimensions provide us with a workable grid which can be placed over the buzzing confusion of human emotionality. This emotional grid is at the core of the "flow diagram" of environmental psychology. An environment causes in us an emotional reaction that is a distinctive, measurable combination of arousal, pleasure, and dominance. This emotional reaction in turn causes us to approach or avoid that environment.

Of the three emotional dimensions, arousal has the most direct connection with environmental load. The greater the load, the higher a person's arousal level. An environment that is novel, surprising, crowded, and complex will produce feelings of high arousal. A person in this environment will become stimulated, jittery, alert, and so on, and the physiological indicators like increased heart rate, muscle tension, and lowered skin temperature will be present. Conversely, a low-load environment will cause feelings of low arousal; a person in it will feel relaxed, calm, sluggish, or sleepy.

As we shall see, however, arousal level is not necessarily the sole determinant of approach or avoidance behavior, although it can sometimes be the major factor. Instead, arousal in some particular combination with pleasure and dominance shapes the overall behavioral response.

Figure 1 specifically shows the combined effects of pleasure and arousal on approach-avoidance behavior (leaving aside the possible

---

* We have all experienced occasions when a certain visual image suddenly comes to mind that is totally unrelated to our current activity or environment. We may be discussing a business problem with a colleague and suddenly get a highly detailed and vivid image from the past of friends lounging about in a college dorm. If we consider how we felt just before the flashback, and how we felt *in* the flashback, it turns out that these two feeling states often have a great deal in common. Indeed, it is this common emotional state which links the current situation to a vivid image of a past event.

This also helps explain the *déjà vu* experience. Sometimes we enter a place and have a very strong impression that we've been there before, even though we know for sure that this is impossible. It is possible that *déjà vu* is not "already seen" but rather "already felt." A new environment may create in us an emotional reaction that is nearly identical to one experienced long ago, caused perhaps by a place that was entirely dissimilar in its physical appearance. We remember the old feeling but not the circumstances that caused it. The congruence of old and new feelings gives rise to the odd have-I-been-here-before? experience.

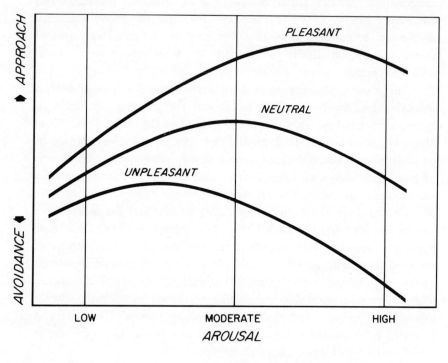

FIGURE 1

contribution of dominance for the moment). Let us start with situations which are neither clearly pleasant nor unpleasant, that is, neutral. Among these, the extremely high-load or low-load situations (meaning those which are extremely arousing or unarousing) are avoided and the moderately loaded ones are maximally preferred. This is the classical "inverted-U" relationship between approach-avoidance and arousal. Situations that produce pleasure are approached more (the upper curve) and those which produce displeasure are avoided more (the lower curve). In addition, the upper curve shows that in pleasant situations we generally expect approach behaviors to increase with the arousing quality of the situation—the greater the arousal, the greater the approach. In contrast, the lower curve shows that in unpleasant situations we generally expect avoidance behaviors to increase with the arousing quality of the situation—the greater the arousal, the greater the avoidance.

Let's take an environment that is high on pleasure and low on arousal. A couple is spending the evening together quietly at home.

One of their friends drops by with a new recording he has just purchased. They begin to interact more with each other and with their friend as they listen to the music. This increase in approach behavior is caused by the higher arousal from the friend's visit and the music. Consider a different situation involving low pleasure and moderate arousal. You are performing an unpleasant task and feel cranky. The increasing noise from a party next door increases your arousal and causes you to avoid doing your task at home. You set it aside or perhaps go somewhere that is less arousing—a library for instance.

An environment that causes a person to feel low arousal, mild pleasure, and some dominance will be perceived as cozy, comfortable, or enjoyable, and the person in it will feel good, relaxed, or content. He will remain in this environment and manifest other kinds of approach behavior, including perhaps a verbal expression of satisfaction. On the other hand, in an environment that causes feelings of low arousal, mild displeasure, and some submissiveness (boredom), the person will manifest avoidance behavior of some sort—staring out the window instead of listening to the teacher, reducing eye contact, leaning away from people in a conversational group, or actually leaving the place when feasible.

But what about individual differences? Don't different people react differently to the same environment? Of course they do, and we shall get to this in a moment. But it is worth emphasizing at this point that people are more like other people than unlike them. The notion that anyone is unique or totally different from everybody else is romanticized wishful thinking. Even cultural differences have sometimes been exaggerated. You can take African mask makers, Fijian basket weavers, and Japanese potters and expose them to paired examples of Western art they have never seen before—classical Greek sculpture, Impressionist or Abstract-Expressionist painting, or whatever—and ask these people to judge which sculpture or painting of any given type or school is the better one. You will find that their judgments are remarkably similar to those of recognized Western experts—artists, gallery owners, graduate students in art history, and so on. Something is crossing significantly different cultures here in a way most people would have said was unlikely.

People are different, of course. The fictitious Sansums I began this chapter with are different in some respects. But Christopher and Linda Sansum are not unique; each, though different from the other, is similar to many other people. That is, each belongs to a large group having similar characteristics or, in short, a type. It has become fashionable to decry all efforts to type people, because sometimes the types or categories to which we assign others are based upon prejudicial notions or imaginary or projected qualities. However part of the time the typing of people results from sharp though possibly untrained observation, and better yet, from research findings.

To type people in our unique framework, we propose that the three basic emotional dimensions also be used to describe different persons' characteristic emotional traits or temperaments. For example, people can have a generally pleasant (or unpleasant) disposition. If you chart various people's dispositions over time, you will find that some consistently feel more pleasant and others consistently feel more unpleasant. No one knows why this should be so, but it is almost certainly something inborn; from the moment of birth some infants smile and chortle a great deal more than others.

The second long-term personality dimension has to do with characteristic levels of dominance or submissiveness. It is likely that this dimension is at least partly influenced by early parental and cultural conditioning, but here again there are also seemingly innate differences. Some babies thump around in the womb like Br'er Rabbit, and others lie relatively still, indicating prenatal tension (arousal plus submissiveness). Most people are remarkably adept at recognizing dominance in others, especially if you ask them to identify leadership qualities, importance in the community, or some other personal or social aspect that doesn't flagrantly suggest a pecking order.

The third and perhaps most important innate personality dimension relates to arousal. The key term here is *stimulus screening*, or how much a person characteristically screens out the less relevant parts of his environment, thereby effectively reducing the environmental load and his arousal level. We're going to have to take some time with this term because it is extremely important for understanding different people's reactions to the same place.

People who characteristically do less stimulus screening, and whom we will call *nonscreeners*, are by definition less selective in what they respond to in any environment. Their attention to the various parts of, and happenings in, their environment tends to be diffuse—they tend to hear, see, smell, or otherwise sense more stimuli. They are less prone to hierarchize or pattern the various components of a situation as to relevance or importance. As a result, nonscreeners experience places as being more complex and more loaded.

Those who do more stimulus screening, and whom we will call

screeners, are by definition more selective in what they respond to. Screeners automatically (unconsciously) impose a hierarchy of importance or pattern on the various components of a complex situation, thereby effectively reducing its load. In other words, their attention to various parts of, or happenings in, an environment is more focused, with the less relevant components having been screened out.

The effectively higher environmental load of the same situation for nonscreeners causes more arousal in them. Nonscreeners have longer lasting arousal reactions to novel, changing, or sudden (i.e., high-load) situations. In contrast, the same situations elicit smaller and shorter lasting arousal reactions from screeners.

Individual differences in screening are most apparent immediately after a sudden increase in environmental load. This is partly because screeners habituate faster than nonscreeners to the irrelevant or less relevant stimuli in a situation, although both eventually habituate to relatively comparable levels of arousal. It is for this reason that arousability—temporary peaks in arousal rather than characteristic or average arousal level—is the most relevant difference in the arousal response of screeners and nonscreeners. Supposing Mr. Jones, a screener, and Mr. Smith, a nonscreener, are in your living room having a quiet, relaxed conversation when suddenly your wife drops a pan in the kitchen or there is a sonic boom. Mr. Smith, the nonscreener, will startle, bolt upright in his chair, and possibly lose his train of thought. Mr. Jones, the screener, on the other hand, will at most turn his head in the direction of the sound. If you charted their arousal curves immediately after the sound they would look something like Figure 2. Mr. Smith's arousal level will shoot up whenever his environment gets loaded (as when something totally unexpected occurs) and will take a longer time coming down. Mr. Jones' arousal level will not go up nearly as high and will come down more quickly. This does not necessarily mean that Mr. Smith is more nervous, anxious, or tense than Mr. Jones. Low levels of stimulus screening simply index less selectivity and therefore more amplified arousal responses to different situations—whether these be pleasant or unpleasant. However, we can say that nonscreeners have a more delicately or more finely tuned emotional "mechanism." They will thus be relatively sensitive to smaller variations in stimuli and may be put out of whack by relatively gross ones.

A nonscreener would show more rapid and higher increases in arousal than a screener if we were to suddenly turn on a strobe light while both were in a dark room, or if they both walked into a crowded

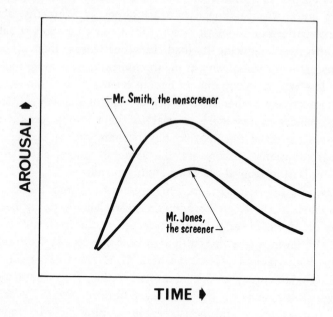

FIGURE 2

elevator, came upon an accident on the freeway, felt an air pocket while on a plane trip, were bumped into while walking on the sidewalk, were told off or insulted by a stranger, or were confronted by a dangerous situation while driving. Similar differences are to be expected in numerous stressful interpersonal situations, such as crowding, the expectation of negative evaluation by others, and the initial moments of encounter with a total stranger.

What are the implications of all this for the environmental preferences of screeners and nonscreeners? Figure 1 shows that among pleasant settings the more arousing ones are approached to a greater extent by everyone. Since nonscreeners are aroused more than screeners in high-load situations, this means that nonscreeners should approach pleasant and high-load settings even more. The bottom curve in the same figure shows that among unpleasant settings the more arousing ones are avoided to a greater extent by everyone. Once again, since nonscreeners are aroused more in high-load and unpleasant places, they should avoid these even more than screeners. In other words, the fact that nonscreeners become more aroused in high-load settings causes them to exhibit more polarized approach-avoidance behaviors to pleasant and unpleasant situations: compared to screeners, they have a stronger approach to high-load and pleasant places, and a stronger avoidance of high-load and unpleasant ones.

There is one more difference in the environmental preferences of screeners and nonscreeners which requires a bit of background to explain. Frequent and extremely high arousal states cannot be maintained by anyone for very long; the body simply won't permit it. The bodily systems overload and fatigue sets in. If the "blown fuse" in the form of ordinary physical tiredness or an avoidance reaction of some sort is somehow overridden, other bodily defense mechanisms kick in and ultimately cause serious physical damage, like ulceration. Your body literally sabotages itself in an effort to get you out of an environment that is causing intolerably high and frequent levels of arousal. But even before fatigue sets in, several signals indicate when too high a level of arousal is being experienced: a thumping heart, clammy hands, and so on.

These bodily reactions to sustained high levels of arousal are part of the General Adaptation Syndrome (GAS). We will be discussing them in greater detail in the next chapter, but it is useful at this point to refer back to Figure 1. The upper curve in that figure shows that among pleasant situations the more arousing (higher-load) ones are approached more, but the curve begins to dip for extremely high levels of arousal. This dip is meant to reflect the limitations our bodies impose on sustaining very high levels of arousal. That is, approach to pleasant and extremely arousing situations is attenuated because it is adaptive to avoid GAS reactions.*

Returning to the differences between screeners and nonscreeners, we can see that nonscreeners reach these maximum tolerable arousal levels more quickly and more often than screeners. This means that prolonged exposure to high-load environments will tend to overwork the nonscreeners' physiological mechanisms more than that of the screeners', and cause them to fatigue faster. Thus, stressful settings, which are not only loaded but also unpleasant, often take a heavier toll among nonscreeners than among screeners. Nonscreeners tire

* As we shall see in the chapters on mental hospitals and prisons, extremely low levels of arousal that are sustained for prolonged periods are also maladaptive, but for different reasons. The lower curve in Figure 1 shows that among unpleasant situations the less arousing (lower-load) ones are approached more, but the curve dips for extremely low levels of arousal. This dip is meant to reflect our psychological limitations in, and lack of preference for, extremely unarousing situations. That is, even while feeling displeasure, there is a limit to how low a level of arousal humans can tolerate.

more easily and are more likely to develop psychosomatic ailments in such situations if they are forced to stay on for one reason or another. Nonscreeners are also more likely to voluntarily drive themselves to their limits of bodily tolerance in more pleasant and loaded situations.

Incidentally, it is fairly easy to discover whether you are a screener or a nonscreener. A high temporary or chronic level of physiological arousal is associated with peripheral vasoconstriction—the capillaries in the hands and feet contract, which means that the skin temperature of these organs is lower than the normal body temperature (lower than 98.6° Fahrenheit or thereabouts). Highly aroused people are thus likely to have cold feet or cold hands.

Take a thermometer which is sensitive to the temperature of the hand when it is held with the thumb and forefinger. The thermometer should be of the kind which registers an increase or decrease in temperature, not the medical kind which only registers the upper limit of a patient's temperature and then has to be shaken to bring the reading back down to a low point. Using such a thermometer, you should be able to take note of the extent to which your hands are colder than your normal internal body temperature at any given time, thus assessing your temporary level of arousal. The higher your arousal, the greater the drop in the temperature of your hands, feet, and skin. By sampling across many high-load situations, you can assess your own level of stimulus screening. Temporary large drops in hand temperature would indicate temporary high arousal and only give you evidence of nonscreening if these large drops were to occur frequently.*

It can be demonstrated that nonscreeners show a high degree of empathy—they are more sensitive to the emotional reactions of others and are more likely to feel or imagine others' emotions. They are more sensitive to subtle changes in their environments and react more vividly to these changes. Results obtained in our laboratory demonstrate that in general there is a slight tendency for women to screen less than men. I hardly want to suggest that all females are nonscreeners and that all males are screeners. But there is a small statistical relationship showing that, on a continuum, more females tend toward the nonscreening end and more males toward the screening end. There are many exceptions, and my example of Christopher and Linda Sansum has been deliberately constructed to show this.

* A more convenient measure of stimulus screening based on a questionnaire format has been developed and is available from the author.

But these scientifically controlled observations correlate well with certain broad cultural or common-sense notions. It has often been remarked, for example, that women are more "emotional" than men, meaning that they react with greater arousal to obviously emotional situations, or that they are emotionally more sensitive to seemingly minute changes in the environment, changes that sometimes are not even perceived by males. Such notions are supported by experimental observations showing that women are more prone to anxiety and fainting and have more emotional empathy for others.

The finding that women tend to screen less than men also correlates uncomfortably well with certain sexist role assignments. Nonscreeners are not going to perform as well in unpleasant and highly arousing environments—settings that involve cut-throat competition, for instance. Nonscreeners are also not likely to perform as well as screeners in situations that are fear-inducing or dangerous.

It is interesting to speculate about the adaptive significance of the slight tendency for females to screen less and hence to be more sensitive to changes in the environment. This tendency probably resulted from natural selection because it favored the species as a whole. Assuming for the moment that divergent sexual roles set in quite early in human prehistory, and that the female confined herself to the local environment in order to look after the young of the species, nonscreening would be extremely useful. The mother who is not very sensitive to minute changes in the environment—a rustle in the bushes, a sudden quietening of birds' songs or her children's play noises—might quickly lose her vulnerable offspring. And it would of course be extremely useful for the species as a whole to have at least half its members temperamentally alert enough to perceive the approach of danger even while secure and at rest.

In the same speculative vein, one might suggest that a general screening tendency of males may also have come about through environmental adaptation. Assuming for the moment that early human males ranged farther from the local environment to hunt or defend territory, it was useful for them to screen more. They were thus better able to cope with dangerous (unpleasant, novel, and complex) environments. And in highly loaded situations like overt physical competition for mates, intertribal warfare, or a dangerous hunt, males who became so highly aroused as to GAS themselves and fail to function adequately were the ones eliminated.

Let's take one last look at the Sansums and see how some of the concepts introduced in this chapter work in relation to them. Both Linda and Christopher arrive home from highly loaded and unpleasant work situations. They have learned that they can create a more preferred emotional state through drastic reduction of environmental loads. The routine—the drinks, the change into comfortable and familiar lounging clothes, the avoidance of people and new places—all serve to lower environmental load and hence lower arousal levels. But there is more to this situation: Linda Sansum is a screener and Christopher is a nonscreener. Even when Linda becomes highly aroused in unusual or complex situations, she tends to come down fairly quickly, and thus will not remain uptight about something for hours. Granted, she prefers considerably lower environmental loads when she first comes home, but this urge on her part is not quite as desperate as it is for Christopher. His loaded job pushes him to barely tolerable levels of arousal and keeps him there. At the office he is likely to be a stickler for routine, procedure, rank, getting things done one at a time and neatly put away. He seeks closure and regularity at each stage because this seems to be his last recourse for reducing the overall load of the work environment.

Even though the unpleasantness and load levels at work are about the same for both, Christopher who is a nonscreener is aroused more. Understandably, then, he dislikes his job more and does everything in his power to reduce its load. When he can't manage that, he begins to get headaches or colds and is sometimes awfully tempted to chuck the whole work routine.

But let us not leave the Sansums on such a sour note; instead, let us give them more desirable work environments to see how they might respond differently. Assume that soon after their marriage they decided to start an educational clearinghouse together, and that an initially small and unstable business has by now grown strong and become extremely lucrative. They have hired a small but efficient staff which consists of people they enjoy working with, and are by now freed of many of the day-to-day chores in running a small business. They have people to whom they can delegate responsibilities, and so it is not necessary for both of them to be at work all the time. This flexibility allows them to take time off to do things—go shopping for a new outfit, plan an interesting dinner for some close friends, or even take occasional long weekends and fly off somewhere for a few days. Over the years, then, the Sansums have managed to create a socially and physically pleasant working situation for themselves that is highly rewarding and moderate in load.

When Linda arrives home after a day's work, she is under no compulsion whatever to seek environments having a drastically reduced load. Quite the contrary. She prefers an environment having a fairly high load and seeks to increase the load at home by having guests over, manipulating the decor, making last-minute domestic decisions, and so on. She even loves to change her physical appearance and hence the emotional impact she has on others. She tries far-out clothes and frequently changes her hair style, makeup, or perfume. Christopher wants the same things and more. He is generally more enthusiastic at work. When he comes home he wants to try new and exciting restaurants and shows; he wants to party it up or even do a little swinging. He is always excited and raring to go and frequently will keep up a joyful and almost frantic social life to the point of exhaustion.

These better environmental cards we have dealt to Linda Sansum (the screener) and Christopher (the nonscreener) help to bring out the interesting differences in the two types. Nonscreeners are essentially more sensitive to the pleasure-displeasure dimension in loaded environments. In the stressful job we dealt him at the beginning of this chapter, Christopher suffered more, got sick more often, and otherwise manifested more avoidance behavior and effort to reduce environmental load. In the job we dealt him next, however, we found him approaching his work and his life with a passion which most screeners would be less capable of. On balance, though, the before and after cards we dealt Linda and Christopher point to the one interesting thing about stimulus screening which sets it apart from other major personality dimensions. Whereas Christopher was worse off before, he is better off now, and it is difficult for us to have an evaluative bias for or against nonscreeners like him.

Suggested Readings

The rationale and experimental support for characterizing all emotions simply in terms of pleasure-displeasure, arousal-nonarousal, and dominance-submissiveness is given in Bush (1973), Mehrabian and Russell (1974c), Osgood, Suci, and Tannenbaum (1957), and Snider and Osgood (1959). Russell and Mehrabian (1974) provided data showing how anger and anxiety are both high on displeasure and arousal, but that anger is a dominant, whereas anxiety is a submissive, state. Opler (1967) showed, incidentally, how these two emotional states occur in different degrees in various cultures. Russell and Mehrabian (1976d) summarized additional data and expressed approximately 150 different emotions in terms of the three basic dimensions.

BASICS

For studies of the cross-cultural generality of "gut level" reactions to stimulation, see Osgood (1960). On the subject of transcultural esthetic judgments, see Child (1968), Ford, Prothro, and Child (1966), and Iwao and Child (1966). For the rationale and experimental data on how to describe people in terms of characteristic (trait) levels of pleasure-displeasure, arousal-nonarousal, and dominance-submissiveness, see Mehrabian and Russell (1974a, chap. 3). Their data show how personality traits such as anxiety, neuroticism, and extroversion can each be expressed in equation form as a function of the three dimensions.

For personality measures relating most directly to characteristic arousal levels, see Mehrabian's (1976a, 1976b) experimental reports on the stimulus screening scale, and Mehrabian and Russell's (1973) measure of arousal-seeking tendency. The basic biological work relating to stimulus screening or arousability is given in Nebylitsyn (1972), Nebylitsyn and Gray (1972), and Siddle and Mangan (1971). Mehrabian and Epstein (1972) provided data on the relation of emotional empathy to characteristic arousal levels and reported females to be more empathic than males. Findings on sex differences in stimulus screening were provided by Mehrabian (1976a, 1976b), and related experimental reports showing females' greater proneness to emotionality and anxiety were reviewed by Anastasi (1958).

Finally, for the theory and experimental data which form the basis for Figure 1, see Dember and Earl (1957), Fiske and Maddi (1961), Mehrabian and Russell (1974a, chap. 6; 1975b), and Russell and Mehrabian (1976a, 1976b).

PART TWO

INTIMATE

ENVIRONMENTS

4

Under the Skin with Drugs

IT'S Saturday night in Manhattan. Let's suppose you live in apartment B of a rather cheaply renovated building. Entirely against your will you are able to monitor the sound levels in apartment A on your right and C on your left. The folks in A are social drinkers and so are their guests. They are jazz and blues buffs. The citizens in C prefer the heavy sounds of Bob Dylan and happen to be frequent marijuana users.

A typical party in A will have a different through-the-walls profile from one held in C. Both parties will start out at about the same level—music fairly loud, boisterous greetings, and so on. But about half an hour later real differences will begin to set in. Apartment A will get louder and louder. There will be increasingly heated arguments, such as whether Cannonball Adderley was ever any good. Blakey's "Jazz Messengers" will shudder thunderously through the floor. There will be a lot of walking about, chairs scraping, feet pounding. C's party, however, will decrease in volume: there will be less movement, and eventually it will evolve into something quiet and soft.

These large differences in behavior result from under-the-skin effects of alcohol. In moderate amounts (a couple of drinks taken over two or more hours), alcohol acts as a stimulant, but in larger amounts (several drinks in an hour), it lowers arousal. In extreme cases when it is used or administered rapidly in very large amounts, alcohol leads to sleepiness and even coma. A person who is using alcohol can regulate his arousal: he can drink slowly to extend the stimulant action or gulp down a few right away to get the sedative action. The experienced drinkers in apartment A have a fair tolerance for alcohol and also knowledgeably pace their drinking to maintain their "highs." In addition, as we shall see, their drinking style helps them feel more dominant.

Compared to alcohol, marijuana has a different effect on arousal. Its main active ingredient acts as a stimulant for about half an hour, thus raising arousal level. After that, the body transforms this ingredient into a depressant, which lowers arousal. For frequent users of marijuana, such as the people in apartment C, the initial stimulant action is absent unless a particularly concentrated dose of the drug is used. In other words, persons who have two to three joints of marijuana daily do not get the initial half-hour arousal boost; in fact, these individuals probably rely on the drug for its consistent arousal-lowering effect. In contrast, the infrequent user who has a joint every one or two weeks experiences the initial heightened arousal with a subsequent arousal drop.

Why do the social drinkers in apartment A approach or create environments having higher and higher loads (more movement, more closeness, and more conversation) while the people in C with marijuana-lowered arousal levels tend not to? The answer is that a moderate amount of alcohol not only increases arousal but, more importantly from a social standpoint, increases feelings of dominance and pleasure. This increase in dominance and the accompanying loss of inhibitions allows people to feel freer to adjust their environments to their needs. They feel freer to act as they choose, say what they want, and approach an environment to whatever degree they wish. People feel—whatever the actual circumstances may be—that they are in control, influential, significant, or at the very least really not accountable for their actions. In vino veritas is a perfectly sensible cliché. It is rendered even more sensible in those cultures, like our own, which tolerate from drunks truth or departures from behavioral norms that are considered unacceptable if the truth-teller is sober.

Dominant-submissive feelings dramatically influence a person's approach behavior toward others. If someone feels dominant he seeks others when the situation is pleasant, particularly when it is loaded. A dominant-feeling individual in an unpleasant situation avoids others no matter what the load. A moderate amount of alcohol, insofar as it makes people feel dominant, aroused, and pleasant, makes them socially more active and exuberant.

Unlike alcohol, marijuana tends to induce pleasant but submissive feelings. A person who feels submissive will socialize at about an average level no matter how pleasant or aroused he feels. This level of friendliness is considerably below that of someone who feels dominant, pleasant, and aroused. A person who has been smoking marijuana is therefore expected to be less friendly even at a pleasant party. His submissiveness is associated with passivity—he becomes a receiver, basking in environmental stimuli rather than making waves of his own. This submissiveness not only expresses itself in the somewhat asocial character of parties where marijuana is smoked, but also in many other situations. As any cop can tell you, someone who is "under the influence" is likely to drive eighty miles per hour in a sixty-mile zone because he feels "on top of" or in control of the road and the car; someone who has been smoking marijuana is likely to be going thirty, because he feels subdued and is especially eager not to make waves.

A consideration of the emotional impacts of alcohol and marijuana, or, for that matter, of any other drug, helps us understand what sort of person will use each drug, or what circumstances will make each drug more desirable. Patterns of alcohol use range from no drinking, to the use of moderate amounts (two or three drinks stretched over several hours), to uses of large amounts (several drinks in the first hour followed by at least two or three drinks in each successive hour, provided the person somehow manages to avoid sleep or a state of stupor).

Small amounts of alcohol which increase pleasure, arousal, and dominance (that is, generate excitement) ought to be generally preferred over large amounts which increase pleasure only slightly, reduce arousal, and probably lower dominance. In fact, persons who habitually drink very large quantities are clearly in the minority, as are situations where most people would be tempted to drink heavily. There are times, however, when someone might prefer large quantities. A person who is temperamentally or temporarily nervous or anxious (feeling aroused and unpleasant) might use heavy doses of alcohol, particularly when he can drink in low-load and pleasant settings. More importantly, those who are temperamentally or temporarily depressed can readily achieve the exact opposite of this feeling with moderate amounts of alcohol—they can shift from the displeasure, low arousal, and submissiveness of depression to a pleasant, aroused, and dominant state. This shift for a depressed person is so dramatic and reinforcing that it can lead to frequent reliance on alcohol. Indeed, research findings strongly support a relationship between depression and chronic alcohol use, particularly for males.

In the case of marijuana, as we've noted, daily use leads to the development of a tolerance to the initial arousing effect; that is, the initial arousal boost is absent and only relaxation results. It is therefore probable that anxious persons who characteristically feel arousal and displeasure, or people who are frequently subjected to high-load and unpleasant situations or events, are more likely to become heavy and frequent users of marijuana. On the other hand, those who generally feel pleasant might use marijuana recreationally and infrequently despite greater opportunities for its use, doing so mostly for its arousing effect.

Here then are some of the general guidelines we use to understand preferences for various drugs. Drugs are used primarily to compensate for unpreferred emotional states, although less frequently they do serve to enhance preferred states. That is, drugs become especially tempting in unpreferred emotional states related to a person's temperament or induced by his environment or activities at work or at home.

The various unpreferred states invariably involve displeasure, especially when it is combined with high arousal. Persons in unpleasant and unaroused states might use stimulants—cigarettes, coca-cola, coffee, tea, small doses of alcohol, infrequent use of marijuana, amphetamines, cocaine, and hallucinogens like mescaline or LSD, provided these can be had in pleasant settings. Those in unpleasant and highly aroused states might seek arousal-lowering drugs (the so-called depressants) such as tranquilizers, muscle relaxants, barbiturates, large doses of alcohol, frequent and larger amounts of marijuana, or very potent drugs like morphine and heroin.

Depressives who temperamentally tend toward displeasure and low arousal are expected to be tempted by stimulants—caffeine, amphetamines, cocaine. On the other hand, anxious neurotics who temperamentally tend toward displeasure and high arousal are expected to rely on depressants—large doses of marijuana, barbiturates, or opiates. Actually, the label "depressant" is a misnomer for a number of these drugs which have the primary function of lowering arousal while increasing pleasure. We will instead refer to these with the more appropriate label "relaxant," since relaxation involves low arousal and high pleasure.

Although temperamental differences are important, the environment at home or at work can similarly affect drug use. People who must function in unpleasant and high-load settings—active professionals working under extremely competitive conditions and businessmen who must administer problem-ridden and complex corporate structures without significant rewards—probably rely on relaxants if they use any drugs. In contrast, those who are subjected to low-load and unpleasant (boring) environments—old, retired people, housewives whose children have grown up and are gone, the unemployed who may be socially isolated and unhappy, and those who perform boring and monotonous work—are likely to use stimulants if they are tempted by drugs.

Stimulant drugs increase arousal and relaxant drugs lower arousal. The reason both classes of drugs are in common use and are usually self-prescribed is that they also increase pleasure levels. In the case of hallucinogens, however, no definite trend toward pleasure or displeasure results from use of the drugs per se. Instead, there is a tremendous and sudden arousal boost which makes the user extremely sensitive to the pleasure-displeasure dimension in his physical or social environment. As would be expected from Figure 1, extreme avoidance reactions ("bad trips") are noted in those who take such drugs and are then confronted with threatening or even slightly disturbing social situations. This is why LSD advocates cautioned novices to first try the drug in comforting and accepting environments, preferably with someone liked and trusted.

Among the various available drugs, choice may also relate to feelings of dominance induced by the drug. Preliminary research shows that cocaine and moderate amounts of alcohol make people feel dominant, and that LSD, marijuana, opium, morphine, and heroin make people feel submissive. In our competitive culture, which tends to reward rather than punish interpersonal or intergroup aggressiveness (dominance), the drugs of choice for those who wish to increase arousal are cocaine and small doses of alcohol. This may account for the steady rise in teenage drinking, particularly in certain minority groups with strong machismo concerns. It also bodes ill for the future uses of cocaine. Those who live in high-load and unpleasant environments but don't identify with the achievement-oriented and aggressive cultural norms (the dropouts) opt for arousal-lowering drugs such as marijuana or heroin which induce pleasant and submissive feelings.

What about the paradox of anxious, nervous, or tense people

who overindulge in stimulants like coffee or cigarettes? In order to explain this, we have to turn to another concept—the General Adaptation Syndrome (GAS).

GAS is a concept first introduced by the biologist Hans Selye to explain human reactions to disease, injury, and poisons. But it is now clear that this concept has a much broader relevance; it also explains our reactions to a wide range of stresses that are common in our daily lives. These everyday stresses may result from decision making, especially under time pressure; interpersonal conflicts; traffic jams; exposure to high concentrations of chemical pollutants; or any other situations causing high levels of arousal and displeasure.

The General Adaptation Syndrome begins with an alarm reaction; the sympathetic nervous system is activated, causing high arousal. When this high arousal is combined with low pleasure and a submissive feeling, we become tense, anxious, nervous. If the stress is somehow removed, we can return to normal levels of arousal. However, when the stress persists and cannot be avoided the second stage of GAS begins; it consists first of weariness, then depression, and then physical illness. The glands involved in supporting the sympathetic nervous activity have by then depleted their resources and the body's further attempts at adaptation are unbalanced and harmful. Symptoms of the second GAS stage include headaches, ulcers, insomnia, colds, flus, cardiovascular and kidney diseases, high blood pressure, and rheumatic or allergic reactions. The third and final GAS stage occurs when the stresses have persisted for so long that the body is no longer able to cope at all. The result is a total exhaustion precluding any normal functioning; one literally does not have the energy to stand up. We'll get into some of the broader social implications of GAS in subsequent chapters, but at this point it is useful to be able to refer to this notion in relation to certain personal habits and needs.

A generally harmless and familiar example of GASing is the feeling of fatigue that gets increasingly stronger during strenuous exercise and which lasts even after we stop exercising. A more extreme example of GASing is the student who has been cramming all week for an important final. He's been getting only a few hours sleep a night and is understandably anxious that he will not be able to do a semester's work in four days. The night before the final he drinks several pots of coffee and maybe even takes a dexadrine or two for insurance. Soon after, he is sound asleep and wakes up hours later both puzzled and alarmed. He has GASed himself. The heavy dose of stimulants has pushed his arousal level—already high and sustained for too long—far too high for his body to be able to tolerate. The bodily systems sustaining arousal simply aborted or disengaged, and the precipitous and rapid drop in arousal which resulted was quite similar to what happens in a fainting spell. One moment he was reading in his chair, and the next thing he knew he was waking up. The coffee and the uppers acted as relaxants rather than stimulants.

People who must function in unpleasant and high-load situations, and whose arousal levels are frequently pushed beyond the limits of tolerance, tend to develop habits which produce a GAS effect. The heavy cigarette smoker who, when you walk into his office, immediately reaches for a cigarette before you even have a chance to say, "I've got a problem with this invoice," is not smoking to raise his arousal level, even though the nicotine in cigarettes is a stimulant. Rather, he is lowering his arousal through overstimulation. Heavy coffee and tea drinkers, knowingly or not, often do the same thing. In some extreme cases of nonscreening and tension, the person is on the verge of a GAS reaction, and a stimulant can rapidly trigger final GASing; even a single gin and tonic might lead to exhaustion or sleepiness. These people are the social bores who become droopy and may even fall asleep in company after a couple of drinks. Other nonscreeners who must function in high-load environments don't even need any drugs; their bodies are often driven way beyond the limits of tolerance and GAS reactions have set in. Such persons give the appearance of fatigue, exhaustion, and, in extreme cases, depression.

It is no accident that people who smoke heavily also tend to drink great quantities of coffee or tea during the day, and use alcohol when it is socially or professionally acceptable to do so. Such persons are trying to reduce their arousal levels; they have learned that coffee, cigarettes, or alcohol in sufficient quantities will do the trick. But they are operating in the GAS levels, and the statistics for this group in relation to GAS symptoms like ulcers, cardiovascular disease, and high general infection rates bear this out.

People with chronically and abnormally high arousal levels—hyperkinetic children and certain kinds of schizophrenics, for example—usually respond with relaxation to stimulants. Reactive schizophrenics who are given LSD show a decrease in arousal, whereas normal persons go sky-high. Hyperkinetic children are often given amphetamines to calm them down. Indeed, recent observations have shown that even two cups of coffee daily go a long way toward reducing hyperactivity in children.

Generally, heavy use of the common and weaker stimulants such as cigarettes or coffee does not always mean that the person is GASing himself. GASing resulting from the use of a stimulant is more likely in a nonscreener than a screener. The stimulant in excessive quantities acts as a relaxant for the nonscreener who is frequently aroused to begin with, but it may simply act as a stimulant, despite its overuse, for a screener who is only infrequently over-aroused.

Needless to say, using a stimulant to GAS oneself and thereby reduce arousal is far more harmful than achieving the same result with a relaxant drug. Frequent GASing simply means that the physiological system is driven to its absolute limits far too often. Sooner or later a vital organ is bound to give out. If you are a heavy user of coffee, cigarettes, or some other stronger stimulant and wonder whether it is the stimulating or relaxing effect you're after (and are concerned about the GASing associated with the relaxing effect), notice whether you get tired easily or whether you have frequent periods of exhaustion in the afternoons. If so, you have probably been GASing yourself with the stimulant. The best way to find out, however, is to give up the habit for a few days. The attempt to give up some sort of habit-forming drug highlights those emotional states during the day when the urge to have that particular drug is strong. If you feel bored at the times you find yourself craving the stimulant, this means you use it to increase arousal. On the other hand, if you crave the drug while feeling highly stressed or anxious, then it is the relaxant effect you seek. A friend of mine who was a heavy coffee drinker and had given it up noticed that these crucial moments occurred in his secluded and quiet office when he was alone with little to do. More generally, he felt a need for coffee when he was bored. On the other hand, he found it very easy to leave a cupful after taking only one or two sips when he was in the company of others or in a loaded environment—outdoors on his patio with friends, eating, and talking. For him, then, coffee clearly served as a stimulant; the urge to have some occurred at those times during the day when neither his physical or social environment nor his job provided sufficient stimulation. In contrast, loaded situations readily allowed him to avoid his unwanted habit.

Nonscreeners who are frequently subjected to stress (highly loaded and unpleasant environments) become more aroused than screeners and are thus especially vulnerable to the temptations of relaxant drugs. Such persons tend to get hooked on these drugs—they reach for a tranquilizer or gulp down two or more drinks as a means of quickly reducing their arousal levels in order to perform needed or desirable tasks like socializing, sleeping, coping. And since women generally screen less than men, they are more likely to abuse themselves in this way if they have the money and connections to do so. Although women's libbers are highly critical of doctors who tend to write off many feminine complaints as "nerves" and prescribe tranquilizers, there is a slender theoretical base for this homespun kind of therapy which works part of the time. Since nonscreeners are emotionally more sensitive, interpersonal confrontations or seemingly insurmountable problems send them sky-high and they take a long time coming down. Troubling social, professional, or physical environments having high loads push them up close to their tolerance levels and almost never allow them to come down. Since complex, highly organized Western cultures place a premium on time and short-term efficiency (getting the narrowly defined job done), there is enormous pressure upon all of us to quickly and conveniently manipulate our arousal levels by chemical means. It is all very well to relate one's general life problems to elaborate past-tense metaphors (Freudianism) or less elaborate present-tense metaphors (Perlsian or Rogerian therapies). But, that doesn't help a lot when you're scared to death because your mate hasn't come home, your child is in the hospital with a fracture, the boss wants to see you about some complaint from a customer, or the Local 45 Grievance Committee is coming in to see you at 10:00 A.M.

The problem of course is that these chemical devices, especially barbiturates, are not efficient in the long run. Barbiturates and other tranquilizers (as well as large doses of alcohol) do lower arousal levels. But they are physiologically addictive, requiring progressively heavier doses to have the same effect. Such relaxants permit sleep, for example, but they do not allow healthful or restorative sleep. They inhibit deep or delta-wave sleep during which the bodily systems repair and renew themselves. As a result, the barbiturate addict or late-night alcoholic eventually turns to stimulants so as to function in the morning. Halfway through the day, the stimulants have succeeded in creating a need for a tranquilizer, and the cycle is on.

Sooner or later, and mostly sooner, severe if not fatal GAS symptoms occur.

For anxious types who must function in stressful environments, then, the cycle starts with heavy reliance on relaxants which eventually necessitates daytime use of stimulants. This cycle is reversed for depressives who function in boring environments. These people are likely to find themselves in a dangerous fix by getting hooked on stimulants. Reliance on high doses of stimulants usually necessitates further adjustments with relaxant drugs, or may automatically lead to serious GASing when the stimulants themselves are used in excess.

My discussion of these excesses will hopefully not be misconstrued as a prescription to indiscriminately fear and avoid drugs. This is especially important to consider here because people who step forward and offer us Science as a sure-fire means of improving our health, happiness, or fortune often have a tricky way of filching back from us our most comfortable pleasures. Suddenly we can't have our fried eggs anymore, or martinis, Pall Mall Golds, chocolate mousses, Buicks, or morning coffee. But having a little practical knowledge of environmental psychology doesn't mean that we have to give our lives over to brown rice, half-cooked liver, jogging at 5:00 A.M., or any of the other hideous personal regimens that are sometimes mistakenly called ascetic.

We've talked a great deal about the abuse of chemical relaxants and stimulants, but there's nothing really wrong with a cup of coffee to get us going in the morning, or a nice Scotch and water for a bit of an "up" feeling at a party. Indeed, small amounts of relaxants have beneficial effects. Since they reduce arousal levels, they also reduce blood pressure and can be helpful, especially to people suffering from hypertension and related cardiovascular malfunctions. But there is something wrong with nine cups of coffee or nine Scotches. Such large intakes don't accomplish what we really want, or accomplish it at a very high cost to our health. One cup of coffee can raise one's arousal level; nine cups in a relatively short period of time will probably have a GAS effect. Beyond a certain level of excess, the more coffee we drink the more tired we get, and hence the more we drink in order to overcome fatigue. This is over-dosing on coffee.

Frequent use of any strong relaxant or stimulant creates enormous physiological stresses and usually entails legal and social handicaps as well. The athlete who uses amphetamines to get that extra measure of performance is driving his body at arousal levels which it won't tolerate—something, probably his heart, is bound to give. The heroin addict who's just shot up will be in a state of extremely low arousal, high pleasure, and extreme submissiveness. Somebody feeling like this is almost wholly incapable of socializing, working, or performing any task at all, including tasks necessary for self-preservation like eating or getting out of the way of a truck. On the other hand, a heroin addict who is withdrawing will be in a state of high arousal and high displeasure. If he is temperamentally submissive, he will suffer from terrible anxiety, and if he is temperamentally dominant, he may not care what he does in order to get his fix.

Another kind of drug abuse results from unknowingly mixing stimulants and relaxants. The result of haphazardly ingesting chemicals with mutually counteracting effects is heavy pollution of the internal bodily environment. We've already mentioned the deplorable upper-downer cycle on which some people hook themselves. But people who regularly lace their grass with amphetamine or cocaine, put brandy in their coffee after a dinner where lots of wine has already been consumed, or make a habit of drinking Irish coffee are also abusing their systems. It is never necessary to mix stimulants and relaxants or use heavy doses of either. A little bit of either usually goes farthest and won't lead to an unacceptably high or low arousal state that requires further radical manipulation. Those who mix, or who try to alter their feeling states too quickly, invariably wind up internally polluted.

I realize that I've been talking about some pretty grim things in this chapter. People can and do artificially alter their arousal levels and feelings of pleasure or dominance by ingesting certain substances, many of which either do not exist in nature or do not exist there in the extremely potent forms that applied knowledge allows us to produce. However, most of these substances work only for a short term: that is their virtue and their curse. As long-term solutions— meaning in relation to reasonably long, reasonably healthy, reasonably untormented, stable, and productive lives—these substances don't work and are in a literal sense self-defeating. We might even make a large philosophical leap and compare the use of these substances to certain actions in the ethical realm: they are a form of lying, conning, cheating, or bullying. One lie, one unethical maneuver, one bluff or unchallenged display of force may be necessary and may enhance our lives. But prolonged lying or cheating will someday catch up with us, and we will sooner or later reach a point where our personal word is known to be worthless and our performance is known to be mostly fake. Anyone who has found himself at such a point of reckoning knows that he is lost, much as one who has burnt out his heart, lungs, or liver at age thirty-five or forty-five knows that he too is lost. By "lost" I don't mean anything necessarily theological, but merely a crushing sense that one has forfeited the chance for a full, rounded, satisfying life.

It is the excesses which make one ask, "Why drugs at all?" Why is it that people rely on these artificial means to modify their emotional states? Certainly, the answer requires a recognition of the many traditions of Western culture which have contributed to this state of affairs. Leading candidates among these are the deference and awe with which medicine and drugs have been traditionally regarded; the emphasis on efficient and rapid change and adaptation necessitated by the increasingly divergent demands placed on humans in modern urban society; the fascination with unusual and mystical psychic states which is part of modern man's continuing efforts to explore himself; or the technological advances which continue to impress and ensnare modern man into simplistic and wholesale solutions (cars, air conditioners, packaged foods) and which invariably seem to lead to excesses, rigidity, and human costs.

Most of this book is about how we can manipulate our environments—whether they be home, office, or fun places—in order to avoid lying to or cheating ourselves chemically in short-term or unnatural ways. The next few chapters deal with certain kinds of more natural or at least less damaging things we can do to manipulate our environments so that our need to control our feelings—our reactions in terms of arousal, pleasure, and dominance—does not exile us from the needs and capabilities of our bodies.

Suggested Readings

For general sources on psychopharmacology, see Aviado (1972) and Clark and del Giudice (1970). Jarvik (1969) specifically considered the effects of drugs on arousal. The psychological effects of alcohol use and personality predispositions to alcoholism were reviewed by McClelland, Davis, Kalin, and Wanner (1972), Mendelson (1970), and by Russell and Mehrabian (1975b). For marijuana, see the *Marijuana Commission Second Report on Marijuana and Drug Abuse* (1973). Also see Nesbitt (1973) for arousal changes among cigarette smokers and nonsmokers after nicotine administration. Ellinwood and Cohen (1972) discussed amphetamines, Siegel (1971) discussed hallucinogens, and Woods and Downs (1973) considered cocaine. A volume on *Altered States of Awareness* (1972) and another by Barber (1970) contain additional reviews of experimental work with marijuana and hallucinogens.

The general problem of drug use was considered by Russell and Mehrabian (1976c) and environmental effects on alcohol use and smoking were experimentally explored by Russell and Mehrabian (1976a). Also, Mehrabian and Russell (1975a) reviewed the available data supporting our discussion of the enhancing effect of dominant (versus submissive) feelings on affiliation or the desire to socialize with others.

Although Selye (1956) is the basic source on the General Adaptation Syndrome (GAS), the following sources relating stress and life changes to illness and psychopathology are also useful: Appley and Trumbull (1967), Levine and Scotch (1970), McGrath (1970), Rahe (1972), and Ross and Mehrabian (1976).

Under the Skin with Music, Exercise, Food, and Head Trips

THERE ARE other things available to us besides drugs for short-term manipulation of our bodily environments, and they don't involve tremendous sacrifices of time and efficiency. These things include music, exercise, eating, and certain mental adjustments like napping, daydreaming, or fantasizing. To use these to advantage, we have to know what we're doing and why.

Let's take music first. A bachelor friend of mine hates basic housework but won't have a maid because he believes semirationally that when you have someone come in to vacuum, or clean the kitchen, you will sooner or later be robbed, not by the maid but by people who've learned to monitor the daily schedules of non-live-in domestics. So this bachelor did the monotonous and unpleasant tasks he despised and wouldn't pay anyone else to do, but found that while he was cleaning the toilet bowl he would have imaginary, vicious conversations with his dearest friends. This disturbed him so much that he developed a technique to enable him to do such monotonous (low-load) and unpleasant tasks without feeling entirely hostile or slavish. What he did was to make tape recordings containing highly arousing and pleasant musical selections—everything from Bud Shank's Latin jazz to Art Blakey's *Orgy in Rhythm* to Archie Shepp's

Mama Too Tight. He plays these tapes at high volume as he goes about his domestic chores. "Without my clean-up tapes, it takes me half a weekend. But when I do my tape number, I get it all done in about two hours."

Boring tasks are boring because they are low-load (simple and overly familiar) and unpleasant. They lower our arousal level, heighten our displeasure and, because we are forced for one reason or another to pursue them, they also encourage feelings of submissiveness. (Low arousal + displeasure + submissiveness = boredom.) By playing music that is loud, exciting, and pleasant, my acquaintance succeeds in increasing both his arousal and his pleasure, thus enabling himself to initiate and complete the boring domestic tasks. The imaginary conversations which increased his arousal and dominance weren't as effective because their bizarre quality not only puzzled him but also increased his displeasure. When I told him about a study showing that supermarket shoppers bought more things in less time when louder music was played, his comment was "It figures."

I'll be talking a great deal more about the uses of music in later chapters, but it is well to note here some simple rules of thumb. The louder and faster the music, the higher its arousing quality (and hence the quicker we move). The more pleasant the music, the more likely we are to display approach behavior in relation to the physical or social environment of which it is a part. Conversely, slow, simple, soft, and familiar music has the effect of lowering arousal levels while usually not detracting from the pleasure dimension, thus giving us a relaxed, contented feeling.

Some modern music is complex, unfamiliar, and dissonant (high-load and unpleasant), with the result that people who must listen to it (as in a formal concert setting) become tense and anxious. As one becomes more familiar with such music, its overall load goes down and preference for it increases. This is what is meant by "acquiring a taste" for anything: reducing a thing's novelty, which in turn reduces its arousing quality, even though the complexity remains intact. Although for a neutral or unpleasant stimulus preference increases as load is reduced (as in acquiring a taste), for a pleasant stimulus preference decreases as load is reduced. This is why overexposure to a musical piece that once charmed us can reduce its load to a point where we don't enjoy hearing it anymore.

Of the various forms of music, electronic music generally involves the highest levels of uncertainty. It is complex, novel, and contains many unpredictable sequences of sounds which make it the most arousing type of music, even more arousing than jazz. This, together with its neutral (neither pleasant nor unpleasant) associations for most people, explains the failure of electronic music to make substantial inroads into the world of popular music. In addition, the typically lengthy compositions in this field make it difficult for the listener to increase his familiarity with a piece by repeated listening so as to reduce its load and arousing quality to more preferred levels. Composers can, however, increase the appeal of their works by giving them a bit more structure, as for instance with the repetition of certain key sequences throughout. On the other hand, it is conceivable that some people will learn to use electronic music to attain heightened arousal by simply combining it with other pleasurable sources. In this case, the pleasure that is provided by the setting or one's fellow listeners will combine with the very high load of the music to yield unusually high levels of excitement.

It is difficult to overestimate the effect that music can have on a person's performance of certain tasks or on the behavior of people in work or play settings. Music can have a stronger and more immediate effect on arousal level and pleasure than, say, several cups of coffee. People who use clock radios to wake up in the morning or put themselves to sleep in the evening are practicing environmental psychology whether they know it or not. The ordinary alarm clock usually emits an unpleasant sound or, more accurately, a noise. I wonder how much getting-up crankiness derives from the fact that people are untimely ripped from their beds and from feelings of low arousal, pleasure, and dominance by a stimulus that is decidedly arousing, unpleasant, and overpowering. One feels, as one stumbles out of bed to turn off the hateful electronic cock's crow, a sudden and diametrically opposed emotional shift for the worse—hardly a good way to start the day.

But clock radios are really not the best device, because it is not usually possible to predict exactly what will be coming over them when it's time to get up. A musical selection may be overly jarring (high-load) or not enjoyable enough for us to make a gradual and pleasant transition to wakefulness. But it is certainly within the technological state-of-the-art to provide inexpensive clock-cassette machines which would allow us to program the sort of music exactly suited to our morning needs in terms of arousal and pleasure. And of course low-load going-to-sleep music could be equally well programmed. After all, the radio is a pipeline to the world; if we are tense and anxious one evening and suddenly hear one of those loaded "we interrupt this broadcast" announcements, it may cost more hours of sleep than we're willing to give up in order to be informed.

All I'm saying here is that music can have an immediate and significant effect on arousal and pleasure levels. In waking up, going to sleep, or perking up, thoughtfully selected music can be an effective substitute for chemical stimulants or relaxants.

Exercise can also work as an effective stimulant or relaxant, though not quite so rapidly. Mild, short-term exercise increases arousal level. Heavy exercise increases arousal level even more and if continued will sooner or later overstress or GAS the body, and hence eventually act as a relaxant. Like any other means of increasing or decreasing arousal level, exercise can be misunderstood or abused.

Taking a bath or shower is not unlike physical exercise. The unevenly distributed high pressure from a shower is arousing. Extremely hot or cold showers or baths cause even higher levels of arousal. If what you need is a lowering of arousal, you should take a tepid bath, one that has a water temperature just slightly higher than internal body temperature. This will cause the blood to move into the extremities, a physiological state equivalent to relaxation or low arousal. A very cold or very hot bath or shower will initially cause the body to suck the blood in toward the vital organs in a kind of shock reaction, thus increasing arousal level. In the same vein, restless sleep characterized by insufficiently low arousal is likely to result from extremely low or high temperatures. While asleep under an exceedingly hot electric blanket, we dream more and have more loaded dreams involving fright, uncertainty, or vivid and complex imagery.

The nonscreener who, upon rising, putters around and fixes breakfast—putting water on for tea, throwing the bacon in the pan, fetching the morning paper from the stoop, and coordinating the whole regimen—may be indulging in just the right amount of physical exercise to raise his arousal level gradually. Such a nonscreener will view with horror those persons who spring out of bed, throw open the windows, and proceed to do twenty push-ups as they listen to the latest stock market quotations. For him to try and do this because it's healthy or because everybody else in his circle does it would be excessively arousing and foolish. This heavier form of morning exercise, however, might be just the thing for a screener—it gets his juices flowing. People who allow themselves to be dragooned into morning routines regardless of their personal needs suffer for it. The nonscreener who jogs before breakfast because his peers do, or the screener who drags through the same old cereal-and-coffee breakfast for family reasons, is acting against his own best interests. The nonscreener will be sky-high far too soon and the screener will be dirt-low when he doesn't need to be.

Light evening exercise is often beneficial to persons who must contend with moderate to high environmental and work loads in the daytime; heavier exercise is more appropriate for those whose daily activities are low-load. Someone who feels tired, unpleasant, and submissive as a result of horrendous days at the office can often benefit from an hour's session at the gym. A very mild and well-spaced workout will raise his arousal level without GASing him. The conversation with a few familiar workout partners will turn around the pleasure dimension, and his skill and familiarity with the equipment and gym environment will cause a rise in the feelings of dominance. On the other hand, if such a person comes to the gym in a highly aroused state, gets involved in open competition, and does a flurry of sit-ups or barbell curls, he will fatigue himself sufficiently to lower his arousal without however being of much use for the rest of the evening.

The gym environment will raise arousal in an especially beneficial way for someone who has boring days. He will perhaps use a more varied workout schedule, socialize more, and overtly compete with anyone who is a realistic match, deriving excitement from bettering his own previous performance or besting someone else. He will enjoy passing on his expertise to others, making new acquaintances, and will savor the stimulating and unspoken competitiveness among a selected group of partners.

Abuse occurs when people allow themselves to get pressured, for one reason or another, into routines for which they are unsuited either temperamentally (permanently) or in terms of immediate level of arousal (temporarily). The following is an example of not terribly serious abuse. Someone who has trouble going to sleep may postpone the going-to-bed experience as long as possible so that he'll be "good and tired" and not toss and turn for hours. Just before retiring, he walks around the house checking locks, opening or closing windows, and perhaps doing a little last-minute fiddling with this or that. These activities constitute mild physical exercise and therefore increase his arousal level, making sleep less rather than more easy to come by. Instead, he would be better off with a bit of light reading to relax him to sleep.

Another example of abuse might be the temporarily highly stressed businessman who pops out to the Y during lunch and feels that he must swim his usual forty laps to keep in shape. The heavy physical exercise may cause him to be exhausted during the rest of his working day. The unwonted weariness may aggravate his concern about his declining physical prowess; so, to reassure himself he might return the following day and again overexert and thereby GAS himself. In fact, a week of unusually high stress at work, combined with a level of exercise that is normally acceptable, may result in severe physical GAS reactions that literally shorten his life.

This kind of thing is the reason behind some strokes, coronaries, and pulled muscles. For males, heavy exercise is perhaps inextricably tied up with things like macho, masculine worth, and dominance, and hence is subject to considerable abuse. The older man who goes out and tries to shovel four-foot snowdrifts out of his thirty-foot driveway after he's just had a nasty argument with his wife or son is probably going to GAS himself and feel low or give himself a heart attack. But men or women who do five push-ups or twenty depending on their clearly perceived needs, are going to feel good because they've manipulated their bodily environments in just the right way.*

The third "natural" under-the-skin thing that can be manipulated for good or ill is food, and this is a common way in which people unknowingly alter their internal environments. I have to confess that the under-the-skin effects of food have been somewhat neglected by environmental psychologists, and that many of my comments in this area represent speculation rather than a summary of hard laboratory results.

We know that hunger causes a rise in arousal level. A feeling of mild hunger (e.g., a feeling that it's time for lunch) will be accompanied by moderate arousal; extreme hunger will result in high arousal. Actual starvation, as when one has fasted or been without any caloric intake for at least three or four days, is accompanied by lethargy—a low arousal, unpleasant, and submissive state—and less

---

* Morehouse and Gross (1975) make a similar point with an exercise program they have devised. The participant determines the amount of exercise to be done by checking his heart rate, which as we know indexes arousal level.

hunger, apparently because the body has begun to tap its own fat and other tissues for nourishment. The act of eating is in itself moderately arousing; this, as we shall see in later chapters, has a number of implications in terms of restaurant design and family eating arrangements. During the digestive process, there is a gradual lowering of arousal as blood is drawn from the brain to the stomach. For this reason, a large meal will sometimes cause us to feel quite sleepy or tired. In general, therefore, we may say that food acts initially as a stimulant and then as a depressant for an hour or longer.

The gourmet who devotes large portions of his leisure time to eating, with smallish, varied portions consumed over two-to-three-hour intervals, has hit upon a way of sustaining very high levels of pleasure and arousal. Although there is no relevant experimental evidence on this point, it is interesting to speculate that cultures as well as individuals tend to opt for this particular source of stimulation and excitement when they are sexually deprived or when sex is not possible. Note, for instance, the heavily food-oriented Catholic countries (France, Italy, South American nations) where, traditionally, sexual activity has been discouraged before marriage and has been economically painful after marriage. Try to remember your own emphasis on food and eating during periods when you were either deprived or had your full share of varied sexual experiences. Consider also single individuals whose sexual life is clearly rich and gratifying and note whether they are less interested in food than other friends whose sexual activities are highly restricted or problem ridden. It is more difficult to assert this inverse relationship between sex and food interest for married couples because of the many unknown variables involved.

Boredom or depression can also be reasons for food-related preoccupations. Bored or depressed people who eat frequently have learned to temporarily increase their arousal and pleasure levels by nibbling or snacking; they do so in preference to staying hungry, which would also increase arousal but would be unpleasant. This is especially true if they eat more loaded foods—anything spicy, sweet, very hot, or very cold like ice cream or frozen puddings, or anything unusual or exotic. Of course, such people will soon pass into a lowered arousal state, thus defeating their real purpose if they overeat—particularly when they consume large amounts of carbo-hydrates, which can send blood sugar levels plummeting. If they attempt once again to raise arousal and pleasure levels, they will then eat more and thus are likely to become overweight. The solution is to eat frequent, small portions of highly loaded foods, perhaps favoring spicy dishes over the equally arousing sweet ones. When the hosts at a dinner party desire sustained and pleasant stimulation for most of the evening from food plus conversation, it makes sense to serve smallish courses, spread out over a two-or-three-hour period, with each course designed to stimulate the palate in a different and striking way.

In a number of the poorer cultures, where the mainstay is a bland but filling carbohydrate such as rice, corn, or wheat, there is a tendency to use extremely spicy ingredients. Indians, for instance, spice their food very heavily and in quite intricate ways, thereby attaining diverse and exceptionally stimulating flavors from very simple ingredients such as rice or vegetable dishes lacking meat, fish, or fowl. Thus, stimulation and arousal from food are enhanced (i.e., food and eating are made more arousing) by introducing either a large variety of spices (complexity) or by introducing extremely hot and spicy (intense) additives to the basic ingredients. On the other hand, wealthier cultures in which a wide variety of agricultural materials are readily available, are less likely to resort to elaborate methods of preparation involving hot and spicy additives, because these are not required as a means of attaining more arousal from food. The North American cuisine is illustrative: cooking styles are rather unimaginative and consist of the relatively simple and straightforward use of a variety of basic raw materials which are delectable in themselves.

Some people use food as a tranquilizer; they have learned to tolerate the initial "high" caused by eating and are instead looking for the longer, lowered arousal state caused by digestion. Such people are likely to "celebrate" by eating heavily when something unusual happens, either bad or good. They may tend to eat very quickly, since the point is not to savor the different flavors and textures of food—an arousing experience—but rather to get the food into the stomach so that the digestive processes may take over and produce a "low." They are also likely to be late-night eaters who've learned that they go to sleep more readily with food in their system, especially high protein or fatty foods that are digested more slowly than carbohydrates. Since people who eat in order to tranquilize rather than nourish themselves are likely to take in more food than their bodies can use, they are likely to be overweight.

An exception is *anorexia nervosa*, where the patient is an extreme nonscreener. He simply cannot afford the additional "high" from eating on top of his already excessive arousal state and loses weight precipitously—to the point of death from malnutrition. Something similar happens when people take diet pills, which are usually some sort of amphetamine (a strong stimulant); they are too highly aroused to seek further stimulation from eating and must be in very low-load environments before food can become tempting.

And then there are others who avoid the arousal-lowering effects of digestion. Such people must often be prevailed upon to "slow down and get a bite to eat." They have learned to avoid those environments which most people find optimal for eating, namely, the relatively low-load ones, and usually prefer to eat on the run (in the middle of a loaded environment) or in loud, noisy, crowded, or exotic restaurants.

So, despite our rudimentary knowledge, there are a few insights that might be applied. If you want to raise your arousal level for one reason or another, don't eat, eat very lightly, or eat larger meals slowly, relying on high-load foods. For example, the student who wants to be very alert for an exam should probably allow himself to get moderately hungry. Of course, extreme hunger may produce arousal levels so high that they interfere with the performance of complex and challenging tasks, and this should be avoided. Athletes sometimes have a big meal the night before a game and then do not eat or just nibble very early the next day. It is interesting that very aggressive athletes, or even aggressive salesmen or stockbrokers, are sometimes described as "hungry."

Eating constantly in order to raise one's arousal level and increase one's pleasure is ultimately self-defeating. As soon as the initial high is gone, lowered arousal and probably displeasure set in and linger for at least an hour. Eating constantly and heavily in order to lower arousal levels is also self-defeating. One tends to get fat, and being noticeably overweight in a culture like our own can have environmental consequences that are counterproductive. One may become an unpleasant and unusual social stimulus, and the likelihood of being rejected as a sexual partner increases greatly, resulting in very high arousal levels in most social situations. If the person turns to food to "celebrate" his often confirmed "unworthiness," this completes the vicious cycle.

The fourth under-the-skin way people have of controlling their emotional reactions to any given environment is what I've called head trips—essentially cognitive devices like daydreaming, fantasy, selective attention, meditation, or biofeedback.

If an environment becomes too heavily loaded, you can control its effect on your arousal level by concentrating on a limited set of stimuli. Experiments have shown that when people are placed in extremely loaded environments—with all sorts of visual stimuli such as mirrors, strobe lights, and wall projections; noises and many different kinds of music; and possibly even odors or strong air currents —they tend to shut off entire sensory channels. If, for example, they are visually oriented people, they attend to a select number of visual stimuli, don't "see" the rest, and don't "hear" anything. People with highly developed auditory channels who are used to absorbing and integrating great amounts of information through their ears— musicians, for example—selectively attend to some of the sounds and ignore the visual stimuli, or translate bizarre visual configurations into their more familiar auditory realm of experience. Others translate auditory stimuli into visual concepts and shapes (one piece of music may be associated with jagged shapes, another with the sounds of ocean waves). Such translation reduces the environmental load by assimilating the excessive and strange stimuli to familiar categories in a sensory channel that is highly developed and can handle more load.

You can find examples of extremely narrow attending in mental hospitals, where certain kinds of schizophrenics compulsively engage in the same simple behavioral routine for hours on end. A patient might walk ten paces in one direction, turn around, walk back ten paces, turn around in exactly the same way, and keep this up for many hours. Such a patient is experiencing intolerably high arousal— either as a result of his physiological makeup or in reaction to the hospital environment—and has learned to lower his arousal somewhat by concentrating on an extremely familiar, extremely structured, extremely monotonous task. In this case a tranquilizer may help relieve the patient from his narrow, compulsive behavioral routine.

But we all narrow our attention radically in certain very trying situations. Many scenes in literature and films are built around our tendency, in moments of great trauma, to concentrate intently on some humdrum, familiar little task. For example, there is a most insightful scene in Vladimir Nabokov's *Pnin* in which Professor Pnin, who has just received the shattering news that he has been fired, starts washing dishes; he scrubs them, rinses off the suds, meticulously dries them, and then delicately stacks them, as though they were the most precious china in the world. And, when Mr. Chips finds out that his wife has been killed, he takes out his watch, sees that his Latin class has a few more minutes to run, and plods on with the conjugations. Concentrating on the dreary little routines of life frequently enables people to go on after some terrible loss or disappointment. By performing such mechanical, low-load tasks people effectively put partial blinders on to screen some aspects of their environment and are able to reduce their extremely high arousal levels.

Various relaxation or meditation exercises also enable us to reduce our arousal levels through a combination of physical exercise and mental concentration. Biofeedback methods designed to induce relaxation simply provide a person with a visual or auditory index of his arousal level (EEG wave patterns or heart rate). He can then try out a variety of bodily, emotional, and cognitive attitudes until he hits upon a method which clearly reduces his arousal, and can then proceed systematically to lower it. If you are without such equipment, you can use the following classic relaxation exercise. Concentrate all your attention on a definite part of your body, tensing it up and letting out half the tension, feeling the residual tension, releasing half of that, and so on. The progression is from the extremities to the center of the body. Start with your fingers, wrists, and arms; then do the same with your toes, ankles, knees, and legs; next go on to the neck, face, and scalp. Finally, do the same with your stomach and chest, moving on to the entire body as a whole, from scalp to toes. Working through each part of the body slowly in this way takes a long time. You put a lot of physical energy and concentration into the selective tensing of each body part and the subsequent gradual draining of that tension. This exercise has proved useful for people who occasionally find it difficult to go to sleep. Others who are extremely aroused cannot make use of such relaxation exercises. For them it is necessary to propose more active exercise, such as lengthy and strenuous calisthenics, and settle for a heavy GAS effect.

Relaxation, meditation, biofeedback, or exercise techniques are active means of reducing arousal; but there is also the very simple passive and universal method of napping. For some people who function at a tremendous pace during working hours, even a half-hour nap—provided they are able to unwind sufficiently for it—can be very refreshing and far superior to drugs, alcohol, or relaxation exercises. In fact, it would be interesting to correlate the napping habits of persons who must function in high-load environments with their sense of physical well-being and illness rates.

Just as there are various cognitive means of coping with loaded environments, there are others for coping with low-load settings. An extreme example of a low-load environment is the sensory-deprivation laboratory, where subjects are placed in soundproof, darkened rooms and are deprived of practically all stimuli. The subjects soon begin to have bizarre thoughts, hallucinations, and an intense and disturbing awareness of internal bodily processes. The hallucinations and other internally generated stimuli function, among other things, to raise an unacceptably low arousal level.

But such things also happen in nonexperimental situations. A colleague of mine was treating a young man who reported that when he was home alone at night he would sometimes close his eyes and then be "attacked" by extremely vivid and frightening visual imagery. For instance, he saw himself running at a hundred miles an hour down a crowded street, with cars rushing toward him. These images would flash before him for a terrifying fifteen to thirty minutes. He felt he had no control over these hallucinations once they began, but could usually guess when they were about to happen.

I suggested that this client was probably suffering from extreme boredom and loneliness at night, and that his peculiar visual imagery was perhaps a costly way of compensating for the extremely low arousal associated with his boredom, which perhaps verged on depression. Indeed, we discovered that the client was lonely and bored, that his relationship with his girlfriend was not going well, that he was now spending a good deal of time alone, and was eating heavily while at home.

I then suggested that my colleague give his client a brief explanation of arousal level and its relation to boredom, and show the client ways in which he could manipulate his apartment environment to increase his arousal as soon as he felt the images coming. For example, he could turn on his stereo at a very high volume or turn on the stereo and the TV and play them both very loud. If he succeeded in raising his arousal level, the visual imagery probably would not be necessary and would cease. As things turned out, the TV wasn't necessary; the stereo alone did the trick. The images stopped, and my colleague and his client were then able to proceed to do something more permanent about dealing with the causes of the client's boredom and loneliness.

We all hallucinate to a greater or lesser extent, in the sense that we all daydream and fantasize. In general, we do this when we are in low-load situations—environments or activities we find boring, monotonous, routine, unstimulating, extremely familiar, and so on. We fantasize in low-load environments to raise our arousal levels, and usually also to increase our feelings of pleasure and dominance. For example, models who must remain immobile for twenty or thirty minutes at a time, surrounded by people who are quietly sketching them, frequently find fantasy the only means of raising intolerably low arousal levels.

The fact that we tend to fantasize in low-load environments has many broad implications, as we shall see in later chapters on schools, prisons, and retirement communities. However, I'd like to point out that fantasy is not always used to raise one's arousal level in a boring environment. There are instances when fantasy or daydreaming has the function of lowering arousal. Take for example the executive who in the middle of an especially loaded day leans back and imagines that he's lying by a pool in the warm sunshine, perhaps reading a book and sipping a nice cool drink. He then imagines an unbroken sequence of warm, lovely days at poolside with no decisions, no hassles, just relaxing, doing what he feels like doing and chucking what Philip Larkin calls the toad work squatting on one's life.* Such a relaxed, peaceful, and pleasant fantasy in effect lowers arousal and of course increases pleasure. This fantasy, like most, will probably turn out to be a disappointment when realized. The retired executive who spends his days lolling about a pool often finds that such a low-load environment drags his arousal level way down—he becomes terribly bored. Similarly, the POW or convict in a dreary, monotonous, and highly regulated environment will fantasize about food, women, freedom, and "doing everything" on the outside. Once such persons are released, however, they sometimes find that the outside contains more load than they can handle—there are too many problems, too many decisions, too many stimuli with which to cope.

Fantasies or daydreams are a resource that can be properly exploited or abused. To cite a positive example, the looseness and flexibility of free associations in fantasy are a significant part of the creative solution of artistic or intellectual problems. With looser associations, one tends to break old mental sets or habitual ways of

* Paraphrased from Philip Larkin's poem "Toads," from *The Less Deceived*, copyright © 1955 by The Marvel Press. Reprinted by permission.

thinking about a problem, and is more likely to connect ideas or events which he would not ordinarily relate. This is how some scientists or artists inadvertently arrive at their most creative solutions or ideas in the limelight zone between wakefulness and sleep, or when they are completely relaxed in a very monotonous, low-load environment and are hardly thinking of their work. The implication of course is not that such persons should habitually isolate themselves in monotonous environments, but rather that they should occasionally be given relief from their typically loaded settings and activity levels.

On the other hand, the socially inept person, whose retiring, passive, or shabby appearance does not elicit a stimulating reaction from others, will often turn to fantasy as a means of increasing his arousal, pleasure, and dominance. He may be the classic Walter Mitty type—a type reincarnated by Woody Allen in the movie *Play it Again, Sam*. His fantasies about seducing women, saving the gold shipment, or being a crack shot with a Weebley may strike us as incongruous, but they have the under-the-skin effect of making Mitty's life a fairly rich one. The pity is, perhaps, that such a person will rely more and more on his fantasy life for stimulation, pleasure, and mastery. He will not work at improving his behavioral repertoire so as to make his actual relations with others more stimulating and enjoyable. And, as we shall see in the next chapter, there are many things one can do to elicit such stimulating and pleasurable reactions.

Suggested Readings

Broadbent (1971) has several observations relating to various parts of this chapter. For some representative studies of the effects of music, see Ayres (1911), Ellis and Brighouse (1952), Rieber (1965), Smith and Curnow (1966), and Zimny and Weidenfeller (1962).

Activity level is a basic component of arousal (see Berlyne, 1960, 1967; Duffy, 1957, 1962; Lindsley, 1957); thus by definition, physical exertion or exercise is associated with high levels of arousal.

See Provins (1966) for the relation between thermal stimulation, as in a shower or a bath, and arousal levels; Jacobson (1938) for the technique of relaxation and its effect on arousal; and Bexton, Heron, and Scott (1954), Burney (1961), Cohen (1967), Gunderson (1963, 1968), Solomon, Leiderman, Mendelson, and Wexler (1957), and Zubek (1964) for representative findings relating to sensory deprivation. Also see Bliss and Branch (1960) about *anorexia nervosa*, and Schachter and Rodin (1974) on evidence to the effect that obese, compared to nonobese, persons are influenced more by environmental rather than internal, hunger cues in regulating their eating. See Osgood (1960) and Marks (1975) for studies of synaesthesia. For studies of biofeedback, meditation, and sleep physiology, see *Altered States of Awareness* (1972). Also see Barber (1970) for studies of yoga and hypnosis.

6

The Person as Environment— Clothing, Cosmetics, and Mannerisms

A FEW decades ago, a problem-solving method called systems analysis came into its own. Systems analysis starts with a precise description of goals (Z) and then works backward to the starting point (A). The end result is a step-by-step game-plan for getting from A to Z. Although quite successful in relation to certain kinds of problems, a pure form of systems analysis has often not been possible because people don't really know what they want—they can't define the Z with enough clarity and precision. And when we get into something like personal relations, the Z threatens to become hopelessly nebulous. What do we want our relations with other people to be like? What do we need and want from others? Such questions tend to slide into the enormous portmanteau: What is the good life?—a question that philosophers, poets, and the rest of the human race have wrestled with for millennia. Although metaphysical dangers abound, environmental psychologists should also have their chance to rush in where angels fear to tread and try to throw their own particular net over the elusive Z.

For starters, we can say that most of the time people prefer that their relations with others be characterized by approach rather than avoidance. You'll recall that approach behavior can be described as having to do with movement toward, exploration, friendliness, improved performance, and expressed liking. You'll also recall that we can effect approach or avoidance behavior by creating a certain combination of environmental load (arousal), pleasure, and dominance.

If we assume for the moment that we want others to approach us, we can say that what we want in general is to cause others to react to us with feelings of high arousal, pleasure, and a bit of dominance. For example, we usually don't want to bore or frighten them, because this causes avoidance and means that we won't get the attention, acceptance, approval, or affection we may need and want. Also, the more pleasure we can generate, the higher the level of arousal that others will tolerate from us; the greater the displeasure we generate, the lower the level of arousal they'll tolerate. This means that an exciting (highly arousing and pleasant) manner usually will attract others more than a comforting (unarousing and pleasant) one. On the negative side, a fearful or anxiety-ridden (highly arousing and unpleasant) manner will drive others away more than a boring (unarousing and unpleasant) one (see Figure 1).

Approval and affection both cause feelings of pleasure and moderate arousal; neither can be part of an avoidance reaction. Attention can be either positive or negative, but in either case people notice us, know that we are alive. To receive attention one must be at least a moderately loaded stimulus; receiving attention causes an increase in arousal level, which may or may not be temporarily desirable. It is safe to say, however, that most people prefer attention, particularly of a positive kind, to being ignored.

Let's take a look at clothing in terms of its ability to produce feelings of arousal, pleasure, and dominance. Clothing that is colorful, bright, and somewhat different from the usual styles is more loaded (complex and novel) and hence more arousing. Clothing that employs complex color patterns which are perceived as garish or clashing will produce feelings of arousal and displeasure. Transparent or semi-transparent apparel that exposes large areas of flesh, or soft, clingy fabrics which reveal every contour of the body, are novel and hence quite arousing. Of course, the high load of nudity serves to polarize attraction-repulsion, resulting in strong attraction when nudity or scanty dress is combined with a pleasant physique or body movements, and strong avoidance for an unpleasant appearance. Nudity per se is arousing only when circumstances make it unusual, unexpected, or novel; hence the often-remarked lack of arousal among long-time nudists or among people who are thoroughly familiar with each other's bodies.

People who select traditional, conservative, and expensive clothing with implications of wealth or social status are primarily tapping the dominance dimension. Those who have large, stylish wardrobes do so in order to arouse themselves and others through variety and novelty. In comparison to those who are stylish, the appearance of persons who seem weird is equally loaded, but unpleasant rather than pleasant. A slight variation of this phenomenon is the "shocking" costumes worn by those who challenge established norms and actually seek avoidance reactions from the conforming masses. This has been called *épater le bourgeois*, or making straights uptight.

People who stick to the same basic and somewhat drab styles, or even wear the same clothes day after day, are not loaded social stimuli. Compare the conservative matron who relies primarily on the same design, colors, and textures in her suits and shoes for months on end with the vivacious college student who changes her clothing in between morning and afternoon classes, and again in the evening before a dinner date.

The sounds made by our clothing and shoes as we move can connote a wide range of emotions: meekness, emotionality, strength, or carelessness. The stiff, crunching sound of some leather, together with its harder look, implies dominance and may explain the preference for suede, which is softer sounding and looking even though less practical. Shoes in particular can be selected to be noisy and rough (high-load in a dominant way), hushed and smooth sounding, or almost totally silent (low-load and submissive). Women today have the option of wearing clogs or wooden shoes to arouse and almost challenge. Taps on men's shoes used to be quite common and corresponded to the desired connotations of masculinity and strength. The classic example is an advertising man or salesman wearing massive and noisy shoes while he visits the typically far less aggressive college professor who wears crepe-soled hushpuppies.

Uniformity in the clothing styles of military, social, political, or ideological groups not only helps to readily identify a stranger's attitudes, primary preoccupations, or way of life, but also tells us something about his emotional preferences. Both the hippie and the beatnik movements rejected accepted social values. However, ideologically, the beatnik movement drew inspiration from philosophies which emphasized despair as the primary emotional reaction to existential dilemmas. The "heavy" beats often chose dark, severe, somber, and more tailored styles. Hippy garb, with its carefree, light, bright, flowery, and complex look, was consistent with its ideology, which emphasized pleasure, doing your own thing (variety), and a "flower-child" brightness and openness.

Western clothing styles and fashions have changed enormously over the centuries, of course, but there are a few constants we can point to. One of these is the dominance connotations of frills, extras, or generally complex clothing which only the wealthy can afford. Renaissance ballet masters trained courtly people to walk and to wear their clothing blithely and with elegance. Clothing had developed from fairly simple garments to elaborate draperies and shoes with long, pointed extensions from the toes that made it very difficult to walk. These masters were hired to train people to walk and move gracefully while wearing such elaborate attire. In this way, functional walking, sitting, and rising evolved into elaborate, graceful, and more deliberate movements that used clothing to advantage; for example, when dancing, clothing seemed to flow and almost served as an extension of the various movements.

Clothing that increases one's size and height also increases one's feeling of dominance. Even long hair and full beards have the effect of making a man look older and increasing the size of his head, thereby increasing his dominance aspect. Since the history of fashion has largely been that of the styles adopted by a dominant, if not all-powerful, cultural minority, it is probably no accident that most finery has historically been both elaborate and bulky—great capes, huge hoop skirts, a great deal of fur, enormous coiffures, and large, flowing, or trailing garments of one sort or another. Of course, there are other factors to be considered, like the lack of central heating in northern climates; nevertheless, most high-status clothing has, in the past, tended to add significantly to the wearer's physical stature. Even today, most women will opt for full-length gowns in formal situations or when they are acting as hostesses. And since the aristocratic or dominant minority had large amounts of leisure time and was often bored, it is natural that they sought to heighten their feelings of arousal and pleasure by wearing extremely elaborate and fanciful styles which their wealth and power were able to command.

Another interesting thing is how fashions change. If you look at what a Roman proconsul in Gaul wore, and compare his attire to that of a Norse chieftain, an Elizabethan courtier, or an Edwardian fop, and then look at the formal wear in the most recent *Gentlemen's Quarterly*, you will note extreme differences, but here we are talking about changes taking place over two millennia.

In comparison, current fashions involve less drastic changes. There are small-scope and frequent changes, however, partly because people get tired of the same old thing. Variations are introduced in order to increase environmental load (novelty) and thereby increase arousal. But as we have said earlier, too great an increase in load is avoided. Recently, for example, the fashion industry got something of a bloody nose when it attempted to shift, in a single season, from the mini to the midi. Most people simply would not buy the midi fashions. However, once the midi had been around for a few months, the transition to the maxi was quite a bit smoother. Somewhat earlier, the Nehru suit suffered much the same fate. During World War II, when large numbers of women entered the labor force, women's styles became less elaborate, more comfortable, and more masculine or dominant. Women began wearing suits with padded shoulders, platform shoes, and slacks or pantsuits. However, some of these fashions have taken more than thirty years to gain anything like full acceptance. Not too many years ago, for example, many fairly high-status establishments barred women wearing pantsuits. Even today, certain intensely bureaucratic institutions like public schools, the armed forces, or very large corporations whose personnel are extremely sensitive to departures from behavioral norms—especially insofar as these departures connote dominance or submissiveness— are likely to prohibit, or at least frown upon, the wearing of slacks by females.

About fifteen years ago, several major U.S. corporations had rules prohibiting their male personnel from wearing shirts of any other color but white. It is likely that color television has played a major role in reducing the novelty of colorful shirts, wild ties, and boldly patterned jackets. These are no longer novel enough to be excessively arousing, but it has taken a good ten years for them to be accepted. Such changes depart sharply from standards accepted for the past seventy years, according to which males could not dress in arousing (colorful) ways. This tradition is partly due to the fact that a few decades ago far more men than women had to work and were subjected to conservative norms of dress at work. The formal and unchanging clothing required of men by businesses made sense in that such attire implied status, respectability, permanence, and trustworthiness (in our terms, high dominance, slight pleasure, but low arousal). Thus, the suit, varying only slightly in cut from year to year and employing dull, low-saturation colors like gray, navy, black, or brown, came to be associated with dominance and a "masculine" role. Women, who remained at home and did not compete in any significant way with men, were expected to introduce variety into their clothing (and hence into their lives), and were of course encouraged to be a source of pleasant stimulation. Colorful attire and the use of cosmetics became identified in the public mind with generally feminine attributes and were therefore shunned by males.

Clothing styles continue to reflect concerns about dominance and sexual roles. For example, many businesses have relaxed their dress requirements for their male employees to the extent that a jacket and tie are no longer de rigueur. Nevertheless, many male employees, particularly those in managerial ranks, continue to wear the suit and tie with its strong connotations of respectability and trustworthiness —dominant status. Also, as the underlying principles of women's liberation have become somewhat more widely accepted, informal male styles have tended to become more masculine and hence implicitly more dominant. They have been modeled after work clothes; many items of military apparel have been introduced; safari or bush jackets have come back; and bulky leather or fur greatcoats are seen more frequently. Recently, the more formal styles have also become more masculine or traditional; suits, jackets, and trousers have eschewed the bolder cuts and hues and have returned to a somewhat more conservative look. The initially feminine platform shoe, which increases dominance by giving the impression of larger size, has also been appropriated by males, either in toto or in the form of somewhat higher heels. Beards and mustaches have made a comeback, initiated mostly by younger males. But it was not long before mature males also began sporting them to show the younger ones who's really "the old bull."

What I have said about clothing in relation to the feeling dimensions also applies to cosmetics and accessories. The more noticeable, varied, colorful, and unusual these are, the more arousing they can be. Jewelry, scarves, or other accessories that are classic in design and extremely valuable primarily serve to connote status and wealth, thereby increasing feelings of dominance. A person who wears tons of jewelry—beads, finger rings, bracelets, earrings, ankle rings, amulets, and so on—and furthermore ornaments his or her body with paint, decals, or tattoos, is striving to achieve an especially strong impact, to be a very arousing social stimulus. The implication is, "I am unconventional and I am open to all kinds of new experiences." But even relatively minor variations—a change in lipstick color, a new belt or purse, new shoes, a tan—can be arousing. Often, when someone returns from a skiing trip or a weekend at the beach, people will compliment him or her; the slight change in skin tint over a brief period of time introduces a touch of novelty and excitement.

The elaborate painted faces of the American Indians, their feathered hats, and their costumes were tailored to suit their festivities —war-related costumes being the most novel and colorful. The height of the feathers gave a man greater stature and implied strength; the number of feathers was a sign of dominance. Makeup for warlike activities was probably intended to frighten and subdue the enemy. To induce fear in another, one must look unpleasant, arousing, and dominant; so masks and wartime costumes were designed to be unusual or even bizarre (unpleasant and arousing) and to increase the size of the wearer.

Mannerisms—by which I mean posture, way of walking, manner of speech, the kinds of gestures one makes, and indeed the whole nonverbal repertory by which we communicate our feelings to others —can have extremely important effects upon our personal relationships. These too can be considered in terms of pleasure (or positiveness), dominance (or implied status), and load (or arousing quality).

Some important indicators of positive feeling are physical immediacy cues such as a close position to another, leaning toward him, touching, and orienting the body and head so as to be facing toward rather than away from him. Positive feeling is also indexed by declarative statement rate (how much we say to the other person), how much eye contact we have during conversation, the positiveness in the contents of what we say, the rate of head nodding, and the rate of hand and arm gestures.

People show feelings of dominance or imply high status by a relaxed posture; submissiveness is conveyed by slight tension. Relaxation while seated is indexed by asymmetry of arm and leg positions, sideways body lean, and a reclining position of the body in the chair. Relaxation while standing is indexed by fewer rocking movements of the body, fewer leg or foot movements, and a greater angle of body lean. Extreme submissiveness is indicated by bodily rigidity and symmetry, as for example in the soldier standing at attention.

Tension in one's posture not only conveys submissiveness but arousal as well. In addition, during conversation a person's arousing quality (load) is indexed by his speech volume, speech rate, and vocal expressiveness. Persons who characteristically talk louder and faster, using more expressive intonation patterns, are greater sources of arousal for those around them.

The emotional significance of specific movements and speech patterns can be interpreted by classifying them according to pleasantness, arousing quality, and dominant quality. To convey respect (positiveness plus slight submissiveness) in a job interview, for instance, we orient, lean forward, and look toward the interviewer, giving fuller answers, avoiding laconic "yes's" and "no's." This gets across the required positiveness; the submissiveness is conveyed by assuming a more symmetrical and forward leaning posture rather than a relaxed backward lean with crossed legs.

An uptight manner is overly tense, implying not only submissiveness and high arousal but some displeasure as well. Pacing—even a relaxed, pipe-puffing, staring-out-the-window sort of pacing a college lecturer might do in front of his class—indicates distress and avoidance reactions. The pacer is attempting to remove himself from the immediate environment. There are many other nonverbal ways in which we signal our feelings to others, but I cannot go into all of them in great detail here.*

We can change our emotional impact on others by altering our clothing, cosmetics, hair style, or mannerisms—changes which tend to reinforce each other's effects. It is much harder to change one's mannerisms than to modify one's clothing, cosmetics, or hair style, but then mannerisms probably contribute the most to emotional impact in the overall picture.

Change is worthwhile when we notice that our emotional impact causes avoidance. Imagine the unpopularity of someone who typically projects a neutral (neither pleasant nor unpleasant) and unaroused feeling. In contrast, if we are in the presence of someone who is physically expressing high arousal and pleasure, we are likely to participate somewhat in those feelings, experience an increase in our own arousal and pleasure, and approach. More specifically, the highest level of approach is elicited by persons who make us feel dominant, pleasant, and aroused. When we are made to feel submissive, the level of pleasure or arousal we feel does not significantly

---

* See my *Silent Messages* for a more detailed description of our nonverbal communication skills.

affect our friendliness toward others. Since a dominant feeling can arise either from the nature of the social relationships or from the environment, the effect of the environment can be extremely crucial in social situations. For instance, an environment which makes the people within it feel relaxed and comfortable (dominant and pleasant) will increase the friendliness among them.

You might do a little research among your friends and ask them to rate your appearance in terms of arousal, pleasure, and dominance. But before you do, keep in mind that a nonscreener will find your appearance more arousing than a screener will, and could in fact find it too arousing. On the other hand, a screener might be inclined to rate your appearance as not arousing enough.

If you find that the consensus is that your appearance is somewhat unarousing, try and introduce a little variety and novelty: get a haircut, try a little more makeup, add a few more colorful items to your wardrobe, vary your perfumes or colognes, pick up a few pieces of costume jewelry, and so on. If you find that your appearance is less than pleasant, consider making changes in your personal hygiene, add or lose some weight, take more exercise or sun. Try to add more mannerisms conveying pleasure to your repertory: smile more often, touch people a bit more, or stand a little closer to them than you normally do. Don't forget that a shy or half-hearted smile or an awkward, tentative pat on the back goes a lot farther than none at all.

If you find that you are judged to appear submissive, try wearing bulkier or more conservative clothing and hair styles. Wear shoes that make some noise when you walk, and walk more quickly. Exercise more to become physically fit, hold your head up, straighten your back. If your gestures tend to be slow and hesitant, speed them up a bit. Even your manner of speech can be changed to appear more assertive and fluent instead of seeming hesitant, pause- or error-ridden.

Transvestites represent the most dramatic example of influencing one's impact on others through the selection of clothing. The transvestite experiences many of the subtle ways in which the two sexes are treated differently. Such a person who occasionally switches the "sex" of the clothing he or she wears can add tremendous variation to his or her effects upon others in a wide range of activities and settings.

The changes in appearance or mannerisms that can significantly affect one's own emotional state, one's emotional impact on others, and one's social relations have been overlooked in most therapeutic schools. Traditional therapies have tended to focus on internalized conflicts and have failed to consider some of the very obvious ways in which a person projects certain feelings, and how others react to those projected feelings. Wilhelm Reich was an exception; he paid a great deal of attention to the postures of his patients, and how posture generally relates to an individual's personality and the effect he has on others. Today's popular Rolfing methods follow Reich's lead in using a variety of massage techniques to ease postural tension and its connoted submissiveness and excessive arousal (anxiety).

Many interpersonal problems can be more profitably examined in terms of a patient's present behavioral patterns and style of self-presentation than in terms of the historical antecedents—parent-child relationships, and so on—of those problems. Someone who is bored, lonely, and depressed may have ceased to pay much attention to his physical appearance because that entails too much effort in relation to his current depressed state. However, his drab or unpleasant physical appearance makes it less probable that he will meet people who will diminish his feelings of loneliness by responding to him in approving or affectionate ways. If the therapist succeeds in getting the patient to dress and groom himself in a more arousing and pleasant way, chances are that the patient will experience a rise in arousal level and begin to feel more cheerful. As a result, he will be more likely to approach and be approached by others. He might even find himself having a little affair, in which case he could find the next chapter worth looking into.

Suggested Readings

For an analysis of, and experimental data on, emotional states that a person needs to create to elicit interpersonal approach (or affiliation), see Mehrabian and Russell (1975a). Note specifically the data presented by Mehrabian and Russell (1974b) on the criteria which make any stimulus (e.g., a person) high- versus low-load. See Osgood, Suci, and Tannenbaum (1957) for qualities (e.g., large-small, heavy-light) which make something or someone appear dominant rather than submissive. For detailed formulas on how to combine pleasure-displeasure, arousal-nonarousal, and dominance-submissiveness to elicit a specific emotional reaction from another, see Russell and Mehrabian (1976d).

Our discussion of large, discontinuous changes in fashions is based on the idea that such changes are unexpected or improbable, highly arousing, and thus unpreferred (e.g., Fiske and Maddi, 1961; or McClelland, Atkinson, Clark, and Lowell, 1953, on the "discrepancy hypothesis"). Evidence of women's greater feelings of arousal and, as a consequence their more arousing quality relative to males, was provided by Mehrabian and Russell (1974a, page 47). Robinson (1975) considered the specific issue of fashion in relation to implied social status.

General discussions of nonverbal communication and data from numerous experiments are summarized by Hall (1966), Mehrabian (1971, 1972a, 1972b), and Sommer (1969). For psychotherapeutic approaches which change the periphery (e.g., postural tension, behavior modification) and expect corresponding changes in personality, see Bandura (1969), Mehrabian (1970), and Reich (1945).

7

Between the Sheets

PEOPLE mainly do two things in bed together: they sleep and they have sex. Both these things are a rich source of conjugal problems, and both can be related directly to the concept of stimulus screening.

We go to sleep when our bodily systems can no longer maintain the arousal states associated with wakefulness. This is reminiscent of GAS reactions—in both instances the body seeks relief from sustained arousal. The difference is that sleepiness is a normal part of daily cyclical changes in arousal, whereas in GAS reactions the low arousal feelings of depression or exhaustion result from high levels of arousal that are sustained for abnormally long periods.

When daily events and settings are moderate- or even low-load, screeners go to sleep more readily than nonscreeners because nonscreeners have more difficulty in shutting out distracting stimuli. This difference is even more pronounced when some high-load events or settings have been confronted briefly, perhaps about an hour or so prior to bed-time. Nonscreeners, in this case, take longer to relax (to lower arousal levels) sufficiently to be able to sleep. The opposite pattern, however, is expected when daily events are high-load or when the activity pace has been especially high so that arousal levels have been raised for several hours. Everyone in this situation will tend to feel fatigued and sleepy earlier in the evening. This will be especially true for nonscreeners because the sustained high loads of the day will have been particularly arousing for them. So, in general, there is more of a tendency for nonscreeners to have greater difficulty in going to sleep, if we assume that low- or moderate-load days and brief, as distinct from sustained, high-load events are more common. In these more common situations, the nonscreeners take longer to fall asleep.

In many heterosexual relationships, the female is likely to be the nonscreener and be the one likely to have trouble getting to sleep; that is, be too aroused for sleep if something unexpected or difficult has happened late in the evening—an accident in front of the house, a spat over the liquor bill, a feverish child, or whatever. She will therefore want to do something routine or relaxing before going to bed—perhaps catching a bit of the late show, doing a little light reading, or merely talking over things with her husband. Her husband, on the other hand, is more likely to be a screener. In the evening, his arousal level is likely to be low, especially after a fatiguing day, so that sleep is almost upon him. He may either retire before his wife or fall asleep almost as soon as his head hits the pillow.

Of course, I do not mean to imply that females always screen less than males. There are many cases in which both mates are screeners or nonscreeners, or in which the male is a nonscreener. The point is that a relationship in which one mate is a screener and the other a nonscreener requires some sensitive adjustment on the part of both.

Excluding the possibility of high-load days when arousal levels have been high for several hours, nonscreeners, who are generally sensitive to minute changes in the environment, may even have trouble with open bedroom windows. A screener will not be kept up by occasional traffic noise or the wind rustling in the leaves outside, but a nonscreener may. Furthermore, minor household stimuli—the ticking of a clock, a nightlight, a dripping faucet—may cause sleeplessness in the nonscreener while not in the least disturbing the screener. Indeed, the mere presence of another body in the bed—touching, turning, emitting grunts or snores—may represent enough load for the extreme nonscreener so that sleep becomes difficult or broken. In such a case, it is foolish for either partner to resist the notion of twin beds or even separate bedrooms. During the night, the nonscreener is more likely to be awakened by something. If that something cannot readily be identified, anxiety may set in, causing the nonscreener to wake the partner and gain reassurance that everything is OK.

Besides problems with sleep, there may be even more serious problems with sex. Leaving individual differences in stimulus screening aside for the moment, we can say that among human beings, frigidity or the inability to achieve orgasm, impotence, and premature ejaculation are the most common sexual problems. In the past, clinicians have often approached these problems mostly in terms of early psychosexual or developmental considerations, and have tended to make much of traumatic childhood episodes—molestation by Uncle John, seeing mommy and daddy "hurting each other" in bed, and other more elaborate, tailor-made, fanciful reconstructions of the past. But these sexual problems frequently have simple physiological explanations and are relatively easy to remedy. In our terminology, these problems have something to do with arousal.

Let's look at the most common male failures first, namely, impotence and/or premature ejaculation. Males achieve erection in two stages. First, there must be a momentary stage of moderate arousal and fairly high pleasure in which the parasympathetic or relaxant nervous system takes over and allows blood to be pumped into the extremities. There is a sphincter-like muscle at the base of the penis which must relax and allow blood to flow in to cause an erection. Then this muscle must constrict and contain the blood, thus maintaining the erection. This second or constrictive stage is associated with high arousal (the sympathetic nervous system), as is orgasm itself. Indeed, sexual excitement and orgasm can be among the highest arousal states a human being achieves.

When the male is for one reason or another anxious about a sexual encounter, his state of high arousal, displeasure, and submissiveness effectively prevents blood from entering the penis and hence impotence results. In situations like this, arousal level must be lowered and pleasure increased. A relaxant, especially a relaxant like alcohol (a couple of stiff drinks), which also increases feelings of pleasure, may help correct this situation. So will a pleasant, low-load environment, or the soft lights and gentle music thought to be appropriate for seduction. However, too much alcohol or any other relaxant will lower the male's arousal level so far that the sphincter-like penis muscle will not constrict sufficiently and the erection will not be sustained.

If arousal level is too low, tumescence will either not occur at all or will be fleeting at best. An extreme screener or older male may have this problem, especially with a familiar sexual partner. In this case, arousal level must be brought up, possibly with a stimulant (a couple of cups of coffee) or some light exercise, including somewhat vigorous horseplay or foreplay. Greater environmental load will also do the trick—loud, fast music, bright lights, a threesome, or whatever. In Truffaut's movie, *Such a Gorgeous Kid Like Me*, the sexually active male cabaret singer invariably tipped off his friends to what was going on by playing racing-car records at very high volumes. Such incisive storytelling can only be attributed to the script writer's familiarity with a character who accidentally must have discovered a miraculous cure for the problem of insufficient arousal during sex.

Premature ejaculation occurs when the erect male becomes too excited (too aroused, too pleased) by the rich and varied experience of sex. This happens especially among young or inexperienced males. Both the sexual experience and the sexual partner are novel (highly loaded) and this sends his arousal level sky-high. The problem is typically exacerbated by excessively arousing foreplay. Experience and increased familiarity with the partner usually will diminish this problem as long as neither partner dwells on it. But if premature ejaculation persists, the male should seek a low-load environment or consider a relaxant.

We are now in a position to understand consistent differences in the problems reported by male and female patients at sex-therapy clinics. The most common problem among females is frigidity or failure to achieve orgasm, which usually results from insufficient arousal. For males, it is impotence and premature ejaculation which result from excessive and early arousal before and following erection, respectively. Insufficient female arousal can be explained partially by conventional male-female positions and activity levels during intercourse. The conventional position has the male on top, free to move about, and therefore better able to achieve activity levels consistent with a high arousal state. Females who are pinned down and generally confined in their ability to move may be unable to achieve arousal quickly enough, or may find their position increasingly unpleasant. The active, highly aroused male (who may not be aware of the pleasure and arousal levels of his partner) is therefore likely to ejaculate before the female has reached the necessary high arousal level. To remedy such problems, males suffering from impotence or premature ejaculation might experiment with more passive and inactive roles, especially during the early stages of the sexual act. Females who suffer from orgasmic incompetence might experiment with more active roles that allow for vigorous freedom of movement.

There are, however, limits to compatibility. A male nonscreener and a female screener may simply not get it on satisfactorily. The male will have climaxed long before the female has reached an orgasmically high level of arousal. This is especially true of sexual contacts in high-load settings or with unfamiliar partners. On the other hand, in a relationship involving a female nonscreener and a male screener, the female is going to get the best of the bargain. Since females in a state of high arousal and pleasure can achieve multiple orgasm, a male screener who takes a long time getting there will provide a great deal of satisfaction.

Everyone is sensitive to the pleasure-displeasure dimension during sex because the higher loads of sexual activity which make it especially attractive when it is pleasant make it particularly repulsive or problem-ridden when it is in some way unpleasant. (This is simply a restatement of the principles outlined in Figure 1.) The point of greater interest here is that since nonscreeners are more aroused than screeners in high-load situations, it follows that they should be even more sensitive to the pleasure-displeasure dimension during sex. Specifically, this means that when the pleasure element is guaranteed by a loving and attractive partner and a generally pleasant relationship, nonscreeners are likely to have a greater preference for sex, engaging in it more frequently than screeners. On the other hand, when there is unpleasantness or a problem during sex, or even in other aspects of a relationship, nonscreeners tend to become more anxious and have more problems during sex. Thus, while experiencing similar levels of displeasure, nonscreeners probably avoid sex more and engage in it less frequently than screeners.

It is understandable, then, that given a relatively fixed emotional effect from the partner in a relationship of long standing, or the usually unchanging emotional impact of the environment in which they have sex, people learn to use fantasies to fine-tune pleasure and arousal levels. Contrary to Victorian attitudes that continue to have a limited hold on popular thoughts on female sexuality, research findings have shown that during intercourse American women engage in a considerable amount of fantasy involving seduction, rape, group sex, and so on. And of course, nonscreening males may just as easily fantasize about low-load and pleasant events to delay orgasm during sex. But fantasies during sex are probably used more often to increase rather than decrease arousal. They may also represent an attempt to increase pleasure, especially when the fantasy involves a substitute, and more desirable, partner.

There are instances in which the necessary arousal for sex is achieved by confrontation. It has often been noted that two people who are extremely close can have a terrific fight one moment and fall into passionate lovemaking the next. This happens most often when one mate is angry (highly aroused, highly displeased, and dominant) and the other is anxious (highly aroused, highly displeased, and submissive). One partner is "blowing his stack" and the other is fuming or sulking. In such lovers' quarrels, the only dimension that undergoes change is the dimension of pleasure. At some point in the argument, the couple may become aware of some absurdity and laugh. Even more importantly, an intimate relationship is bound to involve established patterns of sexual attraction such that specific expressions, postures, or gestures can bring forth strong positive feelings in either partner. This is how, during this highly aroused state, the occurrence of any one of these characteristic, habitual, and positive-toned expressions can cue foreplay—the pleasure dimension shifts from high displeasure to high pleasure, and the partners are suddenly not fighting, but making love instead. After the shift to pleasure and while making love, one partner feels high arousal, pleasure, and dominance while the other feels high arousal, pleasure, and submissiveness.

The aggressor in the quarrel is also likely to be the aggressor in sex because the arousal and dominance feelings don't have to change as he moves from one to the other situation. For the same reason, the victim in the quarrel is also likely to be the more passive partner in sex. Sado-masochistic relationships understandably involve this interplay between aggression and sex in which the sadist shifts from punishing to loving and the masochist shifts from fear and pain (high arousal, displeasure) to heights of sexual excitement (high arousal, pleasure). Extremely pathological manifestations of rapid shifts in the pleasure dimension occur when a victim is first terrorized, then raped, and then murdered.

The dominance aspect of sex is thorny and problematic. Although we now laugh at the Victorian male who, when approaching his wife sexually, told her to "Shut your eyes, dear, and think of England," such attitudes have not by any means disappeared. Not too many years ago a leading young "revolutionary" told an assembled group of male and female civil rights workers that the proper position for women in the movement was "prone." (He meant "on their backs," of course.)

You will recall that one basic personality dimension has to do with one's characteristic level of dominance or submissiveness. Despite the more open discussion of sexual matters today, and despite the liberating effects of feminine militancy, many people still find it difficult to go against the cultural grain and behave dominantly when they have been conditioned to assume a submissive position, and vice versa. A characteristically submissive male may find it extremely difficult to assume a dominant sexual role in relation to his female partner. Similarly, a characteristically dominant female may worry a good deal about her "feminine identity," or perhaps find herself losing male sexual partners if she experiments with or adopts an aggressive role. I suppose the best advice would be, "If it feels good, do it," but I suspect that such an attitude will be acted upon only if both partners feel dominant as well as highly aroused and pleasant. Clearly, it would help if a certain amount of social deconditioning could take place so that males would not automatically become anxious or turned off in the presence of a dominant female.

Confusions deriving from the dominance-submissiveness personality dimension appear to have a good deal to do with the choice of homosexual rather than heterosexual partners. Research has shown that male homosexuals either lacked a father to identify with (the father was absent or emotionally distant) or only had access to a very harsh and punitive father whose dominant role they could not identify with—hence the resulting problems in assuming the more dominant masculine role.

In any case, there doesn't seem to be a great deal one can do about one's characteristic dominance level, at least in bed where people are usually deprived of many environmental props, including their clothing, that can signify dominance. It was Flaubert, I believe, who had intercourse with a prostitute while dressed in top hat and tails—a pathetic and degrading attempt to express dominance which can hardly be recommended. However, some experimentation with personal or environmental props which help a person attain a more dominant feeling might pay off if both partners are fully agreeable.

The bedroom environment can itself be manipulated in order to heighten sexuality for certain kinds of people. We will talk about this further in the following chapters.

Suggested Readings

Masters and Johnson (1966) provided extensive data on sexual problems and various therapeutic approaches to these. For our fundamental distinction between the sexual problems of screeners and nonscreeners, note the more basic physiological data related to stimulus screening (Mehrabian, 1976a, 1976b;

Nebylitsyn, 1972; Nebylitsyn and Gray, 1972; Siddle and Mangan, 1971). Regarding the recommendation of uses of stimulants and relaxants, see the suggested readings for chapter four.

See the work of May (1966) for a discussion of women's fantasies during sex; note Jaffe, Malamuth, Feingold, and Feshbach (1974) on the relationship between sexual arousal and aggression; and refer to Green (1974) for hypotheses concerning effeminate males. Also see *Altered States of Awareness* (1972), Dement (1960), and Snyder (1971) for summaries of findings on dream deprivation and the physiology of dreaming.

PART THREE

RESIDENTIAL

ENVIRONMENTS

8

Today's Homes

NOT MANY of us can afford to hire an interior decorator, and even fewer can afford to have our homes designed and built for us. But the best decorators and architects intuitively create designs which successfully key into the three basic emotional dimensions of arousal, pleasure, and dominance.

The homes most of us are forced to buy or rent, however, are usually built and decorated in accordance with economic considerations and established traditions rather than with serious attention to the emotional impact of the various rooms. They are often rather poorly laid out, consisting basically of a series of rectangular boxes connected by doors of varying widths. If the house is a large two-story structure, the boxes on the first floor are the "socializing" areas like dining room, family room, kitchen, living room, and possibly a den or a library, with the second-floor boxes usually given over to bedrooms and large bathrooms. If the house is a ranch-type structure, all the boxes are of course on the same level. In any case, these boxes often are not situated properly to be used for what they were designed—some may be too far away and inaccessible. For instance, a spacious and attractive patio may be situated to the side of the house, away from the living room, so that the only access to it is via one of the bedrooms. It won't be used; instead, the favorite spot will be a smaller and less attractive patio adjacent to the living room. A "family room" may be stuck off somewhere in a remote wing of the house; it may have a northerly exposure and hence not receive much sunlight; its windows may open onto the neighbor's garage. Also, it may have a long, narrowish shape which precludes informal or circular arrangements of furniture. This room will not be used as a family room; instead, the husband or wife will use it to take naps. On the other hand, the kitchen may be large and bright; it might face the backyard with its trees, grass, or flowers. It may contain a fairly large table with room for books, newspapers, or bills to be spread out upon it by several members of the family, yet not so large that conversation from one end to the other is forced. This will become the family room. Here the members of the family will tend to gather together or at least linger after eating. Friends who drop in during the day will often be received here rather than in other areas of the house. In a more extreme case, and simply due to its strategic location, an austere dining area adjoining the kitchen may serve as the gathering spot for the family and their close friends while a large and luxuriously furnished living room far off somewhere goes to waste.

What then are some of the considerations in deciding whether an area will be used at all or whether it will be used for its assigned purpose? Because a pleasant environment causes approach behavior —causes us to affiliate with other people or simply desire to stay in it—there is no reason why any room in one's house should be unpleasant. Because moderately high arousal levels are needed for people to socialize with one another, all rooms that will be used to entertain guests, or in which the family will gather for any purpose other than dining, should possess a moderately high load. Areas that will be used for tasks requiring relatively low levels of arousal— eating, sleeping, unwinding, or doing complex work requiring concentration—should be very pleasant but low-load. Since few of us will be entertaining heads of state, and since few of us can afford expensive furnishings in areas that rarely will be used, there is seldom need for extremely formal sitting or dining rooms done in classic, costly, dominant styles.

Before further discussion of interior decor and its relation to room choice for different activities, let us contemplate the effects of floor plans on room use. Consider a basic floor plan that would satisfy the needs of most families. Assuming, for the moment, that we are talking about a single-story structure up to $50,000 in price variations of this plan would differ primarily in terms of the size and, to a certain extent, the placement of the bedrooms.

What the plans would have in common is the socializing core, consisting of kitchen, family room, and living room in something like the following arrangement:

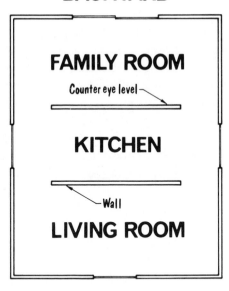

BACKYARD

FAMILY ROOM

Counter eye level

KITCHEN

Wall

LIVING ROOM

FIGURE 3

Even though most of the family eating would be done in the kitchen area, part of the living room adjacent to the kitchen might be given over to more elaborate dining occasions. This kitchen/family room/ living room core would be placed in such a way as to provide maximum sunlight and the most pleasant and stimulating views available —of the grounds, of a garden, of the cityscape, or whatever. Preferably, the family room ought to face the backyard or patio area so that the family could make use of this outdoor space for recreation, games, or barbecues, and still have ready access to the kitchen facilities.

In a servantless household, whoever does the cooking is the crucial person and cannot be isolated, since his or her activities tend to form the center of gravity. In addition, the kitchen is the source of certain elemental blessings—food in the refrigerator, a glass of water, ice cubes, or an ice cold beer. In many households, the everyday liquor is kept in or very near the kitchen, unless there is a separate wet bar and refrigerator somewhere else. In other words, people have many reasons for gravitating toward the kitchen, which tends to form the home's natural heart.

It makes sense then that a kitchen should be livable and attractive. It should be well-ventilated and have good uniform lighting throughout. Surfaces should be easy to clean. Highly textured floors or counters which trap particles are difficult to clean and should be avoided unless they considerably enhance the pleasantness of the facility. The stove, oven, sink, and refrigerator should be arranged so that there is an easy flow of movements without too many steps, with dishes, pots, and pans placed within fairly easy reach. Problems arise when, for instance, the sink and some counter space are along one wall and the remaining counter space is along the opposite wall. If the kitchen is large enough, it is possible to have a central island which includes a stove, grill, chopping-board area, and even an extra sink; located in the center of the kitchen, it minimizes unnecessary movement. Some pots and pans can be hung above so they are readily accessible to the person working at the stove. The logic of minimizing movement also applies to the storage of different items in the various cabinets and shelves. Items or ingredients that are frequently used should be placed in cabinets or shelves that are within easiest reach.

When the kitchen is surrounded by and not segregated from the main living areas in which many different activities can take place— eating, watching TV, entertaining, doing homework, playing games —the result is a functional but nonspecialized core that greatly enhances a family's cohesiveness. This arrangement also lends itself nicely to large-scale entertaining, since one can have a big party without boxing the guests in. They will have room to mingle and also will be able to feel the presence of others in different parts of the core area.

Families which consist predominantly of nonscreeners will require slightly different variations of the basic floor plan than families in which most members are screeners. Remember that nonscreeners, compared to screeners, are more likely to avoid arousing and un- pleasant tasks and environments. Thus, areas of the home where demanding and somewhat unpleasant chores are performed must be especially private and free of distractions (low-load) for nonscreeners. They ought to be able to shield the areas they choose to work in—their bedrooms, studies, or even parts of the living room or den—from noise and interruptions by others. An alternative approach is to make special efforts to create pleasant work areas for nonscreeners who are bound to perform an occasional unpleasant task. A larger chunk of the total floor space of the house could be devoted to individual, pleasant, and more segregated bedrooms to accommodate nonscreeners, whereas parts of the core could just as easily serve as work areas for the screeners. Bedrooms which will be used by nonscreeners as work areas, places to unwind, or to perform complex and arousing mental tasks should not be too highly loaded in their decor. They should be quite flexible in terms of lighting and other forms of controllable environmental stimuli to make absolute silence or darkness readily attainable.

Generally, the design of a house can be improved by observing actual family activity patterns. One can discover how, and how frequently, the various spaces are used and whether the usage conforms to the anticipated functions. This kind of analysis will pinpoint spaces that are wasted and others which serve many more functions than they were designed for. It also will reveal the quality of family life, such as its cohesiveness and the home design features it requires.

The relationship of this core, or the entire home for that matter, to its surroundings can be considered using the idea that more loaded, pleasant environments are preferred to a greater extent, whereas more loaded, unpleasant environments are avoided more. A house that faces unpleasant, noisy, crowded, polluted streets with heavy traffic can be shielded by hedges, a garden, potted plants, or trees; here the challenge is even greater to try to create pleasant and stimulating interior areas. On the other hand, a house that faces a garden with trees in a noise- and pollution-free setting is usually designed with much exposure to the outside, providing stimulation from variations in sunlight, cloud patterns, and wind. This is especially the case when the vegetation, flowers, and trees attract birds, squirrels, and lizards, whose habits and activities can be a rich source of stimulation. Views from different vantage points within such a house enable the residents to have changing input from their pleasant surroundings as they socialize, do light reading, work, eat, or bathe.

When we design and decorate a core area intended to encourage people to interact enjoyably with one another, we must make this area both pleasant and stimulating. Our studies have shown that socializing not only involves conversation but includes the essential element of verbal and nonverbal exchanges of liking. Even though these subtle exchanges, which include eye contact, head nods, and gesturing, are seemingly not attended to, they have a powerful effect on whether people continue to converse and whether they enjoy doing it. Findings have also shown that such exchanges of liking increase in pleasant surroundings; that is, regardless of with whom we converse, we are more prone to be positive if we are in a more pleasant setting.

When people feel dominant, as when they are on their own home territory, environmental load also contributes to their gregariousness. You will recall that two factors, novelty and complexity, combine to give any environment its characteristic load. Even if we furnish a living area in novel, rare, unexpected, or surprising ways, it will sooner or later become familiar and thus less arousing to all but those who haven't been there before. Probably the only practical way to increase the novelty of such an environment is to redecorate from time to time, adding, subtracting, or shifting things around. For this reason, it is a good idea to select furnishings that are light, movable, and admit of several pleasant combinations. Large, bulky pieces that fit only a few corners or wall spaces, or a great many built-ins, will lock you into one static and potentially boring pattern. It is somewhat easier to make the socializing environment a complex one with lots of colors, textures, and other stimuli for the eye and ear. Aquariums, mobile sculptures, and fireplaces are good decorating items precisely because they are colorful and incorporate motion. Mirrors or milar surfaces which are situated so as to reflect the most colorful, warm, and complex areas of a room have the effect not only of increasing the perceived size of the room but also of increasing its complexity. Mirrors placed opposite blank walls or plain draperies should be avoided because of the resulting colder and more distant (low-arousal) feeling. Potted plants and flowers not only contribute heavily to the pleasure dimension but add complexity and novelty through their changing shapes. Also, the different green shades provided by plants contrast sharply, especially with the now fashionable white walls. Tapestries, textured wallpapers, and cork, brick, or wood paneling all contribute more pleasant textures and color combinations of higher load than smooth-plastered, uniformly painted walls.

Aside from all of these primarily static devices for increasing environmental load, there is the tremendous potential contribution of music for increasing pleasure as well as load. Even a single piece of music consists of changing patterns over time; furthermore, a most sophisticated technology allows us to increase the novelty of the pieces we listen to or avoid excessively high-load (overly complex, unfamiliar, or dissonant) selections. The simple act of adjusting the volume of music to the desired level readily alters its load and reminds us of the unusual flexibility of this aspect of our home environments. At a casual get-together, for instance, the complexity, novelty, and intensity of music can be made to compensate for the arousal level of guests. If the pace of social interaction is pretty high, then the volume can be turned down; however, if the activity and arousal levels of guests begin to falter, the volume can be raised to a moderate level with livelier selections.

Lighting is extremely important. Brightly lit rooms are more arousing than dimly lit ones, and so the social area must have a good overall lighting capability. If you do a lot of entertaining—everything from large cocktail parties to small sit-down dinners—you must be able to vary the intensity of the lighting. When large numbers of relative strangers gather, very bright lights might cause them to feel a bit self-conscious initially. Ideally, one should have dimmers so that the lights could be somewhat lower at the beginning of the party and then be turned up as the party progresses. Note that often people will tend to crowd into the kitchen after a party has gone on for some time; the kitchen is usually brightly lit, and the brightness, density, or even cooking odors serve to increase arousal levels. On the other hand, since the social area will also be used for dining where in most cases bright lights will be too arousing, your lighting system should be flexible enough for you to dim the lights somewhat during meals. Because people tend to avoid dark corners, you should have enough lamps and other independent light sources so that all parts of the social area can be lit and hence used. And of course the social area should be placed in such a way as to take fullest advantage of natural light; the changing patterns of sunlight over the course of the day can be both pleasant and stimulating. Particularly colorful areas, tapestries, or large paintings might be spotlighted—where there is no light, there is no color. If you wish, for one reason or another, to be able to make the social area extremely arousing, colored lights might also be used. According to research findings, red lights would be most arousing; hand tremor and fast muscular reaction time, both indicators of arousal, are increased under deep red light. Colored lights also have the effect of changing the hue of familiar objects, making them look incongruous or strange, thus increasing their novelty. But such effects should be used carefully, and only when very high levels of arousal are wanted. For most social situations—unless everybody is drunk or stoned and hence physiologically quite depressed—such lighting or strobe lights may be too novel and cause avoidance. If you do a good deal of entertaining, it will probably be worthwhile to make the guest bathroom a fairly colorful and arousing one; otherwise the contrast between the loaded party environment and a very low-load guest bathroom will be disagreeable.

To use color effectively, we need to know its emotional effects, and these are readily summarized. Color is characterized by hue, brightness, and saturation. Hue is related to wavelength and hence determines whether colors are perceived as red, blue, green, and so on. Brightness refers to the intensity of light that is reflected; saturation refers to the concentration or vividness of the hue. The brighter or more saturated the color, the more pleasant it is. The most pleasant hues are blue, green, purple, red, and yellow, in that order. In terms of arousal, less bright and more saturated colors are more arousing. The most arousing hue is red, followed by orange, yellow, violet, blue, and green, with green being the least arousing. Thus, if we wanted to maximize arousal in a given room, we would probably use flocked, velvety, or otherwise textured deep red wallpaper, carpets, and curtains. Color schemes selected for the social core, for instance, would emphasize the more arousing hues and the more saturated colors. It is probably no accident that extremes of such a decorative scheme often prevailed in the better nineteenth-century brothels.

Lighting and colors may also be used in therapeutic ways. For example, brighter lights and more arousing and pleasant colors may be especially recommended for someone living alone who is prone to depression. If the interior designer manages to achieve a happy feeling within the physical environment, this can help his client to overcome depressed feelings and might even compensate for the client's somewhat nonarousing manner when people are over to visit.

Many living rooms are failures for entertaining not only because they are not colorful and are poorly lit but also because room shapes or the type and arrangement of furniture seriously depress arousal levels. Some rooms feel too large and cold and can easily be made to seem smaller by colors and textures on the walls. Since a high-load surface—one that is heavily textured and contains sharp color contrasts involving arousing colors—appears closer than a low-load one, the perceived shape of a room can be altered dramatically by judicious application of this principle. For example, ceilings can be "lowered" or "raised" by using more or less arousing colors and textures, respectively. When a room feels overly confining, less arousing surfaces must be used. A trick decorators often use is to paint opposite walls darker and lighter shades of the same color, thus making a narrow room seem wider.

Large rooms with furniture, especially long couches, set along the walls at wide intervals prevent guests from facing each other at the proper angles and also introduce too much distance between them. In our experiments, we've manipulated the arousing quality of social settings by having people interact from a variety of distances and orientations. When pairs of strangers are asked to wait in a room together, those who are allowed to sit at greater distances from each other tend to be more relaxed but socialize less. When pairs are inconspicuously positioned to wait together at closer range, there is more tension (arousal) but also more conversation, especially among those who might otherwise be subdued due to their sensitivity to rejection. Of course, too small a distance (less than four feet in a face-to-face position) is excessively arousing and results in avoidance behavior. About four and a half feet is the optimum distance. Many living rooms require guests to interact at distances of nine feet or more and hence create serious environmental difficulties. Shy or self-conscious persons are particularly reluctant to attempt conversation at such distances, and almost everyone tends to lapse into more aloof or formal modes.

The angle at which strangers are seated in relation to each other is another crucial factor in how much they interact. Strangers who are seated parallel to each other, as on a couch, simply will not talk to each other very much. A face-to-face orientation will increase their arousal and greatly enhance sociability. When the angle through which people are turned away from each other exceeds 90°, the positiveness of conversation is curtailed sharply. Since people seated together on a couch are in effect separated by a 180° angle, couches are quite detrimental to social interaction. Couches designed to seat three or more persons become more socially inefficient the larger they get. Two people can orient themselves on a couch so as to face each other, but it is virtually impossible for three or more to do so. As a result, a couch designed to hold four people will usually contain only two. If, in a crowded situation, four people are forced to sit together on a couch, the quality and quantity of conversation among these four will be nothing to write home about.*

* Immediacy—a closer and more face-to-face position—has a beneficial result on the relationships among people provided, of course, that the contact is within reasonable bounds and does not have excessive arousal due to total lack of privacy. Some of the commonly employed encounter group techniques— requiring strangers to hold hands and look into each other's eyes, to disrobe, or to massage one another—increase immediacy and exposure beyond levels of comfort. However, within the confines of the well-defined, socially artificial encounter group, excessively high levels of arousal are tolerated by participants because such interactions are carefully planned not to be threatening and to enhance positive feelings. Also, participants know these to be temporary and feel reassured by the fact that they can return to more normal and more private social conditions once they leave the group.

It is difficult to understand how couches have become such a standard item of living room furniture. If you must have a couch, it is important that it be surrounded by other chairs, as in the following arrangement:

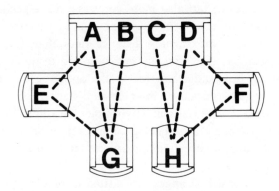

FIGURE 4

In this case, assuming that all seats are occupied, A and E will talk to each other, as will D and F. F and H, E and G, A-E-G, and D-F-H are also possible conversational groupings. But G will tend not to talk with H, nor will A, B, C, and D tend to talk amongst themselves. If you can't manage some such grouping, it would be far better for everyone to stand or sit on the floor or on packing crates than to stick four people alone somewhere on an isolated couch.

It is also better to have a number of smaller, more intimate conversational groupings within the social core rather than one large one. The quality of interaction within each of these groupings will most likely be pleasant and rewarding because people will not feel locked into one particular group. They will feel less self-conscious about approaching the group, as when they first enter, and will feel less uneasy about leaving it to get a drink, talk with someone in another group, go to the bathroom, or whatever. Some of the chairs could swivel so that members from different groups could casually adjust their orientation to interact with someone seated in another group. Furthermore, smaller groupings will in many cases present a more stimulating decor, especially if they give the impression of being randomly scattered throughout the floor space. This would also free areas for people to walk around in and form ad hoc standing clusters in which to seek their own optimum distances and orientations.

The load of the dining area or dining room ought to be lower than that in the living and family rooms. Otherwise the combined arousing effects of the setting, the act of eating, and the associated socializing would be far too high. So, given a choice between lowering the load of the physical setting or that of the food or the social interaction, people generally opt for the former. This helps explain many mealtime environmental preferences, such as a lower volume of music or no music, dimmer lights, special efforts to shut out noise or distractions from outside the home, and, in some homes, a taboo on arguments, discussions of money matters, or generally unpleasant and anxiety-provoking topics.

Bedrooms used primarily for sleeping do not have to be loaded, but they should be pleasant. Children who have difficulty going to sleep and make frequent trips back to the living room after they've been put to bed may be reacting to overly arousing cues in their bedrooms. These commonly include the presence of a sibling, conversation heard from the living room because of poor soundproofing, or noise and lights from outside the house.

A bedroom which will also be a prime sexual locus should probably contain more load. One of the reasons waterbeds are popular in motels which are known to be trysts is that the rocking and somewhat unpredictable motions of such beds serve to increase arousal. There should be a source of music in a bedroom; colored lights might also be considered. Certain motels now offer rooms containing closed circuit TVs or video cassettes featuring pornography; couples who opt for such rooms probably find that the pornographic element provides a desired increase in arousal level. It is likely that some such additional stimulus will gradually enter the private home market. However, among new or inexperienced sexual partners, a too highly loaded environment is unnecessary and most likely will be detrimental, especially to the male's performance.

The placement of bedrooms could involve a subtle design consideration with extremely beneficial effects for people who have problems with waking. Sunshine streaming through a large window in the morning is one of the most gentle and pleasant ways of being aroused from sleep since both the increased temperature and the intensity of light are arousing. When people live on a reasonably flexible schedule, bedrooms can be located with large windows facing southeast so that the early morning sunshine can conveniently and gradually arouse them. The flexibility of schedules is important in that the position of the sun changes during the different seasons and thus the waking time varies as much as an hour. However, it is possible to overcome this aspect by giving the bedroom an extremely large amount of exposure to sunlight, with windows along all walls facing southeast, or even by using skylights. In this case, the position of the curtains can be adjusted so that the desired sunlight reaches the bed at almost exactly the time it is wanted.

Suggested Readings

See Alexander, Hirshen, Ishikawa, Coffin, and Angel (1969) or Alexander, Ishikawa, and Silverstein (1968) for patterns used in the design of houses, and see Fitch (1965, 1972) for a critique of architectural designs. Moriarty (1974) provided a discussion of, and data on, the choice of residential locations. For literature on interior design, see Bedford (1961) and Provins (1966) on thermal comfort; Allen and Guilford (1936), Guilford (1934), and Guilford and Smith (1959) on the effects of various colors; Mehrabian and Diamond (1971a, 1971b) for the effects of furniture arrangement on conversation; and Mehrabian and Ksionzky (1974) for a general analysis of individual differences in gregariousness or affiliation. Mehrabian and Russell (1974a, chap. 4) provided detailed reviews of experimental findings on how different kinds of stimulation in various sense modalities affect pleasure and arousal levels. Mehrabian's (1976a, 1976b) discussion of individual differences in stimulus screening is also relevant here.

9

Tomorrow's Homes

WITHOUT looking too far into the future, it is possible to predict that it will be increasingly more difficult to afford large homes that waste acreage, building materials, and energy. Much of the waste derives from the practice of designing separate rooms for narrowly specialized functions, so that some homes literally contain all of the following: dens, libraries, bedrooms, storerooms, kitchens, breakfast nooks, informal dining rooms, formal dining rooms, sitting rooms, living rooms, two or three different kinds of bathrooms, cellars, attics, recreation rooms, family rooms, and closed porches, open-air patios, interior courtyards, garages, and sometimes separate servants' quarters. Each of these rooms is then furnished in a manner considered appropriate for its specific function. But, as we have seen, many of these rooms are not used for their real purpose or are hardly used at all, and others are used constantly for a wide range of activities. Clearly, tomorrow's housing designs will have to borrow from such traditionally space-conscious cultures as the Japanese or the more communally oriented cultures like certain Woodland or Plains Indians and design primary living areas which permit and encourage a wide variety of functions.

It is important then to overcome the lack of variation and inflexibility in many homes. Variation and flexibility in the shapes of spaces, furniture arrangements, and decor not only provide arousal but a feeling of dominance; in contrast, monotony and rigidity result in feelings of lowered arousal and submissiveness. Those who can afford expensive decorators achieve some variation and novelty of decor by frequently remodeling and even modifying room shapes in their homes. Also, the "in" designs selected for them tend to be the unusual or rare ones. An effective design however must achieve a high degree of pleasure as well as novelty.

Successful decorators don't say, "Let's put a nice, bright looking couch here, a richly grained coffee table there"; rather, they use motifs to attain an integrated and pleasant design which is also novel in the home context. For example, a living room is decorated predominantly in greens, yellows, and other colors and designs reminiscent of spring-time and lush vegetation. The feeling of autumn is conveyed in another room with shades of yellow, brown, and red, flowing together and intermingling through the use of intricate and organic-natural, rather than linear and angular, designs and shapes. There are un-limited possibilities for drawing upon familiar metaphors from nature for decoration to yield the necessary coherence and unusual quality sought.

However, most of us cannot afford expensive and frequent remodeling of our homes; we certainly cannot afford to reshape these interior spaces to suit our needs from time to time. Part of the reason for these limitations is that the home-building industry has failed to incorporate the many technological and cost-saving advances of mass production. Once the mass production of homes gets into full swing, the design of intricate, irregularly shaped living spaces, with flexible partitions and multiple function areas, could be enhanced considerably. But more of this later.

Let's return for a moment to the notion of a core socializing area in which the family can gather to do any number of things together, including entertain guests. Let us assume that certain areas of this core contain conversational groupings consisting of four to six chairs around a small table, with the diameter of the grouping not exceeding six feet. Let us further suppose that in one of these groupings comfortable chairs surround an oak dining table which can be used as a desk, and that the grouping is placed near a window that looks out on a grand old sycamore with squirrels scampering up and down its trunk or bluebirds flashing in and out of its foliage. If other family members are present, this will be a pleasant and mildly stimulating place in which to do certain kinds of routine work—fairly mechanical computations, paying bills, cut-and-dried sorts of homework, pasting in green stamps or recipes, and other tasks that are familiar and simple or actually boring. To approach (perform) such tasks, we must raise our arousal; otherwise we will find ourselves daydreaming, getting depressed, dozing, or manifesting other types of avoidance behavior. This is why such work often is not performed in studies, dens, bedrooms, or other rooms that are supposed to be used for paperwork; instead it gets done in kitchens, dining rooms, or living rooms in which other family members are present and active.

On the other hand, suppose that the task to be performed is complex or involves a high degree of novelty—a very exciting suspense novel, an extremely important report which must summarize and integrate a great deal of data, inductive or essay-type homework that requires concentration, and so on. The load of such tasks is heavy enough so that one's arousal level is fairly high; additional stimuli from the environment might increase arousal to such a point that the task would be avoided. That is, one becomes distracted, annoyed, and frustrated, and performance falls off sharply.*

Now, in conventional housing design this table-and-chairs grouping will be wasted in relation to one's ability to perform tasks requiring low loads. This happens because most rooms, no matter how large or small, are simple rectangles, and a conversational grouping placed this way, for example

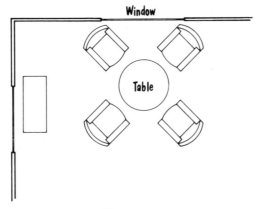

FIGURE 5

cannot be readily isolated from its surroundings. But if the social core were designed properly, it would provide alcoves of some sort

---

* Many middle-class teachers who assign homework to culturally disadvantaged students don't realize that such students may not have one home; that is, they stay with various relatives or friends on a rotating basis. More importantly, these children often cannot work in whatever serves as the home environment because it is far too loaded (extremely crowded, noisy, unpredictable) for performing reading, writing, or computational tasks which are in themselves unfamiliar and complex enough to cause heightened arousal.

which could easily be closed off by built-in sliding panels that are either manually or electronically operated. Thus, people needing a private and less loaded though very pleasant subenvironment could create one simply by flipping a switch, without having to set aside an inaccessible and low-load room in the house that would otherwise seldom be used.

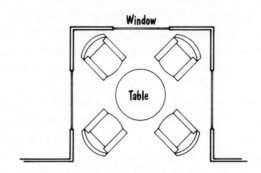

FIGURE 6a

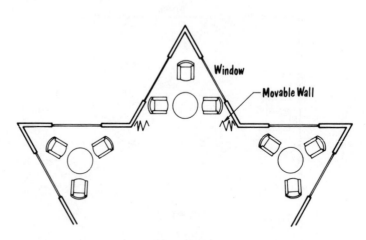

FIGURE 6b

It is possible to carry such a notion one step further and imagine entire houses with movable interior walls that could be raised and lowered to create a wide variety of interior spaces ranging from the cavernous to the intimate and private. Also, when you consider that many bedrooms really exist to provide us with a small, flat area in which to sleep, there is something really extravagant as well as environmentally misguided about many of them. Not only is an entire room often wasted most of the day, but it is usually decorated in expensive and even fanciful ways that belie its main function, which is to provide a relaxing, very low-load environment. In houses with movable partitions, sleeping platforms could be either raised from the floor or lowered from the ceiling; by lowering (or raising) a wall, an instant bedroom could be created when it is needed and then almost literally waved away when it is not. Such houses could also provide a number of interior perspectives, thus overcoming a hitherto intractable design problem, namely, the stasis and hence ultimately lowered arousal levels implicit in an invariable structure. If the walls were painted or papered with designs of varying pleasantness and complexity—everything from restful forest scenes to explosively colorful abstractions—and particularly if some of them incorporated varied colored light patterns, movie screens, or large, TV screen-like panels, the householder could easily create a whole gamut of environments without wasting any of them.

Even in more conventional structures, it ought to be possible to include movable exterior walls or partial walls so that pleasant and stimulating outdoor environments could be incorporated into the home. (Of course, sliding doors do this now, but they have a number of obvious drawbacks: they are poor insulators and all too often people try to walk through them.) For example, bathrooms don't have to be the low-load and neutral or unpleasant areas they often are. It ought to be possible to have an indoor-outdoor bathroom arrangement in which a fully shielded outdoor portion would contain showers or a large bath that could be used weather permitting. Such areas could be planted with shrubs and might make use of colorful textured tiles.*

An alternative to the use of movable partitions inside the house, or in relation to the exterior areas, is to mold intricate, organically shaped living spaces in which the distinction between wall space and

---

* The traditional Japanese baths are an excellent example of the ingenuity that has gone into the design of bathrooms to make them pleasant and stimulating areas of the home and, in particular, of the traditional Japanese *ryokan* (inn). In most of these bathrooms one finds elaborate use of tiles and stones; the bathtubs are usually given interesting shapes, as well as attractive views of the garden. In considering the Japanese emphasis on making a bathroom a pleasant area, we must recognize that their idea of bathing is not simply the act of cleaning oneself. Rather, it is often a pleasant social event in which the entire family participates, and so care is taken to make the bathing area a stimulating one.

floor space all but disappears. Such "organic" homes could have closable bubble-shaped sleeping alcoves or work spaces half way up the wall, various and intricate floor levels incorporating tablelike or chairlike excrescences, larger and smaller conversation pits affording different degrees of privacy, curved tunnels of various shapes serving as corridors, and so on. They might even include depressions that could contain plants, small trees, fish ponds, or even a jacuzzi. Selected areas of the walls, floors, or ceilings could incorporate video screens, speakers, and light sources which could be programmed to provide various stimulus-mixes having definite emotional impacts. One could program anything from the sounds of the gentle summer rain, a color scheme suggesting a peaceful natural environment and bird song, to an extremely loaded cacophony that would make an acid-rock dance bar seem like a walk in the country. An individual could select many environments exactly suited to his temporary needs or to somehow compensate for his temperament. He might want a pleasant but extremely low-load environment for some challenging mental job, but he might want a pleasant but high-load environment in which to wake up and begin his daily routines. A person wishing to deliberately manipulate his environment to create the optimum level of arousal, pleasure, and dominance for a particular activity could do so by using a computer program which would randomly select from a subset of several environmental "packages," all of which would be appropriate for a particular activity and a specific personality. The activity could be anything from giving a cocktail party, having an intimate, romantic tête-à-tête, reading *Finnegans Wake*, waking up, or peeling potatoes. By the time such packaged environments become available, the specific experimental findings that are only now beginning to accumulate will be more complete and will show the optimum emotional state for any activity-person combination.

One can object to preselected environmental packages on the grounds that they are too regimented and represent a formula ridden way of life. But our current interior environments are no less formula ridden, although the present formulas are less well defined. Also, as a result of their inflexibility, our present environments fail to meet our emotional needs most of the time. The high population densities of the future will necessitate technological innovation to impart variation, individuality, and some degree of personalized feeling to the interior space of each home. Even when such variation and flexibility are available, some individuals rigidly adhere to prescribed norms and seek guidelines from authoritative figures or groups. This however should not prevent others from creating interior environments suited to their particular needs. The comparison with the availability of recorded music in the home is useful here. In most instances, prerecorded disks and tapes have vastly contributed to the appreciation of music, and have encouraged people to impart individuality to their homes through their particular inclinations in music listening. The point here is that what is scientifically knowable and technologically feasible can provide people with more choices than they had before.

But there is such a thing as a misused or wasteful technology, and our overreliance upon fossil fuels to heat or cool our homes is a case in point. Consider the enormous waste of energy and acreage in bare rooftops which are seldom properly insulated. During the hot months the sun bakes them, and the heat conducted to the homes often makes air conditioning necessary. During the colder months, and especially at night, the homes lose heat through these roofs and of course through poorly insulated windows and walls. When moderate climates and low precipitation rates permit, flat roofs could be constructed with a gravel bed and a drainage system that would support six to twelve inches of topsoil in which grass, flowers, vines, small bushes, vegetables, or even certain shallow-rooted trees could be grown almost year round. These rooftop gardens could provide restful and enjoyable socializing areas. They could almost double the amount of recreational space in cities where they were feasible, while significantly enriching the oxygen content of the air. If given over to vegetables, they could enliven the family diet and reduce grocery bills. And they would effectively insulate the homes underneath, eliminating the need for air conditioning and causing a reduction in winter heating bills. There must be many, many square miles of rooftops in Los Angeles alone that could be charming, productive gardens, but are instead tar paper frying pans.

There are many other ways in which enlightened construction and the optimum use of vegetation and water can cool homes and at the same time provide pleasant and stimulating environmental variation. A south-to-southeasterly orientation provides a house with maximum heating from the sun's rays, while a north-to-northeasterly orientation keeps such heating to a minimum. In many hot areas of the world, in North Africa for example, city streets that run north and south are often built narrower than streets running east and west. In hot areas of this country, however, such designs are almost never considered, even though narrow, pedestrian-only malls or streets have much charm, quite apart from the fact that they keep shops and apartments abutting on them relatively cool for much of the day.

A body of earth, when it is adjacent to a building, can also serve as an excellent insulator and is especially helpful in creating cooler areas. Cellars have been used for ages as natural refrigerators for food and wine storage. It is possible to expand the cellar concept to the construction of homes in a variety of ways. Homes situated on hill-sides, for instance, can be designed so that rooms which face the hill rather than the view-side serve as cooler areas to be used during the hot summer months. If the design of such homes is flexible enough, it can permit the family to shift its activities during the warmer months to those rooms which are in the cooler part of the home. During the winter months, the center of family activity can be moved to the rooms which face away from the hill and toward the sun. The bonus here is greater environmental variation.

A dramatic extension of the cellar-type design for cooling can be employed in desert areas by building the entire house below ground level. The house can be built so that all the rooms have a view onto exterior or interior courtyards. These courtyards can be shaded by a cross-hatched wooden structure that is simply an extension of the roof which is level with the ground; this wooden structure could support vines and other vegetation. Furthermore, the shrubs and trees planted in the courtyard areas adjacent to the rooms could help to cool the house. If such a house is located on sloping ground, it can be designed with three sides of the house facing courtyards situated below ground level, with the non-southern sides having an open view. The residents will then have beautifully landscaped areas as views from three sides of the house, and an expanded view of a valley or other houses from the fourth side.

Another source of cooling is the evaporation of water. Histori-cally, many clever and economical devices have been used to cool homes in hotter climates. For instance, the Moors in southern Spain or the Mogul emperors in India frequently built pools and water carrying channels into the interior areas and courtyards of their homes. A large room would contain a small elevated pool and fountain at the center. The overflow from the pool ran into small rectangular channels, approximately six inches wide and two inches deep, which were constructed in such a way as to let the excess water run off either toward other rooms or toward a court area. As this water evaporated it absorbed heat and thus acted as a cooling device. Such a mechanism was not only functional but also aesthetically pleasing. Thick walls were used to insulate interior areas from the outside heat, while evaporation helped reduce the temperature in the insulated interior.

In contrasting this type of natural "air conditioning" with the artificial method usually assumed to be the sole means of temperature control in the West, it is important to note that the former, although it fails to maintain a constant temperature in the entire interior region of a house, has other benefits from a psychological standpoint. For example, with natural air conditioning one experiences slight changes in temperature in going from one room to another. The possibility of a breeze or air current wafting through certain sections of the house is also increased, and such air currents can be refreshing. In addition, there are added pleasant and stimulating elements in the visual and auditory realm—hearing the splashing of a fountain, seeing sunlight play on the water, or listening to a flowing stream. Today, small electric pumps can be used to recycle the water in such fountain and pool systems at a fraction of the energy cost required by room or central air conditioning.

Cooler air can be circulated through a house if we recognize that hot air moves in an upward direction. A multilevel house which has vents in the proper places can have air constantly moving from the lower levels up through the higher levels and out, thus creating a refreshing and cooling stream of air. If the areas immediately adjacent to the ground floor vents are usually in the shade and are surrounded by broadleaf, lush vegetation (like evergreen plants, which also cycle a good deal of moisture), the air entering these vents is at least ten to fifteen degrees cooler. If the rooms at the upper levels of the house are properly ventilated—with sealable openings in the roof, for example —a suction effect is created when the hot air from the upper rooms escapes to the outside and the cooler air is pulled upwards through the house. This natural ventilation not only has a cooling effect, but also introduces pleasant and stimulating odors from the ground level plants and flowers. In a similar application, a room which is built to store wines on the lower level of a house could be designed with air vents near the floor and the ceiling. The lower level vents would face six- to eight-foot-wide plantings of evergreen broadleaf vegetation so that the density of these plantings would not allow sunshine to reach the air vents.

For some time now Western architects have been overly impressed with the powers of modern technology and have often created sterile and unstimulating interiors as a result of rigid adherence to accepted standards of "proper" air conditioning. Working with the assumption that human beings have a very narrow tolerance for variations from a presumably optimum temperature, they have failed to consider basic human needs for variable stimulation. In some absurd cases, homes, and particularly office buildings in moderate climates, have been designed without windows or with windows that cannot be opened, to facilitate the air conditioning of an entire unit to a uniform and "acceptable" level. The occupants cannot look out or get a chance to feel a fresh breeze, nor can they change the temperature more than a few degrees within any given area of the building. As a result, many sedentary people find themselves chilled after an hour or two in such an environment, and persons entering or leaving the building experience unpleasantly large variations in temperature. And if, as it can happen, the air conditioning unit should break down, the entire building becomes an unbearable trap of hot, stale air. Surely there is some kind of folly lurking behind all this.

Suggested Readings

The suggested readings for the previous chapter apply here as well. For a discussion of the aesthetic-versus-functional controversy in housing design, see Fitch (1965). Also see Baer's (1969) and Soleri's (1969) projections regarding housing of the future.

10

Apartments

SUPPOSE you and a companion are taking a slow drive in the country. It's a lovely day in the early fall, the sky is a pure blue, and the air is clean with just a tiny nip in it. Some of the trees are already beginning to show their red and gold high cards. Let's say your companion comes from Atlanta, Philadelphia, or New York City. She has a good but demanding job and pays between $300 and $500 a month to rent a two-bedroom apartment in a new high-rise security building with a doorman. As you drive along the straight yet narrow road, you occasionally pass a small, plain house set back fifty feet or less from the road. "All this gorgeous forest!" your friend exclaims with some annoyance. "Why would anyone put a house right on top of the road when they could have it way back in the middle of all those wonderful trees?" If *she* owned all those woods, she'd put her house smack in the middle of it, not right on the road where you can practically get run over on your front stoop!

Such a typical urbanite observation tells us a great deal. City dwellers rarely think of natural environments as potentially nasty or brutal, but rather as pleasant, low-load settings in which to relax and vacation. Your hypothetical companion may never have shovelled snow, and would rightly become extremely alarmed if she found herself separated from the road by a quarter of a mile of eight to twelve foot snowdrifts. For many urban apartment dwellers snow is something the super takes care of, or something that makes slush; it is not something that can besiege or even kill you.

More significantly, many urbanites spend much of their time in extremely loaded environments which are sometimes quite unpleasant. There is often intense professional and even social competitiveness; there is usually a lot of traffic noise; streets, subways, and shopping areas are extremely crowded, especially during the noon and rush hours. There can be jolting contrasts, as when in the dead of winter you pass an old man sleeping barefoot on a stoop under a newspaper, his toes completely rotted away from frostbite—just when you are on your way to lunch at, say, the Rose Room in the Algonquin Hotel. And there is the crime and the antisocial behavior, or the fear of it, invariably generated by extremely dense, complex, unpredictable, and unpleasant environments. People who must live in such high-load and unpleasant environments seek and cherish privacy and its promise of lowered arousal and heightened pleasure. For this reason your companion was somewhat shocked that the rural householders chose to place their homes close to the public road rather than away from it. She could not understand that for them an occasional car or a passing neighbor could represent a pleasant and somewhat arousing stimulus in a basically low-load environment. The low load of rural settings explains why rural folk in many parts of the world are traditionally more hospitable than city dwellers. For them, visitors or strangers represent acceptable and, indeed, sought after increases in arousal level. In contrast, for the highly aroused city dweller, a tourist asking directions, a person collapsed in the gutter, or a friend calling at the wrong moment represent intolerable additional stresses that generally are avoided.

But the intense and sometimes merciless search for privacy and lowered arousal on the part of urban apartment dwellers—a good percentage of whom happen to be single—leads to a dilemma of almost tragic proportions. What happens is that the wealthier, more talented, or more socially adept city dwellers get what they want; that is, they successfully compete for private, low-load living spaces. But in addition to the high rents they pay, the psychological costs—frequent boredom and loneliness or even social alienation—may also be high.

Urbanites today no longer grow up in the neighborhoods of their parents and grandparents. No longer are they surrounded by established networks of friends, relatives, stores, and generally familiar settings providing continuity from one generation to another. Instead, families and individuals are mobile, in search of opportunities which sometimes take them to distant and totally different places. Every time a person moves to a new location he must make new friends and re-establish social ties. The design of housing plays a major role in this process of re-creating a new social circle for the mobile resident and can help or hinder his search for companionship.

Apartments designed to ensure maximum privacy, security, and low loads (good soundproofing, no children, pets, musicians, loud parties, hookers, or door-to-door salesmen) make it very difficult for people to meet other tenants or in general to raise their arousal levels, which sooner or later becomes necessary.

How to provide people with apartments that strike an acceptable balance between needed privacy and lowered arousal on the one hand, and needed social interaction and stimulation on the other, is *the* design problem confronting architects, decorators, and social scientists.

Underlying the paradox of privacy versus social interaction is the phenomenon of territoriality. As we've seen, the insistence on privacy stems from high-load urban environments which include crowds, noise, pollution, and a generally hectic pace of life. Studies of both human and animal crowding have shown that crowding leads to territorial behavior, which in effect reduces arousal. The stronger or socially more powerful members of a crowded social group set aside large areas of territory and protect these from intrusion by others, thereby diminishing the high load of crowded and disorganized social conditions for themselves.

Many social animals, particularly aggressive species, stake out mating or feeding territories which they defend against all other members of their species except their mate and offspring. Usually it is the male who does this, but not always. The stronger, more powerful (and in some cases more canny) the individual, the larger and choicer his territory will be. If two animals of comparable strength fight, the winner is likely to be the one in whose territory the fight takes place. There is a tendency for territorial animals to nest in the center of their territory; the farther away from the territorial center they go, the weaker or less confident they become in relation to challengers. Indeed, the boundaries of a given animal's territory are likely to be defined as the maximum distance it can sally forth and challenge an intruder successfully; that is, without losing that extra edge of aggressiveness or moral rectitude which its own territory confers. Younger and weaker animals can effectively defend or challenge in a territory having a smaller radius than that of more powerful animals.

You can sometimes see territoriality at work among household pets. If you're walking down a sidewalk in the suburbs, some absurd little dog may come charging at you across the lawn, barking and snapping furiously. If you step onto the lawn, encroaching upon its territory, moving closer and closer to the "nest" or house, the chances are good that the dog will bark in an insane, miniature fury. The chances are also good that you will back off, saying to yourself, "What am I doing on this stranger's lawn?"

There is every reason to believe that something very close to territoriality operates in human beings. For example, a study of the seating arrangements in 4,000 U.S. elementary and secondary class-rooms revealed that children with chronic infections and nutritional problems were concentrated in the darkest quadrants of these rooms. For one reason or another, the children staked out spaces that were consistent with their level of physical well-being (strength), which in many cases correlated with their social status within the peer group. Except when conditions become elemental and primitive, adults tend to stake out territories on the basis of economic power and social status rather than physical strength. They are able to claim (pay for) larger, more desirable territories to which access is carefully con-trolled and from which undesirable environmental stimuli—noise, pollution, or whatever—are eliminated. If they are socially powerful they are able to reduce environmental loads by commanding the physical watchfulness and strength of others in the form of doormen, private security guards, policemen, personal bodyguards, and in some cases segments of national armed forces. But we all feel that there is a psychological advantage to being on our own "turf," or at least not on the other fellow's, especially when oneupmanship is involved, such as in a business deal. Hence we tend to prefer meeting people at our place—our home, office, or even a favorite bar or restaurant—rather than theirs. People who are in positions of relatively great power are able to express and enhance this power by insisting that we meet them in their own territory.

Territoriality is especially pronounced among people who must operate in extremely loaded environments, such as crowded and competitive ones. Thus, a citified person is likely to be baffled by behavior that seems in some way to violate unspoken territorial rules, as when a house is built near the boundary of someone's property rather than at its center. But rural environments are not overcrowded or socially arousing. You can be fairly sure that if those little roadside houses the visiting urbanite found so puzzling and disturbing were suddenly faced with a battery of shopping centers, several Mc-Donald's, playgrounds, bars, and high-rises, and their owners had the economic clout to withstand developers and the tax assessor, new houses would be built nearer the geographic and territorial center of their property and the old ones rented out.

We can even see a kind of territoriality operating in the proliferation of answering services and home devices that allow telephone calls to be mechanically answered and recorded. Answering services first developed to meet the needs of a small number of professionals who wanted to be reachable at all times but required a shield from nuisance or nonemergency calls. Today many more people use these services or their mechanical equivalents. The general level of environmental load seems to have risen so sharply that increasing numbers of people regard the telephone not as a communication tool but as an environmental invader—a source of overstimulation rather than welcome stimulation. They purchase such devices to secure more privacy, lower arousal, and increase dominance. (Dominance in the sense that one is free to answer a call or not and has a choice of returning a particular call or not.) But even here there is an increased psychological cost. Suppose you have someone sitting around in his luxury apartment, bored, lonely, and depressed. His arousal level is so low that when the phone rings he cannot make the effort to answer it, at least not for the first five or six rings before the service picks up. He thinks about it for a while and imagines that it's so-and-so; maybe they could take in that new flick at the Bijou. His arousal and pleasure levels go up sufficiently for him to get off his duff and call his service. Yes, it was so-and-so. He then calls so-and-so and gets *her* answering service. So-and-so has, in the meantime, decided to go to bed or watch TV and can't be bothered to answer. Both these people have sharply increased the difficulty of making contact with their friends, and the cost may very well be excessive relative to the benefits.

Territoriality also subtly determines the demand for and hence the cost of different apartments in the same building. Apartments located at the upper levels of a building are more in demand because their superior position implies dominance, a feeling of being above it all, or at least of having more people under than above you. These higher apartments are more pleasant because they are farther away from street noise and provide more stimulating views or panoramas. If two apartments are located on the same high floor, the one with the more expansive view will be more expensive precisely because it contains more pleasantly stimulating environmental features.

Urbanites lower on the totem pole who cannot afford to buy themselves into private but eventually boring or even depressing apartments have rather different problems to contend with. In high-density areas like Manhattan, where land, labor, and material costs are astronomical, developers are likely to want designs which provide the maximum number of units with the minimum expenditure necessary to meet safety requirements and to justify the rents they expect to charge. Architects and interior designers must to some extent work with their clients' expectations; and when they do get a freer hand than usual, they must fight their own training, which strongly tempts them to blow it all on a great looking shell or a really far-out lobby.* In high-density areas apartments are likely to be hopelessly small. If an apartment dweller decorates his one- or two-room apartment elaborately and imaginatively, chances are it will not provide him with the relaxing, very low-load environment he is likely to need on many occasions. If he does it in a low arousal mode, it will not be effective as a place in which to entertain, and will also eventually decrease his arousal level to the point of boredom, loneliness, or depression.

Well, what can be done? The apartment dweller (or decorator if he can afford one) could make every effort within the limits of care, technology, and his budget to make the environment as flexible as possible. Socially ineffective furniture like couches would be avoided, unless of course it is a one-room apartment and the bed has to double as something else. Almost everything would be movable; one would avoid furniture that monopolizes the largest, choicest areas—like a huge Victorian armoire or a bronze-doré desk that refuses to go anywhere but along the only unbroken wall. A flexible lighting system would be essential, with dimmers on every light switch and many independent sources of light—everything from candles to small spotlights to small colored strobes. A good music system also would be essential—a quadraphonic arrangement might be worth the extra expense. Color schemes could be selected for their pleasantness rather than their arousing qualities. Plants would be used generously for their pleasantness and for their associations with the outdoors.

---

* We once analyzed a long list of adjectives that architects and interior designers use to describe buildings and living spaces. Terms referring to the visual properties of environments predominated; terms relating to other sources of sensory stimulation, such as the auditory, the tactual, and the kinesthetic, or terms relating to social and psychological needs, were either absent or under-represented.

Using such parameters, it may be possible for the highly aroused apartment dweller to arrive home after a beastly day at the office and an even beastlier subway ride, and manipulate the home environment so as to create a very pleasant, low-load setting. He could for example dim the lights or gently illuminate only the area immediately surrounding his favorite chair; he could put on some soothing, pleasant music. An hour and a couple of vodka martinis later, he could increase the environmental load by turning up the lights and playing louder, faster music and possibly even rearranging the decor a bit—moving a picture, a chair, a table, a rug, or whatever. When friends dropped by, the lights and music could become even more intense. If a real party got going, he could darken or lighten the apartment selectively, turning the spots on to arousing items—a colorful mobile, or a far out piece of Op art—and deemphasizing the less arousing decorations. He could also introduce his colored moving lights and put on his wildest (most novel and complex) music—electronic stuff or rock-outs. He would then have shot his wad, speaking environmentally.

But what if this person is a newcomer to this city? Suppose he has not yet established a network of stable social relationships? If his developer and architect have provided him with a fifteen- to fifty-story building which is basically a stack job, with elevators opening onto long narrow corridors containing rows of doors, he is not likely to strike up an acquaintance with anyone in that building, not even with people in the adjacent apartments. The opportunities for seeing other tenants are limited, and the corridors, which are usually drably low-load, are not conducive to socializing even if an opportunity should present itself. In such apartment buildings people usually only get to know and like each other if they happen to get stranded in an elevator which has gotten stuck between floors, or if they complain personally about the noise next door and then decide to join the party rather than fight it.

Builders and architects must provide accessible socializing areas where people have the occasion and opportunity to meet each other. If nothing else, they can get the laundry room out of the basement and put it somewhere in the middle floors of the building in pleasant and stimulating surroundings. There should be comfortable chairs scattered around so that people who strike up a conversation about detergents or junk mail can pursue it if they choose. In smaller, older apartment houses, especially those built around a courtyard or walkway, most apartments have front windows. People living in such apartments sometimes are able to sacrifice some privacy and keep the curtains open when they are home. This is effective in increasing the likelihood of social interaction. People passing by on the way to their own apartments look in, see the same face, and begin to feel familiar. This leads to greetings and, at a more opportune moment, to conversation. Some people also leave their apartment door open. But this is really more effective as a means of increasing one's own arousal than of making new friends—people tend to feel uncomfortable looking into a stranger's apartment, avoid following up, and may even hurry past so as not to be caught being nosy.

But it ought to be possible to construct even towering high-rises around small, colorfully decorated, and well-lit interior "courtyards" or lobbies which house the elevators, contain lots of plants, comfortable chairs, and tables in conversational groupings. The apartments grouped around this central core could have windows looking out onto it and thus give the occupants something to look at. Furthermore, at least some apartments would face each other, which is an extremely important factor in whether people form friendships or not. In one suburban community study, for example, some of the houses were built facing each other and others faced away toward the street. People living in houses that faced away had many fewer friendships (4 percent) with people in the community than did those whose homes faced each other (75 percent).

Along the same lines, often some apartments become the common meeting ground for other residents. While part of this is attributable to the personality makeup of the individuals involved, the physical characteristics of the environment also play a major role. For example, the apartment may be located at a major crossing point of pathways. The heavier traffic provides a good opportunity for residents to make frequent contact with one another. In this way, a lively and gregarious person who happens to be located at one of these crossways might take advantage of the location of his apartment to make it an especially catalytic setting for gatherings.

The idea of interior windows in a downtown high-rise apartment may cause people to wonder about security. Most police officers will tell you that there is hardly any such thing as a full-security building. Any professional, or even an intelligent amateur bent on mischief, can penetrate the exterior defenses with ease, and once he's inside he's in an ideal environment for burglary, rape, or what have you. Nobody can see him, nobody can hear him, and nobody knows whether he belongs there or not. Good locks help of course, but the best defense against being ripped off is alert people who share a feeling of responsibility for their floor or mini-community and know enough about the habits and friends of their neighbors to get suspicious about something. As things stand now in many large apartment buildings, tenants tell the manager or the doorman that they'll be gone for two weeks; they wouldn't dream of telling the people who live in the apartments next door. Instead, they leave the radio on and come back to find an apartment that is completely stripped except for the radio, which is still playing.

Owners of high-rise, full-security buildings would be well advised to forget about their closed-circuit TV monitors and electronic garage gates; instead, they should rip out the middle two or three floors (or top floors) and install a swimming pool, a gymnasium, comfortable lounges, game rooms, a handball court, and even a full-service bar. Then their tenants would have some real security, deriving from a crisscross of social relationships and persons sharing a sense of psychological well-being.

In areas which are just now becoming urbanized, builders are providing apartment complexes which do contain common socializing areas like swimming pools, gyms, tennis courts, and even social directors to organize activities and parties. These complexes have, in the main, been financial successes, especially when they have catered to a young, single clientele. Our overemphasis on individualism has led some people—especially the sensitive, shy, and lonely who are greatly in need of environments that encourage social interaction—to reject such places because "enforced friendliness is deeply false" or because "only creeps who can't make it on their own live there." It is also unfortunately true that such complexes are being built where they are needed least, namely, in environments that are actually or in effect still suburban and hence far less loaded than most urban or downtown areas. Furthermore, they tend to be huge, sprawling affairs of two or three stories; even though the socializing core is centrally located, many apartments are quite removed and their tenants must walk considerable distances through endless, dreary corridors to get to the core.

Nevertheless, such apartment complexes represent a step in the right direction—one that more celebrated, more admired, or more chic architects seem not to be taking. I am thinking for example of the use now being made of what probably will become a predominant architectural modality—the mass produced, prefabricated cubic module. The Japanese architect Noriaki Kurokawa and the Israeli architect Moishe Safdi have both used these modules, stacking them in seemingly random ways into playful arrangements of cubes. But the cubes are not stacked randomly; on the contrary, they are placed in such a way as to maximize privacy and minimize interpersonal contact. Kurokawa's Nakagin Mansions were specifically designed for businessmen as low-load resting places where they could relax in privacy during business hours. But Safdi's Habitat in Montreal seems not to have been designed with such a narrow purpose in mind, and we can wonder with some alarm how well such structures will serve as overall living spaces. Good urban design should provide the occupant with privacy when he wants it and at the same time should give him ready access to other people and arousing activities when he wants that. In a bunch of cubes stacked à la Kurokawa or Safdi, varied stimulation is completely sacrificed for the sake of privacy. A person living in one of those cubes will get all the privacy he wants, together with all the boredom, social isolation, and sensory deprivation he can possibly endure.

But if affluent, socially competent apartment dwellers are in a bind, those members of the citizenry who are the recipients of public housing are even worse off. As we shall see in the following chapter, they are forced to choose between what is environmentally the frying pan and the Deep Six.

Suggested Readings

See Festinger, Schachter, and Back (1963) and Newcomb (1961) for data on how the spatial arrangements of apartments can encourage or discourage liking of neighbors and consequently friendship patterns. Related data and more general discussions of the development of liking and friendships among strangers are provided by Berscheid and Walster (1969), Byrne (1971), Mehrabian (1971, chap. 5) and Mehrabian and Ksionzky (1974). See Ankele and Sommer (1973) on some determinants and consequences of apartment choice, and Jacobs (1969) on the importance of commonly shared public areas for neighborhood cohesiveness. Also see the suggested readings of the next chapter for data on race relations, various determinants of neighborhood crime and vandalism, morale, cohesiveness, and other indexes of neighborhood satisfaction.

Representative discussions of the phenomenon of territoriality are given in Ardrey (1966), Braddock (1949), and Carpenter (1958). See Harmon (1945) on the classroom space selections of nutritionally deficient children. Also see Mehrabian and Russell (1974a, chap. 4) for an analysis of architectural and design terminology which reveals the primary visual orientation of these professionals.

11

Public Housing

THE PARABLE of the Talents (Matthew 26:14–30) contains one of the most piercing judgments in all of the New Testament: "For unto every one that hath shall be given, and he shall have abundance; but from him that hath not shall be taken away even that which he hath." As an observation applicable to many realms—the biological, the financial, the social, the spiritual, the psychological—it is brutally accurate.

In terms of housing, what the poor had were extremely loaded and unpleasant living spaces, with the important compensation, however, of many opportunities for social interaction in a stable community. Relationships were developed over very long periods of time. There were extended family ties, friendships of long duration, and general familiarity with the establishments, character, and people of the neighborhood.

In the old-style ghettos, tenements were usually four- to five-story structures that faced each other across the street. The street, the sidewalks, and the large front stoops provided a stimulating and comparatively pleasant socializing area (especially during hot summer evenings, when the ugliness of the street was somewhat softened by twilight and the air was somewhat cooler and fresher than in the sweltering, poorly ventilated rooms). People could meet there to exchange gossip, share a beer, or smoke together; in many cases they could also keep an eye out for their neighbors, thus discouraging felonious or antisocial street behavior like purse snatching, rape, extreme drunkenness, or overt drug use. There were overlapping, very efficient grapevines or informal communication networks that kept people informed of what was going on throughout the block. In emergencies, a friend or relative could usually be summoned quickly. For example, mothers in front apartments could usually keep track of, or communicate with, their children simply by looking or yelling out the window. If a child was hurt, people could call up from the street, and the mother or some responsible adult could be on the scene quickly. In back apartments, the mother could pass or receive messages through her neighbor in a front apartment; and if her child were hurt, someone always knew where she was and could quickly find her.

Most public housing scenarios seem to go something like this. State or federal officials look at a number of large, privately financed, lower-income apartment buildings and pick the one that achieves the maximum number of units in the minimum amount of space at the lowest per-foot cost. The contract goes to the lowest, but not necessarily the most economical or efficient, bidder. Soon after the building is occupied, the tenants report that they feel rootless, unhappy, depressed, lonely. Corridors, elevators, and lobbies are quickly defaced, usually with graffiti of one sort or another. Then more serious forms of vandalism occur—broken windows, jimmied mailboxes, wrecked washing machines, smashed corridor lights. The crime rate soars. The tenants move out, preferring something like their old slum to this new one.

We can understand this abysmal failure of public housing in terms of the higher load due to its more uncertain, mobile, and unpredictable social structure, compared to that of the naturally developed structure of the slum neighborhood. The stable network of social relationships of the older slums is missing for persons who have been uprooted from different areas and thrown together in a single housing project. These families do not have any social ties or shared community feeling despite their similar backgrounds. And as we shall see, the new physical environment usually discourages the development of interpersonal and community relationships. For instance, mothers living in high-rise projects often have no way of keeping track of their children and cannot readily be summoned, either because of the distances involved or because nobody knows whose children they are. Seldom is any attempt made to provide common meeting areas, save perhaps for an inadequate laundry room in the basement. When these projects consist of several huge, separate apartment buildings, they're seldom grouped around a central green area which could, if provided with benches, pathways, and playgrounds, serve as some sort of commons or community meeting place. In other words, these projects are unpleasant and make very little provision for social interaction. As environments, they appeal to the criminal subset; the long, darkened corridors and the social alienation of the occupants form an even better setting for assault and rip-offs than the proverbial dark and lonely alley. Fire escapes, which are required by law, also provide criminals with good escape routes. The anxiety this generates among tenants plus the lack of privacy due to construction (which sometimes is so bad that a sound of ninety decibels produced in one apartment will register eighty-five decibels in the apartments on either side) often combine to make most areas of the project highly arousing.

Slum dwellings, whether of the unplanned variety or the planned, public housing kind, are often extremely loaded and unpleasant. They are crowded, with sometimes as many as a dozen people living in one or two small rooms; frequently trespassed by strangers and salesmen; smelly, with cooking odors saturating the walls; vermin infested; stifling in the summer and freezing in the winter; noisy, with almost no filtering of the voices, fights, and plumbing sounds coming from apartments above, below, and alongside. Thus sleep or relaxation is hard to come by for the highly aroused slum dweller. He is therefore unable to fully restore overworked and frequently malnourished bodily systems, with the result that GAS symptoms, including the "executive" ulcer, are quite prevalent. It is no wonder that a fairly high percentage of slum dwellers have resorted to the heavy use of such arousal-reducing agents as alcohol, barbiturates, marijuana, or heroin. All of these problems are accentuated in the planned slums because of the far greater social load in these settings.

It is under such stressful conditions that territorial behavior increases. Teenage gangs, which stake out turfs and sometimes battle to the death to preserve them, are an expression of this. So is the general and pointed hostility toward outsiders, especially if these outsiders differ ethnically or racially from the majority group. This may partially explain the generalized, as opposed to the earned, resentment policemen experience in ghetto areas.* Policemen, no

* Something like this happened during the war in Vietnam, when an unusually large number of officers were victims of murderous assault by the combat soldiers they commanded. In Green Beret camps, each soldier had his own informal, private territory. This area was off limits to anybody else, including officers, and any of one's comrades-in-arms who intruded would be expelled violently. Such territories permitted the soldiers to enjoy moments of

matter how well trained, experienced, or calloused, respond defensively to such generalized hostility and display considerable avoidance behavior within the ghetto environment. They not only "coop" more often than usual but in many other ways provide sub-par protection to ghetto residents, who are more frequently victimized than anybody else.

Extremely stressful conditions result in aberrant behavior. There have been a number of classic experiments with overcrowding among rats. Even when there was plenty of food and water for all, when crowding was excessive, the rats exhibited a high degree of social disorganization and pathology. Courting and mating behavior fell into disarray. Some male rats became infantile or extremely submissive; others became insanely aggressive, biting everything in sight, including their own tails. Mothers neglected their young. In one study where several pens were provided, a single dominant male took over one of them; he allowed a few females in, but successfully guarded it against intrusion by other males. Even though the social world of most of the other rats was falling into a shambles outside, there was no disruption of normal social organization and relationships within the pen. The male who had successfully staked out one of these pens was able to guard it not only because of his superior strength but also because of his state of psychological well-being.

It is difficult not to generalize from such experiments to our own social environments. We may unfortunately be on fairly safe ground with such a generalization; John Calhoun's experiments with rats were nightmarishly foreshadowed by a similar series of experiments with human beings in the Nazi concentration camps. And although human behavior in those extreme situations was sometimes characterized by heroism, self-sacrifice, or kindness, most of the time it was not. Many survivors reported the kinds of aberrant behavior—and extreme territoriality whenever feasible—replicated by Calhoun in his experiments with animals.*

---

seclusion, privacy, and somewhat lowered arousal during especially stressful periods. This nonmilitary practice was wisely tolerated by the brass, who recognized it as a means of maintaining psychological well-being. It is possible that at least some of the fragging among regular army units occurred because the front line personnel were not permitted some such safety valve.

* Although the statistics have been challenged by some, it seems that the number of reported crimes has increased at a significantly greater rate than the population over the past quarter of a century. It is also my unsupported impression that utterly aberrant crimes of violence—the savage, motiveless mutilation and murder of randomly selected victims—have become more fre-

Similar problems have been noted in the modern high-rise slums. Studies have shown that people who live in single-family dwellings are considerably less neurotic than people who live in the more crowded high-rise buildings. In one experiment, for example, British soldiers and their families were assigned high-rises or separate houses as living quarters. Families living in the high-rises had 57 percent more neuroses. Furthermore, those living in the upper apartments of high-rises were more neurotic, less satisfied, and had fewer friends. People living in houses had twice as many friends and felt far less dissatisfied and alienated. These families were assigned their living quarters on a completely random basis, which rules out the possibility of self-selection factors—neurotics selecting high-rises, for instance. Instead, we must infer that the typical high-rise as a living environment has a devastating effect on the well-being of its residents.

The sense of social alienation prevalent in high-rise buildings is not as prevalent in the low-rise, two- and three-story buildings. In these, a courtyard containing a playground for the children and benches and shaded areas provides a central gathering point which draws the residents together and increases their chances for social interaction. Such arrangements can be even more effective when the entrances to the apartments face the courtyard so that people also pass through the courtyard before they enter their apartments, thus increasing the possibilities for contact. Observations have also shown that sidewalks in ghetto-type neighborhoods function like these courtyards in creating a sense of community. Such sidewalks are used by residents and their children for social contacts; when they need privacy, they return to their individual homes. From the standpoint of esthetics or convenience, the wide sidewalk does not compare with recreational facilities or parklike courtyards. It does, however, provide a very important common ground where people can spend time, meet each other, and form friendships.

In terms of future trends, the advantages of smaller, multiple-

quent in the past fifteen years. The disproportionately greater crime rates in the poverty pockets of major urban areas suggest that environmental stress (unpleasantness and load) contributes to high crime rates and imply that the more general trend of crime rates is partly a reflection of more environmental stress throughout the nation. This means that if the trends continue, in the coming decades many of us can expect to experience something like the high arousal levels and unpleasantness which have traditionally characterized poor urban environments. If this proves to be the case, it will be socially suicidal for us to meet these high-load, low-pleasure conditions by anything remotely resembling today's public housing projects.

unit forms of public housing notwithstanding, high-rise, high-density living spaces are with us permanently, for good or ill. Currently, high-rise buildings—despite the fantastic rents that some luxury high-rises command—are among the least desirable living environments, and it is perfectly obvious that the poor are not going to get the most desirable. But much can be done to improve all high-rise living environments, including those provided for the least powerful, least competent, or simply least fortunate members of society.

Because most high-rise public housing projects are merely cheaper and more cost-efficient copies of middle-class apartment buildings, their floor plans emphasize privacy and look something like this:

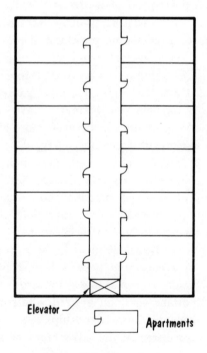

Elevator —   Apartments

FIGURE 7

or this:

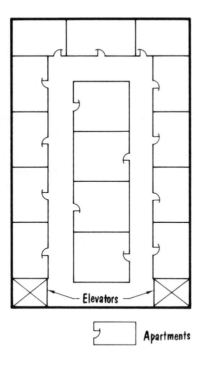

FIGURE 8

There are endless corridors with mirror-image, identical doors leading into identical rooms. Of course, there are sometimes a few additional "wrinkles," like elevators that stop only at every other floor so that some tenants have to detour up or down one flight of utterly barren fire stairs. The corridors are usually not carpeted and are often painted in something suspiciously like battleship gray. To compensate for the monotony and consequent lack of personal identity, residents in these buildings use the crudest techniques to somehow personalize them. They chalk and mark these up to give them a character that differentiates them from other places. Even new buildings are quickly defaced. For example, Eero Saarinen's New York CBS Building—a prime example of modern, cold architecture—was defaced and given a disorganized, cluttered appearance by employees who were probably attempting to individualize their working spaces.

Seemingly endless rows of similar apartments impart a feeling of anonymity. If residents are to have a chance to feel that their housing is somehow special, and if they are to take pride in it, their living spaces must be well-defined, rather than consisting of an endless array of identical units.

Studies have shown that if the number of apartments on a floor is limited to six, dramatic changes in resident behavior result. The corridor suddenly becomes a common space which residents can identify as being partly theirs and for which they are inclined to take some responsibility. They become friendlier with the other persons or families on the floor and so also begin to look after each other's property. As a result, the crime rate drops significantly in buildings having no more than six apartments per floor. Now, architects can offer us many ingenious high-rise designs which incorporate the six-unit concept—with the entire floor at each level of the building segregated into six-unit sections differing in shape, arrangement, color scheme, and so forth. The corridors needn't be decorated with Aubusson tapestries to make them stimulating and pleasant; some nice wallpaper or paint will do, as would a few plants. These corridors would not be defaced. On the contrary, families or residents would probably pitch in and keep them up even if no janitorial services were available. Indeed, residents could be encouraged to add additional decorations—prints, posters, or a shared bulletin board.

Besides the emphasis on enhancement of a personalized feeling, an essential design consideration is the promotion of a social structure. Another series of experiments has revealed how this can be achieved. In a student dormitory project at an Eastern university, it was discovered that couples who lived near the entrance to the building had more friends than those who lived in some isolated area. The heavier traffic at the entrance provided the residents near it with more opportunities for seeing, greeting, and conversing with other members of the building. This made it easier for them to make new friends.

In the average high-rise housing project, chance meetings between residents are usually limited to the elevator. Although people may also run into each other in the corridors, such meetings can occur only among people on the same floor. Furthermore, the dark, unappealing corridors do not provide a pleasant surrounding for socializing. In fact, their unsafe atmosphere would compel residents to scurry back to their own quarters. What is needed, then, are more open areas with activities so that people will be drawn there and will want to stay.

Since in many high-density regions building height does not

represent a problem, two or three floors in the middle of a high-rise public housing project could easily be given over to socializing areas: gyms, basketball courts, party rooms, a nursery school or daycare center, bar and grill, a small movie theatre, and so on. In larger buildings a rooftop garden could be provided. The more such socializing areas there are, the more people in the building can see each other and become familiar with each other, doing so in pleasant rather than unpleasant settings. This in itself will induce them to like each other a bit more, even if they don't get to know one another more fully. This relationship between familiarity and liking has been demonstrated in experiments where people were shown photographs of strangers, displayed in such a way that certain faces were viewed more frequently than others. Afterwards, when people were asked to rate how much they liked the various faces, it was found that they had greater liking for the faces they had seen more often.

The fact that increased contact induces greater liking can be used to reduce racial prejudice. It has been shown consistently that when people of different racial groups are assigned living spaces near each other, the increased visual contacts result in decreased prejudice. A prejudiced person makes inferences about a total stranger on the basis of a few very salient cues like skin color, speech, or manner. Increased exposure to these cues leads the prejudiced person to pay more attention to other interpersonal cues, and hence to receive increasingly complex sets of information which become less and less consistent with his prejudice. But this only happens in pleasant environments which are also arousing enough to cause people to socialize. And it is here that racially or ethnically integrated high-density, low-income, or public housing has fallen flat on its face.

Besides providing a sense of identity and community, public housing must provide privacy, starting with soundproof walls so that residents can't hear each other's TVs, telephones, lovemaking, door-bells, crying babies, or domestic quarrels. For instance, in some British low-income houses the living rooms or bedrooms of two adjacent homes were separated by a common wall. As a consequence, it was very difficult for the families to enjoy privacy either in their living rooms or in their bedrooms; they heard each other's TV sets, felt restrained in their bedrooms, and even smelled the cooking next door. Generally, it was hard to distinguish activities or events in their own homes from those next door. Neighbors were cold and impersonal toward each other and there were feelings of resentment. Some neighbors felt that they were being spied on or gossiped about, and this even affected their own family relationships.

Other low-income homes shared the same backyard area, with low shrubs marking the boundaries. Such boundaries were hardly respected; neighbors walked, talked, played, or barbecued on each other's property. Also, the insides of the homes were visible through windows facing the backyards, resulting in much gossip. Even though privacy could be had at home by drawing the curtains to one's own backyard, the restricted feeling was annoying.

On the other hand, when the setting permitted sufficient privacy, friendly relationships between neighbors did develop. For example, when the backyards of homes were separated from each other by high fences, the neighbors voluntarily initiated cordial conversations across the fences.*

Thus, the need for privacy cannot be overemphasized. Somehow, opportunities for both privacy and social contact are important to a sense of well-being. This is because without privacy people are subjected to sustained levels of high arousal from frequent, uncontrollable interpersonal stimuli. If they have a chance to isolate themselves voluntarily and temporarily from these stimuli, residents can achieve more tolerable arousal levels and will appreciate their neighbors more.

The recent trend toward low-income, one-family homes grows out of a recognition of this necessity for privacy but fails to consider problems of urban design. From a financial standpoint, single-family housing would be a legitimate alternative to high-rise public housing if we had unlimited space in which to expand our cities. It is conceivable that we could manufacture inexpensive but good quality single-family dwellings comparable in per unit cost to apartments in high-rise projects. However, this would only add to the problem of suburban sprawl; it would necessitate even greater reliance on the automobile for transportation. In addition to pollution, automobiles generate tremendous noise, take up large chunks of our urban land surfaces, and increasingly and indirectly add to the cost of housing —gasoline and car depreciation costs are greater for suburban

* These examples of low-income housing in Britain may not be representative, but that is not the main issue here. Our concern is with the principles which relate privacy or the lack of it in housing to inter-neighbor social relations—principles that may be applied in any country and at any socioeconomic level.

commuters. Sooner or later cities are going to have to become more centralized and better planned. In the long run, then, it is more beneficial to invest in research aimed at developing high-density dwelling areas which adequately meet the social, psychological, and economic needs, not only of the poor, but of the general populace.

Suggested Readings

The following sources present evidence relating to the many satisfactions associated with so-called slum life, the disruption of networks of social relations when people are dislocated into public housing, and the undesirable crime, vandalism, and psychopathology which ensue: Chapin (1938), Fried (1963), Fried and Gleicher (1961), Srivastava and Good (1969), and Wilner, Walkley, Pinkerton, and Tayback (1962). Calhoun's (1962a, 1962b) work with rats dramatically illustrated the detrimental effect of crowding in of itself. However, Newman's (1972) analysis showed large-scale differences in the crime, vandalism, psychological health, and general neighborhood satisfaction of small, compared to very large, high-rise structures. Kuper (1953, chap. 2) provided data on the importance of privacy based upon his observations of British housing.

For the basic findings relating people's familiarity to their liking for one another, see Zajonc (1968). Along these lines, generally favorable results of integrated racial housing, which increases familiarity of individuals from different racial groups, were reported by Deutsch and Collins (1951), Jahoda and West (1951), and by Wilner, Walkley, and Cook (1955). See Jacobs (1969) for observations on the favorable effects on inter-neighbor relationships of shared recreational and public areas. References cited as suggested readings for the previous chapter provide additional data on the general determinants of liking and friendship among neighbors.

PART FOUR

WORK

ENVIRONMENTS

CHAPTER

12

Factories

IN a rather unsuccessful poem entitled "The Choice," William Butler Yeats said that

> The intellect of man is forced to choose
> Perfection of the life, or of the work.*

These lines are usually quoted approvingly by artists or corporation presidents who've made a mess of their personal lives, but the idea does have merit, environmentally speaking. Taking the mother tongue and shaping from it verbal artifacts that will endure as long as men read or turning an auto parts shop into a conglomerate with assets of $400 million are tasks that are extremely high in arousing quality and dominance, with pleasure fluctuating wildly in between. For certain people such tasks might well be so absorbing (approach-causing) that little else in life seems worth doing or paying much attention to.

Neglecting one's home or personal life because the job is so exciting and rewarding is not what you'd call a big problem for most factory workers. Factories are generally built around some version of "the line." Workers are stationed along a moving assembly line and contribute one or two behavioral bits—attaching a bumper, soldering the blue wires together, sewing on a pocket—to a partially assembled something. Most such tasks, performed in an identical fashion hour after hour, day after day, week after week, and year

---

* Excerpt from William Butler Yeats' poem "The Choice," in *Collected Poems of William Butler Yeats*, p. 224. Reprinted by permission of the publisher, Macmillan Publishing Co., Inc. © 1933, renewed 1961 by Bertha Georgie Yeats.

after year, probably represent the most monotonous and boring forms of activity human beings can be called upon to do. In other words, these tasks are low-load with a vengeance. They are usually tasks that are not pleasant in themselves and are not performed in pleasant surroundings. The unending, insistent demands of the line plus one's inability to chuck the whole factory environment for some other means of earning a living combine to cause feelings of submissiveness. A state of low arousal, displeasure, and submissiveness—call it despair—is one of the most disagreeable feelings a person can experience. From a work-efficiency point of view, such a feeling is about as nonproductive as you can get: rampant avoidance behavior results in highly defective performance.

I should make it clear that when I refer to the factory worker I am not talking about the man who controls a fifty-ton caldron of molten steel, or operates a crane or stamping machine containing the power of a thousand human backs. Such workers are highly skilled and derive feelings of arousal, pleasure, and dominance from the exact manipulation of almost unthinkably powerful forces. The semi-skilled worker earning $13.50 an hour can also derive such feelings from looking at his paycheck and thinking about the considerably lower pay rates of architects, engineers, or university professors.

Certain old-style managers try to improve performance simply by speeding up the line. This works because arousal levels go up as workers attempt to perform their tasks in less time; productivity improves within fairly narrow limits. But the manager now has workers who are feeling highly aroused, unpleasant, and submissive, that is anxious or tense. If this feeling state is maintained for long, the workers become GASed; there are higher rates of absenteeism and injury, health-insurance plans become more costly, and performance eventually falls off. Furthermore, since anxious workers need only a shift in the dominance dimension to become angry workers, management which relies heavily on the speed-up is asking for fights, union troubles, and ingenious sabotage techniques leading to recalls or other embarrassing experiences in the marketplace.

The many problems facing industrial designers, management, and union leaders include how to increase the load of various factory tasks, how to make the tasks and the settings in which they are performed more pleasant, and how to make the workers feel more significant and more important (dominant) in relation to their tasks.

It may seem odd to talk about making arousal levels go up in factory environments, which often seem to visitors to be hellishly loaded—machinery clanging, hissing, or screeching, people shouting, foul odors, a lot of motion and activity, blinding oxyacetylene flashes, extreme heat, and so forth. But for the visitor this is a novel or unusual environment; its novelty and complexity combine to give it a heavy load which is quite arousing. Complexity is especially high for the visitor since, unlike the workers, he is exposed to many different sections of the factory over a brief period of time. The workers usually function in a limited space and adapt to the combinations of stimuli which surround them, so both complexity and novelty are at lower levels for them. And if routine, low-load tasks are being performed in an environment which has become extremely familiar, arousal levels are bound to be very low.

There is not much that can be done to make a simple, routine, mechanical task intrinsically more arousing. What can and is being done is to vary the tasks each worker performs. Production teams are formed wherein each member does a different job on a rotating basis, either day by day or even more frequently. Since the team as a whole makes a larger contribution to the finished product (for example, assembles a whole engine in an automobile plant), each team member can perhaps feel somewhat less coglike and derive a bit more satisfaction from his role.

The production-team concept was first used for coal mining in England. Before nationalization, coal mining was done in the traditional way, small groups of workers digging into a vein of coal, loading it onto a cart, and pushing it out. The setting was unpleasant and the mines were dangerous but there were strong bonds of friendship among the workers which were important sources of gratification to them, and of course each worker performed a variety of functions. With nationalization, government engineers who attempted to improve the mining technology devised the "long wall" method of mining. In this method, when a vein of ore is found, two parallel shafts are built going into the ore with tracks for moving the dug-out coal along these shafts. Furthermore, a strict division of labor is introduced: one crew drills holes and sets charges to loosen up the coal; a second crew comes in and actually digs out the coal; a third crew shovels the coal into the cars that carry it out on the tracks; as the wall of coal recedes, a fourth crew fills in the emptied portion behind the workers. Different specialized groups thus form two shafts which move into the mountain and fill in dirt behind the advancing wall of coal. Even though the idea looked good on paper, the long-wall method was a terrible failure—productivity dropped and there were frequent delays because one team had to wait for another to finish doing its part so they could proceed to the next step. Social scientists who were called in recommended that the technology be retained, but rearranged the work so that a team of four or five men would be completely in charge of one section of the wall. Each team would do all the different jobs, including the drilling, loosening, digging, loading, and refilling operations. The shift to the team concept resulted in increased productivity and higher morale. What this new method achieved was to give workers a feeling of control (dominance) over the entire process of mining rather than the feeling of being an insignificant part of it; it also added tremendously to the variety (load) of work routines. The change also resulted in closer teamwork and greater social gratifications for workers on each team.

An analogous application of the team concept to a pet food production plant in the United States involved the following change in job definitions. Before its application, one crew would unload the raw materials coming into the plant, several different crews would each take on a small segment of the process of converting the raw material into pet food, and, finally, another crew would load the product for transport. With the team approach, a single team unloaded the raw material and saw it through half of the process while another team carried out the last half of the process and loaded the product for transport. These teams, or autonomous work groups, had a great deal more control and effectively reduced the management hierarchy.

Autonomous work groups counteract the two basic principles of manufacturing organizations, namely, division of labor and hierarchies of control. When these principles were first introduced in young industrial nations, engineers were striving to achieve an economically feasible system of machinery to do each job; whatever could not be done by machines, or was too costly to warrant newly designed machinery, was assigned to workers. Workers were the fill-ins. The management hierarchy reinforced this view of the workers as small cogs in an elaborate system of machinery. The autonomous work group usually eliminates two of the lower rungs of the management hierarchy by taking on those lower level management functions while taking over a greater segment of the production functions. It effectively increases a worker's feelings of dominance and arousal. If the production teams are allowed to work out their own arrangements, it is possible for at least one member of the team to leave the line for an unscheduled but needed break, since another member can temporarily handle two jobs. When such teams are formed, there is an initial drop in productivity because workers have to learn at least five jobs instead of just one. This has occasionally caused such experiments to be discarded, particularly in this country. But such a team approach can pay off, particularly in industries that experience very high employee turnover rates, because high turnover is partly a result of people attempting to increase arousal by changing the work environment.

Interestingly, the team concept opens up many possibilities for workers to introduce innovations in relation to the entire task they perform. Since routines and standardization lie at the heart of the assembly-line process, certain techniques or procedures are used simply because they have worked in the past, not because they are necessarily more effective than others. Recently for example a large metalworking plant was in serious economic trouble. In an effort to preserve their jobs, the workers petitioned management for, among other things, the right to modify production procedures so as to increase output and cut costs. As a result, overall plant productivity went up significantly.

Workers who are able to modify equipment or procedures will naturally feel more significant and useful in relation to the work environment. A dramatically successful case of worker contribution to overall plant efficiency and profits is the incentive plan adopted by a small company, Lincoln Electric. Workers at this factory share equally in the profits and everyone, from the janitors to the company president, is welcome to contribute ideas that might improve productivity. The current income of the average worker at this factory is double that of comparable plants, and turnover is negligible. The effectiveness of the plan hinges on the smallness of the factory, so that the monetary and social reinforcers for those who contribute to the overall success are both immediate and tangible. A similar system is not as workable in large corporations with numerous subsidiaries, since improvements in one subsidiary are diluted by sharing them with others. Also, some cost-saving suggestions, such as buying a part from a competitor of the corporation rather than from one of its own subsidiaries, cannot be implemented. Generally, then, there should be freedom from organizational roadblocks and there should be tangible as well as psychological rewards for successful innovation. There shouldn't be any penalties for changes that fail to produce the desired results, or else workers may wind up feeling that they are exploiting themselves.

To increase the load of the factory environment it is necessary to introduce stimuli that vary over time, or else workers will quickly habituate to the setting. In the classical Hawthorne studies, investigators set out to discover the best environmental conditions for workers. However, they soon discovered that *any* changes they introduced increased productivity. It wasn't a fixed, ideal room color, temperature, or brightness of lighting which caused increased performance, but rather the much needed variability of the surroundings while performing a monotonous task. So, for example, it would not suffice to paint the factory in warmer colors; in time, such a static stimulus would lose much of its arousing value. One could provide visual displays for certain groups of workers: for example, for those who do not really have to look at what they're doing. These displays could include slide shows, film loops, or news stories flashed onto large overhead screens.

Music of course would be an ideal stimulus. People automatically adjust the tempo and rhythm of their movements to the principle beats of their environment. Experiments have shown that even when two people are conversing in an otherwise silent room, each person's gestures and body movements are subtly affected by the other's. A very boring and routine job—folding letters or fliers and stuffing them into envelopes, for instance—can be radically affected by music. If slow, very regular music is played, the stuffing actions will also be slow and regular. If the music is lively and has a complicated rhythm, the stuffing activity will move more quickly and will tend to mirror the rhythms in the music, almost as though the worker were conducting the music—a little flourish here, a pause or an emphatic downbeat there. Such synchrony of movements to music can be planned deliberately to maintain a desired level of arousal or activity pace in the work setting. It may also be used to regulate different levels of activity pace during various segments of the work cycle.

Of course, in extremely noisy factories it is virtually impossible to pipe in music. But if it is consistent with safety, workers in such high-noise environments could be provided with comfortable earphone-type transistor radios which would not only eliminate unpleasant or even harmful auditory stimuli but would replace them with pleasant and stimulating experiences—music, news, ball games, or whatever. Such earphones could even be provided with an open band or an override so that all workers wearing them could receive communications instantly from a central location. It should also be possible to provide two-way headphones so that a group of workers in the same high-noise area could talk to each other, tell jokes, or alert each other to danger, thus creating an informal conversational group even though each worker was isolated by distance and by an otherwise insuperable noise barrier. This idea has special appeal for highly automated plants where workers cannot talk with or even see others who may be spread out over an area the size of three football fields. Provided that conversation with a fellow worker using two-way headphones is not distracting, that is, if the job is not too complex or novel, this possibility would considerably enhance pleasure and arousal levels.

Noise can of course be a source of arousal, particularly if it is irregular, unpredictable, and varied. Factory noise has been studied extensively, usually with contradictory results. Some studies showed that environmental noise detracts from performance while others showed that it has a beneficial effect. These contradictions can usually be resolved by considering the complexity of the work being performed and by recalling that maximum performance is achieved at moderate arousal levels in a pleasant setting. If the task is an extremely monotonous one, then arousal levels are very low and irregular noise, provided it is not clearly objectionable, will increase arousal moderately and consequently result in improved performance. If however the worker is performing a more complex task, one that involves several different steps requiring concentration and judgment, his arousal level will already be moderately high; irregular or unexpected noise will increase arousal too much and will thus cause a drop in performance. Similar considerations apply to the use of music as well. Moderate-load music should be paired with simple, routine tasks, and low-load music with complex and varied tasks.

Interestingly enough, the same amount and type of noise tends to improve performance more in the night shift than in the day shift. A person's level of physiological arousal tends to be cyclical, going from low to high to low again in a biologically clocked rhythm. Many people who sleep during the day and work at night are likely to be fighting a natural tendency for lowered arousal levels during the night and a heightened level when they are sleeping. Furthermore, the nighttime environment is generally less loaded simply because the darkness eliminates or cloaks many environmental stimuli. This is why farmers and other early risers resent daylight saving time: the absence of light causes them to awaken and begin their daily routines in a depressing or low-load environment precisely at the time when they are struggling to raise their arousal levels. In any case, the night-shift worker is somewhat less aroused than the day-shift worker and is likely to benefit from the increased stimulation of music or low noise.

But noise is by definition an unwanted or unpleasant stimulus, and it is far better to increase or decrease arousal by means of a stimulus that is also very pleasant or musical. The pleasantness of an environment is an extremely important determinant of approach or avoidance. Pleasant environments can elicit approach behavior even if there are unpleasant environmental features or tasks to be performed. Indeed, recent research indicates that pleasure plays a significant role in determining what constitutes an optimum arousal level. That is, in a situation of high pleasure, higher arousal levels are more acceptable than they would be if the situation were less pleasant or downright unpleasant.* If, therefore, a worker's job or work environment is such that it causes high levels of arousal, every effort should be made to make that job or that environment as pleasant as possible. The work environment should for example be painted in pleasant colors in terms of hue, brightness, and saturation. Pleasant sounds and odors should be introduced. Communication among employees should be encouraged because this generally contributes to pleasure. And pleasant lounges, lunchrooms, and other meeting places should be provided since these contribute to the pleasantness of factory life as a whole.

Coffee and lunch breaks should serve to increase both arousal and pleasure levels. They can introduce variety into the work routine by allowing a change of environment and by providing an opportunity for enjoyable and stimulating conversation or horseplay. It is considered healthy and proper for sedentary office workers, especially higher-status types, to use most of their lunch hours for a game of

---

* The level of arousal achieved, for example, during the sexual act is so high that if the act does not continue to be pleasant, a powerful avoidance reaction amounting to revulsion can result. This phenomenon has produced, among other things, the experienced bachelor's truism that "bad sex is worse than no sex."

handball, indoor tennis, or swimming in a nearby gym. It has, I think, been widely assumed that mild midday exercise is inappropriate for factory workers simply because they do manual labor. But many factory workers do not do bone-crushing labor; their physical weariness at day's end derives largely from the general environmental conditions of the work site and is at least partially psychosomatic. Workers doing low-load jobs in unpleasant settings could benefit enormously from pleasant and mildly stimulating midday recreation —a swim in a nice pool, a softball game, tossing a basketball around, bowling, ping-pong, billiards, or jogging. Incorporating pleasant, diversified, and accessible recreation areas into the design of large new plants will not represent a prohibitive additional expense, and sooner or later imaginative and empathic union leaders are going to introduce such fringe benefits into the collective bargaining process.

Coffee and lunch breaks should ideally be flexible enough so that they may be taken when the individual worker needs a change in arousal level. If you were to chart the daily arousal and performance levels of a sufficiently large number of day-shift workers, they would start low, rise during the morning, and begin to fall off in mid-afternoon as fatigue starts to set in. Scheduling general mid-morning and mid-afternoon breaks therefore makes statistical sense, especially the afternoon breaks. But there are also many individual variations within that norm; not everybody will benefit equally from a 10:15 A.M. or a 3:00 P.M. break. Ideally, individual workers ought to be able to select their own breaks just when, as a result of fatigue, their arousal levels threaten to fall so low that their performance would be seriously affected. In some factory situations, unscheduled break patterns can create production problems, but even in classic assembly line situations something can usually be worked out. Certainly jobs that are essentially piecework—a daily quota must be met but one worker's production is not sequentially related to another's—can permit wide fluctuations in break and lunch times.

It is important that the break or lunch hour not be taken in the work environment but rather in a very pleasant, mildly stimulating lounge area of some sort that is designed to encourage friendly interaction. Since the purpose of the break is usually to increase arousal and certainly to increase pleasure, this can be accomplished best with environmental change; pulling out a thermos on the work site will not be too effective. The lounge area should be readily accessible and should if possible provide a halfway decent view of the outside; in any case, it should incorporate pleasant, arousing colors and agreeable, mildly loaded music. An excessively loaded lounge area is undesirable since it would simply GAS an already fatigued worker; but the music in the lounge can be of higher load during the mid-morning than during the mid-afternoon break. Ideally, this lounge area should be redecorated from time to time—chairs and tables moved around, paintings changed or shifted—so that the lounge does not become hopelessly static and familiar. If, on the other hand, a good percentage of the workers are performing complex and dangerous tasks, a pleasant, low-load lounge also should be provided so that these workers, particularly the nonscreeners, may bring their arousal levels down to the optimum level.

This brings me to one final point. As we have seen, there are quite consistent differences among people in terms of their reactions to different kinds of work. Lower environmental loads, greater privacy, freedom from distractions, and more predictable and routine work schedules are appropriate when workers perform demanding (complex and somewhat unpleasant) tasks, and this is especially true for the nonscreeners among them. That is, lower performance is to be expected more from nonscreeners than from screeners who are engaged in unpleasant, high-load tasks, and reduction of environmental loads can be expected to raise performance, particularly among the non-screeners. On the other hand, nonscreeners will tend to approach pleasant and high-load tasks even more than screeners. In fact, they are frequently likely to drive themselves to GAS reactions and may find relaxing and calming (pleasant and low-load) homes essential to their health.

Therefore, another way in which worker morale as well as productivity may be maximized is to do some psychological testing prior to making job assignments. At almost any level within any trade or profession there are some tasks that are more regulated and repetitious and others that are more varied, complex, or uncertain, even though these tasks may be comparable in their levels of pleasantness-unpleasantness. At any level of skill or salary, personality selection measures could be used to assign workers to tasks that they would perform better than others. Nobody need get locked into anything, but the use of such prior testing might significantly improve morale and performance for large numbers of workers. It is of course true that the personality of the worker has something to do with the kind of trade he selects and the kinds of positions toward which he gravitates, but many career choices are achieved only after much trial and error. The large majority of workers who apply to giant corporations for positions really have very little idea what their jobs are going to be like. And this is where the employer can judiciously make assessments that will save him and his employees from wasteful false starts, internal departmental conflicts, and less than effective performances.

Suggested Readings

See Roethlisberger and Dickson (1939) on the Hawthorne effect, Taylor (1911) for the basic ideas which have guided factory design for several decades, and Davis and Trist (1974) and Emery and Trist (1960) on recent developments in factory design and management which seek to increase workers' arousal levels by increasing their responsibility and the variability of the jobs they perform. For a review of available experiments and a general theory of environmental effects on work performance, see Russell and Mehrabian (1975a, 1976e). Also see Mehrabian and Russell (1974a, chaps. 6 and 8) for a review of the studies of the effects of noise in factories and for data on the desire to work in a variety of emotion-eliciting work settings. Introductions to behavior modification principles and reinforcement procedures which have possible applications in factories can be found in Bandura (1969) and Mehrabian (1970).

CHAPTER

13

Offices

THERE IS a marvelous office scene in an old movie, *The Millionaire*, in which a multimillionaire gives away his fortune to people he has picked at random from the phone directory. A clerk, played by Charles Laughton, sits at a desk in an enormous drab room filled with row upon row of identical desks. A letter arrives. He opens it and finds a check for a million dollars. He looks at it briefly, rises, and lumbers up the aisle past his co-workers, all of whom have their noses buried in their work. The camera follows him as he opens one door after another, each of which has a bigger nameplate than the previous one, until he finally arrives at a door marked "President." He bangs it open, sticks his head in, puts out his tongue, and makes a huge, fat, noisy raspberry.

Apart from embodying one of the archetypal dreams of Everyman, this scene contains at least one element deserving of comment —the dominance aspect which plays such a large role in many white collar corporations. Few office buildings are designed for a particular company and its particular needs; rather, there is a more or less standard set of floor plans which assume that the company, whether it has forty employees or 4,000, will have a pyramidal organization, with most of the employees forming the base and a handful forming the apex. To properly reflect this dominance hierarchy, the floor plans usually embody a reverse pyramid in terms of space and design, allotting the most space and the most desirable locations to the fewest number of employees. In small, two-story suburban office buildings for example there may be floor plans which provide offices for thirty-two employees on the first floor and three executives and their secretaries on the second. High-rise office buildings designed to be occupied by one corporation invariably set aside the top floors for the executive echelons, frequently with the president or chairman of the board and a few key assistants occupying the topmost or penthouse floor.

In large, older buildings, individual floors often express the dominance aspects implicit in the hierarchy. The corner offices are designed to be occupied by senior executives or heads of departments because these have more windows. The most powerful or dominant executive has the largest office with the most windows. One-window offices are occupied by senior middle-management personnel; junior and more subordinate workers occupy an interior set of windowless and usually doorless cubicles or partitioned spaces. Employees on the lowest rungs—secretaries, clerks, and so on—are placed together in a large, open pit. Even within such a floor plan, there are intricate formal and informal patterns of status. The degree of closeness of a desk or cubicle to the center of power will usually index its importance or power. Also, higher-status offices are generally less accessible. The president's office is the least accessible of all; one might have to go through as many as three doors and then past a receptionist and a secretary to get to its occupant. Such floor plans express and maintain more rigidity, formality, and bureaucratic fussiness than sophisticated managers now consider desirable. Nevertheless, in their rather bare-faced or naive concern for dominance, such old-style designs do sometimes provide environmental features which are almost accidentally successful in providing the required arousal and pleasure levels. I am thinking especially of the central open pit with its rows of desks, sometimes derisively referred to as the "cabbage patch" by office designers or space planners.

The low-status employees assigned to the cabbage patch do low-status work—typing, filing, elementary bookkeeping, or other routine paper work. Although such work may be more complex than certain assembly line tasks, it still tends to be repetitious, mechanical, or monotonous. To perform such tasks efficiently one must have a moderately loaded environment. Unless the pit is run by a complete martinet, it usually is such an environment—typewriters clacking, phones ringing, and, most arousing of all, people moving and talking. It is possible for people to communicate readily by word or gesture; a joke can send ripples of laughter through the whole pit; a spat is electrifying and nobody even pretends not to watch; a newcomer is very interesting, and yet he or she usually is quickly accepted and befriended. More office romances, declared or not, are spawned in the pit than anywhere else, except perhaps among senior executives and their personal secretaries.

In a laudable attempt to give employees more status by giving them more privacy, some designers and managers have tried to completely eliminate the cabbage patch and have provided instead a maze of cubicles. Sometimes these cubicles have floor-to-ceiling partitions; in others, partitions are about chest high. The theory, especially as it relates to the semi-partitioned cubicles, is that people will have the privacy they need but interoffice communication will not be hindered. However, work-related communication is not the only kind there is; people doing low-load tasks can often use simple eye contact, a smile, or a wink. A "How about Ernie's for lunch?" called across three desks, "Ernie's folded last week" coming from six desks across, and "But there's this new place, Jake's, down the block, with good lasagne" from somewhere else will not significantly interrupt work, if at all, but will instead provide a useful, efficient, and pleasant exchange that serves to increase arousal.

But even official interoffice communication sometimes suffers in the newer modularized designs. If someone comes across something on an invoice that looks a bit strange, he might look across the open pit at someone and ask: "Hey, Joni, we got a rep in Bangor, Maryland?" But if he has to stand up, leave his cubicle, and walk ten paces, or shout over two or three intervening modules, he may instead just shrug and pass it on. The defective invoice may get all the way to the warehouse or even farther before it gums up the works. Furthermore, in a cabbage patch you can see if somebody you need to talk to is at his desk, on the phone, or has a visitor. In the modular arrangement you often can't, and must get up and take a look. Since most people are reluctant to impinge upon the privacy suggested by a module, they are unlikely to peek over someone's partition or call out over the top of an intervening one. This means in some cases that a worker will have to rise, leave his module, and walk perhaps twenty or thirty paces only to find his co-worker gone, on the phone, or talking to a visitor. Unless it is extremely urgent, unless he knows the visitor, or unless his colleague indicates that the phone call is not important and waves him in, he is likely to return to his own cubicle with his problem still unsolved and time wasted. If this happens often enough, the net amount of interoffice communication will decline, possibly with detrimental effects on the quality or quantity of work produced.

In general, the lower the load of a task, the more it requires a high-load setting for optimum performance. This is why low-load tasks benefit from the additional stimulation and pleasure that an informally supervised pit can provide. Certain fairly complex jobs that are very familiar so that their overall loads are moderate or even low can also benefit significantly from the stimulation and rapid exchanges of information typical of cabbage-patch arrangements. Several friends of mine had cabbage-patch experiences early in their careers and they invariably recall these work environments with fondness. One of these friends worked as a copywriter for a mail-order catalogue. He remembers a large, windowless, barren, slate gray room in which he and a dozen others sat around and wrote copy for everything from brassieres to grass seed. In addition, there were all sorts of people coming in and out—buyers, layout people, proof-readers, and so on. This was a fairly loaded and, on the face of it, somewhat uncomfortable work environment. Yet the open, informal design allowed people not only to joke or grumble when they felt like it, but also to bounce ideas off each other and hone their verbal skills in an atmosphere of friendly but competitive give and take. Indeed, friendships—some of them rather unlikely—were formed there that have lasted for decades through all sorts of professional vicissitudes. The cabbage-patch arrangement made possible a high degree of interpersonal contact, and the stimulation and pleasure deriving from it more than compensated for the other environmental inadequacies.

A good many interoffice problems in corporations result because marketing doesn't know what manufacturing is up to, and neither knows where finance is until it's too late; all three have set hundreds of people in counterproductive motion. If key executives had the same opportunity as pool typists to interact in their work environments, a lot of problems would never occur.

Management consultants are often amazed at how little many senior executives know about fairly significant interoffice matters. Secretaries get together and compare notes far more often than their bosses do and frequently have a wider and more detailed picture of the whole operation. Parts of this information, in turn, get fed into the grapevine and wind up in a cabbage patch ten floors down, with the result that someone in the steno pool or the copying room knows that two top executives have had a big fight and are subtly undermining each other's efforts, while the rest of management hasn't a clue.

Although the really sticky problems that nobody at a lower level can or wants to handle generally reach the executive hot seat, top executives are not always dealing with spicy meatballs or making big-picture decisions. There are plenty of moments when they're reading reports, winnowing through all kinds of dull proposals, or wondering how to answer some housewife who found a dead spider in the cat food manufactured by a West Coast subsidiary. That is, there are often times when executives must wade through low-load paper work that calls for a fairly high-load environment. And a huge, somewhat formal and isolated office done in black leather and beige is not the most arousing or effective setting.

Finally, there is a good deal more loneliness at the top than need be. Some executives try and overcome this by taking occasional strolls in their dominions on the lower floors. But they often find that they have become so isolated that subordinate workers clam up, get anxious, feel they're being evaluated, or otherwise exhibit avoidance behavior. And top executives are likely to be so impressed by their own colleagues' status and dominant surroundings that they are overcautious about engaging them in friendly, informal, and continuous contact.

There is then justification for less emphasis on executive privacy and greater efforts to create accessible channels of communication and contact both among executives and between executives and lower-echelon personnel. Executive as well as middle level offices ought to be provided with ample means for altering the work setting in the direction of low or high loads. These should always be pleasant, of course, since a pleasant environment invariably causes approach. Whenever possible, they should downplay if not actually eschew the accouterments of dominance, if for no other reason than the fact that intuitive or informed persons will wonder why a given executive has chosen to emphasize his dominant status at the expense of his own comfort and a more open, relaxed, or friendly setting. The answer in some cases could be insecurity deriving from real or imagined incompetence. An interesting solution to this problem which I've observed in a small corporation is that none of the doors have locks. People within the company can drift in and out, exchanging ideas, opinions, or maybe arguments. Nobody even closes a door unless there is a "fire drill"—an emergency which requires meeting a deadline. Even the president's office is open. In fact, he has a large storage space in his office so when others cannot find brochures or other sources of information, they try his office. This casual atmosphere is well liked and is made possible in part by having a good security system which screens people from outside the company. The only entrances to the building are a number of doors reached from the parking lot which require knowledge of the combination (changed from time to time) and passage through a large reception room. All visitors are screened in this room so that additional security becomes unnecessary.

Since lower-echelon employees who are assigned offices need privacy and low-load settings for occasions when they perform loaded tasks, such offices should have doors. Doorless cubicles do not afford protection from extraneous environmental stimuli—people walking by, a conversation down the hall, and so on—but do on the other hand tend to isolate workers from one another. That is, doorless cubicles provide a less flexible work space than cubicles with doors; if a worker needs complete privacy, he cannot get it without a door. On the other hand, a worker in an office with a door can have privacy, and he can get more stimulation from the environment if he needs it by leaving his door open. Workers at all levels should be permitted to have and play desk radios, since these provide one of the few means available for manipulating arousal and pleasure levels within the office context. And of course employees should be permitted to personalize their work spaces as individual differences dictate; some might prefer or need a more (or less) loaded environment than others. This last point may seem obvious, but not many years ago a major corporation had its headquarters designed by one of the great modern architects. The building was completed after his death, and its interior designer came up with all kinds of rigid schemes regulating personnel minutiae—whether employees would be permitted to have on their desks framed photographs of their families or sweethearts, or whether the color scheme of any given office favored red as opposed to yellow flowers. The utter folly of this sort of thing was ultimately recognized, but not until considerable interoffice resentment and strife had resulted. Employees should definitely be allowed to introduce prints, paintings, posters, plants, and appliances (including coffeepots) as a means of making their work spaces as comfortable, pleasant, and loaded as they wish. It is of course equally foolish for someone in a position of authority to walk into the office of a nonscreener who performs complex and somewhat unpleasant work and drop veiled hints that the office needs a bit more "life." That particular office and that person may need no such thing.

In the same vein, a worker ought to be able to leave his office door open if he wants to. While doing demanding (high-load and slightly unpleasant) work, people tend to keep their doors closed and make efforts to maintain a noise- and distraction-free work environment. However, while doing pleasant and complex but extremely familiar tasks (the familiarity of which makes them relatively low-load), workers might prefer to be with others and to discuss things; they might be more productive that way. During such work, non-screeners are expected to benefit even more from companionship than screeners. On the other hand, while under pressure to meet a deadline (high-load and unpleasant task), a nonscreener might be especially annoyed by clutter in his office, visits by people who are just dropping in, or by phone calls. On such days we would expect him to avoid the crowded coffee lounge that is readily at hand and to enjoy his coffee less.

Since, as I mentioned earlier, increased visual contact with others tends to increase liking and often leads to more substantial interpersonal relations, it is a good idea for all office buildings to provide a common lounge area in which people can get together during breaks or gather to eat their lunch. Such a socializing area would be especially effective in the center of a cluster of offices. Workers could pop out of their offices when they needed a change from too much privacy, or when they needed to communicate with a number of their colleagues. Many offices are quite small and barely have enough room for two or three people to stand in. Although most office buildings have conference rooms, these are often quite forbidding and are placed deep in executive territory.

I recall a particular lounge, situated in the executive wing of a small corporation and surrounded by the top executive offices. It was almost never used for two reasons. First, it was not on neutral ground; employees had to go out of their way to get there and understandably felt reluctant to be seen relaxing or socializing by company officers who were not doing so themselves, or who had no idea whether the employees were on a break or were just goldbricking. Second, the area was furnished like a formal living room—a long couch, a few side chairs—and hence did not encourage social interaction. Instead it served as a waiting room for visitors calling upon the various executives. All the employees, including the executives, socialized in the lunchroom, which was considered neutral ground since it was shared by the entire company. The lunchroom had vending machines, posters on the walls, many movable small tables and chairs, and a view of the lawn. At first it seemed as if this lunchroom would not be used by top management personnel because it utterly lacked any dominance aspect—plastic chairs, rather tacky posters instead of oil paintings, beverage and soup machines, and so forth. Due to its informality, however, this lunchroom encouraged cross-status exchanges, which are usually more stimulating, and was thus the favorite socializing place in the building.

A readily accessible, properly furnished common lounging area is a particularly valuable asset in academic or other office buildings housing any business that is basically informational. It is extremely important that faculty members and administrators have an opportunity to exchange ideas and to challenge and stimulate each other. Most of the really interesting breakthroughs in the world of ideas have come about when the findings of one discipline have interpenetrated with the findings of another. Unfortunately, the tendency has been not only to house each academic department separately, but often to widely space these on campus, with few if any common socializing areas. Even within departments there has been a trend toward lessened interpersonal contact. In the less affluent days of one university department, for example, the entire staff shared a three-story building and people crossed paths frequently. Now they are scattered throughout an eight-floor office building having a standard corridor floor plan. This has had a dramatic impact on the social structure of the department, which has become much more fragmented. The few opportunities for informal or extended discussions are provided by chance meetings among faculty members while they are picking up their mail in a small and congested mail room.

Office buildings that are shared by a number of different companies could also benefit from the cross-fertilization which might be promoted by a central socializing area available to all occupants of the building. This area would not be designed in the conventional coffee-shop style. Instead, there would be only two or three conversation pits. The limited number of separate areas and chairs would force strangers into the same conversation pit. A building that housed legal offices, a publishing house, a data-processing firm, a finance company, an architect, a theatrical agent, an importer, and the sales offices of a company manufacturing hang gliders or surfboards could be the perfect setting for an exciting, enjoyable, and perhaps even commercially profitable exchange of ideas, provided the various employees had a chance to meet each other and talk. And even if no new business ventures were generated and nobody got a single usable idea or bit of information, such a central socializing core would still go a long way toward enriching the impersonal, alien, and sterile atmosphere of many office buildings, especially the newer high-rise variety.

The cold, distant, aloof functionalism of many ultra-modern, high-technology office buildings poses an interesting dilemma for professionals, especially young doctors and lawyers trying to build up a practice. Assuming for the moment that economic considerations are not important, the young doctor can opt for a spanking new high-rise medical building having firmly professional connotations of prestige, status, prosperity, and impersonality. Or he can select a smaller, older building, possibly even a large house, with a more comfortable, informal, and personalized quality. This smaller building will probably be located in a less congested and more pleasant sub-urban neighborhood, one that is easier for clients to reach by car. Let's say that our young doctor has a maddening but fairly typical image problem—he looks about twenty-three. He has tried a mustache and a beard, but that makes him look nineteen, and he knows he'll be getting an "Are you the *doctor?*" reaction for another ten years, at least. Such a young professional could possibly benefit from the prestige and status associated with a high-technology medical build-ing. He could decorate his office in a dominant mode which would reinforce his patients' submissive feelings—a big desk placed between himself and his patients, a rather dark or somber color scheme, towering bookshelves, and so on. After he has gained experience, self-confidence, a good reputation, and a lucrative practice, he could then afford to move to a less formal and more friendly environment that would be conducive to relaxed, open, and confidential relation-ships with his patients; he wouldn't need dominant environmental cues or props to reinforce his own or his clients' confidence in his ability.

Of course this is not the way things usually work. For economic reasons, the young doctor usually starts out in a cheaper, friendlier, and more informal office setting and then makes his move to the cold, prestigious, high-rise medical building when he can afford to financially but no longer needs to psychologically. New medical buildings do have advantages—more of those little treatment rooms so that a greater volume of patients can be processed; convenient diagnostic or lab facilities so he doesn't have to do microscope work anymore; automated billing services; and of course a large number of colleagues whose expertise he can call upon in emergencies. But they also have disadvantages. Not infrequently, patients with whom he has built up rapport in the more relaxed, comfortable, and personalized office are put off by the crowds, noise, and parking problems of the areas where high-rise offices are usually located and by the colder, less pleasant, more dominant atmosphere of the new office. They begin to mutter, "Boy, Doc so-and-so is beginning to turn into a real factory all right; he can barely spare you a minute anymore. It's getting to be a real stick-your-tongue-out-and-pay-on-the-way-out kind of operation." Actually, Doc so-and-so may in fact not be seeing a significantly greater number of patients or devoting less time to any of them. It just seems that way because of the glassier and more formal setting. And, of course, some of these patients hear about a nice young doctor —"Really a friendly sort of guy; none of this professional voodoo, you know; he really listens to you"—and decide to try him instead. What they're really trying is another comfortable (pleasant, low-load, low-dominance) setting in which they feel far less anxious and are less aware of a discrepancy between their own status and that of the doctor.

Since the doctor's waiting room is where his patients spend a large part of their visits, the design of such rooms also can make a difference. Most waiting rooms, especially in the newer medical buildings, have furniture, usually couches, arranged along the walls, with a few coffee or end tables offering a selection of magazines. The room is often painted a clinical white rather than a more pleasant color, and is brightly lit. In such a situation, the lighting should be bright but not excessive; sufficient so that it doesn't promote the feeling of a bar or a cafe, but rather that of a more professional atmosphere. The magazines can be a useful distractor and help the patient forget his troubling thoughts for a moment. But research has shown that people under stress have a distinct preference for socializing with others, this being especially true for the somewhat dependent or submissive. Socializing under such conditions diminishes anxiety because it turns around the pleasure dimension, thus helping people tolerate the high levels of arousal often occasioned by a visit to the doctor. But standard waiting rooms, like many quasi-formal living rooms, do not encourage people to interact.

If waiting rooms were arranged so that two or three circular coffee tables were surrounded by comfortable armchairs, the chances for conversation and other forms of personal interaction would be greatly enhanced. Studies have demonstrated that if there were three such conversational groupings with only three people in the waiting room, each person would probably sit at a different table. If however there were more than three persons present, the arrangement would necessitate at least two or more people sharing the same table. Given a nice view, interesting art work, or other conversation pieces (and especially if the magazines were removed), there is a strong probability that conversation would ensue. People who interact with strangers in stressful waiting situations tend to come away with a greater liking for one another and, of equal importance, a greater liking for the environment in which the pleasant interaction takes place.

Quite often the waiting rooms in older, smaller office buildings are more conducive to pleasant social interaction, especially if as sometimes happens the building was not originally designed to contain a doctor's office. Such waiting rooms have a cozy atmosphere; there are often more easy chairs than long couches, because smaller and more irregular rooms will accommodate the former but not the latter. As a result, more people tend to face each other or to be seated at right angles to one another, which increases the likelihood of personal interaction among strangers. The light sources are usually floor or table lamps rather than ceiling fixtures, and contribute to a cozier, more homelike atmosphere. If the doctor is really just starting out, he may have said to himself, "Well, I can't afford to make it elegant, but at least I can make it comfy"; he may have put in some plants, hung a few of his own prints, thrown in some of his own furniture, and in fact decorated his waiting room as though it were part of his own home. His own office might convey the same kind of informal, comfortable feeling, with its more colorful decor and a small desk placed against a wall so that he can directly face his clients rather than view them across a large, formal-looking desk.

Suggested Readings

Zajonc (1965) explored some beneficial effects of the presence of others on a worker's productivity. See Gordon (1961) on "brainstorming," and Davis and Trist (1974) and Emery and Trist (1960) on new approaches to management that are designed to increase the arousal of the worker. For a general theory and a review of available evidence concerning environmental effects on work performance, see Mehrabian and Russell (1974a, chaps. 6 and 8) and Russell and Mehrabian (1975a, 1976e). Other discussions of office design from an environmental standpoint are given in Manning (1965) and Wells (1965, 1967). See Sommer (1969) for seating preferences in waiting situations, and Mehrabian and Ksionzky (1974, pp. 48–50) for the effects of anxiety or stress on a person's desire to affiliate with others.

CHAPTER

14

Schools

ASKING what a major social institution is good for is a little like asking what a poem or a mountain is good for. Nevertheless, most people will tentatively agree, I think, that public schools exist in part to shape certain kinds of behavior; this is, depending on your perspective, a more accurate or more faddish way of saying that schools exist to provide young human animals with skills that society as a whole deems essential or worthy of reward. There has been much controversy about what these essential skills are or should be; like soap operas, curriculum controversies bountifully reflect the society which produces them. In the past fifteen years there have been aggressive calls for educational programs that: provide career education or sensitivity training; teach Johnny how to read, write, count, and know the basic facts; teach linguistic, mathematical, and other cognitive skills to enable him to organize and interpret data and evaluate facts; inculcate patriotism and a belief in the free enterprise system, in traditional American values, in a supranatural origin of the species, and incidentally get prayer back in and sex out of the schools; or prepare him to be a responsible citizen by giving him complete access, starting in kindergarten, to the best and most recent findings in economics, anthropology, American history, mathematics, sociology, political science, and psychology.

I certainly don't want to put my oar into the curriculum controversy, get involved with broader social and moral issues, or deal with questions relating to how and why children should be taught. Rather, I'd like to talk about what can be done to make elementary and secondary schools preferred environments—places that have a positive effect on one's ability to perform work and on one's desire to stay, explore, and interact with others. It seems to me that those responsible for maintaining the public school system—legislators, boards of education, superintendents, principals, supervisors, teachers, parents, and students—can have no serious quarrel with positive performance, affiliation, exploration, and a desire to remain in schools as broad, systemic goals. Parents, educators, administrators, and others who resent efforts to make education fun or relevant, demanding instead that the schools be run in a highly disciplined, tightly structured way, have failed to make a necessary distinction between the school environment and school tasks. Clearly, subjects or structures of knowledge have many rules and disciplines built into them and cannot be assimilated or understood if children are exposed to them in a sloppy or unsystematic way. But tightly disciplined and highly structured subject matter which may be threatening, boring, or unpleasant is not best taught or learned in an environment that causes avoidance. Indeed, the contrary is true: tasks that in themselves cause avoidance behavior must be done in preferred environments or they will be done resentfully, poorly, or not at all.

It may be proposed as axiomatic that any system which requires people to perform work in an unpreferred environment will have pronounced authoritarian features. The most obvious of these features is that a small number of people occupy positions of relatively great dominance—persons who command resources enabling them to reward greatly or punish severely. If you examine an authoritarian system even cursorily, you will find many behavioral and environmental cues designed to proclaim and reinforce the dominance of the few and the submissiveness of the many.

Those who call for a rigid, Spartan, no-nonsense school environment are in effect urging that an unpreferred environment be used to promote the performance of unpreferred tasks. Such a procedure creates the need for increasingly disproportionate punishments (or rewards) in relation to the stipulated tasks or performance objectives, that is, extremely authoritarian and discipline-oriented education.

There is an interesting etymological metaphor in the words student, teacher, and education: a teacher is one who guides or shows the way; a student is one who is eager or zealous; an education is a bringing out, a leading forth. A good case could be made for the claim that all too often the image lying just beneath the surface of today's educational experience has to do with guards, prisoners, and forced labor. One of the complaints frequently heard from teachers is that they are forced to spend most of their time maintaining order in the classroom and therefore have relatively little time left for teaching. When questioned as to why this is so, some teachers blame the kids, their parents, or their backgrounds; others blame the entire system or one of its features, like pay scale, grades, cognitive emphasis, or the school board; some even blame themselves. But very rarely does anyone say, "It's the environment."

Preoccupation with discipline and authoritarian measures is largely absent at the college and graduate levels, partly because traditional academic reinforcers such as grades remain potent. Most members of the student population respond to these reinforcers as a result of a conscious decision to do so, because they realize that what they are engaged in is essentially vocational training. More importantly however, as environments, most universities are preferred more than public elementary and secondary schools. These environments are arousing and pleasant in that students usually have a large variety of settings and physical activities during the course of a single day— walking across campus to get to different classes, sitting in different classrooms with different people, being exposed to a variety of teachers, or meeting friends during breaks. Thus, unlike the public elementary and secondary students, they don't fidget, misbehave, or plot to upend the teacher's cool just to have some fun and increase arousal in an otherwise monotonous and restrictive environment. As a result, at the university level, environmental and behavioral cues relating to dominance-submissiveness are far less blatant and less critical to the system's operation. Faculty members tend to address even undergraduates in reasonably polite ways, students are allowed and expected to manage their time and tasks with little direct supervision, and so on. Under normal circumstances, the more pleasant and more stimulating university environment reduces the need for the obvious formulae of authoritarian control. There are fewer of the totalitarian absurdities which prevail in some public junior and senior high schools: where, for instance, students must obtain written passes to the bathrooms, or where first-graders are allowed to leave the school grounds to go home for lunch but twelfth-graders are not.

The importance of a pleasant and sufficiently loaded environment is illustrated by the case history of a library in a good-sized elementary school which was not distinguished by its large quota of highly motivated students. The librarian, who was young, eager, and had the support of her principal, bought a lot of popular paperbacks full of violence and suspense in the hopes that if the children found something they liked to read they would eventually go on to better things. This worked with a few pupils, but only a handful. Her training as a librarian caused her to overlook the library environment, which was drab, looking very much like a large classroom except for the books along the walls, the card catalogues, and the long tables. Then someone donated a large, fluffy, shaggy, deep red carpet and a bunch of colorful pillows to the school. Nobody knew what to do with them. At her wit's end, the librarian asked for and got the carpet and pillows, had most of the tables and chairs removed, and put the twelve by twelve foot carpet in the middle of the library and scattered the pillows around it. So many kids flocked in to sprawl on the carpet and read that she eventually had to ration space.

In our terms, what the librarian did was to create the only arousing and pleasant subenvironment in the school building. It was arousing because it was novel and colorful (the red carpet being especially serendipitous); it was pleasant because among other things it was comfortable; it also elicited less submissiveness because children were not constrained by the unyielding spatial arrangements of tables and chairs and could lie on their backs, sit up, or stretch out on their stomachs or sides to read.

And one other extremely important thing: it allowed children to affiliate, which served to heighten both arousal and pleasure. It may seem heretical or downright unprofessional for a librarian to allow her domain to be used as a place where people can interact socially. Luckily, this librarian, who had already broken most of the rules, decided to go all the way and let the experiment play itself out. What she found was that at first there was a great deal of giggling, whispering, poking, and in a few cases some tentative, friendly wrestling matches. It took a lot of restraint to let that go on and not step in, but her restraint paid off; after twenty minutes or so they settled down and started to thumb through the books in their hands and eventually began to read. Her only rule was that you had to have a book in your hand to get on the carpet. There was still some interaction in the carpet area, but it was considerate of others. Because children could lie close together, it was possible for them to whisper to each other without greatly disturbing others. And since such whispering was permitted, it was not unusual or defiant, and hence was not distracting to others. The children moderated their own behavior to be considerate of others without any intervention from the librarian.

Significantly, it was a librarian who, having failed to attract pupils and being bored with the monotony of her working life, welcomed the changes brought on by the new decor and did not insist on silence. Unlike her, many teachers in elementary and secondary schools are suffering from overarousal and impending GAS reactions. Their working days are spent in almost constant contact with about thirty children, each with an individual personality, particular problems, and daily variations in mood—not to mention the many possible combinations of relationships which can arise within a group of thirty kids. Confronted with a potentially complex and unpredictable situation, teachers and school administrators foist a large number of rigid rules and regulations upon students so as to make their behavior far less varied, more uniform, and more predictable—in short, to achieve low-load classrooms.

There is a dilemma inherent in a situation where one adult must spend most of his or her working hours with a group of thirty active children. Whereas the teacher is responsible for and must cope with a room teeming with kids, each child is primarily responsible for his own conduct and occasionally relates to the teacher or a few others of his choice. Given the fact that the typical school environment is neutral (neither pleasant nor unpleasant) or slightly unpleasant, the adult is bound to seek a low-load physical environment and will also try to regulate and reduce variation and uncertainty in the group. The children, in contrast, are going to feel confined and bored, and end up trying to generate arousal and pleasure by interacting amongst themselves. In the ensuing battle, the more dominant members of the school community extend restrictive regulations which even make it tough for kids to communicate with each other, to share laughter or hurt, or to spend relaxed or thoughtful time together. When you consider the documented needs of children and teenagers for peer-level interaction in which to probe and define themselves in relation to others, the restrictive school environment—no talking, no laughing, no passing notes, keep moving in the halls, line up, stay at your desk, homeroom and free periods are for studying—makes little sense.

Any viable solution to this dilemma of restrictive regulation and insufficient arousal for kids and potential overarousal for adults is bound to involve environmental changes and instrumentation which will provide teachers with relief from intensive contact with large groups. This means that individualized or small group learning centers (such as those mentioned in the next chapter) are needed. Children could then select audio- or video-recorded programs, and teachers, instead of acting as sources of information, could act as consultants on the choice of programs and their sequencing. Such systems would provide necessary relief for teachers and would also give the students more loaded, flexible, and pleasant learning environments. Three or four children watching the same program could stop the tape when they wished and could then discuss it or call something to the attention of the teacher; they could simply stop it to take a break, or they could select another program farther back or ahead in the sequence to recall or anticipate something that they were curious about. Allowing children to pick their desired program and to pace their rates of learning can be a tremendously effective way of letting them function at optimum arousal levels with a greater sense of mastery (dominance and pleasure).

In the absence of some of these anticipated developments, the question is how to ameliorate some of the problems by considering the physical environments in which students are taught. Specifically, if the majority of school tasks are avoided because they are too loaded (too novel, too complex), too boring (too routine, too repetitious, too simple), or somewhat unpleasant, what can be done to make the school environment an appropriate place in which to perform these tasks?

It is first useful to think about the options for organizing the interior spaces of a school. As in the case of other small-scale communities, these spaces can be arranged so as to encourage people to cross each other's pathways and thus encourage them to interact. Opportunities for informal social contacts among school children should contribute to their arousal and pleasure levels, and are enhanced by designs such as this:

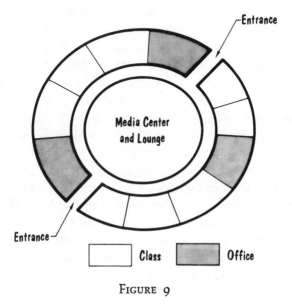

FIGURE 9

The focal point of this particular school is a central book, videotape, and film library referred to as the media center, with an adjacent casual lounge area. The periphery consists of classrooms and various administrative offices, and access to all areas is through the single circular corridor. Such an organization of space contributes greatly to opportunities for contact among students from different classes and permits them to study together or interact casually in the centrally located media center and lounge. The architects were especially attuned to the necessity for adequate sound insulation in this arrangement; they were careful to shield the sounds of corridor traffic from both the peripherally located classes and offices and to shield the noises of the informal lounge from the study areas of the media center.

The success of such designs hinges on making the school environment as pleasant as possible, because only then will higher loads be tolerated by teachers and administrators. So, the first step is to give the whole school interior a good paint job. Every room in the school—from the principal's office to the bathrooms—should be painted in pleasant colors.

Next, consider the curriculum and decide which subjects have a high-load (are complex, novel, or difficult in relation to the students' backgrounds and capabilities). It is not difficult to figure this out; a beginner's typing class attended mostly by juniors or seniors whose next "course" is varsity football, baseball, or track is going to have a different load than a ten o'clock sophomore honors biology or trigonometry course. Naturally, administrators or teachers whose schools are on some kind of variable modular scheduling will be able to put their hands on such data more readily than others; nevertheless, informally asking students and teachers what they are doing and how they feel about it will usually work just as well. Students and teachers who perform low-load, slightly unpleasant tasks should be assigned to high-load and highly pleasant classrooms. Complex and cheerfully painted interior decor and furnishings, windows which provide stimulation from the outside, music, and student participation in frequent redecoration of the classroom in terms of themes taken from the subjects of study can all contribute to the load and the pleasantness of the work environment. Also, furniture arrangement and the various activity centers in a classroom should encourage children to move about, work with different partners, sit in different seats so as to have different vantage points of the class or of the outside, and in general to provide them with a greater variety of physical activity and stimulation in the classroom. This becomes essential when we consider the fact that physical confinement to the same chair in the same place in a room for a large portion of the day is almost inhumanly restrictive for the adult and even more so for children, who derive a great deal of their arousal from physical rather than conceptual activity. On the other hand, at times during the day when students and teachers are performing complex, unusual tasks, they should be assigned rooms that are very pleasant but low-load. I don't want to make this analysis of tasks sound easier or more mechanical than it is. It takes a certain amount of expertise and empathy to realize that teaching children to write "My mother got mad because of the rats in the kitchen," when their natural and more poetic idiom suggests "Rat he come in. Mama she done got mad" is an extremely loaded task for both teacher and pupil.

The next thing to do is to arbitrarily select some of the classrooms in the school, discard the combination chair-desks, and start experimenting with other, less formal furnishings, or even minimal furnishings—highly textured and brightly colored carpeting and large pillows or cushions, for example. If a teacher is going to use mostly inductive-type instruction, it is far better to do it in a flexible, comfortable environment in which pupils may readily group themselves in a circle or a series of concentric semicircles around the teacher. During free periods, the children should have permission and room to move around, set up their own social groupings, and talk freely. Free periods in a large room with permanently fixed desks may make attendance-taking easier, but also make flexible, conversational groups impossible.

Many of the fads in education are simplistic all-or-nothing solutions adopted by opposing camps without regard to basic environmental and individual (temperamental and skill) variables. Consider the controversy surrounding structured versus unstructured classrooms and instruction. Children differ in their ability to cope with informal and unstructured learning environments because of varying degrees of familiarity with such situations at home. Some homes are informal learning situations where children have ready access to books, magazines, and other educational materials, and where frequent discussions and explanations are common. For these children, the high load of the complex and unstructured classroom, when combined with familiarity, yields moderate arousal. The same setting is excessively arousing to a child whose home life is devoid of books or intellectual discussions.

One recent line of thinking on early education—the hypothesized importance of infant stimulation at home and in daycare centers—is useful to consider in this context. Even though related research has yielded inconsistent findings, there has been an effort to popularize the idea that stimulating infants and children in loaded daycare and school environments contributes to their rapid cognitive development. Research methods here have ranged from (a) placing mobiles of various kinds above infants' cribs; (b) adults interacting with in- stitutionalized children who are generally deprived of such social contact; and (c) intensive stimulation projects extending over several years, notably the Milwaukee Project. The effectiveness of these procedures has been assessed by examining, respectively: (a) the in- fants' continued interest in the mobiles; (b) their ability to engage other adults in conversation; and (c) a variety of tests of general cognitive development. Without going into a detailed discussion of these studies, it is fair to say that procedures which combined pleasant and high-load stimulation led to greater interest in the stimuli and contributed to opportunities for learning and cognitive growth. In contrast, procedures which inadvertently combined unpleasant and high-load stimulation (such as ugly or frightening mobiles) resulted in the infants' avoidance of the stimulation.

Stimulation per se, then, cannot be viewed as the final answer. If high-load toys are introduced into an infant's play area or crib, it is important to assess the pleasure-displeasure producing effects of these toys. Certainly, more contact between institutionalized children and understanding, responsive adults can increase the children's pleasure and arousal levels and will encourage them to approach other adults. However, it is also important to remember that many children, particularly the nonscreeners, suffer from over-stimulation in un- pleasant or at best neutrally pleasant settings such as disorganized (high-load) homes or daycare centers. Increasing the load of such places by crowding more children into a room or by introducing a greater variety of toys and tasks would hardly constitute an improve- ment and would be detrimental, especially to the nonscreeners.

There is no need here for undue repetition. Previous chapters contain enough examples about how to make environments more pleasant, how to make them high- or low-load, and how to match them to the screening and skill levels of the individual. The central problem of the teacher, the administrator, or the parent is overcoming a resistance to thinking about classrooms and the school environment in the same terms that are used for thinking about more personal home environments.

I have resisted getting into facts and strategies that might serve to make learning tasks themselves more arousing, pleasant, and less restrictive. Standard curricula, syllabi, methodology, and publishers' product in almost any content area are miles away from the hypotheses and experimental results that more than three-quarters of a century of psychological research have produced. But the implications of environmental psychology for the classroom have been neglected even more, and these are what occupy center stage for us here.

Suggested Readings

See the following sources for data and analyses of various issues considered in this chapter: Barker and Gump (1964), Cohen (1973), Doll and Fleming (1966), Featherstone (1971), Illich (1971), Jackson (1968), Leonard (1968), McReynolds, Acker, and Pietila (1961), and Moore (1969). Also see the entire issue of *The University of Chicago School Review* (1974) devoted to environmental analyses of schools.

For some examples of research on infant stimulation, see Rheingold (1956) on the effects of increased adult contact for institutionalized children; see White and Held (1966) for a study which increased stimulation by introducing mobiles above cribs; and note the comprehensive report on the Milwaukee Project by Heber, Garber, Harrington, Hoffman, and Falender (1972). A general review of environmental intervention studies was provided by Horowitz and Paden (1973), and a theoretical base for the effects of environmental stimulation can be found in Falender and Mehrabian (1977).

CHAPTER

15

Libraries

LIBRARIES have an ancient, honorable history. More than five thousand years ago, the Sumerians stored clay tablets containing agricultural and other records in temple buildings. Rameses II (1292–1225 B.C.) set up a library of sacred literature. In the seventh century B.C., the Assyrian ruler Assur-bani-pal established several royal libraries, one of which contained more than 20,000 clay "volumes" recording many of the most important Near Eastern literary works. The famous library in Alexandria, Egypt, held as many as 900,000 papyrus rolls which, in effect, contained the whole culture of the ancient Greek world. When this library burned, a considerable portion of Greek civilization was obliterated. By 300 A.D., there were twenty-eight public libraries in Rome as well as many extensive private collections. About a hundred years later, many of these "pagan" libraries were destroyed or allowed to fall into ruin. As a result, what we speak of as the classical heritage is a relatively meager collection of leftovers, not the banquet, preserved in part by copyists in medieval scriptoriums.

Because libraries have historically served as the seedpods or memory centers of human culture, it is understandable that librarians have tended to be a conservative breed. In fact, the plan of most medieval libraries (usually found in the monasteries) was more akin to that of museums, designed to discourage the use and/or borrowing of the precious, rare volumes. This is part of the tradition which modern librarians have had to overcome. Even today, it is probably not unfair to say that most librarians would put books first, people second, and buildings last. But librarians also want to get books and people together, which means that they usually want people to come into their libraries and stay awhile. And this means that libraries must be preferred environments.

There are of course libraries and libraries. Enormous, venerable institutions like the Bodleian, the British Museum, the Bibliothèque Nationale, the Library of Congress, some university libraries, a few great publics like the New York Public Library, and specialized, privately endowed collections like the J. P. Morgan or Huntington are essentially research libraries. Such libraries, containing many millions of volumes, including some rare or priceless items, have too many worries vis-à-vis space and security problems and need not be overly concerned about attracting scholarly types who'll go there regardless of environmental conditions. But most people are under no great compulsion to visit or remain in the more common variety of libraries. Public school, local community, and some undergraduate libraries need all the environmental help they can get if they are to fulfill their functions.

Let's start with the dominance aspect. Most libraries elicit a good deal of submissiveness from their users; one's library behavior is extremely circumscribed, requiring a hush-hush, tip-toeing degree of self-control amounting almost to the reverential. As we shall see, this temple-like behavior is really not always necessary or desirable if libraries are properly designed.

Access to the stacks is another facet of library design that can sometimes needlessly detract from one's feeling of competence, control, or freedom within the library environment. In older libraries, books were usually laid horizontally on shelves or tables and were often chained to them. In the post-Gutenberg era, when the number of books began to increase exponentially, books were stored vertically on wall shelves. Still later, shelves were placed at right angles to the walls, forming small alcoves in the process. In the mid-nineteenth century, the British Museum, under the direction of its librarian, Antonio Panizzi, was the first library to segregate its book storage areas from its reading rooms. In many libraries that follow this arrangement, the stacks are often not open to the general public. People have to locate titles they want in the card catalogue, fill out a complicated request slip, wait in line to hand the slip in at a delivery desk, and then wait until the book is located and delivered—or not delivered if "in use," or "at the bindery." This may be the only way to go for libraries having enormous noncirculating collections that must be stored as economically as possible in labyrinthian stacks, but it is a time consuming and frustrating procedure that may even turn off some motivated readers. Unfortunately, many medium sized undergraduate and public libraries have adopted this procedure quite needlessly. Some people who have access to university libraries would rather use their local public branches for generalized research in areas outside their own specialties. If they know only one title in some field they're trying to learn more about, they can locate that title in the catalogue and then go to the stacks and look at the other books in the immediate vicinity. There is bound to be something there that they can use, even if the book they are looking for is out. Moreover, since most books in a small public library circulate, if they find something they'd like to read, they can take it home.

Most research libraries today are undergoing a technological revolution which is bound to lead to a far greater sense of dominance for the user. Computers are now being introduced into libraries for catalogue and bibliographic search. Imagine the difference between systems before and after the installation of computers: an involved search through a complex cataloguing system one does not understand, a visit to the stacks to get some idea as to whether the books selected are appropriate, or a long wait at the desk for some of the books to be delivered *versus* simply walking up to a computer terminal, typing in a few key terms (such as "libraries," "technology," and "environmental psychology"), and having an immediate visual display of those volumes which are the intersection points of these topics. Add to the latter alternative the convenience of next requesting abstracts of journal articles or volumes in order to scan any particular source and determine its relevance.

A second convenient (pleasure- and dominance-inducing) trend associated with technological advances in library design is the addition of storage media which supplement the printed page. Microfilm, microfiche, punched cards, perforated tapes, magnetic tapes, and many types of digital and graphic techniques are now available for the storage and transmission of textual or pictorial materials. The advantage of facsimile transmission when such media are used is temporarily offset by the cost of specialized display stations for the user. However, as such display stations gradually become more common in libraries, it will be possible to view materials stored in other libraries. This will minimize the necessity for each library to duplicate materials housed in others and will allow for more specialization. Given the escalating rate in the outpouring of books and journals, libraries would have a choice of providing incomplete coverage across different fields of specialization or specializing and then relying on network transmission with other libraries that have different fields of specialization.

Another aspect of libraries that has been conducive to a more comfortable and more dominant feeling for the user is the idea of the circulating collection, which in time will include audio and video cassettes as well. The idea of a circulating collection of popular reading matter was put into practice for the first time by the Boston Public Library in 1854. It was a good idea because it gave people an opportunity to read books in an environment that suited them, thus allowing more control or independence. Often, the great libraries are too possessive about what they will permit to circulate; but if they made their reading rooms more preferable, it wouldn't matter nearly as much. Even libraries which have good-sized circulating collections often make the use of their books more circumscribed or more difficult than need be. For example, the cataloguing system is frequently complicated enough to befuddle even experienced adults, who sometimes find themselves searching for some title in the wrong place because they fail to notice a letter or number which indicates that the book they want is in the Rare Book Collection or in the Young Adult Section. It would be relatively easy to color code the cards; for example, you could instantly recognize from a blue card that the book you want is in reference, not in the stacks.

Recent experiments in certain circulating libraries also indicate that the common practice of limiting the number of books one may check out during a visit, and the period of time for which books in a given Dewey classification can circulate, together with the system of fines, may not be the most efficient way of running a library. Some small town school and public libraries have completely done away with the whole business of library cards, checkout procedures, and fines; instead, people are given unrestricted access to the circulating collection. They walk out with as many books as they want and bring them back when they feel like it. To the great surprise of those librarians who've tried this experiment, the number of books taken out goes up and the rate of nonreturns (and also of damage) goes down significantly, sometimes by as much as 10 percent. The lesson in all this seems to be that if we increase people's sense of independence and control (dominance) in a small community, we will also increase their sense of responsibility to the community. At any rate, there won't be any overdue library books at home ticking away like taxi meters.

A collection of books is not a library but a warehouse. A library is by definition a place where books are used, and if a library environment is such that the use of books is discouraged, those responsible for administering the library have failed to perform one of their essential functions. What then are some of the things that can be done to increase preference for the typical public or under-graduate library? Besides environmental load, which we'll consider in detail shortly, it is important to increase the comfort (pleasure- and dominance-eliciting quality) of the library. We have so far noted the dominance aspect of libraries. To see how something as elementary as pleasure is ignored in most library designs, consider the stacks, which are often drearier and more uncomfortable or inconvenient than they need to be. Since these are essentially storage areas, one's impulse is to make them economical storage areas. But there is such a thing as being penny-wise and avoidance-foolish. For example, the shelves, invariably painted a dull gray, are usually metal. Many libraries also have floor surfaces which cause a person shuffling along them to generate a good deal of static electricity. The result is that people are constantly being shocked when they inadvertently touch the shelves, which is a classical avoidance conditioning situation. That's the way you get people to stop doing anything; it is certainly not the way to encourage them to approach and explore a situation.

To encourage exploration, stacks should be as pleasant as pos-sible. Special displays, which are usually set up in library lobbies where they are least needed, could be incorporated directly into the stacks, thus providing variety and relief from the endless row-upon-row effect. Also, stacks are often too close together, so that two people looking at opposite shelf spaces cannot both bend down to examine the contents of a low shelf without bumping into each other. When the stacks are far from the reading rooms, it is convenient to be able to examine books with some care on the spot rather than carry a whole pile of them somewhere else. In such cases, the stacks could be provided with upholstered benches so people could sit down in relative comfort. People with two or three books in their hands could then sit down and peruse a fourth before deciding whether it's what they want. They wouldn't have to sit on the floor, which is invariably covered with dusty and heat-conducting (cold) tile. Many newer libraries are getting back to the older practice of making some of the stacks part of the reading room environment, thus providing subject-area alcoves:

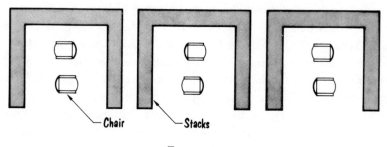

FIGURE 10

This is somewhat inefficient in terms of space, but far more efficient in terms of getting people to explore a pleasant and moderately loaded book-filled environment.

The most important aspect of library design is careful consideration of the load in the various facilities. Most of us try to adjust the environmental load while reading. For example, when reading at home, many people turn on soft music because loud music or news over the radio or the TV is too arousing. We know that people prefer less loaded settings when they read difficult (complex and slightly unpleasant) materials, but that they prefer more loaded places for light, pleasant reading. Since environmental preferences while reading are dictated by one's ability to comprehend, recollect, and enjoy what is being read, this means that libraries should have more loaded places for persons who are doing fun reading and less loaded places for those doing complicated reading and research.

An example of the incorporation of more loaded areas is to have a central patio and surrounding terraces entirely within the confines of the library. There might be a variety of snack shops, comfortable lounging areas, or even places to stroll among plants and where conversation is acceptable. Once a person enters the library through one or more of the checkpoints, he would be free to take whatever books he has selected to one of these areas. He could visit these areas after periods of intense concentration, or when he is fatigued, to increase his arousal. Such casual areas within the confines of the library would eliminate many unnecessary logistic problems. Most people are reluctant to check out books and have briefcases and bags examined in crossing a checkpoint in order to leave the library for a snack; instead, they either speed up their reading and leave to do other things, or they are forced to stay on while feeling uncomfortable, hungry, or tired.

Unlike the traditional severe and somber library environment, a library which had such terraces and snack facilities would provide many behavioral alternatives for the visitor; the result would be a feeling which most people call "comfort," namely, dominance and pleasure. Users would have the option of selecting places within the library to suit their kind of reading material or their emotional state. We mentioned in passing that concentrated reading leads to fatigue, which is a low arousal and unpleasant state. Since performance— ability to concentrate and recollect what is read—deteriorates with fatigue, it is important that libraries provide opportunities for periodic relief from demanding work. Casual outdoor areas would be ideally suited for much needed, varied physical activity. People differ in the ways in which they relieve the low arousal state associated with fatigue. Given such areas, some might socialize; others might choose to keep to themselves and daydream while drinking a cup of coffee; and still others might seek stimulation from a small snack or a short walk. In any case, when a library provides opportunities for any of these alternatives, the users have the advantage of taking breaks without having to check out and can conveniently maintain an optimum level of arousal and pleasure for the work they are doing.

Libraries possessing a variety of high-load areas for fun reading and low-load areas for demanding and somewhat unpleasant reading would greatly appeal to nonscreeners. Needless to say, such libraries would also be valued by screeners, but not to quite the same extent.

The various spaces that constitute the traditional library can be analyzed in terms of the appropriateness of their respective loads. For example, one local public library is set up something like Figure 11. The reader who has followed our discussion thus far will recognize that the Reading Room, with its small, round tables surrounded by four or five chairs, has a design that strongly encourages personal interaction or socializing. As a result, nonscreeners or those engaged in high-load, difficult work shun this room in the late afternoon and early evening when students from the nearby high school use the area to complete research projects assigned as homework. The latter usually amounts to copying things out of encyclopedias or other standard reference works. Such boring or low-load tasks demand an

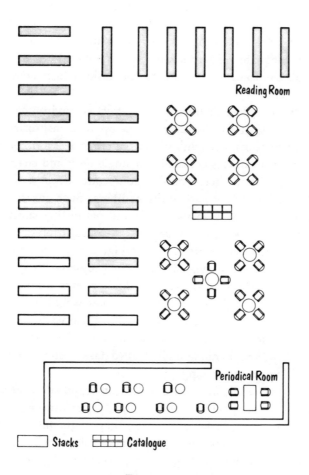

FIGURE 11

environment that is moderately loaded and pleasant. The high school students can create one instantly by looking at each other, giggling, talking, and teasing the poor librarian, who is desperately trying to maintain a proper low-load environment. On the other hand, the Periodical Room is mainly furnished with comfortable armchairs, far enough apart so as to discourage personal interaction. It is an ideal place for somewhat complex reading tasks except that it is difficult to perform research and note-taking assignments which require keeping several books handy for constant cross-reference. Although this area contains a very good collection of domestic and foreign newspapers, it only provides one smallish table to spread a paper out on.

Since it is difficult to hold and read a nontabloid-size newspaper for any length of time, the newspaper collection rarely gets the use it deserves. In effect therefore, a small community library possessing more than adequate resources has been sabotaged by its failure to provide sub-environments suited to the tasks which could be performed in them.

In order to make this library more effective environmentally, one would have to split the Reading Room up in a task-oriented way. For demanding tasks, a modularized area is needed—preferably consisting of doored cubicles containing a single desk and chair in which people could, if they chose, smoke, pour coffee from a thermos, or open a lunch box without disturbing others. Such measures would be aimed at increasing pleasure levels and permitting short smoking and munching breaks as fatigue sets in. Meanwhile, the cubicles would shield their occupants from the higher loads outside, such as more varied and complex visual stimuli or people walking about.

For moderately loaded tasks, a lounge area containing comfortable armchairs with small, movable tables would be appropriate, especially if these chairs were grouped along the walls to discourage interaction. Some small tables seating no more than two would also be provided, although moderately loaded tasks tend not to require a lot of writing or note-taking.

A third, pleasant, and more loaded environment would also be provided in which people could optimally perform more routine, repetitive, or boring tasks, and where they might take their breaks to increase their arousal levels. This room might be given over to round tables as in the Reading Room pictured in Figure 11. Ideally, a separate conversational lounge (similar in spirit to the casual patio-terrace-snack areas already noted) would also be available in an adjacent area. Friends doing their homework at the round tables could then get up and stretch their legs, take a break on the lounge chairs, rest their eyes, or even indulge in a short snooze. Students, professional colleagues, and others might also carry on discussions here in a normal or even animated tone of voice. Frequently people come across things in the course of their library work that they like to talk about with others but usually cannot unless they leave the building. This conversational lounge should of course be pleasant and fairly arousing in decor.

The Periodical Room shown in Figure 11 probably could be abolished as a separate room, assuming the library abandoned the typical but completely unnecessary rule that magazines and newspapers must not be removed from wherever they're displayed. The Periodical Room could either be integrated with the conversational lounge or the moderately arousing Reading Room. People merely wanting to flip through an issue of *Town & Country* could do so without being in the least distracted. Those wanting to read a complex journal article could take the journal to a less loaded part of the library.

The casual and informal areas should occupy the bulk of the space and are especially important in public libraries located in working-class or low-income neighborhoods. These informal areas should be as pleasant as possible, with lots of plants, comfortable chairs, pleasing color schemes, and a minimum of rules, regulations, and other dominant aspects. Only then will the library begin to fulfill its potential as a community resource center, or "people's university."

In the not too distant future, libraries will probably begin to take over some of the functions now served by schools and universities, especially those functions having to do with basic education or elementary instruction in a given discipline. Indeed, the learning-center concept used in some of today's more progressive colleges is approaching this goal. At Oklahoma Christian College, the top two stories of a three-story learning center contain over 1,000 electronically connected carrels, with each student having complete and private access to one of these. The lower floor of the center is the library. Students have access to a centralized bank of audio tapes which they can request and listen to in their individual carrels. In addition, a scheduled series of audio presentations is accessible from each carrel so students can hook into a scheduled program if they see fit. To use visual materials, students check out projectors and films to watch in their carrels. A more expensive setup in the future might include individual TV-style monitor screens in each carrel with video tapes stored at the central bank, thus allowing students to watch any educational program without having to leave the carrel to obtain projection equipment or films. Since the carrels are individualized, students are encouraged to decorate these according to their individual tastes, that is, at the pleasure and load levels they desire. And of course the flexibility of the setup provides a strong boost to the students' dominant feelings. Soundproofing allows students to meet friends in the carrels, either to listen jointly to a program or to discuss work they share. It is therefore not surprising that there has been a 40 percent increase in the rate of book and journal use at this particular library.

Such developments in our colleges make a lot of sense when we consider that most introductory courses, especially those at the college level, are given as lectures to anywhere from fifty to 500 students at a time. Instructors often lack the preparation, social skills, or personality to make these presentations stimulating or entertaining; furthermore, most students do not have the stenographic skills necessary to take good notes. This results in inadequate notes based upon lectures that are less informative and less well organized than standard textbooks in the field. But in fields requiring laboratory experiments, three-dimensional models, or the demonstration of the proper use of tools, even the best textbooks are not always the most effective medium of communication.

There is a tremendous amount of creative talent available today, of which only a small portion finds expression in feature films or TV productions. It ought to be possible for educators and creative media artists to get together and produce vivid, exciting films or video tapes presenting the most up-to-date basic findings in each field. These films or tapes would therefore constitute the basic texts for many introductory courses. Since they would be used on a nationwide basis, they could be budgeted and produced within the same economic parameters as feature films. Students and members of the general public could then have access to these educational media through local public libraries, either checking them out for home viewing or availing themselves of library facilities. This would enable individuals who for a variety of socioeconomic reasons cannot attend college to expose themselves to educational materials of the highest caliber and to study at their preferred rate of speed.* It would also free faculty members from wasteful and ineffective procedures for which they are not intellectually or temperamentally suited. Research-oriented scholars could do what they do best and not fiddle around with lectures, tests, and so on. Educators could do what they do best and not have to engage in halfhearted research banalities to justify their university positions. They would instead be responsible for

---

* The latter would be a considerable improvement over the traditional classroom, where everyone moves along in lockstep fashion. In the latter situation, some students are overly aroused because the rate of progress is too fast for them, while others function below their optimum arousal levels and are bored with the pace because it is too slow.

172

updating, summarizing, and transmitting existing knowledge to the general public (including the undergraduate public) through the most effective and sophisticated communication channels modern technology provides. Public libraries are natural distribution centers for such educational media. Public schools and universities could then concentrate their physical and human resources on more specialized, more advanced, or more dynamic learning contexts.

Suggested Readings

See Dupuy (1968) and Enright (1972) for general discussions of library design. Check back to the suggested readings at the end of chapter two for references on environmental load. Russell and Mehrabian (1976e) provided a general theory of environmental effects on work performance and showed how the theory applies to specific data obtained from college students (Mehrabian and Russell, 1974a, chap. 8).

PART FIVE

THERAPEUTIC

ENVIRONMENTS

16

Health Spas

IN THE DAYS before Freud and psychoanalysis, it was not uncommon for a physician to send his "nervous" patients to a health spa or on an extended vacation in a peaceful country setting. These neurasthenic patients usually had recurrent problems which did not seem to have any definite physical origin. But even if their symptoms were identifiable, they did not respond to drugs known to be generally effective. In some cases, patients simply complained of general malaise —fatigue or a draggy, ill-at-ease feeling.

For a long time, health spas were the standard recommendation in these cases and seemed to work reasonably well. The patient usually spent a month or two in a spa, taking hot water baths, mineral waters, mud baths, salubrious air, or any combination of these. Activities at the spa were largely relaxing, involving walks through the surrounding countryside or within specifically designated areas inside the spa, concerts in open-air theatres, and so on. A variety of therapeutic activities, such as bathing in hot mineral springs or special kinds of exercise and massage, were part of the regimen and also tended to be relaxing. Such spas still exist in some European nations; one can see the patients taking leisurely walks, sipping mineral waters out of their special cups, or socializing. The calendar of events in these spas is carefully regulated so that many diverse yet relaxing programs are available to the patients. There is little demand upon them to face the uncertainties of decision making or any of the other stresses common to urbanized life.

These patients' recurring and occasionally nonspecific ailments which seem so difficult to cure can be understood in terms of the

General Adaptation Syndrome. GAS was initially an explanation of human reactions to disease, injuries, or toxins. But it later became clear that the concept had much broader relevance for studying physiological reactions to different forms of stress that are so much a part of our daily lives. These everyday stresses may result from decision making under pressures of time, interpersonal conflicts, professional vicissitudes, and so forth. That is, a GAS reaction is set off by highly arousing and unpleasant stimulation from the environment. If stress persists, initial feelings of nervousness and anxiety lead to physical diseases and finally to total emotional exhaustion.

Health spas, then, are de-GASing centers. You will recall that in chapter four I talked about the General Adaptation Syndrome in relation to the "fuse-blowing" effects that stimulants can have on an already over-stimulated system. People who must operate under conditions of sustained high arousal will ultimately blow their own fuses without any additional help. Many of us have had the following somewhat puzzling experience. We undergo some personal or professional crisis—a court case, for example, or a crucial project with fierce deadlines—and come out of it all right. But instead of feeling elated and ready to go out and celebrate, we feel weary or depressed. During the crisis our arousal levels have been maintained at a high level by the pressure of the situation and the uncertainty of the outcome; very likely we also have not slept well or enough. When the extremely loaded, crisis-filled environment dissolves, our arousal levels fall precipitously, causing a feeling of extreme fatigue or depression.

If people are forced to maintain high arousal and displeasure levels month after month, year after year, with only an annual two- or three-week vacation that is also novel or hectic, they will begin to manifest second stage GAS symptoms like headaches, frequent colds or allergic reactions, ulcers, high blood pressure, or cardiovascular and kidney ailments. If these symptoms are ignored or merely patched-up, sooner or later the third GAS stage will assert itself either in the form of total exhaustion or else as a major systemic collapse from which, because of adrenal and other glandular depletion, the body will recover very slowly if at all.

In the nineteenth century, and even into the Edwardian period, the one- or two-month visit to a health spa served not only to remove people from highly arousing and unpleasant environments but also to place them in low-load, extremely pleasant surroundings in which their bodily systems could both "come down" and gradually restore themselves. This helps to explain the many successes claimed for particular health spa mineral waters, baths, or exercises. The general change to a relaxing and unstressful environment was probably more beneficial than any of the cure agents.

There is something terribly quaint sounding about the *haute bourgeoisie* "taking the waters" at Baden-Baden or Saratoga Springs, but there is nothing at all quaint about the GAS reactions that sent them there. Recent research shows that GAS phenomena are even more pervasive in our everyday lives than they had been thought to be. A relationship clearly exists between the amount of change that occurs in a person's life and his subsequent diseases or illnesses. Changes in one's life—the death of a spouse or a close family member, divorce, a jail term, marriage, retirement, the birth of a child, the purchase of a new home, a change of job, or even a change of residence—reverberate through many different aspects of one's daily activities. For example, the birth of a child requires major changes in a couple's daily schedule and weekend activities. A new job or place of residence may necessitate adjustments to a totally different environment, including a change in climate, new friends, new working conditions, and possibly even a very different life style. Retirement represents a dramatic slowdown in the general pace of life and in many cases a dramatic loss of status. Not all of these changes are associated with unpleasant feelings, of course. For example, retirement or marriage may come as a welcome change. But common to all these changes is a sense of heightened arousal resulting from new environmental complexities and improbabilities.

Researchers have assessed the amount of continued and excessive arousal for a given period of life in terms of the number and severity of the changes during that period. These researchers first scaled each type of change by having the subjects rate the severity of adjustments to everyday activities necessitated by each change. For example, they found that marriage involves a greater amount of adjustment than does a change in one's line of work; the latter in turn involves more change than taking on a mortgage or a loan in an amount less than $10,000. Consider for example the purchase of a new home and the changes that this might entail. A mortgage is usually necessary, together with other new financial responsibilities. There are unforeseen problems with the movers. The owners find themselves learning how to negotiate with contractors, finding skilled laborers such as carpenters to build new cabinets, or workmen to put in a new barbecue. With the pride of ownership also come gardening and maintenance chores. Owners must adjust to new neighbors and expend time and energy getting acquainted with the new community in order to discover the best places to shop for goods and services.

Life changes such as these, once scaled, were added together to obtain a total life change score for any six- or twelve-month period of a person's life. Next, these total life change scores were related to the individual's physical health, emotional well-being, or even accident proneness in the following period. It was found that the frequency and severity of a person's illnesses in one year were directly related to the amount of change experienced during the preceding year. Some of the illnesses correlating with high change rates were cancer, heart diseases, skin diseases, and even the common cold.

In one study, the amounts of change in the lives of men in the Navy were measured for the six-month period prior to sea duty. Illness rates for the high- and low-change sailors were then compared for the six-month tour of duty. Those with higher change scores during the preceding six-month period were ill more often during the cruise.

In another study, football players with more life changes in one year were found to suffer from a greater number of personal injuries during the succeeding year. This suggests that owners and coaches who are constantly trading athletes will have more injured players than those who keep their trades to a minimum. It also suggests that coaching staffs which undertake to alleviate their players' off-the-field worries will have more successful teams.

Some other examples of situations or experiences that are extremely arousing and, if sustained, can lead to physiological malfunctions are participation in competitive sports, military training, prolonged hospitalization, surgery, major examinations in school, frequent emotional interviews necessitated by a poor job market, or the bizarre perceptual distortions associated with hallucinogenic drugs. Even visits from mothers-in-law are frequently reported as preceding the onset of various illnesses. This is because the presence of a house guest introduces many changes in a home: there may be changes in household schedules; one may have to dress more formally at all times; there may be less privacy or even a feeling of overcrowding. In addition, a mother-in-law may have suggestions about ways to do household chores or ways to arrange the furniture, discipline the children, or whatever. Her visit will probably cause increased activity in terms of sightseeing and visits to relatives, which are often reciprocated. Such activity will be arousing in itself. Understandably, then, a prolonged period of heightened arousal resulting from an extended visit can have serious negative effects.

An extremely dramatic change in the pace of life was experienced by American prisoners of war returning home from Vietnam. After spending sometimes as much as seven or eight years in isolated environments, they were suddenly confronted with a tremendous amount and variety of stimulation. The attention of the entire nation was focused on their every move and word. At home they faced the necessity of readjusting to the routines of family life. In some cases they came home to children and wives they could barely recognize, and there were many emotional reunions throughout the extended family. The ex-POWs were also confronted with many small, daily problems like choosing what to wear, what to do, or where to eat— choices that had been taken away from them for several years. This transition from an extremely monotonous and highly regulated (low-load) environment to one that maximized novelty, unpredictability, and complexity (much decision making and intense stimulation from others) was severe enough in many cases to induce exhaustion. Psychological problems also occurred, and some suicides were reported. Military psychologists could have anticipated the high rates of physical ailments or accidents for these returning POWs. Thus, even though it might have seemed cruel, unusual, or suspicious, it probably would have been better for the men if they had been gradually eased back into everyday life rather than being plunged into it under the glare of TV lights.

But one doesn't have to choose extreme situations to find damagingly high levels of arousal. Commuters on high-speed freeways are under considerable physiological stress. However habituated the commuter may be to freeway conditions, his brain tells his body that driving at sixty-five to seventy-five miles per hour on a four-lane freeway while separated by no more than a car length in any direction from other cars going at the same speeds is extremely dangerous. The businessman driving one hour each way to and from a highly arousing and often unpleasant job is a good candidate for a GAS reaction. We have seen that many inner-city residents live in anxiety-causing environments. In fact, many urban and suburban dwellers are being exposed to everyday environments that are becoming increasingly loaded and unpleasant because of overcrowding and general environmental deterioration. Furthermore, many people work in places and at jobs that are highly loaded and unpleasant. All this adds up to an over-stressed population that is finding pleasant interludes harder and harder to come by.

So today, with all our psychological sophistication and medical progress, it looks as if we may have to come full circle back to the old psychiatric cures. Visits to a health spa may once again have to be recommended as the most effective means of recovering from the ill effects of the pressures and changes of everyday life.

You may be tempted to ask: What about the change from one's everyday schedule to the health spa environment? Does that also contribute to change and therefore become harmful? The answer is yes and no. It contributes to change, but it is not harmful. The spa environment is designed in such a way as to minimize arousal and increase pleasure—remember that higher levels of arousal are preferred in more pleasant settings. Each spa has a carefully planned schedule of activities, and there are physicians and nurses present to see to it that visitors follow this schedule and benefit from it. The visitor plays a passive role. He has few decisions to make. His environment and his activities are regulated by others. All he need do is bask in a state of passive enjoyment. In other words, the initial novelty of the spa environment is more than offset by its overall low-load and high pleasure.

We can therefore expect to find an increase in the popularity of a variety of healthful programs set in peaceful country surroundings. These may be designed to help people give up some undesirable habit, lose weight, or learn a sport. All are modern analogues of the traditional health spa. They are for the most part expensive analogues. The more exclusive fat farms or drying-out places often charge more than $100 a day. But these programs are still worthwhile to people who can afford them and who are aware of the limitations of medical intervention in curing or alleviating their chronic diseases or non-specific feelings of malaise—those who know that drugs only bring temporary or even dangerous relief. Most people, however, cannot and will never be able to afford $1,000 to $2,500 for one to two weeks at a traditional or contemporary health spa. And besides, two weeks often isn't long enough anyway for people in the second or third level GAS stages.

Another alternative is to take several extended vacations. The standard American practice of granting employees a two-week vacation is an abomination. It makes people feel that they must cram a whole year's worth of living into two weeks, with the result that they go flying off somewhere, keep on the go constantly, seeing or doing this and that, and then scramble madly back in time to get to work on Monday morning more GASed than ever. Instead, an annual vacation of at least a month would allow people to travel in a leisurely and relaxing way to their chosen vacation environment, and would remove most of the time pressures once they got there. So what if they don't see the cathedral at Chartres on Tuesday? Wednesday or Friday will do just as nicely—"Let's have a nice picnic today instead." People could also more economically invest in a distant second home or cabin if they knew they could spend a month or two a year there, instead of ten days or less.

The one-month vacation, as well as a healthy two- or three-hour lunch, has been traditional in several European countries, and is admirable. Unfortunately, the Americanization of European industrial procedures has begun to make inroads into such eminently civilized and psychologically sound traditions. Fortunately, perhaps, the emerging worldwide energy and environmental crises may lead to a reassessment of our social and economic goals. As a result of these crises, we may ask, in our eminently practical way, what has a nation profited if its indexes of disease and anti-social behavior continue to "out-perform" the growth rates of its GNP?

Suggested Readings

Selye's (1956) concept of the General Adaptation Syndrome provides the framework for relating stress to physical and psychosomatic illness. Experimental findings relating life changes to illness and accident rates are reported and reviewed by Holmes and Masuda (1970), Rahe (1969, 1972), and Ross and Mehrabian (1976). The following three volumes of collected readings also provide a broad-based discussion of various aspects and consequences of stress: Appley and Trumbull (1967), Levine and Scotch (1970), and McGrath (1970).

CHAPTER

17

Mental Hospitals

AFTER the 1906 San Francisco earthquake, psychiatric patients in the Napa State Hospital had to be housed in tents because of heavy damage to the building. Physicians and administrators at the hospital were astounded to find immeasurable improvement in their patients' health under these somewhat unusual circumstances. When the building was repaired and the patients were moved back, their behavior deteriorated; they reverted to their more disturbed and bizarre behavior.

These puzzling changes can be explained if one considers the environments of mental hospitals at about that time. In the early 1900s, mental hospitals served primarily as custodial institutions. They were drab and unstimulating, both in terms of the physical makeup of the wards and also in terms of the lack of activities, recreation, workshops, or therapy sessions for the patients. Among the few gratifications available to these patients were the infrequent personal attention they received from staff and medical personnel. Such attention was usually forthcoming when patients exhibited new and "interesting" symptoms such as elaborate hallucinations or fanciful delusions. For patients who had spent years of their lives in these monotonous and unstimulating (low-load and unpleasant) hospitals, opportunities for exchanges with ward physicians in their more pleasant and comfortable office surroundings were not unlike the proverbial oasis to the desert traveler. If their increasingly disturbed and bizarre behavior attracted more attention and concern, and thereby produced temporary relief from unpleasant and low-load settings, then such behavior was understandably offered more often.

When the earthquake occurred, a good deal of excitement and variability must have been injected into the hospital community. The circumstances were somewhat unpredictable; living in the tents was novel, and the staff did not have a chance to organize the everyday routines and make them stable and totally predictable. The variety, unpredictability, and greater pleasantness of not only the physical setting but also of the interactions between patients and staff temporarily eliminated the reinforcing value of symptomatology, especially since staff members were preoccupied with such mundane matters as the arrangement of patients' new lodgings, how to get food to them, and so forth. As a consequence, patients appeared much improved.

Studies of the physical makeup of mental hospitals have a lengthy history and constitute an important base in the early development of environmental psychology as a discipline. Before the 1950s, mental hospitals functioned primarily as places of incarceration rather than therapy. They were extremely monotonous and drab: uniformly painted in serviceable colors (neither pleasant nor arousing); lacking decoration; designed without concern for facilitating social interaction. Psychologists and other professionals visiting such hospitals intuitively sensed the inhumanity of these unstimulating environments and recommended that they be furnished with colorful carpeting, paintings or posters, and reasonably comfortable furniture. Areas were also set aside in which the patients could socialize comfortably. Beginning in the mid-1950s, television sets were introduced; these could be sources of pleasure and arousal, especially when placed in lounging areas so that patients could share their reactions— laughter, excitement, disbelief, horror—with others.

These particular recommendations, which were made on intuitive and humanitarian grounds, proved to be effective in improving the behavior and mental health of many patients and provided some important clues: that patients' behavior becomes less bizarre and more cooperative in more loaded and pleasant environments is expected and normal. That is to say, one can almost always expect people to exhibit approach behavior in a moderately loaded and pleasant environment, especially when they have come from one that was neither. It is also possible that these patients were reacting normally to environments that approximated the low loads of places deliberately designed for sensory deprivation. We know what happens to normal people in extremely low-load settings: they hallucinate, get disoriented, and become bizarrely aware of internal bodily processes and stimuli. The symptoms displayed by many mental patients in the 1940s and earlier were quite similar; they included hallucinations, elaborate scenarios of persecution, obsessive self-manipulatory movements like rocking or even self-flagellation, and echolalia (emitting a variety of sounds and then echoing them or repeating them back to oneself in different forms). The condition of such patients also tended to deteriorate progressively the longer they were hospitalized, to the extent that patients who had lived in such hospitals for ten or twenty years were almost hopelessly gone. Their symptoms may be viewed as the attempts of reasonable people to increase their arousal levels under enforced and prolonged sensory-deprivation conditions.* With the subsequent design modifications in mental hospitals which enriched the lives of patients, many of these classical symptoms became quite rare, to the point that by the mid-1960s it was difficult for ward physicians to find interesting examples of textbook cases for their resident students; echolalia, for instance, is now virtually extinct.

The implicit distinction I've made between normal and abnormal mental patients is not nearly as outlandish as it may sound. Many mental patients are admitted after a diagnosis of schizophrenia. According to one school of thought, there are only two basic kinds of schizophrenia rather than four basic types with dozens of idiosyncratic subcategories. In one type, process schizophrenia, the patient demonstrates extreme avoidance behavior from early childhood on. His behavior becomes increasingly aberrant, withdrawn, or autistic (with self-imposed isolation making it easier for him to develop bizarre ideologies or hallucinations) as he grows older, until at about age twenty he becomes unfit to care for himself and must be put away. Such patients almost never get better and usually spend the rest of their lives in mental institutions. The other type is reactive schizophrenia. Reactives usually have normal medical histories. They also tend to have been high achievers whose relationships with others have been energetically approach oriented. At some point in their lives reactives come under a great deal of stress—usually intensely

---

* The lower curve in Figure 1 shows that among unpleasant situations, the less arousing (lower load) ones are approached to a greater extent, but the curve dips for extremely low levels of arousal. This dip is meant to reflect our psychological limitations in, and lack of preference for, extremely unarousing situations. That is, even while feeling displeasure, there is a limit to how low a level of arousal humans can tolerate.

felt personal loss with which they cannot cope as a problem to be overcome by hard work or by "toughing it out"—and go to pieces. They exhibit bizarre behavior of one sort or another, usually accompanied by intense feelings of guilt or anxiety. Indeed, during these periods of crisis they usually appear more disturbed than process schizophrenics, who often display a curious feelinglessness or emotionless self-absorption that psychologists call "flat affect." But given a reasonable therapeutic environment, reactive schizophrenics usually quite literally pull it all together after awhile—usually within a period of one year—and frequently emerge from their breakdowns as more integrated personalities than they were before. But nobody can get better in an environment that calls forth extremely aberrant or bizarre behavior, and it is likely that pre-modern mental institutions, rather like pre-1850 medicine, harmed more people than they cured.

The problems of process schizophrenia are probably of physiological origin where genetic factors are strongly implicated. I suspect that many of these persons may turn out to be extraordinary non-screeners. In any case, the prognosis for process schizophrenics is extremely poor, and it seems more worthwhile to concentrate on the reactives who have a good chance of recovery.

The concept of environmental load is critical for understanding the effects of the physical design of hospitals on such patients' activities and their welfare. For example, in one study patients assigned to large, multi-bed rooms were found to spend about 70 percent of their time on their beds, awake or asleep. In comparison, patients who occupied semi-private rooms were socially more active. These findings can be explained in terms of the loads of the different rooms. The larger rooms lacked privacy and were highly loaded and unpleasant, so that patients preferred social isolation as a means of lowering their arousal levels. In contrast, those in semi-private rooms could achieve reasonable privacy (moderate arousal and pleasure) and could enjoy the companionship of a roommate.

To draw up general guidelines concerning suitable environments for patients, it is important that a distinction be made between the newly admitted and the long-term patient. Many persons entering mental hospitals are extremely anxious (feeling high arousal, displeasure, and submissiveness). This anxiety usually subsides as they become familiar with the setting and recover somewhat from the crisis which drove them to the hospital in the first place. Thus, incoming patients and those who are acclimated to the hospital setting require separate facilities differing in load.

We must remember that being admitted to a mental hospital for the first time can be a traumatic experience. The incoming patient has experienced overwhelming problems that seem beyond his control and with which he cannot cope by himself. Added to this source of anxiety is the excessive load of an unusual array of interactions with staff members at the hospital. Staff members are often intrusive in their examination of the problems which brought the patient to the hospital, and the patient is frequently forced to recount his intimate problems to a variety of strangers. In addition, the patient feels a great deal of uncertainty about just what is wrong with him, what will happen to him, and how long he must stay. Such questions are difficult for the staff to answer and usually are left unanswered, thereby perpetuating those uncertainties and associated high arousal levels.

The admissions sections or wards of a hospital should therefore be structured so as to minimize novelty, since excessive environmental loads can only contribute to the patients' anxiety and discomfort, leading to further deterioration of their mental health. Wards to which patients are initially admitted might consist of several small buildings grouped around a courtyard, with private or semi-private rooms furnished in a comfortable, homelike manner. And since higher levels of arousal can be tolerated in pleasant environments, these rooms should be pleasantly decorated. If possible, patients should have pleasant views of the courtyard or other grounds from their windows.

The same considerations do not apply to patients who've been around for one or two months. Even if the initial physical and social environments of the wards once seemed strange to these patients, they have had many opportunities to adapt. These patients do not need familiar, unstimulating environments; they need settings that provide considerable variety and rewarding social interactions. It is important that they have hobby shops, workshops, exercise rooms, and interactions in the form of group psychotherapy, and that their environments be generally free of the routines so typical of custodial institutions.

To appreciate how improperly planned hospitals can be needlessly and excessively arousing for incoming patients, we need only recall that not too long ago typical hospital routines subjected patients to very severe and abrupt changes upon admission. Their clothing, personal belongings, and jewelry were taken away, and they were required to wear unfamiliar and often uncomfortable hospital uniforms. Patients were also subjected to a barrage of interviews by various staff members about extremely personal matters. In addition, they saw the bizarre behavior of the other patients in the ward. The ward in many cases was literally a madhouse.

Let us consider this last point in some detail. The weird and unpredictable ways in which other patients behave can be extremely unsettling for an incoming patient. When we greet a normal person we can expect a predictable reaction; in a typical discussion with him, we have reasonable expectations of kinds of answers that will be forthcoming or topics that are likely to be discussed. We do not expect intimate self-disclosures from total strangers; if such disclosures are made, their novelty, their unpleasant contents, and the implied demands for reciprocal disclosures which amount to invasions of privacy usually cause avoidance. A hospitalized schizophrenic may react in ways that are at considerable variance with what most people are used to. These include an associative response to greetings ("Hello." "Monday, Friday, Saturday."), eccentric nonverbal behavior, and inappropriate topics of conversation. The tremendous novelty built into a mental hospital's network of social relationships can be frightening for the incoming patient. Of course, as he becomes familiar with the behavior of various patients, their extreme load is reduced and they become less of a problem.

It is not surprising therefore that a newly admitted patient clings to any means or clues that might provide him with some direction, that might help him understand what is required of him in the hospital and generally what to expect. If other patients spend the bulk of the day in bed, then the newly admitted patient thinks this is the thing to do. If other patients are not hesitant to discuss bizarre and very personal matters with staff members, then this again serves as a cue. In general, a well-defined network of social relationships exists in any hospital and a new patient quickly finds a niche within this network so as to minimize uncertainty. For example, a patient is supposed to be sick and to talk about his problems; the doctors who interview him are usually not interested in hearing about his hobbies or his past successes, so he talks about what they want to hear.

The patient's attempts to reduce uncertainty (and therefore

arousal) during the initial admission period also lead him to become extremely sensitized to subtle cues from various physicians that might indicate how he is expected to behave or what they expect him to talk about. For example, physicians who followed the once-popular psychoanalytic orientations, expressed interest in, and probed at considerable length for, aberrations or problems in the sexual area. They were similarly preoccupied with aggressive contents and seized upon and questioned any statement by the patient which hinted at a tendency toward aggression or a fascination with gore.

Suppose a patient described one of the Rorschach cards that has red ink blots as a situation involving spilt blood ("There has been an accident and here is somebody's blood"). The physician would question the patient at some length about what he meant by blood and what other ideas he had about spilt blood, and so forth. The patient, who was terribly uncertain about just what was required of him, would suddenly find himself confronted with a man of authority who was interested in bloody stories, so he would elaborate upon these. With a few interviews of this kind, the patient would learn to develop his interview style, elaborating upon fantasies or daydreams which he might have had a long time ago and which somehow related to people getting injured or hurt. Since he knew that these stories were attention getters with the hospital staff, he would refine and expand upon them as he went along, also beginning to take some of these stories more seriously himself. In this way, the patient's file took on a well-defined direction as that of someone who was preoccupied with aggressive fantasies and hallucinations. Interviews with the staff revolved around these issues, resulting in an assigned identity for the patient.

Thus in highly loaded environments, patients who had little knowledge or understanding of their own psychological problems were led, by means of selective questioning, to elaborate upon certain minor and sometimes even consequential thoughts, ideas, or incidents from their past. As these were elaborated, they become more central in the patients' thoughts about themselves. Since staff members expressed the greatest interests in the most bizarre ideas and events reported by patients, it was quite natural that the latter should become more and more preoccupied with such bizarre notions or events, thereby losing all sense of perspective. These weird things may in fact not have occupied anything like center stage in their everyday lives prior to hospitalization.

Mental health professionals who currently use the principles of behavior modification realize that the verbal and nonverbal behavior of a helpless and highly anxious individual can be shaped readily in any direction desired by an authority figure. In the more progressive hospitals, patient interviews are therefore attuned to the strengths which patients can draw upon to reintegrate their lives and make a successful re-entry into their everyday communities. Efforts are made to discourage any elaboration of bizarre episodes or preoccupations in a patient's past which he may think somehow relate to his present condition.

It is worth discussing the role environmental load can play in the rehabilitation of mental patients. At some point during hospitalization the patient may show considerable improvement. His ward behavior becomes normal and he interacts in reasonable ways with other patients and the staff. It seems that the time is right to get him back to his family and his job. But when the patient is sent home, there is a sudden and unexpected increase in his anxiety, and he manifests symptoms which were characteristic of his behavior in the ward during his worst period.

This sort of thing happens often enough so that it is important to understand. What happens is that the shift from the relatively stable and routine life of the hospital ward back to the family, the community, and the work situation is too large and discontinuous a change. The patient is suddenly confronted with curious relatives and neighbors who want to know if he is really OK—a phenomenon poignantly portrayed in the movie, *A Woman Under the Influence*. The return home is marked by a tremendous increase in the amount of social interaction, which contributes to heightened arousal. If the patient goes back to work, this constitutes a drastic change from his hospital environment where he did not work or have any joblike responsibilities, not, at least, in most hospitals two decades ago. As a consequence, the home and work environments are considerably higher in load and more problem ridden than the one he had learned to cope with in the hospital. The novelty and complexity of the outside environment create excessive levels of arousal; the patient experiences the same tidal anxieties which led to his breakdown and hospitalization in the first place. So he is hospitalized once more.

A patient's rehabilitation can however be structured so that he gradually and increasingly gains exposure to hospital activities that approximate the load levels typical of his everyday life back home.

This is the rationale behind halfway houses, which have the feeling and supportive quality of the hospital environment and yet are located in the community to allow patients to accommodate themselves gradually to increasingly complex and uncertain situations. While he is in a halfway house, a patient can take on part-time jobs, make friends with people in the immediate community, use community recreational facilities, and visit with members of his family.

Hospital routines can themselves be modified to approximate the external environment. As patients improve, they can be assigned jobs within the hospital community: they can work in the cafeteria, the laundromat, or on an adjoining farm. They can be required to take a greater part in social activities and even to take on responsibility for guiding some of these activities.

Ideally, then, patients should make a gradual comeback to the community, moving step by step toward the patterns of social interaction and activity which they must ultimately assume. This implies that the physical and social environment of mental patients should involve a progression of settings increasing in load through which the patient must move in the course of his hospitalization. This progression begins with the extremely low-load environment of the newly admitted patient, shifts to the slightly loaded and peaceful setting of the one-to-two month resident, and finally reaches the moderately loaded environment of the nearly recovered patient where the physical setting may resemble that of the intermediate stage, but is augmented by an active work load and a social program. Patients should be allowed to pace themselves in their progression through these settings and those suffering from occasional setbacks could return temporarily to the less loaded environments.

Since psychotherapeutic techniques used in hospitals and in private therapy also differ considerably in their loads, a parallel course of increasingly loaded methods of treatment is also recommended, beginning with individual psychotherapy in low-load settings and gradually progressing to group therapy sessions with ever-increasing loads. Therapy groups, for instance, can range from those in which each person presents a dramatically different (high-load) psychological problem to those in which every member of the group basically has the same kind of problem. Group activities can range from the intensely novel or unpredictable—nudity, much physical contact, or extremely aggressive truth-telling—to the relaxed, friendly, or polite, in which people are allowed considerable reserve. Groups demanding intensive, intimate interaction among strangers having quite different problems create enormously high levels of arousal in combination with at least some displeasure, and are rarely to be recommended except for well-adjusted persons, preferably screeners. Unstable persons or nonscreeners having no prior group experience have been driven to psychotic breakdowns in such encounter groups, not only in those groups "facilitated" by inexperienced or unscrupulous persons but also in those conducted by trained personnel in reputable institutions.

If therapy is genuinely needed (as opposed to being a faddish social experience), it is far better to start out with the fairly relaxed or reserved setting and with participants who have the same basic problem or symptom. A group for example consisting of a married couple having sexual problems, an alcoholic, a homosexual, and an adolescent suffering from an identity crisis is going to require each member to process a great deal of discrepant or unfamiliar information, much of it not bearing in any direct way on his or her own problem. This will make the somewhat unpleasant group experience needlessly arousing and will lead to avoidance, which is the opposite of what is wanted.

Once group members have had a chance to get to know each other better, and have explored in a nonthreatening way the problem which they all share (a moderately arousing and not too unpleasant an experience), they can be encouraged to become more penetrating in their reactions to one another. After a good deal of familiarity with group therapy—and presumably after having gained some perspective on his own problem and a degree of self-awareness, self-confidence, and so on—a person might very well benefit from a group whose members have rather different problems. In such a group, fairly stable, fairly integrated members can often bring interesting and helpful insights, generated by widely different perspectives, to bear on a particular question. A therapy group consisting for instance of the same six male homosexuals who've been meeting once a week for three years will ultimately run out of fresh perspectives on any issue. Indeed, the group might very well begin to be counterproductive in the sense that it might tend to maintain the problem in a position of central or even obsessive prominence rather than allowing it to assume a less preoccupying place in the members' lives. At some point, members of such a group might very well benefit from interaction with straight couples having marital problems, people with alcohol or drug problems, and so on. But such a newly formed group should begin with fairly polite techniques and then progress to more loaded and possibly unpleasant methods. "Too much, too soon" applies not only to show business but to a great many other contexts as well.

Suggested Readings

Osmond (1957, 1959) was one of the first environmental psychologists to draw attention to hospital design and its effects on the social interaction of patients. Specific discussions of hospital ward design were also provided by Ittelson, Proshansky, and Rivlin (1970, 1972). Goffman (1961), Laing (1968), and Laing and Esterson (1964) presented sociological analyses of mental hospitals. Behavior therapists discussed the undesirable consequences of a hospital staff's preoccupation with the bizarre ideas and symptoms of patients (e.g., Bandura, 1969).

For a review of evidence on arousal among schizophrenics, see Broen (1968). See Buss (1966), Higgins (1964, 1969) and Zigler and Phillips (1962) for discussions of and data on the process-reactive distinction in schizophrenia, and Lemkau (1955, p. 381) on the psychologically harmful effects of a person's social isolation. Also see the following sources for general reviews of findings on the effects of sensory deprivation: Bexton, Heron, and Scott (1954), Cohen (1967), Solomon, Leiderman, Mendelson and Wexler (1957), and Zubek (1964). For a discussion of some of the catastrophic consequences of group therapy see Shostrom (1969).

18

Prisons

SOME READERS may legitimately balk at the idea of prisons as therapeutic environments. I don't want to get into a complicated analysis of what prisons are really for, but perhaps a few paragraphs on the subject are warranted.

People are sent to prison because they have broken rules of social conduct that a given society considers serious enough to punish by taking away the offender's freedom, or even his life. Some of these rules are essentially meaningless, but many of them are fair, necessary, and wise. For instance, rules which prohibit and punish certain kinds of assault, theft, or murder are eminently reasonable in relation to the needs of most communities.

Those who argue against prison reform feel that it is unjust to punish a rapist, bank robber, or a bunco artist by sending him to a relatively pleasant place in which his human needs are perhaps more alertly and compassionately looked after than they would be if he were an ordinary, law-abiding citizen. And these people have a point.

But prison reform of the compassionate variety is considered because the hard-nosed approach to prisons seems to have failed. Prisons have not served as a deterrent to criminal acts. Indeed, evidence strongly suggests that typical prison environments contribute significantly to the overall crime rate. A low-status youth who gets drunk and has a car accident in which others are injured or killed can get sent up on a felony charge. He may emerge from prison embittered, depraved, and knowledgeable about little else but criminal behavior. He is no longer an accidental criminal, but a deliberate one.

Since most first-time offenders are not given life terms, it is entirely reasonable for a society to take steps to ensure that the persons it imprisons do not leave penal institutions more dangerous or violence-prone than they were when they entered. This is especially the case when we consider that it costs more to keep a man in prison for a year than it does to send someone to college for a year. Taxpayers are clearly not getting their money's worth from penal institutions that turn out graduates who for a number of reasons are very likely to commit additional, even more serious crimes.

To make prisons more effective as correctional institutions, the first thing that has to be done is to make them more pleasant and more loaded. The extreme importance of this idea becomes evident when we consider some of the worst kinds of prisons—those used for political and sometimes military prisoners. Brainwashing or so-called thought reform methods invariably involve the combination of displeasure and sensory deprivation for the prisoner—a reduction of his environmental load such that there is little variation in visual, tactual, kinesthetic, or auditory sensations. In laboratory studies of sensory deprivation, a person is confined to a bed in a dark, soundproof room where he is not allowed to move. His arms and hands are placed in large, soft gloves so that touch, kinesthetic impressions, and other sensations are minimized. Since the room is dark, visual experiences are eliminated. In other experiments, subjects lie in shallow water tanks, using snorkels to breathe. Their eyes are covered with halved ping-pong balls, the room is dark and soundproofed, and stimulation from the water over most of the body is uniform. Usually, subjects in these situations first go to sleep. When they wake up, they are extremely disoriented, display an undue preoccupation with their bodily sensations, hallucinate, have bizarre ideation, and generally manifest a great deal of psychological disorganization.

Such results of sensory deprivation show that humans require some minimum environmental load to function normally. The extreme case of near-zero load is psychologically maladaptive and is associated with a craving for any kind of stimulation, accounting for the hallucinations, preoccupations with internal bodily sensations, and bizarre ideas.

Thought reform methods use this craving for stimulation when people are deprived of sensory input—placed in solitary confinement. The isolation is usually accompanied by artificially manipulated surroundings which simulate daylight for from two to five hours, thereby contributing to a further sense of disorientation and a craving for information. In this state, any stimulation is welcomed by the prisoner, even prerecorded propaganda messages or benevolent (pleasant and considerate) guards or officers who seek concessions, such as confessions or information, from him.

The example of thought reform illustrates the extreme vulnerability of humans to understimulating environments, particularly of the unpleasant variety. When placed in such environments, most people try to compensate by engaging in a variety of routines, exercises, or fantasy. When this is not possible, or when the sensory isolation is extreme, they exhibit many of the signs of severe psychological maladjustment observed in schizophrenics.

Even though modern prisons do not approach the low levels of load found in solitary confinement or other sensory deprivation experiments, they nevertheless represent extremely low levels of environmental load, frequently for several years of a prisoner's life. Most prisons are extremely drab, unarousing environments. Usually they are painted gray, have almost no visual perspectives; what can be seen, even in the yards, consists mostly of sky, gray walls, and physical and human symbols eliciting submissiveness. Prison life is usually extremely regimented. Inmates make almost no decisions about working, eating, sleeping, or recreation, and have almost no options in relation to a myriad of domestic tasks—what clothes to wear, what hair style to choose, how to arrange and decorate one's room, how to entertain oneself—which most of us take for granted. Such a simple and utterly predictable environment produces extremely low levels of arousal.

It is not surprising, therefore, that many prisoners invest considerable emotional and intellectual effort in devising elaborate plans for escapes or future "jobs." The complex and stimulating task of planning an escape or a crime—or even the frequent recounting of criminal pasts—serves both to raise arousal and to provide an opportunity for intensive, friendly socializing among a select, intimate group of inmates. It has the side effect of schooling less experienced inmates in the finer points of criminal behavior.

Many of the problems common to modern prisons—corruption, assault, drug abuse, violent homosexual cliques, strong-arm hierarchies, racial tension—are in part behavioral responses to environments that create prolonged and uncomfortably low levels of arousal. A prison beset by these problems will also provide large numbers of inmates with feelings of excitement, fear, or anger—high-arousal emotions. Furthermore, racial and sexual cliques, fights, gang rape, and homosexual pairings enable at least some inmates to experience feelings of dominance in an environment where they would otherwise have almost no control. Temporary compensation for the prolonged submissiveness demanded of prisoners, then, is an added motive for these aberrant prisoner behaviors. A measure of the extreme submission-demanding quality of prisons is the prisoners' inability to have territories which are exclusively their own. There is no place in the prison that cannot be visited by guards and thoroughly inspected; even personal lockers are frequently examined in this way.

Prison riots also provide a means of generating excitement and feelings of dominance. Riots gain the attention of the general public and the news media; prisoners are interviewed or are able to express their views through spokesmen. At such times, prison officials must negotiate with inmates, thus temporarily increasing prisoner status. And of course riots are also effective in bringing about certain permanent changes in the prison environment. But even if they don't, their negative results—punishment, loss of privileges or parole possibilities—are partially offset by the temporary but much needed boost in arousal and feelings of dominance.

The low-load prison environment has an equally corrupting effect on the employees of these institutions, leading them to sanction and relish prisoner generated excitement, as noted in the following observation of an ex-convict:

> It's like when a man escapes. Supposedly every available free man in the prison is required to go out and search for him. During an escape the atmosphere becomes charged with excitement, practically everyone is issued a hand gun or a rifle, the cars are readied, the local police are alerted, and the chase is on! Even if the escapee is an insignificant little alcoholic check-writer, impulsive enough to get himself rearrested immediately, anyway.
>
> I know of at least one associate warden in the system who has left express orders that he is always to be informed, even if he is away on vacation, whenever there is an escape. As soon as he hears of an escape, he runs home (he lives on the grounds) and changes into tall leather boots, large Western hat, leather jacket, and completes the regalia with a riding crop—along with his heavy holster and gun, of course. And then, for him, the fun begins. I would love to talk with him about some of the feelings he has while tracking a man down.*

* This excerpt from pages 54-55 of *The Time Game: Two Views of a Prison*, by Anthony J. Mannochio and Jimmy Dunn, is reprinted by permission of the publisher, Sage Publications, Inc. © 1970.

Informal observations of prisoners suggest that at least a few find the extremely low-load and routine quality of prisons almost akin to the spa environment. Such persons, who are probably in the minority, go on a very high-paced binge full of excitement, thrills, uncertainties, and drug or alcohol use upon their release from prison. They regard their return to prison as a rest period, a period in which to build themselves up physically and psychologically for the next binge on the outside. These are the prisoners who ultimately spend the bulk of their lives in prison, but find it soothing and restful rather than a hardship. For them, the brief period of exposure to excessively high-load environments on the outside has a GASing effect, resulting in feelings of exhaustion, depression, and possibly even physical ailments. A sudden release of such persons to the high-load outside environment is especially maladaptive; instead, a graduated transition is essential to ensure that crime does not become a reinforcer (i.e., lead to a much needed, low-load prison setting).

Some prison administrators both here and abroad have attempted to create appealing prison environments that are more complex, less routinized, and more pleasant. One notable example in Fort Worth, Texas, contains both male and female inmates. Prisoners are allowed to wear their own clothes and can get their hair cut in whatever fashion they please. They usually live two to a room, although individual rooms are available on the basis of seniority or good behavior. Inmates have keys to their own rooms and are free to enter or leave them when they choose—there are no cell blocks that clank open and shut at specified times. The guards are not armed, and it is frequently difficult to tell prisoners and prison staff apart. All the inmates have jobs, working in the business office, cafeteria, laundry, and so on. But most significantly, inmates have access to the surrounding community. Many attend nearby colleges during the day; others work for charitable organizations. Furloughs are granted frequently, enabling prisoners to make trips that range in duration from a few hours to a few days into the surrounding community.

Although men and women are housed in separate quarters and sexual relations are not permitted, there are a number of opportunities to interact on the grounds, both informally and in the course of work or therapy sessions. And they may of course get together on the outside during furloughs.

This particular prison has been in operation for about two years. It is relatively small—about 530 inmates—and costs more than twice as much per prisoner than larger, traditional institutions. Only inmates having two years or less of their time left to serve are admitted, and prisoners having histories of violent behavior are excluded. Many of the inmates are in their early thirties, although there are also some old-timers who have done forty years or more; many are "nickel-and-dimers," drug cases, or those convicted of other nonviolent felonies. The escape rate is quite high, and not enough statistics are available on the recidivism rate. Nevertheless, prison officials are understandably encouraged by the almost complete absence of convict "games" or problems typical of most penal institutions.

The community-access part of this prison experiment is especially sound. Someone who has been confined to a low-load setting for a long time is likely to find the outside too complex and unpredictable. It is not surprising therefore that an ex-convict gravitates toward old and familiar hangouts, friends, and ways of making a buck, or, as Raymond Chandler put it, "an old con always goes back to look at the piece of sidewalk he slipped on."*

Since at least some convicts are likely to have psychological problems, the sudden burden of an overwhelmingly loaded environment is likely to cause a recrudescence of these problems, much as it does with mental patients who are suddenly released from low-load hospital settings. A program of graduated exposure to the myriad sights, sounds, decisions, and responsibilities of the outside world will certainly give ex-cons a better opportunity to adjust. It will also give the community a better chance to respond in positive or at least nonhostile ways to those members of society it was forced to temporarily segregate for unacceptable behavior.

The foregoing environmental analysis of prisons yields the following suggestions for their reform. To counteract the well-known effects of prisoner education in criminal life, the physical environment, social structure, and activities of the prison can be modified to segregate experienced, hard-core criminals from novices who are incarcerated on minor offenses. There is no need to reiterate the importance of increasing the load and pleasantness of the prison environment, as well as that of the inmates' activities. Along these lines, contacts between prisoners and the community can be increased using a two-pronged approach. First, various community organizations (a "Prison Corps") can be encouraged to visit prisons and to

* This excerpt from page 138 of Raymond Chandler's *Trouble Is My Business* is reprinted by permission of the publisher, Houghton Mifflin Co. © 1950.

establish one-to-one contacts with individual inmates. Second, prisoners can be allowed to visit the community and such furloughs can be made contingent upon good behavior. This process of contact between prisoners and the community would be overseen by counselors in the prison system whose main task would be to provide constructive channels of communication and to select outside contacts from which prisoners would profit the most.

Both measures would provide a much needed increase in the load and pleasantness of prison environments. Prisoners currently rely on the many variants of aberrant and maladaptive behavior to accomplish this, meanwhile schooling themselves in antagonistic attitudes and behavior toward authority and society in general. The proposed changes would provide most prisoners with realistic and adaptive alternatives. Furthermore, contacts with the members of the surrounding community would provide them with many opportunities to discover educational and career possibilities, training programs in various technical schools, and generally to be exposed to a social outlook which goes beyond the narrow confines of the ghetto perspective over-represented among prisoners.

Suggested Readings

See Manocchio and Dunn (1970) for an insider's perceptive view of prison life, and Wicker (1975) for a detailed case history of a prison riot. Note Haney, Banks, and Zimbardo's (1973) dramatic experimental analysis of the social environment of prisons. The contribution of peer group pressures to delinquency and crime among institutionalized adolescents was reviewed and documented by Buehler, Patterson, and Furniss (1966). Agron (1974) and Glaser (1964) provided environmentally oriented analyses of prisons. For representative findings on sensory deprivation, see Bexton, Heron, and Scott (1954), Burney (1961), Cohen (1967), Solomon, Leiderman, Mendelson, and Wexler (1957), and Zubek (1964).

PART SIX

PLAY

ENVIRONMENTS

Movies and
Movie Theatres

MOVIES are probably the major art form of the twentieth century, and environmental psychologists are likely to approach such a subject warily.

Movie theatres can be enormous, quasi-baroque, reserved-seating palaces; chi-chi, medium-sized first-run houses with lines going around the block twice; comfortable old nabes showing double spaghetti westerns or *Les Règles du Jeu* and *Les Enfants du Paradis* for $1.50; or porn houses in which more is going on in the balcony and the johns than on the screen. Some moviegoers are overworked intellectuals who go to wallow in cops-and-robbers, people who want to find out if they'll faint or get sick while watching *The Exorcist*, or buffs who go to *Citizen Kane* for the umpteenth time to argue about whether a certain frame was really Gregg Toland or Welles. Movies themselves go from *Fantasia* to *Fritz the Cat*; from low-tacky tearjerkers to high éducations sentimentals like *Casablanca* or *In Which We Serve*; from dim thesis films like *The Hellstrom Chronicle* or *Soylent Green* to serious, well-scripted idea things like *He Who Must Die* or *Z*.

How does one deal with the infinite variety that any rich art form encompasses, especially a truly popular one that not only cuts across class lines but also engages the consciousness of the most as well as the least perceptive members of a given culture?

PLAY ENVIRONMENTS

The reader who has kept company with me this far knows that I will somehow manage to bring in things like arousal, pleasure, dominance, and stimulus screening; but first I'd like to talk about movies and dreams. It is not uncommon for people within and outside the movie industry to refer to Hollywood, meaning one of the movie production centers, as being or as having been a "dream factory." If by dream one means a relatively compact, complex, and arousing perceptual episode in which things happen that are alien to our everyday experience, yet related to our human potentials and yearnings, things that are fairly rapidly combined in ways we find meaningful or cryptic, problems posed or solutions offered that have somehow eluded our day-to-day processes of cognition and evaluation, then all art is dream. Hopefully, this disposes of the parochial and chauvinistic notion that movies are more dreamlike than poetry, opera, mural painting, or a good spy novel. And, I'm not going to contest the idea—occasionally put forth in tipsy moments by specialists in Edmund Spenser or William Blake—that our next Shakespeare will be a script writer.

The arousing quality of movies and moviegoing is probably the most important single factor to consider. Movies, even though they involve fantasy and identification with imaginary events and characters, are ways of enriching one's world. They explore the limits of human experience—events, places, and emotions that are not readily available to most of us in our everyday lives. By identifying with someone else, we see and do things in his ways. Movies, then, introduce variability and novelty into our lives. It is this quality—the exploration of the possible realms of human experience, with a particular emphasis on highly emotional experiences—which in a very basic sense makes movies comparable to the various art forms. This is achieved not only by using emotional episodes but also by portraying places and events that are either extremely different from those encountered in everyday life or by showing common events of human existence in such great detail and with such sensitivity that the viewer cannot help but notice aspects of life which he ordinarily overlooks.

The intense and tremendously varied visual and auditory stimuli of movies are presented on a large screen. In the darkened movie house, the bright screen is a preemptive stimulus, and is arousing for this reason alone. People and objects on the screen are quite large, especially in close-ups, thus decreasing the perceived distance and heightening arousal. Even in middle-distance shots actors appear quite large. We often aren't aware how much larger they seem until we encounter a well known "heavy" actor pushing a shopping cart in a supermarket and note to our astonishment that he is a full head shorter and forty pounds lighter than we are. Part of the effect is due of course to the fact that a smaller scale, usually seven-eights, is used in the construction of most movie and TV props and sets. Thus, the size of doors, windows, tables, or chairs makes the actors and actresses look larger.*

These factors—the relative intensity of the screen, the greatly exaggerated size, the movement of the actors or the camera, the colorfulness, and the many sounds—all tend to make movies intrinsically arousing, regardless of their particular content.

The McLuhan thesis that TV is a "hotter" or more involving medium than movies because the TV viewer must subconsciously resolve or recreate the picture from a pattern of dots may have some merit. But the fact that movies are intrinsically more arousing than TV is revealed by the rather different directorial styles employed by those who make movies and those who make TV dramas. In movies, medium, long, and panning shots are far more common, and the close-up is employed far less than in TV. A movie director can afford to show his actors walking, fidgeting, or pouring drinks as whole people in a given environment. This can happen because on a movie screen a medium shot showing two actors talking to each other in a drawing room will still give us persons who are at least ten feet tall. In this way movie scenes generally provide a more complete account of action in a physical context—they are more heavily loaded. In contrast, a TV director must avoid medium or long shots because his whole actors, even in a medium shot, will objectively appear to be from six to twenty inches tall. He will tend to employ close-ups so that an actor's face is approximately life-size. For this reason, on TV there are a lot of quick cuts from one face to another, and many more camera angles than would occur in a comparable movie scene.

* Although the sound is not actually coming from the screen, we tend to locate it there. This tendency to make the screen the locus of all stimuli is so strong that when we see a foreign film with subtitles we often imagine that the actors have actually spoken the lines given in the subtitles, especially when the language they are really speaking is not one we know well. Furthermore, when a foreign film is dubbed into a second language, or when the lip-synch is out of whack, we are intensely conscious of discontinuity; only then do we become aware that the sound is omnidirectional or at least not coming directly from the screen.

The TV director will tend to reserve the middle and long distances for action shots or more motion-filled and arousing contents—a chase, a mob scene, a fight. You might sometime just count in a *Hawaii Five-O, The FBI, Cannon, Mission Impossible,* or other action TV drama how many times the main characters—to say nothing of the minor ones—are shown full-figure. Even in the so-called establishing shots, as when he wants to show that someone is traveling by plane, the TV director will tend to use stock footage showing airplane tires hitting the runway. In movies, it is more likely that there will be a panoramic shot showing the whole plane landing on a runway.

It is interesting that highly arousing movies, especially in the cops-and-robbers or thriller genres, tend to employ a relatively greater number of the less arousing TV directorial techniques. It is also interesting that some made-for-TV movies which are leisurely, serious, or documentary employ movie directorial techniques. *The Autobiography of Miss Jane Pittman*, a TV movie which was widely praised for its slow-paced, spacious, nonhysterical, documentary quality, did in fact employ a relatively large number of medium and long shots. The ending, which was built around a thematic and dramatic climax in which a 110-year-old ex-slave drank from a "Whites Only" drinking fountain, was shot almost entirely in medium and long. This produced both a sense of documentary reality—you could see whole people with their feet on the ground and trees over their heads—and a thoughtful, nonexaggerated quality. An ancient woman, however strong her spirit or her anger, is a small, frail thing, and it takes time for her to get where she's going; it takes time for her to get helped into the back of a pickup truck. Long as opposed to close-up shots give us a much truer and ultimately more moving perspective on this.

Consider also the different environments in which we watch movies or TV. A movie theatre is a public place, and even though we've been there several times before, the public is not the same, but a crowd of different people each time. To get to the movie theatre we must travel, whether it's just a long walk or a considerable drive. In any case, a visit to a movie theatre represents a change from a private to a public environment, which is usually arousing in itself.

Sometimes, however, this difference in arousal can be excessive. Several years ago, movie-industry people found out to their great surprise what moviegoers knew from just standing in line—that a large percentage of patrons were young and more highly educated than the national average. Producers responded by making a lot of trashy, youth-oriented pictures, but more importantly, they began to starve the neighborhood theatres and instead built smallish first-run theatres near universities. The result has been that married, middle-aged, middle-class people must travel to more congested communities and face horrendous traffic and parking problems, huge lines, and so on. These people consequently may find the moviegoing environment too arousing, too hassling, and too unpleasant, and tend to stay away, demanding more movielike entertainment from their TV sets at home.

In relation to almost any movie theatre, the environment in which we watch TV is usually not particularly arousing. We are in a familiar room, either alone or among familiar people. The presence of our mates, children, or friends can increase arousal, because peoples' emotional reactions tend to reinforce each other: one laughs a bit louder, longer, and with more pleasure if others are laughing too. But such reinforcement is far greater in a theatre with a capacity audience.

While watching TV, we can focus on many other elements in the immediate environment, especially if the TV has been an extremely familiar stimulus since childhood. In contrast, we hardly ever shift our attention from a movie screen. This comparison suggests that TV is not a very "hot" or superinvolving thing for many people. They turn the TV on and then do homework beside it, or they wander around the house doing chores, talk on the phone, read the newspaper, or chat with others. Few people find TV a preemptive stimulus to the extent that they can't tear their eyes away, or can't carry on a coherent phone conversation while the TV is going. Those who can't are often people who for one reason or another did not watch a lot of TV as children and don't have years of practice turning it off perceptually.

We feel more dominant in our homes than in a movie theatre. Our behavior is less physically and socially constrained at home, and we are therefore more likely to do things which distract our attention from the TV screen. We can move around, put our feet up, eat something a little less manageable than popcorn or a candy bar, write letters, or scan a magazine during commercials. In addition, we are free to watch or not watch a particular program. We can simply change channels and get something else. We can usually adjust the picture to suit our own color preferences, and we can certainly adjust the volume. At the movies, we can only stamp our feet if the picture is out of focus; if the sound track is too loud for our taste, we are helpless; and if the movie is a bummer, we can only walk out, regretting the money wasted.

Aside from making one feel more submissive, the many factors which combine to make movie watching a generally more arousing experience than TV watching include: the size of the screen; the manner in which one's attention is focused on it; the presence of a crowd of strangers which heightens emotional sensitivity and expression; the variable, possibly new, setting represented by a particular theatre; the change in daily routines and environments involved in simply getting to and from the movie house; and finally, the gamble represented by paying beforehand for something we may not like.

The less arousing quality of TV is eminently sensible considering that Americans spend several hours per day watching TV. Imagine an entire nation GASed by its favorite entertainment medium! One could predict therefore that those who have especially hectic work schedules or highly loaded work environments, particularly if they are nonscreeners, will not be likely to go to the movies often unless the experience is also a highly pleasant one.

And it is in the pleasure dimension that TV has a great advantage. I am not talking at this point about the content of movies or television programs, but rather the environments in which they are watched. People tend to put their TVs in the most comfortable rooms in the house—living rooms, family rooms, or bedrooms. People watching TV can therefore sit in a comfortable chair, sprawl on the floor, or relax in bed. They can do things to make themselves more comfortable: if it is too cold, they can turn up the heat, throw on a blanket or a sweater; if it is too hot, they can turn up the air conditioning, open a window, or take some or even all of their clothes off. They can fix hot soup or a cold drink. In short, they can do anything they normally do at home to increase their pleasure. This is not possible in most movie theatres. One has very little control over the physical environment of the theatre, and the presence of others exerts considerable control over our behavior. Many people will sit in discomfort rather than get up in the middle of a picture and stumble over a row of people to go to the bathroom. In some theatres it is almost impossible to stretch one's legs or even get enough leg room. Often there are gum, popcorn containers, and other garbage in the seating area. One is not free to open candy wrappers noisily, talk, smoke, or engage in other behavior that might tend to increase one's own comfort but decrease that of others, especially if they are strangers and their reactions cannot be readily predicted. One's view of the screen can be obstructed by a large person in the next row; one can find oneself next to or in front of someone with a tubercular cough, an unpleasant laugh, a foul odor, or some other disagreeable characteristic.

Pleasure is of course a feeling dimension that has a great deal to do with approach behavior. For movie producers or TV execs, approach behavior means box office or ratings, plus quality-of-audience—the consumer-dollar-rich eighteen to thirty-five group, or the over-fifty set. When you consider that people who feel pleasant are most likely to manifest approach behavior, it is no wonder that TV has captured an enormous segment of the entertainment market.

TV people often test their pilots in a movie theatre made even more arousing by testing devices which require viewers to record their reactions by twisting dials or participating in filmed and recorded group discussions. This leads TV programmers to under-estimate the entertainment load requirements of viewers who will be watching the same programs at home, and explains their reluctance to produce extremely arousing or controversial shows. Our theory suggests that in a pleasant environment people are able to tolerate more, not less, arousal. Indeed, a good number of successful TV programs or specials have been inordinately successful precisely because they have been quite arousing compared to the usual fare.

Movies on the other hand have tended to respond to the competition from TV by presenting high arousal works containing language, sex, or aggression considered too heavy for TV. Films explicitly designed for the whole family have usually not been too successful, often because they have been insufficiently loaded. One critic has also suggested that movie makers have become too sophisticated to produce successful family movies; they have usually been unable to provide stories in which likable, four-square heroes battle impeccably against unlikable, four-square villains and triumph over them in such a way that family values of truth, justice, honesty, and worthy effort are positively reinforced. All too often the hero or dominant character of a modern movie is tainted with lawlessness, brutality, greed, or other undesirable characteristics, thus making the movie too complex and possibly confusing for the children, while providing better entertainment for the parents.

Films that are essentially entertainment can be distinguished from films that are serious works of art in that the former are far more conventional—they are governed more by artistic conventions typical of a particular genre. Horror movies, thrillers, westerns, cops-and-robbers, samurai flicks, and drawing room comedies all constitute genres. They tend to have certain standard elements, settings, characters, and in general rules which govern what is appropriate and what is not. Genre audiences tend to be sophisticated. They are consciously or subconsciously familiar with the governing conventions, and hence appreciate (are pleased and aroused by) imaginative variations played upon these conventions. Good genre pieces tend to push almost dangerously against the limits of what is appropriate. For example, in one episode of the TV serial *Maude* (which like its parent *All in the Family* and its cousin *Good Times*, is essentially drawing room comedy) the character Walter got nasty-drunk and slapped his wife Maude. This was shocking enough in relation to the conventions of drawing room comedy to elicit audible murmurs of dismay and protest from the studio audience. It was an extremely arousing moment in that it was totally unexpected. Now, a single slap in the kisser would not be especially arousing or unusual in a cops-and-robbers regular, in which people expect at least one corpse, one violent shoot-out, and who knows what else.

One could argue that there are two cardinal rules about genre movies: first, that you can play interesting variations on the theme of a genre piece, but you cannot utterly violate the conventions; and second, that a scene, word, or action can be quite arousing in relation to the general level of arousal sustained by the film, without having to be intrinsically hideous, horrible, grotesque, or violent. The TV cops-and-robbers serial *Columbo*, for example, is arousing, yet rarely contains violent scenes. Even the murders which bring the character Columbo into the case are seldom brutally or grotesquely depicted. Movie makers who forget these rules, ultimately defeat themselves by producing genre pictures in which for example law enforcement officials are more vicious, unscrupulous, or unlikable than the criminals they are seeking to capture, or in which the average level of arousal is pitched so high that the climactic scenes must be nightmares of grotesquerie.

I except from this generalization directors like Sam Peckinpah, for whom violence per se is not merely an arousal device but a thematic resource or a subject as well. It is interesting to note that

Peckinpah's movies are also usually high on pleasure. They often contain not only a good deal of scenic beauty but also many moments of deep or even hilarious comedy. And this is perhaps the crux of the often expressed dissatisfaction with much contemporary movie making —the failure to provide pleasure. High arousal movies that neglect the pleasure dimension create extreme anxiety or anger, and these anxious or angry reactions spill over into calls for censorship or have other negative social manifestations. Indeed, one can argue that the genius of someone like Peckinpah lies partly in his exploration, conscious or otherwise, of the sometimes incongruous episodes that provide relief from anxiety. There is for example a brilliant little scene in *Straw Dogs* in which one of the villains besieging Dustin Hoffman's house gets on a child's tricycle and pedals around gleefully. In a very tense scene in *The Wild Bunch*, just before the killing starts, Ernest Borgnine gives a little laugh that contains both tension and pleasure. It should also be noted that Peckinpah rarely seriously violates convention. "Bad guys" usually lose; "good guys" usually win. And in *Getaway*, in which bank robbers "win" in that they are not brought to justice, the protagonists are so attractive that we don't mind if they escape to Mexico, as long as they aren't free to remain in the United States, the scene of their crimes. And despite all the exciting killing that Steve McQueen does—in which some moviegoers can take pleasure because of the marvelous way in which this violence is filmed—he never kills a cop, only the bad conspirators.

On the other hand, equally violent movies like *Magnum Force* contain little in which the audience can take pleasure. As a result the extremely high levels of arousal generated by the violence are also accompanied by feelings of displeasure, which as we know can result in a turn-off or create disgust or revulsion. Most successful horror films, which presumably create fright (high arousal, low pleasure, and submissiveness), usually have campy moments or incorporate monsters, fantasy creatures, cartoons, and other unreal agents or episodes. These enable people to distance themselves from the events on the screen, thereby lowering the load. In any case, the genre is so well-established that people who go to horror films feel dominant in relation to the genre, and often derive pleasure from the realism of the makeup and so on. It is also interesting to note that people who are overly aroused by horror films usually know when a particularly gruesome moment is coming, having been forewarned by changes in the background music. They can cover their eyes or watch through a slit between their fingers, thus reducing the intensity of the screen's stimulus.

The issue of filmic violence and its effect on general social behavior has become a subject to which increasing numbers of people have turned their attention. I think this issue has become prominent not so much because movies have become more violent, but rather because they have become more violent, less pleasant, and less observant of familiar conventions. These conventions, when observed, result in lower levels of arousal because they coincide with cultural expectations of "good" and "bad" violence.

Psychoanalytic theory provides one approach to the analysis of this issue in terms of the notion of catharsis which it borrowed from the classical heritage (from which, being a literary discipline, it borrowed many other of its terms and metaphors). In the *Poetics*, Aristotle spoke of the catharsis or purging of the emotions of fear and pity. Early Freudian theory used the term catharsis to mean the expression of strong emotions associated with a problem, and assumed that the expression or reliving of these emotions was an important step toward healthy psychological adjustment. If one hated one's mother and were encouraged to fully express or vent that hate in a therapeutic environment, the theory was that this hate might in some way be purged or rendered less potent simply by letting it out instead of bottling it up. Some neurological and ethological evidence confirms this notion, in addition to the experiences of many people inside and out of the confessional. In any case, this psychoanalytic notion of catharsis was subsequently reapplied to the arts, the assumption being that people who watched plays or movies which created strong emotions would thus be similarly purged of these emotions; they would vicariously experience them and would not need or be tempted to experience them in real-life situations.

Today's concern with violent movies is quite the opposite. People are asking if the exposure to, and vicarious experience of, aggressive emotions will not be likely to cause viewers to feel these emotions outside the movie setting. The basic question is, "What happens after we have spent some time experiencing certain emotions? Are we more, or less, likely to continue feeling the same way afterwards?" Whereas the classic catharsis hypothesis suggests that we are less likely to continue feeling the same way, present-day concern over aggression in the mass media suggests the opposite. These contradictory positions can be resolved by using what we know about emotional reactions to sustained high arousal. We know that continued arousal at a high level (whether in real life or in an artificial environment like a movie theatre) cannot be tolerated by the human organism and that it results in GAS reactions of fatigue and exhaustion. It follows that continuous highly arousing emotions cannot be sustained—one arrives at the condition Milton aptly called "all passion spent." So in the case of sustained high arousal, catharsis in the neoclassical sense is a reasonable hypothesis. If you are standing on a movie line when an earlier performance lets out, you will sometimes hear people say, after they have looked at the patrons filing out, "It must be a good one." They have observed that the patrons are thoughtful, subdued, or at least aren't jabbering and laughing and otherwise being animated. The thoughtful or subdued demeanor of the patrons suggests that the movie has been intense and sustained enough so that these people have been GASed, or at least fatigued by the emotional experience.

On the other hand, we can experience intense and brief arousal. This might happen with a ninety-minute movie which has an extremely exciting or laden finish, lasting perhaps ten minutes. In such a case, the emotions induced in the audience are very strong, but of short duration. The high arousal state is not maintained long enough for the feeling of exhaustion and fatigue to ensue. Rather, the audience leaves the theatre in a highly aroused state, probably feeling the kinds of emotions generated in the last few scenes. If the movie creates extreme feelings of elation and excitement, we expect these feelings to persist when people leave the theatre. If, on the other hand, the movie instills feelings of suspicion, paranoia, and anger, then these particular feelings are likely to be felt by the audience as it leaves the theatre. Indeed, experiments have shown that if you expose people to brief, highly arousing films, they are likely to demonstrate increased aggressive behavior immediately afterwards. Adults who watch a short film of a boxing match will afterwards behave much more aggressively toward those who temporarily come under their sway. For example, they will administer more and severer electrical shocks to experimental subjects they think are actual recipients of the shocks (but who in fact are only pretending to be experiencing great physical discomfort). Also, children will engage in more aggressive play after having seen a brief, violent episode on TV or at a movie if they believe that the violence they have seen is real—with the impression of reality making it a more loaded stimulus.

The brevity of one's exposure to arousing vicarious experiences thus has a great deal to do with whether one's emotions are carried over into real life. This is especially significant in relation to commercial television where dramatic presentations are often split up into fifteen minute segments punctuated by commercials. The breaks allow viewers to leave the environment in which they have been watching TV and go get a beer or something to eat, or at any rate deflect their attention from the drama. Brief, highly arousing TV episodes in which the characters express negative emotions can thus be expected to have a negative carry-over. Highly arousing episodes having a positive emotional tone—the expression of love, faith, or honesty—can similarly be expected to have a positive carry-over.

In a way, the increasing sophistication—and even the increasing humanitarianism or at least good observation—in recent films and TV programs has exacerbated the problem of negative carry-over. It may be that some popular entertainments have become too unconventional for their own good. We are not disappointed or outraged when a cops-and-robbers movie is stacked, because we expect it to be. We know who will win, but can still derive high arousal and pleasure from the unequal game. Some of our satisfaction with this convention may be connected with our perception that in the real world the resources of the social group are, and indeed should be, vastly superior to those of the criminally deviant.

There is nothing wrong with a movie thoughtfully exploring this convention or even overturning it. But my impression is that such conventions are increasingly being manipulated by high-arousal films in ways that leave audiences with intense feelings of displeasure and ambivalence in the dominance dimension precisely because the cops won. To achieve this effect, all you have to do is present a criminal or psychopathic hero in a favorable light, portray his victims as deserving of whatever happened to them, and present those who are trying to stop him as basely motivated, unpleasant creatures reflecting in miniature a larger social group having these and only these characteristics. Then, in the last few minutes, have these unpleasant "cops" apprehend or murder the nice "robber" in a way that offends one's sense of fair play or justice.

The point is that any particular combination of filmic techniques and resources can leave moviegoers in a state of high arousal, high displeasure, with seesawing feelings of dominance and submissiveness. If the stimulus package or entertainment goes so far as to indicate a legitimate target for aggressive display, then it immediately becomes propaganda. As such, it is an agent of social change, and may then properly be evaluated by sociopolitical criteria as well as by aesthetic ones.

Suggested Readings

Not much is available in the way of environmental analyses of movies or movie theatres. McLuhan (1964) provided a general discussion of various media, and Handel (1950) studied details of audience reactions to different categories of movies. See also Berkowitz (1962, 1974), Feshbach and Singer (1971), Lorentz (1966), and Milgram (1965) for analyses of aggression and catharsis.

Theatre

FOR the purposes of this chapter, "theatre" means any live artistic performance and the environment in which it takes place. Thus, La Scala or similar opera houses, multipurpose concert halls like the Dorothy Chandler Pavilion in Los Angeles or the Academy of Music in Philadelphia, the Old Vic, the Globe, or the ruins at Epidaurus are all theatres; so are band shells, the Hollywood Bowl, Ravenna, Woodstock, burlesque houses, jazz joints, grungy little fifty-seaters off-Off Broadway, or working-class repertory houses in Manchester. A performance by the Rolling Stones in the Los Angeles Coliseum is theatre; so is an *Il Trovatore* at the Met, *Les Huguenots* in a high school auditorium, a standup comic at Las Vegas' Sands Hotel, a drag show in a Berlin nightclub, a Sibelius *Second Symphony* at Tanglewood, and Gary Davis singing in front of a storefront church.

As physical environments, theatres are usually loaded and pleasant (exciting). Opera houses, concert halls, and legitimate theatres are often fairly high-status environments. Money, brains, and craftsmanship have gone into their construction because people who can afford to pay $10 to $25 or more a ticket for halfway decent orchestra or grand tier seats can also afford not to, and will tend to stay away unless the theatre environment is reasonably pleasant. Lobbies are usually plush and impressive; it is interesting that a good many theatres are carpeted in red, which is the most arousing color. Theatres traditionally have bars which lend a festive flavor to the intermissions. This emphasis on luxurious and stimulating lobbies and intermissions in live, as compared to movie, theatres fits a more general pattern of differences between the two. Stage plays cannot use rapid scene changes to achieve the tremendous loads that are readily attained in movies. Within the constraints of each scene, plays must strive for greater complexity and novelty to increase load and thereby heighten audience arousal. Understandably, then, they require more exciting stage settings and more stimulating lobbies and intermission activities to sustain the heightened levels of arousal during the breaks in performance.

Specifically, anything the theatre can do with sets and lighting can be outdone in movies: a detailed presentation of exotic and hence highly loaded locales; rapid shifts in perspective, as when the camera shows a long, scenic view of a mountain valley and suddenly shifts to a startling close-up of a man looking down into it; scenes of cars colliding and exploding as well as other high-load action; and, of course, tremendous detail shots in which the screen is filled, for example, with the image of a man's face and a few flies crawling on it. But the variability and intensity of the screen stimuli are achieved at a price, namely, a reduction in the number of stimuli (complexity) available in each scene. In a live stage play, opera, or ballet, there are usually a number of performers on stage. True, directors tend to block out the most climactic scenes so that the audience's attention is focused more directly on the main characters. They might use dramatic lighting, get the characters center stage and near the footlights, or have the chorus or corps de ballet form a semicircle around, or otherwise direct attention to, the main action. Nevertheless, the theatre audience is still free to choose from—or forced to integrate—a wider range of stimuli than is the moviegoer. Even if only two characters are center stage, a theatre audience can choose to concentrate primarily on one of them, noting delivery, costume, movement, and so on. In movies we are not free to do this because the camera provides a single frame in which the movie director, not the viewer, decides which actor to concentrate on, even to the extent of deciding what angle the actor will be viewed from and how much of his body will be shown. If the director chooses for example to film a conversation over the shoulder of one of the characters, we obviously cannot interpret that character's facial expressions or notice if he shuffles his feet nervously, stamps them in anger, or whatever. In opera, ballet, or stage plays, on the other hand, all these stimuli are visible to members of the audience. Theatregoers who equip themselves with good opera glasses are in effect giving themselves one of the options of a movie director, namely, to achieve a close-up at the expense of losing sight of whatever is occurring outside the binocular field. Although I have known people who, it turned out, were intently studying a member of the corps de ballet during the first-act mad scene in *Giselle*, it is interesting that most people do not use their opera glasses during dramatic moments of a live performance. Indeed, they instinctively put them down, because the narrow though more intense visual field has the effect of reducing the totality or complexity (and hence the arousing quality) of the scene.

The fact that movies reduce the complexity and immediacy of a live performance can be seen in certain filmed versions of ballet or opera performances in which the camera is placed so as to provide a view presumably similar to that of a member of the audience seated in the center of the orchestra. Ballets or operas filmed in this way are almost invariably boring in comparison to the exciting live performance. Thus, directors who are responsible for making such films invariably opt for a number of close-ups or unusual angles which show the corps de ballet from above, or film in slow motion from below to give the impression that the dancer is soaring endlessly ten feet off the floor, and so on. Although some of these shots can give us unusual perspectives, they usually offend people who are accustomed to live performances and want to see what's going on where the camera isn't looking. Furthermore, close-ups often provide details that are either unpleasant or bear no relevance to the total performance—veins bulging in the soprano's neck as she hits her high C pianissimo, or sweat coursing down the face of the Odette. Stage plays filmed with movie techniques tend to make the actors look a bit corny, since good stage technique requires somewhat broader or less subtle acting than do movies or TV. Also, filmed plays cause audiences to feel impatient, because they expect the camera to "get outside" the particular setting and vary the scenes and perspectives instead of poking around like a blind mole within the confines of the stage set.

In opera especially, the reduced size of performers viewed from a great distance in a large house can, paradoxically, be a source of great pleasure and arousal if the artists are outstanding. Imagine being seated in the last row of the orchestra of a very large opera house just as Tonio in *I Pagliacci* emerges to sing the "Prologue." Although he may seem a mile away and about a foot high, a magnificent baritone voice can literally fill the theatre, and at certain moments seem almost to reach out and press you back against your seat. The contrast between the small human figure so far away and the huge, beautiful voice so near can be uniquely arousing. People who talk about amplifying opera houses to give a discreet boost to the singers are talking about depriving us of a precious and astonishing experience—hearing a great vocal artist sing to 6,000 or 7,000 people and reach them all in such a way that there is no longer a distinction between the first and the last.

The difference between a concert and a recorded musical performance may also be discussed in terms of complexity. Even when flawlessly recorded and played back over the finest system, a tape or record lacks many of the stimuli that contribute to the environmental richness of the concert performance, including of course the entire visual dimension. It may seem a bit strange to speak of the visual dimension in relation to a concert performance of say Beethoven's *Fifth* or Mahler's *Eighth*. But being able to see the conductor, to see two dozen second violins vigorously sawing away, or see an enormous choir singing contributes greatly to the overall load and hence to arousal. It is interesting that people who frequently attend concerts tend to play their stereo systems at concert-hall volumes, while people whose musical experience derives mostly from tapes or records tend to play their music louder than it would normally be performed in the hall, as if to compensate for a missing load factor that they cannot add imaginatively.

We can use the concept of immediacy to order the wealth and intensity of stimulation in various entertainment media. Ranked from the most to the least immediate are live performances, movies, TV, radio broadcasts, and audio recordings. The more immediate media combine stimulation from several sensory channels and contain a greater number of those detailed sources of stimulation which we've noted in the preceding pages. In other words, the more immediate media are more loaded and hence more arousing for the audience.

Another element of the more immediate media is the presence of an audience which we can see, hear, and feel. Being part of an audience can add greatly to one's enjoyment of a performance. Not only is being in a crowd an extremely effective way of achieving heightened states of arousal, but the presence of others permits the expression of heightened emotions in the pleasure and dominance dimensions. People in a mob situation are more likely to experience an intense crescendo of feelings than if they were alone. This same contagion of feelings is at work in a theatre. The laughter of others at a comedy somehow adds to the general sense of enjoyment and amusement. At a tearjerker, the sobs and sniffles of a nearby person seem to remove all barriers for freely expressing one's own emotions. It is fair to say that it is the more emotionally sensitive members of the audience, the nonscreeners, who act as a sort of pacemaker for the rest of the crowd. Their reactions—bravos, clapping, screaming, or rhythmic bodily movements—serve as high-load cues for other participants, over and above the stimulation coming from the stage.

I don't know anyone who likes to go to an opera, concert, or play alone. The fact of being alone—not being accompanied by someone, or even worse, not knowing anyone in the audience that one can approach during intermission, or before or after the performance— almost invariably detracts from the enjoyment of the overall ex- perience. It is relatively easy to see how a tourist who goes to the theatre alone feels a community around him and is acutely conscious of not belonging to it. Being aroused and pleased by the performance, he is likely to want or expect to affiliate and has an ill-defined feeling that "something's wrong" if there is no one to talk to.

Theatre design can maximize the effects of audience participation and interaction. Some theatres are arranged so that members of the audience can readily observe the reactions of others while watching the performers, as in small theatres or theatres-in-the-round. This proximity maximizes the impact of stimulation in all sense modalities. We may be aware of the performer's feelings of excitement, un- easiness, anxiety about errors or not being received well, and perhaps even his embarrassment in taking on certain roles. During the per- formance of a play in a small theater-in-the-round, we may feel embarrassed ourselves, as though we were intruding on someone's private life. In very large theatres, on the other hand, it is more difficult for the audience to express itself collectively or to take in all the details of the performers' gestures, facial expressions, and other facets of the performance which contribute to the overall effect. For much of the audience the performers are far away; the stimuli are less immediate and consequently less arousing.

There is also the tradition in older theatres of setting aside one section for standees. The standees are often students or others with an interest in theatre who cannot afford the seats. Frequently these standees express the greatest excitement and enjoyment. Part of their increased excitement can be explained in terms of the greater muscle tonus (a correlate of arousal) associated with standing as opposed to the more relaxed seated position. Also, standees are frequently packed together; there is intense stimulation from other persons in one's immediate vicinity—not only visual, but tactile, kinesthetic, and even olfactory cues may be present.

The communal feeling at a live performance includes the performers as well, and this aspect is mostly absent at a movie or while listening to a recording. People tend to applaud after a fine movie that has genuinely impressed or moved them. But it is always a tenuous, hesitant, short-lived sort of applause, as they quickly become self-conscious about the fact that there is really nobody to applaud. In a live performance, on the other hand, there is somebody there, somebody whose artistry you can applaud, who comes forward as a person, not as a character, and personally accepts the gratitude and appreciation of the audience. This applause represents an enormous release—and something more—for the audience. You can sense the frustration felt by an opera audience in sceneless things like *Otello* or certain Wagnerian works, for example, which do not allow people to express their approval of particular arias. For instance, there are marvelous moments in *Otello* where people want to exclaim, "Stop the show!" or vent their approval of, say, the "Credo" or "Niummetema," but usually hold off out of respect for the dynamics of the work as a whole. Under extraordinary circumstances, even sophisticated audiences disregard protocol and applaud and shout approval to their heart's content. And if the conductor does not fold his tent for a moment, the audience is willing to sacrifice the next few minutes of music in order to get it off its chest. Having a live performer to applaud not only allows members of an audience to express their feelings, but also has something to do with creating a sense of community. If somehow one perceives oneself to be alone in such a community, one feels alien, unfulfilled, or unrelated to something important.

Many performers have emphasized the importance of the audience, and it takes much persuasion to get some of them into a recording studio. A bond somehow develops between the audience and the performers in sharing the many strong and often personal feelings generated during a live performance. This bond is lacking when we attend a movie or listen to a record.

These reactions to the performers, the other members of the audience, and the setting in which the performance takes place can all contribute to an escalation of strong emotions. That is, there are many ways in which two or more of these elements of a performance can combine to intensify the dominant themes or feelings which one of these elements might inject into the entire scene. For instance, the higher the levels of pleasure and arousal in the audience resulting from the setting, the greater the ease with which the performers can achieve their desired effects. In this sense, it is easy to understand why open-air music festivals like Woodstock or the marathons at the Hollywood Bowl tend to be successful. The audience is already in an excitable mood and can be easily swayed to greater heights of excitement: the less formal and more pleasant environment does not inhibit exchanges among members of the audience—exchanges which help generate and maintain that excitement. In such festivals—where people are free to move about, stretch out on the grass, select their seats without regard to price, bring along food and wine in a natural, open-air setting—another emotional undercurrent is the feeling of dominance.

It is no wonder then that television and radio recordings increasingly rely on performances with live audiences. The hope is that the spontaneous excitement from the audience during the recording session will be transmitted to the home audience. This is particularly effective in comedies, where the laughter of the audience creates a jovial mood and also cues the home audience in about a joke. It also adds an extra dimension to the televised performance; you can see the actors timing their lines, allowing the audience a good laugh, and deciding when to continue. With a good script and a good audience, there is a considerable amount of cooperation between the actors and members of the audience. In live slapstick, the laughter of the audience can be so infectious that the performers themselves are affected, causing them to break character and giggle to the extent that they can't deliver their lines with a straight face. It is almost unheard of to record a comedian's routine without the presence of a live audience, whose laughter adds considerably to the overall humorous impact. In this case, the laughter of the audience is set off partly by the facial expressions and gestures of the comedian. Audience laughter on a record or tape acts as a cue to help listeners become involved in the general feeling of the performance, and possibly even to visualize the comedian's expressions and gestures. It is easy to demonstrate the tremendous effect of audience laughter on such a recording by simply presenting an edited tape of the jokes to one group while presenting the original recording with the jokes and laughter to a second group, and compare the reactions.

A pleasant, high-load performance is preferred, and an unpleasant, high-load performance is avoided. The greater the load of either, the greater the degree of approach or avoidance, respectively. This means that approach and avoidance reactions to a performance will be more polarized to pleasant versus unpleasant events when a large, spontaneous, informal, and expressive crowd gives an additional boost to the load of a performance and hence to arousal levels. A similar consideration applies to the different reactions of screeners and nonscreeners. Since nonscreeners are likely to become more aroused at a performance, their reactions to pleasant compared to unpleasant performances will be more polarized than those of the screeners.

When a performance is slow-paced and lengthy, our attention wanders, and we find ourselves daydreaming or fantasizing even though the performance is pleasant. The load is just not high enough; it is not a "captivating" performance. Traditional Japanese theatre had this leisurely quality, but then, social motives behind theatre attendance in Japan were not unlike those governing a family outing. The audience would bring some food along, socialize during the performance, or get up and leave the hall for a break while performers were on stage. These flexible rules of theatre conduct provided the audience with relief from the possible monotony of a performance and their physically confining (low-active) seating positions, and helped them overcome fatigue from extended concentration. Our own performances come in shorter and more concentrated doses. Nevertheless, a pleasant and extremely high-load performance which manages to sustain peak arousal levels for an hour and a half can drive audiences to GAS themselves.

Aside from the many things that can happen simultaneously to determine the impact of a performance (the crowd, their actions, the proximity of the performers, the load level of the performance itself, and so forth) there are a number of temporal and sequential factors which are also important.

One of these temporal factors is how pleasant or unpleasant a person feels because of events that occurred before a performance. For example, a hungry person watching a performance is likely to feel some discomfort, and if the performance is extremely high-load, he might even feel tense or anxious rather than excited. Similarly, if he has encountered several difficulties—hassles with parking or an argument just prior to entering the theatre—he is less likely to respond positively to the performance. Prior events can also affect arousal, and combine with the emotional impact of a performance to yield somewhat extreme results. Thus, if a person has had several cocktails and a large meal prior to attending a show, and if the performance is not particularly loaded, he may doze; the food, the alcohol, and the slow-paced performance combine to depress his arousal level too far.

The programming of a concert performance (or the "programming" or scripting of a play or opera) can have a marked effect on its overall success or failure. The initial piece (or opening scene) should, ideally, create an emotional set for the audience that will be consistent with the overall emotional effect desired. If the purpose of the performance is to create high levels of excitement in the audience, it is important to begin with one of the more exciting pieces. This will create levels of arousal and pleasure that will produce approach behavior in the audience, especially if unfamiliar or less pleasant items follow. Since a sustained level of high excitement cannot be maintained for too long a period—it will GAS the audience—it is important to change the performance load at certain intervals by going to something slower, more familiar, or relaxing.

One pattern for such a concert might begin with a highly exciting piece (which would warm up the performers as well); continue with a few moderately stimulating pieces; then include one or two more melodic, peaceful, and relaxing compositions; and just prior to the intermission, end with something extremely exciting. The audience would then exit for intermission at a high peak and their conversation would help to maintain that level of excitement. When they returned to the hall for the second half of the performance, it would be possible to resume with moderately exciting pieces and gradually build up to a finale of intense, frantic excitement. The ending of the concert would thus represent the highest levels of arousal and pleasure. This is, of course, only one among several possible arrangements specifically designed to pay off in terms of audience appreciation.

These suggestions on programming are based on research findings which have demonstrated the importance of what are called *primacy* and *recency* effects. Primacy means that the effect of a series as a whole depends more on the elements at the beginning of the series than on elements contained in the intermediate stages. Recency means that the overall effect of a series is influenced to a disproportionately greater degree by the last elements of the series. It follows that when a performance is designed to have a certain overall effect on an audience, it is important to set the stage with an initial piece which will get the audience into a mood approximating that effect.

Also, in order to capitalize on recency, final pieces should contain the highest doses of the required effect. However, to avoid monotony and to provide contrast and variation during the intermediate stages, it is important that the same mood not be maintained for too long a period—no longer than about fifteen minutes.

The intense levels of arousal which are generated in the public performer take a tremendous toll. Some performing artists are so highly aroused before going on stage that they become physically sick every night, even during a long run. Such artists frequently manifest GAS symptoms; they also tend to have short careers; they just burn out. Other artists, probably the nonscreeners, find the extremely high levels of arousal and pleasure generated by successful performances so approach-causing that they over-perform and either ruin their gift (this being especially true of singers) or push themselves to such an extent that fatal GAS reactions result.

A performer's level of arousal is affected by, among other things, the extent to which the details of his performance are specified in a script or a musical score. An act or a musical set can range from complete improvisation without any prior practice or predetermined structure, to the more frequently encountered type of improvisation where variations of the same form are frequently performed, to a firm script of the performance where every sentence or musical note is predetermined. A performer who is improvising for the first time and is experimenting with a new idea he has not rehearsed is in a highly aroused state. The performer who is following a written script to the letter and has rehearsed it on numerous occasions is to that extent less aroused. (Of course, if the performer is doing a well-known work with which many members of the audience are familiar, then he has another sort of problem; he cannot afford to make obvious errors.) The extreme uncertainty and arousal of the performer who is improvising can be a tremendous burden. His improvisation can either degenerate into a terrible failure by not managing to capture and involve his audience, or his experiment may pay off dramatically and excite the audience, generating more excitement and pleasure for him. The possibility of such disparate outcomes will affect the nonscreening performer more than the screener. The nonscreener will more readily get caught up in a positive cycle of success and further effort to outperform himself; but, by the same token, he will also be more easily discouraged at the first sign of failure, with consequent rapid deterioration of his act.

Both the performer and the audience recognize the risk inherent in improvisation. Audiences take chances when they attend jazz jam sessions, for example, since they don't expect to have a thrilling evening every time. Instead, they are usually content to settle for moderately successful improvisations; they attend these impromptu concerts repeatedly in the hopes of hearing the rare, exceptional, never-to-be-forgotten performance.

The performance situations of improvisational artists contain a great deal more uncertainty and novelty than those of traditional performers. For example, the uncertainties for a jazz musician are greater than those of a well-established classical musician. The latter's occupational subject matter and environments are less loaded—more structured, more rule-governed, less improvisational, and more predictable. The contrast between the jazz musician and the classical musician has interesting results in terms of the effect of extended and unavoidable uncertainty (and hence sustained high arousal levels) on psychological health and physical well-being. For instance, the number of deaths among jazz musicians due to severe physiological malfunctions, car accidents, and so forth, is far greater than the corresponding figure for classical musicians—the average life expectancy of the former is considerably shorter. This difference in life expectancy for the two groups highlights the maladaptive consequences of unavoidable and extended stressful experiences or uncertainties in one's profession. Humans generally avoid continuous, high-load stimulation. But when such avoidance is not possible, they resort to temporary means of reducing their arousal levels. Ways of achieving this include the use of alcohol, tranquilizing drugs, and severely addictive relaxants such as heroin. Excessive reliance on tranquilizers or stronger relaxants to reduce arousal levels is common among those professional groups which are forced repeatedly to cope with high-load situations, and the notably high rate of heroin addiction among jazz musicians is part of this pattern.

Suggested Readings

See the following sources for data and general psychological analyses of art: Berlyne (1972), Child (1968), Hogg (1969), Valentine (1968). For a discussion of differences in the intensity and multi-channel nature of various media in terms of the concept of immediacy, see Mehrabian (1971). Also see D'Atri (1975) and Wheeler (1966) on the arousing effects of crowds. Primacy-recency effects are discussed by Murdock (1962) and Postman and Phillips (1965). Drug use, as it is determined by situations and personalities, is discussed in chapter four.

21

Museums and Galleries

ALTHOUGH we tend to think of museums and galleries in thinking of art, actually art in its many diverse forms has a pervasive impact on most aspects of our everyday environments. It influences our architecture, interior design, including the design of furniture, wall, and floor coverings, and even appliances and utensils. We can consider these influences of art by understanding which of its forms are likely to be preferred and to become parts of our environments—that is, by examining the artistic products themselves within our framework. It should then be possible to consider the emotional tone of a people in relation to the arts it produces and the resulting "culture" which permeates its living and working spaces.

All works of art, including the paintings, sculpture, and other fine art that most museums and galleries are designed to display, may be considered forms of experimentation. Just as scientific theories and experiments are created to express and explore the realms of actual and possible events or entities, so are works of art. The novelist who invents a character and then makes him undergo a trauma is in one sense saying, "Let's see what happens" or "I believe that this character will behave in such-and-such a way given the conditions confronting him." The painter, as he combines oils on canvas, is usually testing or expressing certain hypotheses about alternative ways of making painterly combinations. He is also experimenting with particular perceived or imagined objects, colors, textures, spatial relationships, and so on.

The end products of scientific and artistic experimentation are thought to belong to entirely different orders of things largely because the emotional dimension plays a considerably larger or more obvious role in art than it does in science. Scientific work is, however, no more devoid of emotional content than any other kind of work. Productive scientists always have a strong emotional commitment to their research, and are likely to view their results and those of other scientists at least partly in aesthetic or emotional terms. Scientists may on occasion knowingly set out to produce work that will instill feelings of admiration, anger, frustration, or excitement. But they rarely do work that is capable of engendering emotions of pity, terror, disgust, embarrassment, or lust. In general, we may say that the range of emotional effects produced by artistic experimentation is far wider, particularly insofar as scientific experimentation seldom results in verbal or other artifacts that arouse negative emotions.*

Without getting into the various controversies about what art really is, or what artists really intend to accomplish, it is fair, I think, to say that art has a large emotional component. It is not necessary to decide whether this emotional component is the essence of art or merely one of its major by-products. In either case we are dealing with, among other things, the expression, exploration, or experiencing of a wide range of human emotions, and to this extent we may bring our dimensions of arousal, pleasure, and dominance to bear on a discussion of art. Indeed, we may say that any aspect of human emotion that is represented by the diverse combinations of these three basic dimensions may legitimately constitute, if not the content, then the comet's tail of an art form.

When we consider pleasure as it relates to art, it is clear that in the visual arts we have always had extremes along this dimension. For example, the art of the Middle Ages often contained considerable gore and horror—bloody crucifixions, chopped-off heads, skeletons walking around in robes. Modern counterparts of ugly or disgusting art are exemplified in the work of Edward Keinholtz. These works seem to make a special effort to arouse disgust by putting some of the less savory aspects of modern civilization into sculptural form. One example is a piece portraying a woman in the midst of an abortion. Keinholtz also uses materials which in themselves have a rotting, deteriorating, and dirty feeling. Indeed, forms which arouse

---

* When scientists knowingly or inadvertently do something that produces negative emotions, as did the nuclear physicists who produced the gigantic mushroom clouds at White Sands or Eniwetok, there is usually a good deal of shock and soul-searching among them and a feeling that somehow science shouldn't be concerned with such things.

disgust or revulsion have become quite common in modern art exhibits. Daniel Spoerri, a noted Yugoslav artist, specializes in table-tops containing the remains of meals, where utensils and plates are covered with leftover food, sauces, or meats, and ashes and cigarettes are stuck into the leftovers. Other artists, such as Tetsumi Kudo, concentrate on sculptural representations of dissected internal organs or imagery resembling dissected human innards. I am not describing these more negative or unpleasant types of art to imply that they preclude the more beautiful or pleasant forms, but simply to note that art is not exclusively pleasant in quality.

It is, of course, important to consider the arousal dimension in describing art.* Basically, the length of time during which a given art form can continue to have an arousing effect on its audience is a measure of its life span. Given two paintings, the one that is more colorful, complex, and readily amenable to a greater number of different interpretations will continue to be arousing for a longer period of time. Extending this idea a bit further, we can say that art forms which are changing, mobile, and which contain stimulation in multiple modalities are likely to be more arousing over time than those which are unchanging, static, and restricted to only a single modality, such as the visual one. Even relatively simple objects which are inherently low-load can be made more arousing by being situated or used in ways which increase their impact. For example, a polished, flat coil might be suspended from a string so that it can rotate randomly with the air currents and reflect sunlight shining upon it at different angles during the day. Other instances are Calder's mobiles, the various arrangements of colored lights which randomly flash on and off, pieces that make sounds when they are approached, or more interestingly, a set of mirrors and reflected laser beams positioned so that the beams form intricate and changing patterns of colored lines in space.

The load of various art forms can also be analyzed in terms of the intensity of the initial stimulus. Some art forms have an extremely intense, almost shocking impact upon first viewing—an effect which rapidly dissipates as we become more familiar with them. This happens, for example, in pornographic works or in paintings depicting

---

* James Joyce's crack to the effect that his books would keep graduate students busy for a couple of hundred years is a put-down having so many edges that its affirmative relevance to the world of creative work—the issue of sustained arousing power—has not been adequately stressed.

executions. Other, more subtle artistic creations always seem to yield something new. Because such works are usually quite complex, they are somewhat arousing at first sight but also repay continued study. For example, Maurits Cornelis Escher has an etching in which lizards emerge from a sort of chessboard, crawl onto and down objects, and then retreat back to the chessboard. This cycle of events only becomes evident with continued scrutiny. Escher's work is complex and involved, and hence arousing. It holds one's attention, at least until one discovers the hidden order within it.

An artist can also increase the load of his work by incorporating unusual or improbable contents. Notable examples are the ideas one finds in surrealistic works, such as the floating figures in Marc Chagall's paintings, or the unusual combinations of human and inanimate forms in many of Salvador Dali's paintings.

Then of course there is the possibility of creating a visual display which is akin to music in its sequential variations. Since arousal increases with the changing quality of a stimulus, it follows that a visual display which leads the onlooker from one element of the sequence to another over time will be more arousing. An example of this would be a series of photographs exhibiting some sequential relationship. The onlooker simply follows the sequence at his own tempo, moving from one photograph to the next and possibly back, then skipping ahead two or three photographs, and so on. On different occasions, he regulates and enhances the arousing quality of the entire sequence in this way. Another way to increase arousal is to portray the same figure with different colors (as when the same portrait is shown through variously tinted filters), which yields marked contrasts in the colors of the subject's face and clothing. A third idea, more closely related to musical concepts, is a sequence of paintings of drastically varying sizes, intensities of color, and detail, all arranged to create changing dynamics for the eye as it moves across the sequence.

It is a great challenge to an artist to create fixed visual art forms that have the sustained power to arouse his audience, because these basically static forms—whether paintings, sculptures, or architectural structures—become less loaded over time or with increasing familiarity. This may in part account for the relatively rapid rise and fall of schools and movements in the fine arts. There is of course a strong economic motive as well. As one school falls into disfavor, its representative works become undervalued and make good speculative investments in relation to an almost inevitable revival of interest two or three schools later.

Museums and galleries can also be considered in terms of their load, or arousing aspect. Despite the treasures they may contain, many museums can be very low-load—every room is more or less like another, with a single row of paintings girding the walls at about eye level. The average visitor who tries to see everything often finds himself getting bored after trooping through several rooms. This happens because museum designers seldom consider it essential to make the setting in which art is displayed an arousing one. They are partly correct in being apprehensive that high-load settings will detract from the appreciation of the art itself. Nevertheless, certain devices are available which should not pose much of a problem in this respect. If some effort were made to select hues appropriate for the paintings or the sculpture displayed, darker and more saturated colors could be used on the interior surfaces, and these would be more arousing than the bright colors (whites) generally in use. Also, rug and wall colors and textures could be varied from one room to another. In one study it was found that visitors to a museum covered more space per unit of time when the walls were rich brown than when they were pale brown: the more arousing color increased their activity. The visitors' liking of the exhibit was not examined, although it could have been measured in terms of the length of time they spent in each display area.

Fortunately, some museums are beginning to experiment with multimedia displays which incorporate visual, auditory, tactile, or even olfactory stimuli. In an unforgettable exhibit of African art, particularly masks, in Munich, the room in which the masks were displayed was wired for eight-channel sound. Music providing examples of the sounds of various African instruments came from different parts of the room. Movies were shown periodically of different aspects of African culture, such as the festivities in which some of the masks were used. A parallel exhibit of modern art, with definite family resemblances to some aspects of the African art, was juxtaposed with corresponding forms of the latter. The exhibit as a whole was a very thorough creation of an exciting, complex environment.

Aside from being generally low-load, museum and occasionally gallery environments induce a submissive feeling in the visitor. In most older museums or galleries one is required to be quiet and to behave in a formal and subdued way. The rooms are often immense and almost depressive in their architecture and design. The Louvre is a prime example. The building is large and has many intricately connected rooms, making it difficult to find one's way around. It is not well lit, and whispering is the norm. In some newer museums, however, notably the Louisiana in Denmark, a homey, pleasant, light, and colorful environment is created for the visitors. There is a primary linear progression through the rooms, and in some outdoor exhibit areas normal voice levels are of course allowed. When a museum is informal or resembles familiar settings in this way, the visitor is more likely to feel dominant, or at least not feel submissive.

Submissive feelings experienced by a typical visitor to a gallery or museum can be due to his lack of understanding or his feeling of incompetence in judging the various art forms displayed. It is of course very difficult to feel dominant in relation to anything that is utterly incomprehensible, that bears absolutely no relation to your experience or needs, or that is deliberately attempting to shock you. In a subtler vein, it is also difficult to feel dominant in relation to work that for one reason or another defies or at least fails to demand and repay serious attention.

The feeling of incompetence in art appreciation is not restricted to those extreme cases where the work is even incomprehensible to the knowledgeable. Rather, it is a common problem resulting from the fact that much fine art was commissioned by wealthy patrons (or by wealthy institutions like the Church), and is still closely associated with a small, high-status minority. Many visitors to museums are unlikely to have experienced these art forms as part of their everyday culture, or as familiar and sometimes even useful elements of familiar environments. Accordingly, galleries dealing in prints, lithos, or woodcuts are less likely to induce feelings of submissiveness than are galleries dealing in expensive oils. Many more people decorate their homes with prints and are more likely to be shopping rather than looking at things they know they can never afford to own.

Sometimes paintings and sculpture create feelings of submissiveness and awe by virtue of their subject matter. This is especially true of works with religious content, but can also result from the heavy and durable quality of materials, or the grandeur, scope, or size of the work. Michelangelo's *Moses* or the Sistine Chapel ceiling can evoke feelings of awe and humility in those who are quite unaffected by the religious associations. The murals of a José Orozco, David

Alfaro Siqueiros, and Diego Rivera can have a similar effect, even on those who are quite unmoved by political sentiment. And of course somewhat less worthy feelings of awe and submissiveness can be engendered by the "pricelessness" of an Old Master, especially when a museum has spent three or four million well-publicized dollars to acquire it. On the other hand, art forms, portraits for instance, that elicit feelings of pity, disgust, and contempt or feelings of relaxation and self-satisfaction are associated with a more dominant feeling in the onlooker. Also, in high-status museums, the more traditional and familiar works are likely to be the most popular items, because the onlooker understands them and does not feel at a loss.

One can make a good case for the assertion that artists, like certain theoretical scientists, tend in some way to reflect or otherwise anticipate in their work broad cultural or social developments before these developments have emerged into the general public consciousness. Be that as it may, artists create works whose emotional component represents a certain distinctive combination of arousal, pleasure, and dominance. When significant numbers of artists adopt similar changes in technique or content, a school or movement emerges that projects, among other things, a certain distinctive emotional tone or impact. It is possible I think to relate the popularity of artistic schools or movements to the emotional needs or emotional state of a given culture at a given time.

The bored aristocracy of a few centuries ago understandably appreciated the higher loads which even the realistic though detailed and vividly colored paintings provided for their spacious and sparsely decorated halls and rooms. The same aristocracy and the wealthy who had similar unarousing life styles and high-load environmental needs continued to patronize and, in fact, welcomed the Impressionist painters of the mid-1880s and the various nontraditional schools of art which subsequently flourished. Deviations from realism were novel and involved unexpected color combinations, shapes, and unusual subject matter. Abstract Expressionists such as Oscar Kokoschka asserted the excitement rather than the logic of life by using strong and bizarre colors (for example, a green face), heavy, dynamic brush strokes, and even distortions of figures and faces, such as enlarging an eye out of proportion to the rest of the face. These artists stressed the extremes of our three dimensions: arousal, dominance, and pleasure.

Today's wealthy patrons of the arts, and even of the artistically oriented architecture or furniture, are usually highly involved in complex and extremely competitive segments of our society. Understandably, then, the bias is in favor of simpler, less cluttered designs in art, architecture, and furniture. Note, for example, the strong influence of the architecture of Mies van der Rohe or of the streamlined effect of Scandinavian furniture.*

The revival that more representational works are currently undergoing—new things as well as American primitives, nineteenth-century genre articles, and even recorders or illustrators like Frederic Remington or the senior Andrew Wyeth—provides some arousal simply because these things represent a change. Representational works tend to be relatively complex (and hence somewhat arousing), but not as intensely arousing as "wooly ruins," paint-covered nudes rolling about on a canvas, or sculptures that explode or are smashed to pieces by their creator. People can of course take pleasure in a great many things, including the act of destroying something. But there is a special pleasure to be found in the painterly translation, or virtually photographic reproduction, of relatively familiar scenes or objects. Even those who have never tried to paint can respect and respond with pleasure to the skill involved in getting people, places, or objects onto canvas in some recognizable form. Cognoscenti mock, sometimes with considerable justification, the philistine reaction to a good deal of totally nonrepresentational art ("A chimp could have done that," "Hell, I'm a house painter and my drip cloth looks like that," "Sure, if I wanted to drive my car off a cliff I could be a sculptor too"). But they often fail to recognize in such reactions a sneaking if not deep-seated respect for the artist as an exceptionally skilled craftsman who does special things most people cannot do—special things like carving a beautiful woman out of hard stone, or putting a storm at sea on a piece of canvas, or even etching and coloring lovely animals on the back wall of a cave.

Today's return to realism has a special slant—exquisite attention to detail of features drawn to scale. Features are highlighted beyond the extent revealed by a casual observation of the person or thing portrayed. The realist achieves a moderately arousing effect, unlike the caricaturist who goes all out to make his point. The former highlights, without distortion, the subtle qualities of the expression,

---

* It is interesting that someone like Norman Rockwell, who was most popular during the stressful '30s and '40s, is now enjoying a slight revival of interest in the equally stressful '70s.

clothing, or posture of his model. Caricature is less disciplined in that it emphasizes one or more features at the expense of the others; it is arousing because the features that stand out give one a new, usually humorous, yet truthful perspective on the subject.

One might suggest for example that the recent movement away from highly arousing abstract or Pop forms toward more representational works implies a broadly felt cultural need (felt even by the more expert art-world elite of museum directors, gallery owners, patrons, and the artists themselves) for less blatantly arousing art with its rapidly dissipating effect and more moderately arousing and pleasant forms. A Campbell's soup can, when displayed in the form of a twenty-foot model, had two elements that made it quite arousing. First, it was exceedingly novel to see this familiar household item in the form of a gigantic sculpture in a museum. Second, the very large scale highlighted the design details and allowed for heightened visual discrimination. In addition, Campbell's soup cans are usually a deep (saturated) red, which is a most arousing color. The same general observations can be made for gigantic comic strips. But most Pop objects were not complex enough to repay close and continued scrutiny as art works and were rather passing cultural phenomena; although initially arousing, they were too minimal to sustain anything like the load we expect from art. There was some pleasure (humor) associated with them, but lurking in them too was a relatively subtle put-down.

An interesting example of the relationship between cultural-emotional needs and art appreciation may be found in Japan. The most respected form of Japanese art, traditionally favored by the nobility, religious institutions, and higher classes, is called *Shibui* and is characterized by restraint, subtlety, harmony, and peacefulness. Indeed, one could define *Shibui* art works simply in terms of their common emotional impact—pleasure and low arousal. For example, the peaceful quality of the Shinto shrines is quite remarkable, even in relation to their peaceful Western counterparts, certain monasteries. Such shrines are usually set in beautiful, quiet gardens with ponds full of carp and goldfish. Careful attention is paid to the selection of trees which yield beautiful blossoms and to the aesthetic quality of the placement, size, and shape of the stones in the walkways, bridges, and areas surrounding the ponds. The style and scale of the buildings are designed to be compatible with the scale of the vegetation and trees in the shrine area. The shrines themselves are usually devoid of any ornate decoration, frequently consisting of very simple rock gardens placed behind an arch fashioned from three simple beams, with white banners hanging from the arch.

The tea gardens, another extremely important Japanese institution, again have the same emotional tone of beauty, subtlety, and peacefulness, as evidenced by carefully tended aspects of nature. The tea ceremony itself is a highly ritualized, repetitious, almost hypnotic event that goes on and on. The tea is served using gestures that are rigidly predetermined. The feeling of monotony for the Westerner is extreme, but for the Japanese participant the understanding and appreciation of the skill with which the movements are performed transcends the boredom.

Thus, *Shibui* art is lacking in strong contrasts or active temporal variations in any sense modality. In fact, according to traditional Japanese cultural and aesthetic precepts, garish or extreme color combinations or loudness of voice (both of which can be highly arousing) are considered signs of bad taste and poor breeding. The *Shibui* art forms are appreciated for their subtlety rather than the sudden arousal value associated with much Western art. Incidentally, the appreciation of this subtlety has traditionally been part of the sophistication available only to the wealthier groups. As a consequence, some of the most important aspects of high-status culture—for example, the architecture of the home or the garden, the prized possessions—have not been readily evident to the poorer masses. Thus, the Japanese home and its furnishings seem to lack the obviously discrepant levels of conspicuous consumption that often characterize differences between the homes of the wealthy and the poor in Western cultures. These differences have tended to express themselves, however, in other, often brutal, ways.

Many other aspects of traditional Japanese taste can be seen as being heavily influenced by *Shibui* art. For example, the most common pet in Japan is the carp, not the dog or cat as in the West. The graceful, gliding, and peaceful movements of the carp are far more conducive to a feeling of low arousal and pleasure than are the more jarring and noisy movements of some Western pets. Traditional Japanese clothing tends to be rather uniform, thus providing little variation in basic design or in color. Even the bolts of cloth from which the kimonos or yukatas are made are of uniform width and both of these garments are made without modifying the width of the cloth—without cutting it to a narrower width before preparation of the garment. Slippers used to be made only in one size for males and in a second size for females. Even today one is likely to have trouble finding slippers differing in size in the smaller towns of Japan. Japanese habits in relation to their environments and travel tend to emphasize low arousal. Their homes are very simple, without elaborate variation in color and design; however, there is a hint of subtle elegance in the traditional ikebana arrangement placed in one corner of the living room.

All these facets of Japanese art and general aesthetic appreciation point to an insistence on pleasant low loads in their art forms and in related aspects of their lives. One way to understand this definite preference is in terms of the physiological makeup of the Japanese, who tend to be nonscreeners. And Japan is of course an extremely competitive and crowded nation. The high load of crowding and the often unpleasant consequences of extreme competition, when combined with the national trend toward nonscreening, help explain the general preference for low environmental loads and the reverence for art forms which are low on load and high on pleasure (peaceful, relaxing).

Incidentally, even though the Chinese live in comparably crowded environments, they do differ considerably from the Japanese in terms of their screening. The Japanese show a much greater postural tension and muscle tone which clearly indicates heightened arousal in relation to the Chinese. The Chinese have a freer, looser posture, with many more sweeping or relaxed gestures. Compare, for example, Chou En-lai's loose-wristed, graceful gestures and often slouchy posture while seated with any of the Japanese leaders, including the somewhat westernized and ebullient Tanaka. The Chinese also happen to have a generally more cooperative and less competitive set of social traditions compared with the Japanese. This, and their tendency toward higher levels of screening, explains the absence among the Chinese of continued pressures to reduce environmental loads. The traditional Chinese art forms do not necessarily rely on the extremely subtle, quiet, and peaceful qualities that are so characteristic in Japan. In a related area, Chinese festivities are frequently characterized by considerable noise, color, and movement, as are many of their less public social occasions, which frequently involve group gambling. Banquets held for weddings, birthdays, and other special occasions generally involve gambling which contributes to even higher arousal levels. A special form of gambling accompanies each festival, like the New Year or Moon Festival. The gambling is sometimes a family activity in which children participate alongside their parents. During the Moon Festival, for instance, the whole family plays a game of dice to see who can win the most moon cakes.

Aside from a person's cultural membership, his level of sophistication can also influence his preference for certain load levels in art. Students of art are more likely to show preference for more complex or less predictable displays. Such persons, as a result of their familiarity with a wide range of art objects, experience a lower load from a very complex piece of art than do inexperienced or infrequent visitors to art exhibits. Thus, if he is to excite the knowledgeable in art, an artist must strive for a degree of novelty and complexity in his work that might involve too much load for the uninitiated. On the other hand, if the artist wishes to enhance his mass appeal, he must use familiar themes or subjects, and arrange his displays in combinations that are extremely pleasant but low-load (simple and familiar). Needless to say, popular art forms that are successful with both sophisticated and unsophisticated audiences have effected ingenious compromises that manage to satisfy or please—elicit approach from—both groups. A work of art that over time arouses and pleases only the naive will not survive, because the naive are for the most part not the curators and preservers of culture in the elitist sense. They have more pressing survival needs which legitimately demand to be met, and if it means making a tent or a poncho out of an El Greco canvas, so be it. But all truly sophisticated people possess—and recognize that they possess—naive emotional needs. If an art work fails to arouse them, it too will be ignored or used for something better or more satisfying, or be consigned to nonattention.

One of the oldest debates among serious art appreciators is whether functional objects may be considered legitimate art forms. To consider this issue, we must go back to the notion of art as an endeavor which seeks to explore or has the effect of exploring a wide range of human emotionality and emotional expression. Functional art, like nonfunctional or theoretical science, necessitates a restriction in the realm of emotions, and consequently imposes a restriction on artistic expression. For example, if a creative artist designs a chair, he will not want it to be uncomfortable (unpleasant and also excessively arousing). It cannot for instance consist of very stiff protrusions and nail-like objects which would arouse the body to a high degree and also create unease and feelings of displeasure. In that form, it would not be a chair in the usual sense, but would be something else—a rare instrument of torture. Thus, functional pieces, which may be designed and made by fine craftsmen whose skills are comparable to those of the finest artists, are bound to involve certain restrictions. Usually, the arousal level elicited by functional crafts cannot be too high; they must elicit a feeling of dominance (one can use them for something), and they must elicit feelings of pleasure. Functional objects that are aesthetically appealing often no longer possess a real function, like nineteenth-century dueling pistols or even powerful, aesthetically appealing sports cars, which must be driven to the supermarket according to the same rules governing a boxy old passenger sedan.

Another issue in the definition of art forms is the question of permanence. Are sand castles built at the beach worthy of being considered art when we know that their life span is necessarily limited to a day? And what about paintings drawn on sidewalks or on the exteriors of buildings, where wear and weathering will limit their life span? In one sense, the permanence of an art form is irrelevant as a factor in determining whether it is art or nonart. Lack of permanence does not limit the emotional range and emotional impact which can be achieved by art. Indeed, the transitory quality of an aesthetic experience is an element which is likely to add to its uncertainty and consequently to its impact. This is one of the things that makes a sunset, or for that matter an aerobatic show by a perfectly coordinated Blue Angels squadron of Navy jets, a profound aesthetic experience. The onlooker is likely to be more aroused and to appreciate the spectacle more because he knows it won't last long and that its recurrence for him is very uncertain. Similarly, a sand castle or a display of fireworks which is bound to come to a quick end may have a greater initial impact than an art work displayed in a museum that has survived 1,000 years and can last quite a bit longer.

On the other hand, we human beings tend to respect time, even if only because each of us has so little of it. We are awed by, or tend at least to treat in a gingerly manner, things that have lasted a long time. Human artifacts have survived for the most part because somebody made an effort to preserve them; whether that effort was motivated by greed, hostility, love, or respect doesn't really matter in the long run. One of Oscar Wilde's aperçus goes something like this: a thing is not necessarily true because a man dies for it.* Such

* From page 194 of A. Redman's *The Portrait of Mr. W. H.* Reprinted by permission of the publisher, Dover Publications, Inc. © 1959.

an assertion tends to be shocking, because ultimately many people obscurely and perhaps rightly believe the opposite to be true: an idea or an artifact that has come down to us like a proud or wayward family gene does acquire stature and does acquire a somewhat disproportionate value. And so a sand castle that has been preserved since 500 B.C. through diligence, love, superstition, or worship will inevitably be valued more highly than a sand castle we build today and aggressively protect from today's high tide, yet with few regrets relinquish to tomorrow's.

Suggested Readings

See the following sources for data and general psychological analyses of art: Berlyne (1972), Child (1968), Hogg (1969), and Valentine (1968). Srivastava and Peel (1968) conducted the study in which museumgoers' pace was affected by the color of the walls.

22

Inside Books

IF you arrive early at a party whose host has a large personal library, and there are a lot of bookshelves in the rooms in which most of the socializing will take place, observe the guests as they come in, especially if a group of them enter at the same time. At least one of the guests may make a rather awkward or self-conscious entry, spot the books, and head for them eagerly, almost aggressively, head cocked sideways to read the titles, hands jammed into the pockets. He will largely ignore the other guests, as though they were distinctly less interesting than the rows of books and as though much more of importance might be learned about the host from scanning his library than by talking directly to him.

In this chapter I hope to discuss briefly magazines, textbooks, novels, and poetry under the general rubric of "books," and to make certain generalizations about all of these. The bookish person at the party will serve to illustrate some of these ideas. In relation to other entertainment media and loaded (uncertain, novel, unpredictable, or complex) environments involving social interaction, books usually provide lower loads and heighten feelings of dominance. I don't mean to suggest that books are always low-load; if they were, there would be no such thing as best sellers. But books—almost any kind—are familiar to bookish people. Most truly experienced readers can tell by examining the first paragraphs of a novel whether the author has talent, what his models are, and, within fairly narrow limits, how this particular book relates to the known universe of other books. There is nothing mysterious about this, any more than there is anything mysterious about a jeweler who can pick up a precious stone and assess its value within fairly narrow limits with his naked eye. But even an exciting (loaded and pleasurable) book with deep, complex, rare, or surprising style or contents is not likely to have the same load as a party of friends and strangers. Books, especially unillustrated ones, provide only limited visual stimulation. They don't move, make sounds, or give off odors. They can't wound you with an unkind remark, refuse to go home with you, prefer another reader to you, or press you with demands for attention, approval, or difficult decisions. And they can't respect you, like you, laugh at your jokes, touch you, or make love with you.

This is not to say that bookish people invariably prefer to experience life secondhand, or after it has been shorn of most of the stimuli associated with personal interaction; nor does it mean that any dreary old cocktail party will inevitably be more stimulating and personally rewarding than a good book. But there are many, many times in the life of a bookish person when he chooses—almost under duress—to read a book rather than to interact socially, because he has learned that social interaction will cause him to feel highly aroused, highly unpleasant, highly submissive, or all three at the same time.

The pleasure dimension vis-à-vis reading books is more problematic in the sense that it is more variable. Something you are reading (or writing) can produce feelings of extreme pleasure or extreme displeasure. But unless you are forced by outside pressures to read something disagreeable, you retain a sense of dominance; this means that you can, at the very least, close the book. If you are very aroused and very displeased by what you are reading (or writing), you'll usually still remain dominant, which means you can throw the book against the wall, kick it across the floor, or even burn it. There are documented cases—I'm thinking particularly of the poet Hart Crane— in which writers have been so displeased at their progress and yet have felt so dominant that typewriters bearing the offending (blank) page have been hurled through windows.

Perhaps this is the point at which to indulge in some speculation about why people write books. It makes no significant difference what sort of books we're talking about—whether they're six-page, single-spaced memos addressed to one's corporate superiors, or a great play, poem, or novel addressed to one's social superiors, to one's Muse, or to the ages. It seems that a large percentage of important authors in the realms of literature and science display—in their lives or in their works, and usually in both—"symptoms" consonant with dominance and nonscreening.

Consider the three persons whose published ideas have probably had more impact on twentieth-century Western culture than anybody else's—Einstein, Freud, and Marx. All three can probably be considered "scientists" despite the fact that they developed ideas that were not in toto or even largely verifiable at the time in which they wrote. All three were synthesizers, thinkers who pulled together large numbers of ideas and data that were floating around and imposed comprehensive patterns upon them. These theories may disappear through inutility, but have not to this date been replaced by ideational structures having the same scale or power to compel.

The scientific urge to impose order upon large amounts of otherwise intimidating and seemingly disconnected data is characteristic of dominant nonscreeners who find chaotic and disorganized phenomena both unpleasant and overly arousing. That is, it is an urge to reduce the arousing effect of unpleasant complexity and uncertainty by imposing patterns upon it—which is also part of a characteristic urge to dominate. This is especially true of Einstein who spent the last forty or so years of his professional life fighting certain literal uncertainty data and theories growing out of his own work. Einstein responded both to Heisenberg and to the failure of his own attempts to develop a unified field theory by saying, "God is clever, but not malicious," or "God doesn't play dice with the universe," meaning that there must be a set of overarching physical rules that govern the behavior of the microcosm and the macrocosm, and that nothing is random. Freud's basic premise too was that nothing humans do is accidental or random—everything is determined. Most novelists, whether celebrated or unknown, seem to be guided by the same beliefs, at least to the extent that nothing can be random in their own works. Many of these authors feel compelled to dominate not only their own characters—whom they can literally kill off when and in what manner they choose—but also physical reality. By describing something in precisely the right terms, the writer not only dominates his medium but also in some semi-primitive way ensnares, uses up, and kills off parts of the observed world. Once a writer has, for example, exactly "caught" a squirrel hopping across a suburban lawn, chances are that another one will never hop through his work; and he may in fact cease to observe squirrels carefully in real life. Extremely conscious verbal artists like John Updike and Vladimir Nabokov have often been quite explicit on this point, as have a host of minor academic novelists who fail to produce any significant verbal artifacts and yet get all hung-up on the effects upon themselves of doing literature.

There are real satisfactions associated with authorship, quite apart from financial rewards or other forms of approval. I remember congratulating a poet once upon the publication of his first volume of verse. He grinned and told me that one's first book was "like having your first woman." For an author, no matter what his or her genre or subject matter—be it a manual on how to raise radishes organically, an epic poem on the subject of Lithuanian forests, or a short story about a man who gets shot by his wife on a hunting trip—there are moments during composition, while correcting galleys, or when the bound books arrive from the publisher that combine high arousal, high pleasure, and high dominance in ways as to be comparable with other rare triumphal experiences—great sex, a great meal, a great personal victory in sports or war.

The idea that "all art is miniaturization" goes a long way toward explaining the talismanic, magical quality associated with certain forms of literature, especially with poetry and the novel. If magic is designed to give those adept in it a certain amount of control (dominance) over what would otherwise be an uncommandable sea of phenomena, we can understand why, for example, novels that "create a world"—and contain that world in a relatively small physical object—are among the most popular and cherished by readers in any genre. When people say that the novel is dead, they mean, I think, two things: first, that there have been few contemporary serious novels that have been able to miniaturize large physical and temporal chunks of reality; and second, that some if not all the special techniques employed by early twentieth-century masters have been taken about as far as they can go. Some contemporary experimental works have in fact made the world of the novel more complex and unpredictable (loaded) than the real world; they have failed to give pleasure and have induced submissive feelings in all but those few readers who have devoted their professional careers to the exploration and explication of these works. But the novel is not dead; it has simply gone elsewhere—to unusual locations and professions where it is still possible for talented authors, as opposed to towering geniuses, to provide readers with a sense of place and time and a small but distinctive "world." It is no accident that many recent best-selling novels have been historical in nature, or have involved unusual and narrowly circumscribed professions (politicians, spies, criminals, bacteriologists), or that detective and science fiction stories have continued to be written and have in fact enjoyed a modest renaissance. If you examine, for example, the science fiction novels which have received the big awards or have sold extremely well, you will find that most of them are "big" books; that is, they attempt, with varying degrees of success, to deal with enormous themes, not excluding the birth and death of the human species or of the universe itself. I'm thinking of *Childhood's End, Foundation Trilogy, Perelandra Trilogy, Cities in Flight*, and *Dune* and am also including in this category *The Lord of the Rings*. I'm not suggesting that such novels have more merit than *Clarissa*, works by Dickens, Conrad, or Henry James, or *La Comédie Humaine, À la Récherche du Temps Perdu, The Gift, Ulysses* or *Finnegans Wake*, or *Der Zauberberg*, but that some of the impulses of their authors are the same—to dominate materials of enormous scope. These motives and rewards are shared by readers as well— they too feel that they have incorporated and, to a certain extent, dominated huge portions of the real or imagined universe.

Poetry, one of the oldest art forms, is as inexhaustible a subject as that of language itself. One might even suggest that poetry is the research lab of human language in the same sense, perhaps, that certain forms of higher mathematics provide the laboratory setting in which human cognitive abilities are experimented with, or as atomic accelerators play with the essential constituents of matter. Be that as it may, we can say that poetry—spanning a verbal universe containing everything from nursery rhymes and limericks to proverbs and forms of spoken or written language in which word associations and syntax are so decontrolled as to resemble the associative babblings of certain kinds of schizophrenics—achieves many of its effects by manipulating the various elements that comprise environmental load. That is, in "primitive" poetry, pattern, repetition, similarities, and predictability play an important role: rhyme, meter, stanzaic constraints, and so on, are uppermost. This explains why poetry was the principal medium for the transmission of culture before written records were widely used: it was easier to remember. Even today, people tend to remember things by putting information in essentially poetic forms of language. Someone who has to remember which way the one-way streets run in Manhattan is likely to remind himself that "east is even," meaning that even-numbered streets run from west to east. The patterns, both oral and visual, are far more likely to be readily grasped and retained than the prosaic "odd-numbered streets run from east to west." It is interesting and significant that young children learning their mother tongue often make errors that adults find delightful without realizing why. These errors usually result from the child's attempt to impose regularity or pattern upon language in places where it departs from pattern. A child will say "foots" for feet, or "falled down" instead of fell down, trying to form the regular plural or the past tense by the normal addition of *s* or *ed*. Children also derive a great deal of pleasure from the congruence of sounds (rhyme), a delight that seemingly survives in most adults as a love-hate for puns, or occasionally in the form of laughter at a foreign name or word possessing completely different vowel-consonant combinations than those they are used to. But it also survives in some adults as a love of poetry, especially the kind that has a regular rhythm and rhyme scheme, lots of alliteration, and perhaps a heavy dose of sentiment. Other adults who strenuously deny that they have the least bit of interest in literature can still quote gobs of Kipling, Poe, or Edgar Guest with great pleasure and accuracy.

As poetry becomes more complex and significant, the regularities —rhyme, meter, and so on—become less salient and are increasingly warred against by verbal combinations that are novel, surprising, and complex. Syntax becomes disjointed or almost nonexistent. Key words are allowed to resonate in such a way that semantic associations are decontrolled.*

What the great poets do is provide artifacts (poems) combining lines or images of enormous complexity with certain intense verbal regularities and patterns (meter, an occasional surprising rhyme) that not only impose and betoken enormous constraint, but also provide experienced readers with great pleasure and in a way confer upon those who recite these lines a sense of almost talismanic dominance. Parties at which after several hours of fairly hard drinking only a handful of hard-core literati remain, almost invariably lead to recitations from memory of certain peak literary experiences—something

---

* To take a simple example, the word *chest* may be used so that it is no longer contextually controlled to mean a box that things are locked in. The difference between the sentences "Long John Silver buried his chest twenty paces NW of a stone thirty paces above high tide on Long Island" and "Long John Silver / his chest full / augered the beach" is that *chest* in the latter instance can now mean not only a treasure chest but also Long John Silver's rib cage, which may be full of other things—sorrow, years, an enlarged heart, and so on. In other words, there is a quantum jump in complexity.

from *The Wind in the Willows* or the last sentence of *The Wings of the Dove* or *Under Western Eyes*. And then, one is bound to get the last lines of "Sailing to Byzantium," "Among School Children," "Little Gidding," "The Domination of Black," or even "Dover Beach." To watch such people declaiming, with faces flushed, eyes gleaming, bodies tense—often struggling to rise from their chairs; their voices sharp, controlled, and rising; their cigarettes, drinks, or lousy sex lives utterly forgotten—is something both to be cherished and wondered at. That a dozen or so lines of drab little printed symbols should confer upon otherwise ordinary people such arousal, such pleasure, and such dominance can cause one who doesn't share such feelings a moment of real unease—perhaps the same sort of fear that led unlettered Anglo-Saxons to derive the word *glamor* (mystery) from the word *grammar*.

The failure of nonliterary types to like, appreciate, or otherwise respond positively to significant novels or poetry, or indeed to any complex and difficult subject matter, is of course the bane of teachers. Experienced teachers wisely avoid authoritarian encounters with their students about "who is the greater poet, Wallace Stevens or Rod McKuen?" Instead, they patiently work with McKuen as though he were in fact a poet, and let their own love of Stevens shine through as a beacon. Such teachers have intuitively grasped certain important environmental principles, and know that to arbitrarily insist upon the high value of their beloved subject matter is simply to increase both the displeasure and submissiveness of their students, thus making the learning environment less conducive to approach or improved performance.

Any subject matter that is perceived to be complex, novel, unfamiliar, incomprehensible, or literally meaningless will be too arousing and unpleasant to cause approach. Anything that is too simple, familiar, trite, or old-hat will also not elicit approach—it will be dismissed as boring. The art of teaching is, in essence, similar to many other acts of persuasion or entertainment—one must provide enough novelty but also enough familiarity to make the content moderately arousing. The arousal levels one can demand (or which correspond to maximum approach by the student) increase proportionately with the pleasure one provides through jokes, displays of affection, respect, or whatever for one's students or paying customers.

Almost all successful artfulness—teaching, popular forms of entertainment, selling cars, soap, new tax legislation, or defending a client in a courtroom—follow this formula. High art, extremely complex forms of scientific thought, or complicated, specialized bodies of law also follow this formula, but the complexity baseline is simply displaced upwards as a result of the expertise of a specialized audience —that is, the audience, as a result of its greater familiarity with the subject, can tolerate higher loads at the same pleasure levels. This is why, for example, all elementary textbooks in any field tend to be illustrated profusely and colorfully, whereas at graduate or specialist levels they tend not to be. The illustrations are there not so much because they are more arousing (they provide more stimulation, but usually of familiar things and thus with little net increase in load), but because they increase pleasure levels. If you look at a typical elementary-grade social studies text, for example, you will find that it contains pleasant photographs of kids playing or doing ordinary kinds of things, not photographs of unusual events. As the grade level goes up, the illustrations become more loaded (partly because the text does not) and include unusual old prints, historic art photos, and so on.

General magazines as opposed to more specialized ones also tend to be interestingly illustrated. General news magazines like *Time* or *Newsweek* have loaded, grabby covers and also are fairly heavily illustrated—they aim for high pleasure and high arousal. More specialized news magazines like *The New Republic, American Opinion*, or the various journals devoted to foreign policy, government, and so on, are not as preoccupied with the pleasure dimension and tend to be sparsely illustrated, containing at most a couple of cartoons. Sometimes an economic factor is involved; to be profitable, specialized magazines such as *Golf Today, Psychology Today*, or *Tractors Today* tend to offer a loaded, colorful, usually pleasing bonus to their readers (and can also accept glossy, four-color advertisements from car or liquor manufacturers). The latter is a must for general magazines, which operate on the assumption that the load baseline of their readership is popular rather than expert—higher pleasure levels being required for the same load by the popular than by the expert reader. Popular magazines therefore keep articles short, edit them in an informal or jazzy tone, lay them out so that someone thumbing through the magazine will find lots of punchy headlines, a number of front-page spreads rather than one article which he must read through before coming to another one, and so on. More specialized magazines assume a great deal of interest on the part of their readers and are designed differently and more economically. The style in which articles are written or edited is also different. In specialized magazines, the author is recognized by at least some of the readership; the response is likely to be "Aha, let's see what so-and-so is saying now." In general magazines, on the other hand, the authorship is less important, and articles tend to be set up in a way as to upend the usual reportorial model. That is, in newspaper journalism, the classic way to set up a story is to give the gist of the story, then some details, and then some further human interest minutiae, on the assumption that the city desk will cut from the bottom up, and that subscribers will read from the top down. In general interest magazines, the author or editor will begin with some human interest details to catch the attention of the reader, next get into the meat of the article, and then progress to details of background, qualification, or whatever. Again the assumption is that the editor will cut from the bottom up, but the secondary assumption is that the first paragraphs have to grab the reader, not so much in terms of the facts, but rather in terms of familiar human experience.

When we talk about plots in fiction we are also talking about the foundations or overall structures of a story. All writers must assume that the reader will find the plot reasonably familiar, since there are only so many ways to build a foundation. Much experimental fiction expends a great deal of ingenuity and energy disguising or exploding the plot, much as a good deal of modern music avoids melody, which is another form of horizontal (temporal) organization. The result in both cases is that the art work is too unfamiliar (too loaded) and also usually lacks pleasure-giving elements. Detective or spy fiction is a specialized genre that deliberately plays a game with the plot, concealing its true outlines and yet offering the reader clues by which he may indeed predict the outcome in very narrow terms—such as identify the villain. Most successful detective-fiction plots are built on an arousal pattern similar to that found in a well-planned concert. That is, fairly quickly a high-load event takes place—for example, a murder—and then there is a period of a certain amount of low-load consolidation, in which characters, locale, and so forth, are set up. The reader is given some sort of experimental base upon which to solve the crime itself, or at least to develop plausible, if mistaken, hypotheses. Thereafter, the amount of information and hence arousal level slowly rises toward a climax, the peak occurring near or at the very end of the book. Successful plots do not defy analysis, but unsuccessful ones positively beg for it. Unsuccessful detective fiction either provides obvious clues, so that the reader has figured out the plot long before he has finished the book, or else—as is far more common—there is so much uncertainty that the reader cannot possibly "solve." This excess load usually occurs in two places: very early on, so that the reader becomes too aroused at the beginning of the book and cannot sustain this level throughout, or else at the very end of the book. In the last few pages the load (in the form of clues) increases at such a rapid rate that the reader feels that he has been cheated—given information necessary to solve the crime which should have been presented earlier, in smaller doses, so that it could have been absorbed or weighed.

Pacing—how quickly information is presented to the reader—is thus another aspect of a book's load and is something all good novelists instinctively vary. There are many ways in which this is done, but one of the standard ways is through conversation, even the traditional "he said," "she said" variety. You will usually find that writers instinctively place conversations at the most dramatic moments in a plot, and that these very loaded moments are usually preceded by several long paragraphs or pages of exposition which function as stage directions. Conversation, when it is skillfully done (and does not for example come from indistinct characters serving as mouthpieces for the author's views) can represent an enormously rich or loaded medium for the reader. One can tell immediately a great deal about characters from what they say and how they say it. Good novelists are aware of the research finding that people are the single greatest source of arousal for other people and instinctively give us human voices when we are threatening to drown in descriptions of flowers, apartments, streets, or squirrels hopping across lawns.

Suggested Readings

See Munsinger and Kessen (1964) for findings on preferences for written material of varying complexity. Bellugi and Brown (1964) provided analyses of children's grammatical errors. For data and general analyses of people's preferences of things varying in pleasantness and load, see Mehrabian and Russell (1975b).

23

Bars and Restaurants

LORD BYRON may have been exaggerating when he wrote that man, being reasonable, must get drunk.* Nevertheless, drink-oriented establishments are important social environments fulfilling a wide range of human needs. In pre-Prohibition America, for example, working-class bars often served as centers of ward politics—a man could get a free (though often salty) lunch with his beer, could blow off steam, and could talk to the Man about a job for himself or for his cousin, newly arrived from the old country. Today's midtown watering hole—in which the commuter stops by for a few quick ones before catching the 6:17, nibbles on high-protein hors d'oeuvres, unwinds with friends, and catches up on the latest industry gossip—fulfills a like function.

There were restaurants in the city of Ur in the year 2100 B.C. These restaurants were actually market stalls where people could buy food that they were too poor, too busy, too hot, or too lazy to prepare for themselves. Today's restaurants, whether they be a Jack-in-the-Box or a Lutèce, offer the same basic convenience. But the act of sharing a meal, whether of barbecued frankfurters or paté de foie gras, has always had important social implications. And in Western societies at least, sharing a meal has usually also meant sharing something alcoholic to drink—mead, Coors from paper cups, or Château Haut-Brion. In the United States, bars and restaurants often have a certain connection with each other—a connection in some cases imposed

* From Canto II, Stanza 179, of Lord Byron's *Don Juan*. Reprinted by permission of the publisher, Random House, Inc. © 1951.

by state or municipal statutes requiring that bars offer some sort of food, or imposed by an informal operation of the marketplace requiring that restaurants invest in beer or liquor licenses to ensure their profitability. And of course many restaurant owners have found that a large, comfortable, well-stocked bar with generous bartenders contributes substantially to their trade, or that the three-martini lunch is among their chief moneymakers.

But for every successful restaurant there are three or four failures. There can be two bars on the same block, one doing a booming business and the other verging on bankruptcy. What are the environmental factors that make for a successful bar or restaurant? One way to answer such a question might be to set ourselves a design problem, namely, to design an establishment containing a hypothetically ideal bar and restaurant.

Let's stipulate that our hypothetical establishment must be open for business from 11:00 A.M. until 3:00 A.M., seven days a week. It must cater to a large luncheon crowd from 11:00 A.M. to 3:00 P.M. This luncheon crowd, most of it deriving from neighboring office buildings, includes expense-account people seeking to flatter, impress, or otherwise deal with important clients; secretaries and other office personnel looking for a place to get a decent lunch at a reasonable price or an interesting place to share a meal with friends; and local construction workers looking for the same things.

There will be an après-work crowd from 4:00 to 7:00 P.M., including blue-collar workers, the commuter set, and lower-level corporate personnel who, depending on their mood, may be eager to rub elbows with either of the other groups.

There will be a dinner crowd from about 6:00 to 12:00 P.M., including those seeking the privilege of truly elegant and fastidious dining, those who have come hungry and excited from the theatre, and those for whom an evening meal out is convenient or mandatory for one reason or another.

There will be a fun crowd from about 10:00 P.M. till closing. This crowd will include the bored but prosperous plumber's apprentice and the equally bored but rather strapped junior executive. It will include the eighteen-year-old who is surly and stiff because he or she doesn't know any better, and those half a century older who are ungracious because they do. It will include the boisterous and the aggressive, the lonely and the shy, and all the other needy ones. It will include those who are blind-dating, and those who are accompanied by their husbands or wives of twenty-seven years. It will include those who want to get out of the house for a little peace and quiet, and those who are being driven up the wall by peace and quiet.

How does one create a place—an environment—for all these different people with their manifold needs and wants? It is likely that, given such a design problem, the environmental psychologist will approach it in a spirit of humility and suggest that the ideal bar-restaurant, perhaps like an ideal church, will be a house of many mansions—a place containing many environments in which people may be secure, comfortable, or happy according to their needs.

Our ideal establishment will be constructed according to several rules-of-thumb with which you are already familiar. The first of these rules is that the various environments in our establishment must all cause approach, meaning, in this case, that people will enter, stay a while, enjoy themselves, and spend money in the process. The second rule is that people come from environments and activities widely differing in load and may require recreational environments that compensate for the varying loads of their work settings. Thus our ideal establishment will consist of environments that range from the highly loaded and extremely arousing to the slightly loaded and relaxing.

At the high-load extreme, there should be a large dancing bar featuring 120-decibel acid rock, strobe lights, and a laughing, pushing, shouting, sweating mob. There might be smaller rooms off the main dance floor featuring a variety of raucous, surprising, or wicked entertainments that push to the limits of the so-called community standard. Since novelty contributes significantly to load, these smaller rooms and entertainments could be changed frequently. The strobe-light patterns and colors could be kaleidoscopic, and films might be projected on the walls or onto the crowd to increase the sensory over-load. It is important that liquor be easily obtained at many points throughout this bar, because many patrons will feel a strong need to lower their arousal levels in order to make such an extremely loaded environment a tolerable one, especially early in the experience. It would be a great mistake to place a main bar right by the dancing floor and force hundreds of patrons to compete for the attention of four or five bartenders. Rather, there should be many smaller, well-manned bars placed along the periphery or in convenient, some-what less loaded alcoves. Patrons needing a drink will be seeking to lower their arousal levels, and a hopelessly crowded bar may constitute the straw that causes an arousal overload and hence avoidance of the entire environment.

At the opposite end of the environmental load spectrum, there should be a separate, quiet, clublike bar with comfortable armchairs placed in such a way as to ensure privacy or minimize personal interaction. The decor should include carpeting, many plants, magazine and newspaper racks, and a lamp for each armchair or small conversational grouping. There should be no music at all, or else something very low and restful. The waiters should be modestly if not drably uniformed, not startlingly interesting in appearance or manner, and should accommodate the needs of their patrons quietly and quickly.

Both the dancing bar—which we might call The Crazy Place— and the clublike or living room-like bar—let's call it The Sitting Room —are highly specialized environments. The former is deliberately designed in such a way that it might, in laboratory miniature, drive experimental animals mad; the latter might easily cause them to doze. Yet it is entirely possible that both The Crazy Place and The Sitting Room could represent ideal environments for the same person on the same day.

Take for example a young businessman whose day has gone something like this: He's had to conduct several delicate interviews with a number of people he'd never met before; he's had to make several important decisions on the basis of insufficient data; sales were down today and hence the boss has been prowling the office in a kick-the-dog mood; a valued subordinate has presented him with a hairy personnel problem; new carpet was being laid in the office, so half his files were stacked in cartons in a corner; late in the afternoon his wife called to say that somehow all her credit cards were missing from her purse.

This man has had an extremely loaded day. His arousal level has remained so high for so long that a GAS reaction is beginning to set in. He can't face the rush hour. In his highly aroused condition, the lemminglike comings and goings, and the grotesquely crowded and noisy subway will be too much. His arousal level will be sustained beyond the breaking point, fatigue will set in with a vengeance, and he will arrive home wrung out and in no shape to enjoy the Ortizes, with whom he and his wife have planned an evening out. So instead of going straight home, our man pops over to The Sitting Room, flips through the latest issue of *The New Yorker*, reading only the cartoons and the ad copy, and even takes a short nap. The private, restful atmosphere and the nap combine to lower his arousal to the point where he feels like getting up and about; the now slightly less hectic subway ride will in no way overstimulate him.

He arrives home. He and his wife talk sensibly about the stolen credit cards. He showers, changes, and they go out for a bite at a neighborhood restaurant, where they meet the Ortizes and then go to a movie, which proves to be rather boring. All four then repair to a local pub for a beer, which for some reason is empty. The quiet dinner, the boring movie, the empty pub, and the now lagging conversation have brought arousal levels to the point where some interesting stimulus is sought and accepted in the form of, "Let's all be trashy and go to The Crazy Place." They all go trooping off to this new environment and enjoy it because the noise, the lights, the mob, the porn, or whatever, do not constitute overload but rather an acceptable increase in arousal level. After an hour or so of dancing, drinking, and getting spaced, arousal levels begin to fall again as everybody gets tired, and they all leave for home.

Although The Sitting Room and The Crazy Place have entirely different load characteristics, they do share one element of environmental design: neither is set up to encourage interaction among strangers. The widely spaced armchairs and muffled, library-like atmosphere of The Sitting Room clearly encourage subdued and solitary behavior. The noise level and the self-absorbed, manic crowd at The Crazy Place also discourage the tentative, exploratory conversations which lead to companionship among people who have never seen each other before. At best, The Crazy Place is only good for a quick pickup, based on a shouted "Let's get outta this madhouse!"

Therefore, our hypothetical establishment should contain a bar specifically designed to make it easy for strangers to meet, talk, and decide that they like each other enough to do something about it. In a perhaps regrettable excess of sentiment, let's call this bar One Enchanted Evening, or The Evening for short. The Evening cannot be a high-load bar, nor can it be radically low-load. Ideally, it should be sort of lower-middlish. There should be music so that awkward or abrupt lulls in conversation will be masked. The music should be constant, but not loud, dissonant, or completely unfamiliar, which means that there should be a good selection of "oldies but goodies." The lighting should be somewhat muted but not too dim, so that people will neither feel that every wrinkle in their suits or in themselves will be highlighted nor feel so deprived of visual cues that they become wary or uneasy. The general decor should be Standard Bar, or even somewhat on the old-fashioned side, so that people will feel that the environment is basically a familiar one. It would be an error to make this environment too old-fashioned, with too much leather, frosted glass, and mahogany or polished oak, because it would then take on a perceptible upper-middle-class tone that could be inhibiting to large numbers of prospective patrons; rather, it should be perfectly vague or redolent of a wide variety of bars. People who are seeking companionship are usually fairly aroused in anticipation of strangers' unknown reactions, and it is neither necessary nor desirable to present them with a physical environment unique enough to cause additional arousal. Furthermore, there will be a few unavoidably novel elements in this strangers' bar, and these elements should be compensated for by a decor that is simple, familiar, and in general low-load.

The most novel element will be the shape of the main bar. Most barrooms have a long rectangular bar like this:

FIGURE 12

When people are seated next to each other at a bar, it is uncomfortable to turn sideways to talk to someone sitting alongside. Our experiments have shown that such side-by-side seating along a straight line discourages conversation among strangers. This is why, when all the bar stools are occupied, most of the animated conversation usually goes on at the corners. People who are seated at right angles will talk to each other more than if they are seated side-by-side. You will notice too that the bartender, if he is sociable, will tend to gravitate toward the corner, unless the cash register or the well is placed in the middle of the bar so that he must walk back and forth a great deal from the corners. Good bartenders function partly as hosts; they can be very helpful in starting or carrying conversations, and tend to move to those areas where this function can be performed most economically.

You will also notice that in barrooms that have both a long bar and a smaller, circular piano bar, there is more animated and friendly conversation at the smaller bar, especially when the performer is taking a break. This happens because the lines of communication—particularly nonverbal communication in the form of a smile, nod, or gesture—are far more open and complex at the smaller bar.

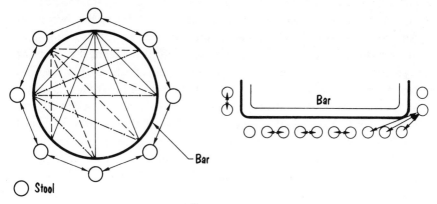

FIGURE 13

For The Evening, we want a bar that enables people to take a seat with a minimum of anxiety and self-consciousness and, more importantly, one which enables them to face others and gives them a chance to talk to more than the person on their immediate right or left. The following zigzag bar accomplishes this.

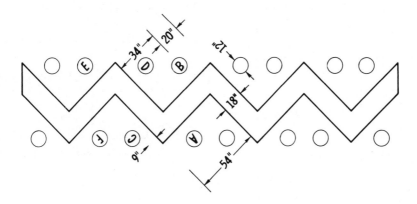

FIGURE 14

Each bar stool should swivel, thus enhancing a patron's ability to face and talk with at least three others and usually more than that. The traditional long mirror, designed to increase the drinker's field of vision, but frequently reinforcing his self-consciousness and sense of isolation, would of course be eliminated.

A personal-interaction bar like The Evening should not contain separate tables. Research has shown that people will not sit at a partially occupied table unless the pressures are quite intense, or unless there has been an unmistakable signal from the occupant. Among strangers, such a signal is not likely to be forthcoming, and in its absence, people do not risk a violation of someone's privacy or rejection in one form or another. It is conceivable then that the first two people who enter The Evening would sit quite far from each other at the zigzag bar, but after a while when the place starts to fill up, people would have to sit in positions such that they would face each other with only a small swiveling adjustment. Each person sitting at a given point would have the option of talking to at least four different persons: person C could readily talk to persons B, D, E, and A, or even swivel about to talk with person F.

When a single zigzag module is used by itself, as in the previous illustration, patrons would probably have to be served by waitresses, or possibly be accommodated by two bartenders, one on each side of the module. Alternatively, modules could be combined in some such arrangement for convenient service:

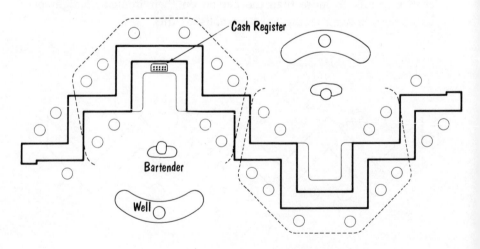

FIGURE 15

Assuming that The Evening will eventually become filled, we should take a modified leaf from the cocktail party and provide room for people to walk around and seek different conversational groupings. This space must be designed carefully, however, or people will tend to align themselves along the walls in typical wallflower fashion. Shy or insecure people tend to seek the walls in a crowded bar for a number of reasons, but do so often merely because there is some sort of benchlike seating provided where they may sit down and take stock for a moment, or at least put their drink down to light a cigarette or whatever. In The Evening, the walls should not function as a convenience or a haven encouraging immobility and insularity. Instead, small tables and banquettes would be placed away from the wall in a random pattern. People who want to set their drink down, snuff out a cigarette, or just get off their feet would therefore be forced to opt for some sort of nonlinear arrangement. Tables and chairs would be arranged so that those who might be tempted to lean against the wall would find it inconvenient and uncomfortable to do so. The tables and chairs would be simple and readily movable to encourage the formation of small informal groups and easy contacts among persons seated at different tables.

There is a second reason for the scattered arrangement of tables and chairs when we remember that an informal social environment is needed to encourage strangers to mix. An irregular arrangement of tables forces a person wanting to walk from one end of the place to the other to almost weave his way around the tables. This introduces some discomfort (insofar as efficient movement is concerned), but efficiency is not a prime consideration. What is gained, instead, is considerably more exposure and eye contact in this process of having to walk around others' tables. It also adds to the informality of the setting.

Our ideal establishment now includes three barrooms. But given the original design problem, it needs more. It needs a neighborhood bar where people who do know each other may gather for the evening. Our neighborhood bar should be designed as a pub where a great proportion of the population will feel comfortable. Most working-class pubs share one interesting feature—they have windows, suggesting an unabashed or rather social attitude toward drinking— that it is not something to be done in the dark, shielded from the eyes of passersby, the law, or the community at large. Anyone on the street can look in and see who's there and then decide whether to enter.

Most working-class barrooms tend to be fairly low-load: they are well lit, they are modest if not drab in decor, and the bar is always long and straight. The prices of drinks, always low, are often prominently displayed, so there is no uncertainty from this source. Usually there is a jukebox, but it is silent more often than not. The bar is the place for the so-called serious drinker who is someone temporarily bent on lowering his arousal.

All these features should be retained for our neighborhood bar, and added to in the following way. There should be many tables and booths of various sizes, perhaps separated from the bar proper by an eye-level partition. At these tables friends may gather over a pitcher of beer or whatever. There should also be an area for darts, pinball or bowling machines, a pool table, and perhaps a piano for patrons' use. The decor should be very simple—plain wooden tables and chairs, for example. Tables might well be provided with dishes of peanuts, pretzels, pickles, or hot peppers, since the free offering of food is a principal means of indicating both hospitality and communality. There might even be a little sawdust on the floor, suggesting, among other things, a name for our hypothetical neighborhood bar: The Sawdust. Most of the patrons would be regulars; they'd know each other and gather in the evening to drink, nibble, and amuse themselves at relatively low cost.

Ideally, The Sawdust should also contain a delicatessen-style kitchen offering inexpensive but filling food during the lunch hour and well into the evening. The simple, familiar, low-load environment, together with cheap, hearty food, will encourage a wide variety of people to approach this bar, especially during the lunch hour in the middle of a high-density business district. The construction worker will be able to enter and order a hot pastrami sandwich and a mug of beer and carry his tray to a small table to eat alone or join his co-workers at a larger one. The lab technician, programmer, or secretary can do the same.

Our hypothetical establishment now contains four bars: the extremely low-load Sitting Room, the low-load Sawdust designed principally for people who know each other, the moderately loaded Evening designed to promote comfortable social interaction among strangers, and the high-load Crazy Place. These four environments will accommodate many different kinds of people and, hopefully, meet their manifold needs.

But what about dining? What sort of restaurants should our

establishment contain? We can say that people eat out in order to take in nourishment more or less conveniently, but beyond that no really inclusive generalizations are possible. There is gourmet dining, an intensely refined sensual and aesthetic experience. There is what we might call pseudo-gourmet dining, where food is not really the central element of the experience but remains subordinate to the high-status decor, service, and inflated prices characteristic of most gourmet establishments. Then there are several varieties of eating out in which the visit to the restaurant is merely one aspect of an exciting evening and may include professional entertainment during the course of the meal. And then there are several varieties of what might be called functional eating out, in which the main purpose is to ingest food with a minimum of delay, expense, and hassle. Having lunch at our hypothetical Sawdust would fit this last category, as would a visit to Chock full o' Nuts, McDonald's, or the corner hot-dog stand.

Gourmet dining requires an environment which causes low arousal, pleasure, and feelings of dominance. Superbly prepared food lies at the heart of gourmet dining, and the environment is designed around this core. Although there are tales of smoky little hole-in-the-wall places with four rickety tables where a gum-cracking waitress slaps a magnificent *boeuf périgourdine* down in front of you, these are merely legends of high sentiment. Great food—which must start with premium-quality meats and produce which, increasingly, can only be obtained through great effort and at great expense—is almost inevitably offered in a high-status environment designed to pass inspection by those who know and demand the best.

The decor of a gourmet restaurant makes use of elements that are consistent with established good taste. This means that the tables, chairs, and other furnishings bear a family resemblance to Chippendale or Queen Anne rather than to Art Nouveau, Bauhaus, or any other style that tends to be designed for looks rather than comfort. The tables are irregularly arranged in alcoves, different rooms, or sections separated by low-level decorative partitions or planter-dividers, so as to provide privacy without isolation. Tables are widely spaced so that people may talk in normal tones, and the restaurant, even when full, does not appear crowded or sound noisy. Plants and flowers are used generously to contribute to a tranquil and pleasant background. Since diners are attuned to and can appreciate the way in which their food is displayed, this means very good lighting, white tablecloths, and relatively plain table settings. The color of the wine and the colors and textures of the various foods are enhanced when set against a white tablecloth, whereas a red tablecloth, for instance, would dull these effects. Even the plates are not cluttered with colorful and elaborate designs which would interfere with a beautiful presentation of each dish. There is no music since nothing in the environment is meant to contribute to arousal except the food and perhaps the conversation.

Because attention to detail is a crucial factor in the gourmet experience, the sight of a half-smoked cigar poking out of the pocket of the maître d'hôtel is quite enough to cause the prospective diner to sour or become intensely suspicious. Such slovenliness may mean that other details have also been neglected. This is not snobbishness on the part of the diner but rather an intense concentration upon every single perceptible detail contributing to the total experience. As an accomplished cook in his own right, the gourmet knows that his grouse may well have been dropped and kicked halfway across the kitchen floor by a waiter hissing venomously at an assistant chef. But if the waiter does not serve that fallen grouse skillfully and indeed lovingly, or if the grouse has in some way picked up an extraneous flavor, such shortcomings in the dining experience will instantly be noticed, and connected in the diner's mind with that hideous cigar.

The gourmet diner experiences a feeling of dominance in relation to the entire environment and particularly in relation to those who are serving him. There is often an elaborate and clearly defined hierarchy of personnel—maîtres d'hôtel, head waiters, senior waiters, apprentice waiters, and busboys, with the chef and sommelier occupying the somewhat ambiguous rank of all artists or artistic experts. Hierarchies are especially cherished by those who perceive themselves to be at the top, and diners are made to feel that all these people exist to serve them. Service is ideally flawless, but does not call attention to itself. Waiters instantly perceive the diners' needs; it is unthinkable that a diner should have to look around and struggle to get a waiter's attention. This would constitute a distraction from the table or the conversation and would be arousing and unpleasant.

The subtle assumptions of dominance—and these assumptions must be subtle or unspoken—are perhaps best illustrated by the fact that the service staff in first-class restaurants is almost always male, the assumption being that it is within the range of anyone's expectations to have a female serve him, but that only high-status males or females are able to exact skilled male servitude. There is, furthermore, an additional assumption that truly accomplished service is the result of a lifelong professional commitment and that only males are capable of such a commitment. Despite recent agitation in the waiters' unions, it will be very interesting to see if females are in fact absorbed into the gourmet dining environment.

Incidentally, consider the different emotional experiences of those diners in a gourmet restaurant who can readily afford it compared to those who are with some difficulty splurging on a special occasion. Unless the latter are terribly insecure, they too are apt to feel dominant. But there is a difference in the arousal levels of the two kinds of diners. Those who usually cannot afford the restaurant and who cannot ordinarily assume the dominant role experience the event as an especially significant or unusual one—for them it is highly arousing. On the other hand, those who can afford it take it in stride and experience it as something familiar and probable, therefore unarousing. As long as the restaurant is designed and managed in such a way as to heighten the pleasurable qualities of the meal, it can safely remain a preferred setting even for the aroused clientele who are having a one-time bash.

The differences between gourmet dining and what I've called pseudo-gourmet dining can be almost intangible or can be laughably great. In the latter category, I recall visiting a small restaurant in a midwestern college town which was indubitably the best for miles around. The environment was almost classic: there were but ten or twelve tables, spotless white linen tablecloths, a very good silver service and in general a well-lit, two-star French country inn decor. The waitresses were all dignified, middle-aged women who looked like retired grade-school principals. It was a cool fall day, and clam chowder was on the luncheon menu. I asked the waitress if the chowder was prepared New England-style, and she answered, with pleasing deference, "No sir, it comes from a can."

The principal difference between gourmet and pseudo-gourmet dining is, of course, the quality of the food. In many pseudo-gourmet establishments, the food is inferior to that which a somewhat inexperienced cook could produce by following a good recipe with scrupulous care. All other differences derive from this difference. The service personnel are likely to be a bit snobbish in relation to manifestly insecure patrons, as though the waiters were unable to resist displaying their superior knowledge of etiquette. On the other hand, patrons of the pseudo-gourmet establishment are likely to revel in the dominance aspects of their dining experience, and are more likely to assert rather than simply assume their superior position. In truly great restaurants there is often an underlying sense of communion between service personnel and patrons, a sort of mystique or acknowledgment that both share a commitment to an almost impossibly high standard. In the pseudo-gourmet establishment, this sense of a shared mystique is usually broken off by one side or the other.

Nevertheless, our hypothetical establishment should contain both gourmet and pseudo-gourmet restaurants. The gourmet room will be smaller and will cater to perhaps 1 percent of the total restaurant-going public. The pseudo-gourmet dining area, The Ritse, can be considerably larger, but should still contain the same basic design elements; it might, for example, resemble the main dining room of a very grand old hotel. Such an environment may be ideal for persons who are entirely too aroused—perhaps because of critical personal or business decisions that must be reached during the course of the meal—to pay very much attention to what they are eating. For such persons, the dominant, pleasant, and low-load environment will be just what the doctor ordered, and short-notice reservations will be fairly easy to obtain.

Both the gourmet and pseudo-gourmet restaurants provide meals at great cost and are thus inaccessible to most on a regular basis. Our ideal establishment will therefore have to contain the popular variety of restaurant that most of us can afford to enjoy frequently. Typically, such popular restaurants in the community tend to be crowded, noisy, and even overheated; there are often long waiting lines; the decor tends to be unusual or striking; the staff usually includes sexy, costumed, or sometimes even seminude waitresses; service is frequently poor; and diners must often compete ferociously for the attention of the harried waiters or put up with curt or plainly rude behavior from them. Some restaurants of this type feature professional entertainment. A few even encourage diners to pound on the table with their spoons, insult their companions, pinch the waitresses' bottoms, throw food, and in general indulge in what ordinarily would be considered intolerable boorishness.

How can such high-load eating environments be successful when they run counter to everyday eating traditions? When people eat at home—especially if they are entertaining guests who are not old friends—they tend to eliminate loaded cues: they lower or turn off background music, dim the lights, put the dog out, close the windows if there is street noise, and often segregate the children. Some families have a flat-out rule that unpleasant or controversial topics should not be discussed at the dinner table, and most people instinctively avoid bringing up matters which can lead to personality clashes or heated arguments. If one's arousal level is high, one tends to eat faster, which can cause tension and is certainly not good for the digestion. Indeed, we can say that, at least in most Western cultures, the optimum eating conditions are those of low load and pleasantness.

Yet many successful restaurants do not meet these emotional requirements. Such restaurants work because the food is acceptable and usually reasonably priced. More importantly, they work because people who approach them are not necessarily looking for a pleasant dining experience but are seeking an exciting evening out in which entertainment and stimulation are the goals. These restaurants—and we must have several of them in our ideal establishment—thrive on environmental features that contribute to a fairly high level of excitement without pushing arousal to an extreme.

In our version of such a restaurant, tables are rather close together and have colorful and stimulating place settings. Waiters and waitresses wear unusual costumes and are encouraged to display their personalities and bodies—crack jokes, flirt with the patrons, and so on. Diners are likewise encouraged to wear striking or imaginative ensembles. The lighting is dim enough so that diners do not feel their every move is subject to scrutiny, yet bright enough so that there is some visual stimulation from the other clients. There is some music to mask conversation, but care is taken that it does not make intimate talk utterly impossible or drown out the general murmur. Liquor is served, of course, to enable overstimulated patrons to lower their arousal to acceptable levels.

The food is ethnic or otherwise unusual; it need not be excellent, but merely good or acceptable, especially if it is of a type the majority of patrons tend not to prepare for themselves—for example, Mexican, Greek, Chinese, Japanese, Italian, German, Soul, or Middle Eastern. The decor is appropriately ethnic. The restaurant is touristy only in the sense that people knowledgeable about, or seriously interested in, the various national or ethnic cuisines will not visit it primarily to enjoy the food. If and when they come it will be with the intention of sharing an exciting evening out in the company of others.

If a serious attempt is made to provide professional entertainment, it is usually best if show times are specified or otherwise staggered, so that the entertainment begins after most people have finished eating. Otherwise patrons will be distracted, confused, or aroused to such an extent that the experience will become distinctly unpleasant, and the performer or the diner suffer for it.

In addition to three or four such loaded restaurants, our hypothetical establishment should also contain one or two low-load, pleasant, and somewhat intimate eateries in which people may take a quiet meal, either alone or with a companion or two. These restaurants should feature small tables segregated from one another by partitions, statuary, plants, lighting patterns, and so on.

Many people find eating alone in a restaurant to be an extremely arousing and unpleasant experience; they feel self-conscious, exposed, lonely, and in crowded places they are often rushed by waiters who would rather be serving a table of four. Many of these unpleasant feelings grow out of a sense of being observed or scrutinized. A restaurant catering to single diners or couples who would prefer not to be noticed should not contain unobstructed lines of sight. It should not make the diner feel small by placing him or her at a table in the center of a large room, and hence at the real or imagined center of interest. It should not place tables in lines of traffic, where people entering, leaving, or going to the restrooms will troop past the solitary diner. For many single diners, a regular arrangement of tables throughout a dining room which lacks partitions would be arousing and unpleasant. Most people would shun the tables located in the center and instead would seek tables, especially booths, along the walls.

In our social interaction bar we employed a zigzag arrangement in order to facilitate conversation and companionship among strangers. In our singles restaurant we might use zigzag partitions for precisely the opposite purpose, as in the Figure 16.

If such a floor plan were complemented by low-load decor, subdued lighting, and an abundance of plants, diners could feel comfortably alone—alone with themselves, their true love, their waiter, or their perverse and ungovernable urge to lick the plate. The food could be Standard Menu. The waiters would not be especially skillful, charming, or attentive, so long as the diner had an unobtrusive and effective way of summoning help—perhaps a button that would signal the waiter electronically. A good many people would be willing to pay slightly higher prices for the resulting sense of privacy and security, even if the food were just average.

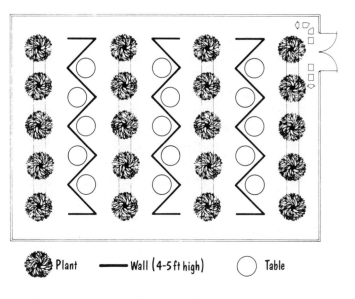

Plant ——— Wall (4-5 ft high) ◯ Table

FIGURE 16

Our hypothetical establishment has now become quite large, containing four barrooms, two high-status, low-load restaurants, four rather loaded restaurants, and at least one restaurant designed for the single diner seeking a nonthreatening, low-load environment. But we should add one final element to our establishment—a sidewalk cafe.

Sidewalk cafes function as a sort of theatre, the street being the stage and the passersby the show. People-watching from a cafe table can be a moderately arousing activity, but unlike legitimate theatre, it does not create a sense of involvement or community. The cafe tables are usually small, discouraging the formation of large groups that would distract one's attention from the street. The tables are even arranged in tiers, so that tables situated farther back have an unobstructed view of the madding crowd. The traditional practice of European sidewalk cafes—that one may buy a drink or a cup of coffee and nurse it for hours—is essential. It tends to create a sense of leisure, relaxation, or at least a feeling that it is legitimate to remove oneself from the social mainstream and simply observe it for a while.

In the environment we've postulated, our version of the sidewalk cafe will probably fulfill several purposes. It will represent a place where the over-aroused may gain some relief by passively observing, having a slow, sippy kind of drink, or possibly getting a plain sort of sandwich. On the other hand, those who have been rather isolated in their home or work environments may raise their arousal levels somewhat by watching large numbers of people—with all their different mannerisms, assorted dress, and manifest destinies—parade by.

Having rounded out the various environments in our ideal establishment with a cafe, we now need to house them somewhere. A fairly large building will do, in which case it is wise to place the less loaded environments on the first floor. This makes them the most accessible so patrons do not have to cope with elevators, crowded stairways, and excited or boisterous persons in order to reach them. Thus, The Sawdust, The Sitting Room, the gourmet restaurant, and the singles restaurant are all to be found on the same floor. This arrangement violates a deep-seated cultural sense of propriety, namely, that high-status environments should literally be placed high, in physical imitation of metaphysical hierarchies. Since our establishment is hypothetical, we can afford to wonder if environmental convenience will win out over an uneasy feeling on the part of the gourmet patrons, and perhaps even some diners in The Sitting Room, that their environments ought to be on the topmost floor.

The exciting restaurants and The Evening are placed on the second floor, and The Crazy Place occupies the entire third floor. Patrons may subconsciously associate the different floors with different levels of arousal and mentally refer to themselves as needing a first-floor, second-floor, or third-floor level of stimulation. They may even learn to play these various environments, moving from one to the other on the basis of felt needs. None of these environments is unique, of course; what is unusual, however, is the fact that they are gathered together under one roof and invite quick and effortless passage from one to the other.

One further point deserves passing mention. Many sensitive and sophisticated people feel and express distaste for environments that pretend to be all-encompassing, to "serve all your needs" or provide package deals that purportedly contain everything ye need to know or do. Examples include the high-status Watergate complex; walled-in suburban communities, each with their own shopping centers, schools, and power sources; perhaps even luxury apartment complexes with their own pools, party rooms, and gymnasiums. Sometimes these "complete" environments are constructed along stereotyped class and status lines which may be responsible for a good deal of outsider dissatisfaction with them. Our hypothetical bar-restaurant complex does not, however, contain environments designed to cause avoidance at a particular class or status level; rather, it is designed to cause approach on a more humane and individualistic basis. I hesitate to say that this basis is more humane because it is more scientific, but there is much wisdom in the old cliché that to know is to sympathize.

It is tempting to add a fourth floor to our hypothetical establishment. This floor might very profitably be given over to comfortable bedrooms where couples or those who, for one reason or another, do not feel up to going home might spend the night. Our establishment has, after all, been constructed in such a way as to accommodate the needs of people who are, among other things, temporarily bored, unhappy, depressed, lonely, or hungry in various literal and figurative ways. At our establishment people may eat, drink, and make merry as they choose. But all revels end, and many are the revelers who dream mostly of sleep.

Suggested Readings

See Mehrabian and Russell (1974b) concerning the effects of environmental feaures on arousal. Also see Sommer (1969) and Mehrabian and Diamond (1971a, 1971b) for a discussion of the effects of furniture arrangement on conversation and approach among strangers. In particular, note Mehrabian (1971, pp. 16–22 and chap. 5) for a detailed discussion of the zigzag bar and related experimental findings.

CHAPTER

24

Home Away from Home—
Travel

OUR everyday lives at work and at home have many ingrained routines that form a thickly textured but almost invisible background for our daily activities. These routines are so familiar that most of them have become habits to which we pay little conscious attention. We only notice them inadvertently, as when we wake up at 10:00 A.M. on a mid-week day off and bolt out of bed in great alarm—the bedroom is too light, we're late for work! People who use their cars mostly to drive to work sometimes find that when, for instance, they're taking the kids to an early Saturday morning dentist's appointment, that they've turned left out of the driveway toward the office, rather than right toward the dentist's. Those who drive away from the house in a hurry and unknowingly skip one of their semi-conscious morning routines—a few sips of coffee, a glance at the headlines, making the bed, locking the door—often have a strong nagging feeling that they've forgotten something. This feeling can be so strong that they actually pull over and check to see if they have forgotten their wallet or purse, checkbook or briefcase.

When we stay at home during our vacation, we continue to be enmeshed in the routines that are part and parcel of our everyday lives. These routines have certain strong associations, and frequently set off thoughts about work and all the tasks we have to do in order to maintain a home. We often find ourselves saying, "Well, I should really get this done." And since the things to do are right there, we either go ahead and do them or feel uneasy about not doing them. For married males, in particular, being at home during the day can be a mildly arousing experience. But the novelty quickly wears off, frequently resulting in lowered arousal verging on boredom. If the wife does not work, the husband's vacation time can represent for her a greatly desired change of environment, and a failure to go somewhere during this time can cause much disappointment or bitterness.

Travel is appealing partly because it allows us suddenly and almost magically to cast off our many familiar daily routines. If we are on the road or flying from city to city, there are often no set places to eat, sleep, wash, shower, entertain, or meet people; wherever we do these things is usually a new, unusual, or unfamiliar setting. Many things that we take for granted in our daily existence are missing; we consequently don't have any definite expectations about what will happen next. We don't have the familiar restaurant or cafe around the corner; we don't have our friends to telephone, we don't have our homes with the associations that these set off for us. So, the novelty, and hence arousal, associated with travel can be extremely high.

But high levels of arousal are only preferred when they are accompanied by pleasure, and this explains most travelers' choices of places and activities. People selectively travel to pleasant places, but more importantly, they are very selective about what they do in the places they visit. Unlike the native residents of the places they go to, travelers do not have much in the way of responsibilities. They do not have to work or clean house and are not burdened by the chores and responsibilities associated with everyday routines. They are free to enjoy the best things any location has to offer and constantly strive to take in the most pleasant or most interesting places and events.

We often find that we live for years in a famous city yet hardly ever get a chance to appreciate most of its various landmarks or special attractions; indeed, we visit some of these only because relatives or friends come to town and expect to be shown around. But when we travel, special landmarks and attractions are our prime targets. This goes to show that travelers have special attitudes and prerogatives, amounting to an ability to rape the land—see the best that it has to offer, eat at the most interesting restaurants, attend the best concerts, and see the best plays or shows. The combination of highly loaded and highly pleasant environments frequently results in feelings of excitement or elation. This is what makes travel a favorite leisure pastime, one that is becoming a major world industry.

Another element that adds considerably to the excitement of travel is the fact that most people set aside only two weeks out of an entire year for this purpose. This makes the vacation a brief period laden with tremendous emotional and financial investment, and disproportionately significant within the context of a year's activities. Frequently the pace of activity is great. The traveler or tourist may find himself doing five times as much in the course of a single day as he ordinarily would do. The energy to explore and to try new things is far greater than that with which most people go about their regular routines. This sustained high pace would certainly be avoided in the home environment, but, even at the risk of an eventual GASing, is preferred during travel because of the accompanying pleasure. The reason is that we can tolerate a great deal more arousal when it is combined with pleasure than with a neutral or unpleasant feeling.

In this context of intense, pleasurable activity, the tourist or traveler, who has no set routines to inhibit and restrict him to his characteristic ways, becomes more uninhibited or free (dominant). Most of our behavior is set off by and tied to the stimuli which surround us. When our familiar stimulus-set is almost wholly replaced by new and unfamiliar locations, there are far fewer behavioral associations, and a "when in Rome . . ." attitude develops. It is much easier to be uninhibited and willing to experience novel things as well as to do things differently. Consider someone who never drinks beer at home because it is fattening or because he has other well-established habits and preferences related to alcohol. He may find himself tasting and immensely enjoying beer in an English pub or a Canadian beer parlor. Someone else who would never consider going to a strip joint in his home town may find himself enjoying one in Copenhagen, where it is one of the primary tourist attractions.

The type of clothing one wears can also be an element of uninhibited experimentation. For example, guests staying at traditional Japanese inns are provided with a *yukata*, a lightweight cotton kimono-type garment. The guest is expected to wear this while he is in his room, when he takes a walk in the garden of the inn, and, in smaller resorts, possibly even when he goes for a walk in town. The experience of wearing a totally novel garment can be very arousing, since one becomes aware of unusual bodily sensations while moving or sitting.

People may also wear more extravagant clothes with louder colors and flashier cuts when they travel—items which they would be reluctant to wear on their home ground.

Another aspect of stimulus variation in travel is, of course, the people. One often encounters and befriends individuals who might be out of bounds or inaccessible in the home community. There is generally a less inhibited feeling about starting conversations either with the natives or with fellow travelers. Since there is less commitment to long-term friendships or social exchanges, one may be more willing to start conversations with others who ordinarily might be disqualified on the basis of age, socioeconomic standing, profession, or physical appearance. For instance, an older couple might befriend a young pair while traveling and find the company unexpectedly refreshing. Someone whose friends at home are principally professionals in his own line of work may find interaction with professionals or craftsmen in different fields to be stimulating and perhaps even more rewarding.

The feeling of dominance is an important factor in the high levels of sociability often found among travelers. Since whole industries if not whole economies are built around the tourist, great pains are taken to make him feel important. He is usually treated deferentially, most of his whims are catered to, and he is generally looked after by people whose lifework is to serve visitors like himself. Our research has shown that dominance is a major factor in affiliative behavior. If a person feels dominant and pleasant, he will be extremely sociable; if he feels dominant and unpleasant, he will be extremely unsociable, to the point of being rude. Since the vacation-travel environment is one that usually creates feelings of pleasure and dominance, there is a high degree of gregariousness. This is especially true in self-contained vacation environments from which potentially unpleasant stimuli have been eliminated—cruise ships, for example, or certain resort areas. Needless to say, persons whose livelihood depends upon tourists must take special care to maintain relatively high levels of pleasure for their guests or clients. The highly aroused, dominant tourist can become a nasty customer indeed if his pleasure level drops sharply.

Exceptions to the modal travel style described so far are determined by an individual's finances, temperament, and normal environmental load. When, for example, economic considerations limit the luxury in travel and increase the possibilities of hassles and problems, we can expect travelers to prefer low-load experiences, and such preferences should be especially pronounced among nonscreeners. On the other hand, people in general, particularly nonscreeners, should show a preference for higher levels of arousal when finances or other factors permit trouble-free travel. Sometimes, however, it is not the pleasure levels during travel which influence preferences for various levels of arousal, but rather the typical load levels of the home and work environments of the traveler. Persons, especially nonscreeners, who come from exceedingly high-paced and hectic jobs are expected to prefer low-load and pleasant (relaxing) vacations; in contrast, those who leave routine jobs and sedentary life styles, are expected to relish higher loads in travel.

The fact that many travelers come from highly stressed (high-load and unpleasant) work environments helps explain the success of travel guides, travel magazines, tour companies, packaged vacations, and all the various means whereby a traveler's activities and itinerary are structured and made more familiar. Independent travelers have too many decisions to make: hotel reservations, restaurant choices, means of travel, how the day will be spent, and so on. Some, as they face the uncertainties and problems of travel find themselves desperately trying to reduce these uncertainties and unpreferred high arousal levels. One option available to the overaroused and troubled traveler is to find something familiar in the generally unfamiliar place he is visiting, something that resembles what he has at home and which will therefore be less arousing. This is why we find Americans in Americanized coffee shops in Rome or eating steak in Tokyo, or see Englishmen spending their afternoons in Yugoslav hotels drinking beer and socializing with their own countrymen. A second option open to the potentially overaroused traveler is to travel as part of a group and thus make a minimum of decisions. In this case, the schedule is predetermined by the group leaders, the reservations are made in advance, and almost all the decisions regarding the daily sightseeing and other activities are taken care of. So group travel guarantees a certain level of security and comfort while minimizing risks, problems, and possible unpleasantness—it allows the traveler to passively enjoy whatever has been planned. In short, group travel reduces arousal and maximizes pleasure.

Of course, a rigidly scheduled itinerary can be vexing to some people; they may not want to plod through the umpteenth national monument and would prefer a quiet Pernod at a sidewalk cafe or a stimulating stroll through the shopping district. As a person becomes more expert at traveling, he becomes knowledgeable about ways to find transportation, lodging, food, and entertainment in a strange city.

For such a person, traveling does not include high uncertainty, but rather consists of an alternative set of highly practiced routines. The shift from his daily routine at home to a second set of routines while traveling contributes only moderately to his arousal.

This is the reason why we often hear someone say that the excitement of their first overseas vacation can never be matched. Young people who leave home for the first time find the many uncertainties awaiting them abroad tremendously exciting and invigorating. With repeated foreign travel they become more confident and blasé (dominant), no longer becoming anxious about problems which arise, but also being less excited by the highlights.

Similar considerations apply to people who choose to camp or stay in their summer place during vacations. These periods are not laden with uncertainties and disruptions of daily activities, but simply consist of well-practiced alternative routines somewhat different from those at home. The emotional tone of such vacations tends to be low on arousal and fairly high on pleasure and dominance, thus yielding feelings of contentment and relaxation rather than excitement.

Our analysis of travel and vacation styles applies equally to the selection of familiar versus unfamiliar modes of transportation, and to possible future developments in the design of passenger seating areas, dining sections, or lounges on planes and trains. Roughly, passengers would be given a choice of relaxing (pleasant and unarousing) or exciting (pleasant and arousing) accommodations. Thus, a novice air traveler who is apprehensive, or someone who is trying to get away from a hectic schedule, could opt for a more relaxing compartment, relaxing forms of entertainment, and comforting services. Such sections might, for instance, be designed in pleasant and unarousing color combinations. On the other hand, the experienced air traveler who is bored and impatient to get to his destination could benefit from a compartment that is designed to intensify social interaction and to maximize varied and unpredictable experiences. Lounge areas on some of the larger planes (and of course on trains) could be deliberately designed to be relaxing or exciting, using some of the ideas suggested for the design of bars and restaurants in the previous chapter.

National travel styles can also be examined in terms of emotional needs. The Japanese travel style presents a striking contrast to the American one. The Japanese usually travel in groups. It is not unusual to find a group of twenty or thirty Japanese tourists walking through a city with a guide carrying a small triangular flag which group members can readily see and follow. Different group guides carry flags of different design, thus avoiding possible confusion. Such groups may be seen touring museums, historical sites, or even hotel lobbies and shops. In contrast, even though many Americans join tours, the general trend is to be more individualistic; Americans prefer to travel alone or in small family groups, often expressing scorn for guided packages which specify what they'll see and when.

The unusual consistency in travel styles among the Japanese is consonant with other aspects of their culture which we have discussed. Since, as a nation, they tend toward nonscreening and live under extremely crowded and competitive conditions, they understandably value relaxing (low-load and pleasant) art forms and settings. To them, travel, despite its necessary variety, novelty, and uncertainty (high load), is paradoxically appealing because of the worldliness and elevated status it implies. Those Japanese who choose to travel, then, try to keep the lid on arousal while accentuating the pleasurable elements.

We might mention a third style of travel, characteristic of many continental Europeans, but especially noticeable among Germans. These travelers tend not to travel in large groups or in structured tours but often make serious efforts to reduce the novelty and complexity of new or unusual environments. They prepare for their travels by reading as much as they can about the country they intend to visit. They often make an attempt to learn some of the language of the country they are visiting, and they know approximately how much things should cost. They have read up on the sites they especially want to see and know exactly what they are looking forward to experiencing, whether it is a particular ruin or a special national dish. Such intensive preparation can be viewed as an attempt to reduce the novelty of travel and hence its arousing quality. In fact, anyone who prepares intensively for anything is making a similar attempt.

Suggested Readings

See Mehrabian and Russell (1974a, chap. 5; 1974b) for a general discussion of environmental information-rate (load). See also Mehrabian and Russell (1975a) for the effects of dominance on affiliation.

25

Sports Arenas

SPORTS are distinguished as a subset of games because they involve more than a minimal amount of physical activity. This is why chess, bridge, or poker, despite the enormous drain upon the bodily systems that championship-level play involves, are considered games rather than sports. Marathon walks, golf, mountain climbing, yachting, and car or horse racing are considered sports because the participants are physically active or express themselves through active animals or machines, both of which represent extensions of human motor skills.

Indeed, heightened arousal for players and spectators alike is the key to most sports. For a participant, any sport involves very high levels of arousal. First, there is the physical activity, which is arousing in itself; the more activity, the higher the arousal level. Ignoring individual differences for the moment, we can say that a pitcher is likely to be more aroused than his right fielder, or that a fraction of a second after the snap, a defensive tackle is likely to be more aroused than a safety, simply because one is more physically active than the other.

The pace of a sport is important in determining its load. On the low-paced end, we have sports like baseball, golf, bowling, or horse racing. When a pitcher is warming up between innings, there is really not much happening. But every once in a while all the bases get loaded and the spectators' arousal shoots up. After that inning, arousal levels immediately drop down again. The general level of spectator arousal in baseball may be a little higher than normal in an important game or toward the end of a game in which the score is tied. In general though the pace is slow, marked only occasionally

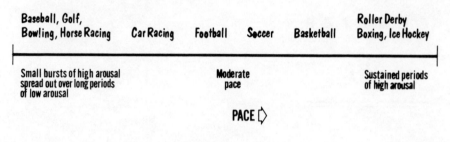

FIGURE 17

by peaks of load and spectator arousal. In golf also, arousal level is generally low because the activity of the athlete is slow paced and there isn't much happening. However, here again there are those occasional spikes in arousal, as when the golfer is putting for $30,000 on the final green.

In soccer, basketball, or football the pace is much faster, with

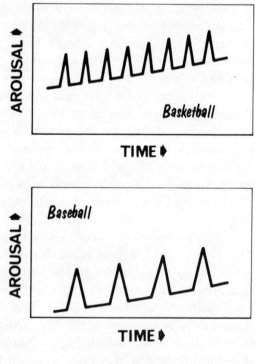

FIGURE 18

basketball being even faster than the other two. Pace in this context means that the spikes of arousal tend to occur more frequently. Then there are the extremely loaded sports such as ice hockey, boxing, and roller derby, where the arousal spikes are almost continuous and tremendous concentration is required by spectators to see all the action and subtlety of a game. The speed of these events (the speed of the boxers' movements, the speed of a hockey puck) is so fast that spectators have to be highly aroused to keep up with what is happening.

In general, team sports tend to be more complex than those in which a single competitor is pitted against another, against a field of individual competitors, or against the forces of nature. A golfer or a miler, to take an obvious example, has less information to process and more time to do it in than, for instance, a quarterback or a goalie in hockey or lacrosse. Team sports tend to provide more intense stimulus cues because of the violence involved, even in so-called noncontact sports like basketball. Of course, some non-team sports also provide intense stimuli—in boxing, bullfighting, or car racing, for example, the participants face the possibility of serious injury or death. Most team sports also tend to have a higher degree of novelty or uncertainty because more individuals are involved and more things can go right or wrong. This was one of the reasons why the "amazin'" Mets were once so popular despite their poor record—people used to go to the games just to see what new way the Mets would find to blow a five-run lead or otherwise botch things up.

Another factor contributing to the load of a sport, aside from the number of participants, is how much each of these participants controls the outcome. When a single individual controls most of the activity, it is easier to predict the outcome. For example, in baseball attention is focused disproportionately upon the pitcher. If a particular pitcher is known to have a good fast ball only, we can anticipate that an opposing team can put in a pinch hitter and turn the game around. In football it may be the quarterback who commands attention. Some quarterbacks (whose careers, incidentally, tend to be brief) have a tendency to become predictable. It is known that in a certain situation they won't get a touchdown because they are simply not good enough or don't have a sufficiently complex bag of tricks.

Although purists will offer a number of cogent reasons why the new designated-hitter rule in baseball is not a good idea, the fact remains that it is designed to increase the complexity of the game and make it more arousing for the spectators. The rule changes in basketball were instituted for the same reason. It seems likely that something will also be done about the field goal in football. Since the high loads of football constitute its greatest asset, it seems probable that anything which serves to reduce this load—in this case by reducing uncertainty—will sooner or later be modified or eliminated by those for whom football is a profit-making venture.

In contrast to baseball and football, volleyball and basketball are such that the players have relatively equal responsibility for the outcome of a particular game. When the action is distributed in this manner, we need to concentrate a great deal more to be able to fully appreciate the game because the combined moves of the various players contain a great deal more complexity and uncertainty.

Singles games in tennis are low-load, not only because just two players are involved, but also because professional games tend to be highly predictable. The server usually wins the game, and reversals only occur in those rare cases when the opponent somehow manages to break the serve. This, together with the strict protocol for spectators, who are usually as restrained as a concert hall audience, implies that neither arousal nor dominance are especially important at these events. Rather, it is the graceful and highly coordinated movements unfolding against a manicured background which appeals to the spectators.

Equality of participants in determining outcomes also means closely matched opposing individuals or teams. Remembering that high uncertainty contributes to load, we can say that games in which the scores are closer or which are characterized by more frequent reversals are more arousing—a fact which sports promoters are aware of and acknowledge through their efforts to have closely matched competition. In drafting new football players, the best teams have the last choices, which gives the poorer teams a chance to improve. The idea of handicapping is based on a similar principle: by extraneously equating the chances of the various participants to win, the game's load is increased.

But teams or single players are not always equally matched, and this often results in feelings of elation and enthusiasm (pleasure and arousal) for winner(s) and stress (displeasure and arousal) for the loser(s). As we know, high-load situations are more arousing for nonscreeners than for screeners. It follows that the nonscreening members of a losing team will experience greater arousal and stress, with consequently greater deterioration in performance than the screeners. On the other hand, nonscreeners are expected to feel greater elation while winning and may outperform the screeners in this case. This has some interesting implications for player substitutions during games. Coaches who pretest their players' screening levels at the start of each season can judiciously substitute their best screeners during those stressful moments when their team is in trouble on the field. Moreover, they won't have to rely on the same players when fortunes are reversed and their teams are ahead, because at such times they can profitably rely on their best nonscreening players. Similar considerations apply to spectators. The nonscreeners become even more involved and enthusiastic or otherwise display approach behavior when their side is winning, but are more readily discouraged and possibly even leave the arena when their side is losing.

High school and college athletic contests, especially those between small schools, tend to be somewhat more arousing than professional contests taking place in large stadiums. In the smaller gyms or football fields, proportionately more members of the audience are exposed to high loads from the playing field; that is, they are closer to the action and hence see a lot more detail. Bleacher seats in a huge stadium radically reduce the load and cut down on the intensity of the stimuli—you can't distinguish the facial expressions of the players or spot many of the fouls. Closer seats cost more because they provide greater arousal for their occupants. For similar reasons, seats nearer to the diamond tend to be the preferred ones in baseball because there is more continuous (arousing) action in the infield than in the outfield.*

Even though, through zooms and instant replay, TV can provide a spectator with greater detail than he might be able to get in a sports arena, it cannot replace the crowd which, with the exception of certain sports like golf or tennis, tends to be extremely uninhibited. During a good game—one that has a high uncertainty level because the contestants are evenly matched and there is a seesawing score, or one that is heavily loaded as a result of much complexity and activity—spectators often yell, scream, throw things, and generally

---

* Considering the effect on spectator arousal, probably the most important feature of sports arenas is not arena size, but crowd density. In so far as small arenas are easier to fill, and spectators in such arenas are more likely to have better views of the events on the field, these arenas should be highly arousing. However, when a very large stadium is filled to capacity, the overall impact of the emotional expressions of a tremendous mass of people adequately compensates for the greater (less arousing) distances and results in what are probably the most arousing spectator experiences.

express intense feelings in ways they would not while in their homes or in most other public places. The congregation of large numbers of highly aroused, uninhibited people who share similar interests and attitudes is also conducive to socializing; it may lead to the development of new friendships or the renewal or intensification of old ones. Attending a sporting event in the company of a friend or relative is almost a universal trend; only a small percentage of people go alone. This tells us something about the kind of emotional experiences people look forward to at such events. Being with others helps one to achieve higher levels of arousal, but also of dominance. In the generally pleasant setting, then, gregariousness is further enhanced.*

Aside from its contribution to gregariousness, the dominance dimension plays an important role in sports. The need to win, "drive," and many other terms describing aggressiveness in the sports environment have a strong dominance component. Indeed, overtly aggressive behavior is impossible without accompanying feelings of dominance. Part of the dominance felt by athletes results of course from their training, from mastery of the various physical and mental skills involved in their sport. In many team sports the players tend to be unusually large or strong, and great size or strength tends to make people feel naturally dominant in relation to others in a variety of environments. Also, the competitive nature of most sports tends to favor those individuals who are temperamentally (permanently) high on dominance. This is because if two players are equal in all respects other than temperamental dominance, the more dominant player will outperform the other athlete.

The dominance aspect is also quite important for spectators, so much so that most spectators find it impossible to watch a sporting event without choosing sides and rooting for one particular player or team. This is also one reason why teams which win most of the time draw the best crowds: their fans can count on a dominance-producing identification. Temperamentally dominant fans who find their favorite team on the losing side have a great many psychological devices at their disposal to negate the physical reality of submission. They can find fault with referees who supposedly fail to call fouls on unfair plays by the opposing team; they can be critical of the coaching (strategies, player substitutions) their favorite team receives; or they can boo and throw things at the "villains" out on the field. All such actions reflect the common elements of dominance and arousal.

* In a somewhat different context, the large-scale civil rights and Vietnam demonstrations often served a similar purpose, although these gatherings tended to be more disciplined and inhibited than a sports crowd.

Spectators who have no reason to identify with either side—no school, city, or regional associations, no money riding on the outcome, no real continuing interest in the sport—will often pick one side or the other on the basis of seemingly frivolous things like the color of the players' uniforms, whether some players have long hair, or whether one team is heavily favored to win. Indeed, if a majority of spectators at a sporting event didn't care who won—if they didn't make an "us-them" distinction and direct their feelings either for or against a temporary hero or villain—an atmosphere that is somehow alien to the very nature of sports would result. People even tend to resent or become impatient with national sportscasters who carefully control their biases and give evenhanded descriptions rather than overtly favoring certain teams.

Sports differ in terms of how much freedom (dominance) they allow spectators. Spectators at a tennis match are quite inhibited. At baseball games you are assigned a seat and regulated as to when you can stand up in your seat; there is, for example, the etiquette of the seventh-inning stretch. Then there are events such as sports car racing at a place like Laguna Seca (near Monterey, California), where you are free to find your own mound, sit or stand, eat, move around to another place, talk to friends, or come and go when you please. The greater the freedom of the spectator or the less inhibited he feels, the higher is his feeling of dominance.

For participants and spectators alike, there are wide fluctuations in the pleasure dimension. Players may take pleasure in a successfully executed maneuver, a score, crowd approval, the actual activities involved in the performance, or the environment in which the sport takes place. In golf tournaments or yacht racing, for example, the physical environment is often spectacularly beautiful and tends to create feelings of pleasure. But pleasure levels can shoot down as well as up, and pain, a bad call by a referee, a muffed shot, or losing can create intense feelings of displeasure. Players and spectators can thus find themselves in emotional states ranging from ecstasy or joy (high arousal, high pleasure, dominance) to anger or fury (high arousal, low pleasure, dominance). This is why fights on the field or frequent fouls tend to occur when one team is clearly losing; some losing players express their anger in ways that are not part of the game's rule-governed violence.

Similarly, when spectators identify very strongly with one of the teams, as at neighborhood or international soccer games or high school football or basketball games, there are likely to be a number of fights after the game. A loss can create feelings of intense displeasure among spectators who have a large emotional investment in the success of their team. And, highly aroused, very displeased persons who feel dominant in the company of several friends who'll back them up are going to be spoiling for a fight. Further, although the spectators have been highly aroused by the events on the playing field, for many of them this arousal will not have been intense enough to cause fatigue or a GAS reaction. Unlike the athletes, who, after a physically grueling contest, are likely to be too exhausted to sustain the high levels of arousal necessary for a fight, many of the spectators will still be experiencing heightened arousal for some time after the contest has ended. Thus, if large numbers of spectators from both sides are present and must mingle on the way out of the stadium or gym, it is almost inevitable that there will be at least a scuffle or two. Other, less harmful manifestations of strong, pent-up emotions occur when spectators storm the field, knock down a goalpost, and tear it to pieces. Interestingly, on-the-field brawls more often than not involve players who have just come off the bench, rather than players who have been in the game for ten or fifteen minutes and who are likely to be fatigued.

Since the promoters of most sports are primarily interested in providing excitement (especially arousal) for spectators, there seems to be much potential for use of electronic music to manipulate and reinforce crowd feelings—rousing pieces played during time-outs or other slow moments, pieces conveying apprehension prior to penalty shots, and "aggressive" tunes played during high-scoring periods by the home team. Of course, this can be extremely controversial, since it might give the home team a psychological advantage. But since it is also in the interest of promoters to prevent riots, it might be worth experimenting with musical means to raise pleasure levels among the home-team fans whenever their team gets into trouble. Visiting players might also welcome such an experiment if it succeeded in reducing the number of epithets or beer cans thrown in their direction.

Suggested Readings

For the arousing effect of activity, see the suggested readings for chapter five. Mehrabian and Russell (1974b) provided data on what makes a situation (e.g., a sporting event) more arousing; Wheeler (1966) discussed the arousing effects of crowds; and Zimbardo (1969) considered the increased anti-social and aggressive behavior which seems to be facilitated by the high arousal states in mob situations. See Osgood, Suci, and Tannenbaum (1957) for a discussion of the correlation between size and strength to feelings of dominance or power.

26

Stores

FOR the sales clerk who's been on her feet all day or for the guy who popped into a discount department store on the way home to pick up some underwear and was banged five times in the knees by old ladies swinging shopping bags seemingly filled with machine parts, it may come as a surprise to find stores included under the heading of play environments. But since shopping is a source of pleasure and excitement for many people, I've considered places where consumer goods are displayed and sold as basically fun environments.

Even buying groceries can be an enjoyable experience. Many people who can walk to their markets or stop off at them on the way home buy something every day. They could buy for the entire week and even save some money, but the daily contact with the shop owner, the pleasant and mildly exciting displays, the fresh and varied foods available, and the possibility of meeting and chatting with neighborhood acquaintances all cause them to prefer their little einkauf, or daily purchase.

Environmental conditions that make for maximum buying, namely, conditions that provide heightened arousal, heightened pleasure, and mild feelings of dominance, are the same as those which make a place fun for shoppers. The classic example is when shoppers feel themselves to be part of something larger, like a boisterous crowd or mob. In a mob, people are highly aroused, physically active, and uninhibited (shouting, screaming, or jostling); they are also highly attuned to others and to the general environment. They are also extremely suggestible; they'll often do what others do, and will respond positively to the blandishments of an orator or a tradesman. If the moblike levels of arousal are combined with high levels of pleasure, people will buy frantically and impulsively. Such conditions are usually created best in a fair or bazaar type environment.

I'm thinking in particular of the large, centrally located outdoor markets that used to be found in many major American cities and are still to some extent typical in Europe. These are pleasant, enjoyable, exciting, and colorful environments offering all sorts of produce, meats, and flowers for sale. They often have the quality of an auction, with retailers from all over the city bustling about in the early morning under the pressures of time and competition, bidding for their day's stock. But there are also housewives milling about, free to come and go as they choose. The old-fashioned, centrally located outdoor market is attractive to a wide variety of people because it is fun to walk through and has something for everyone.

The open-air aspect—sunshine, blue sky overhead, a sense of openness, naturalness and freedom—is pleasant but not absolutely necessary. Many of the great central European markets are (or were) housed in great hangarlike buildings; the bazaars of Turkey and Iran are covered and resemble labyrinths. These markets are exciting because they are usually crowded and have a great number of stalls, each selling something different. We are not used to seeing cheese, flowers, vegetables, and clothing sold in such close proximity; the combination of odors, colors, feelings, and associations as one walks from stall to stall is varied, novel, and extremely exciting.

The economic pressures being exerted on the large urban markets are such that many of them are being forced out of the central city into less accessible locations. Historically, these markets have been located in the middle of town, but as cities become more congested, it becomes increasingly difficult to get produce into the downtown areas from the farms and shipping centers. And since the markets are operated largely by small entrepreneurs—some of the tiny stalls have been family-owned for hundreds of years—the general economic factors favoring large corporations with centralized decision making, purchasing power, and distribution facilities are also working against them. The final and fatal blow is dealt to these old markets when they are forced to move to suburbs lacking crowds and atmosphere—retailers go there because they have to, but nobody goes there because they want to, and so the exciting, complex, heterogeneous, bazaarlike atmosphere is lost. Even old-fashioned fairs are becoming a thing of the past for the same reason—they can no longer be set up in areas that are accessible to many different types of people in large numbers.

The high-density crowds don't materialize because substantial investments are needed to advertise the fair and because adequate public transportation to the site is usually not available. Crowds are essential to a bazaarlike atmosphere; if enough people do not show up, heightened levels of arousal are not achieved, visitors are not particularly excited, and they don't buy enough to make it worthwhile for the merchants.

Large department stores holding warehouse clearance sales often attract huge crowds, but these crowds are usually drawn from the store's regular clientele and hence lack the heterogeneity of the bazaar or fair crowd. Furthermore, the sale crowd tends to be far more purposeful; most people are there specifically to buy certain items or advertised specials and become quite annoyed when these items have been sold out. Hence, although the arousal levels achieved at such clearance sales are frequently very high, the pleasure levels often are not, causing many people to avoid the situation entirely or bringing out anxious or even downright antisocial behavior in those who attend.

Filene's basement in Boston is the classic example of a high-load and invariably crowded department store. Filene's buys merchandise from stores that are going out of business and then sells it in its basement with a regular schedule of price markdowns. This basement, dubbed The Snake Pit, is often a mob scene. Customers buy almost with a sense of desperation, undressing in the aisles, fighting with each other over items, and coming away with many unnecessary things.

The huge success of Filene's derives in part from its greatly reduced prices; if one is lucky or aggressive enough, one can find a most unusual bargain. The shopper's feeling of uncertainty is enhanced by the very disorganized (complex) displays. Things are constantly moved around and piled on top of each other in frenzied disarray. There is no orderly way to separate the valuable items from the junk; one may discover a bargain hidden away in some corner at any moment. And the personnel don't seem to care what you do. Dominance is enhanced by a feeling that you can look anywhere, rummage around, and handle everything. If you know what you want and can distinguish a real bargain, the store is a high-load environment in which to explore and have fun. A feeling of gambling for an exceptional buy keeps bringing back lunch-hour crowds day after day.

Some people who can afford to pay the higher prices in expensive and well-organized stores nevertheless avoid such places. For them shopping is a hobby and a challenge to beat the odds. They love the excitement generated by uncertainty, and the varied shapes, colors, odors, and associations. Stores can be designed in an almost hide-and-seek fashion to give customers the impression that they are making discoveries not readily accessible to other shoppers. Of course, the game is only successful if it is not obvious. Then there are shoppers who can't spare the time and would rather pay the extra premiums. To attract them, additional floors or sections are needed where different kinds of merchandise can be located readily and which are staffed with competent sales personnel.

Even further removed from the disorganized and inadequately staffed stores are the exclusive, high-status establishments featuring beautiful merchandise artfully displayed in uncrowded and well-organized (low-load) settings. In most cultures, including our own, personal possessions serve in part to indicate a person's status and wealth; something that is purchased at an exclusive shop has high status associated with it. So, high-status stores are specifically designed to appeal to a wealthier clientele. Apart from being quite pleasant, these stores offer "climates" which make clients feel socially dominant, important, and part of a select group—a feeling strongly reinforced by the behavior of the sales personnel.

We can draw a distinction between exclusive and pseudo-exclusive shops based largely on the manner in which the sales personnel behave. In exclusive shops, sales personnel tend to act much the same as waiters in true gourmet restaurants: they are instantly available to and at the disposal of the customer; they are expert and knowledgeable, but they are unobtrusive and submissive and do not impinge upon the customer's privacy or freedom of movement or decision. In the pseudo-exclusive shop, the setting may be impeccable, as may be the merchandise, but the shop personnel tend to be somewhat pushy or snotty. The customer finds himself under pressure to buy something conforming to the tastes of the salesperson or to somehow justify his presence. It is understandable of course that someone who has spent much of his life handling beautiful things he himself cannot afford to buy may develop a feeling of dominance through intimate association with the luxurious merchandise. He is sometimes likely to become impatient with a customer who is indecisive or unsure of his status or his ability to afford some item. But such salespeople effectively destroy the main things an exclusive shop has to offer, namely, pleasure and dominance. Persons who are unsure of their status will feel deeply inadequate, and those who are confident of their status will be annoyed and may feel obliged to assert themselves; in either case there is a distinct loss of pleasure.

Actually, a person who feels somewhat inadequate or unsure of himself in a luxurious, exclusive shop places the sales personnel in an unusually advantageous position. If they treat the customer with implicit trust and understanding, connoting unquestioned acceptance, the customer is privately relieved and grateful and probably won't hesitate to return to that store. On the other hand, if they threaten his feeling of belonging, the customer may make a purchase to prove them wrong, but avoid the store thereafter. In terms of long-range customer relations, it is far better to make the customer feel dominant by means of respectful attention; he is more likely to make a purchase, and more importantly, to return and make future purchases even after he can actually afford to.

Of course, in stores having little in the way of exclusive merchandise, sales personnel tend to be slightly aggressive (unpleasant, arousing, and dominant). People go to such stores because the merchandise is cheaper (or because they think it's cheaper, having no basis for comparison) or because they feel less inadequate in such stores than in "fancier" ones. However, anxious persons and nonscreeners are especially apt to avoid the aggressive salesman or the unpleasant and disorganized shopping scene. Cluttered stores, if they are to attract such customers, must emphasize the pleasure dimension —relying possibly on friendly personnel. In fact, all types of clientele are more readily attracted by a pleasant store. This is why, aside from careful consideration of their visual aesthetics, some stores are designed to pleasantly stimulate the other senses as well. Music, even though it may not be the item on sale, is an obvious choice. The olfactory sense can be pleasantly stimulated through the use of perfumed sprays—a practice now in use at some exclusive stores.

Another way to achieve moderate arousal and pleasure for nonscreeners or impatient and hurried customers who are also overaroused is through an action- or context-oriented grouping of merchandise. Department stores are generally organized according to fairly traditional ideas. There are separate areas or floors uniformly displaying furniture, dishes, cooking utensils, and separate sections for women's, men's, and children's clothing. As we walk through a big department store, the uniform low load of these displays bores us; things are just there and have no context to set off associations and remind us that we actually could use them. Most department stores rarely gather together in one place more than a fraction of the items actually used in the typical kitchen: stoves are in one place, blenders in another, glassware is somewhere else, tablecloths or other linens are on a different floor entirely, cookbooks are in the book section, tiles or wallpaper suitable for kitchens are in the basement, and so on. This is one reason why people often forget to buy the things they intended to unless they make lists—their normal associations are fragmented.

Displays compatible with usual combinations of everyday things are more likely to stimulate buying, if only because they invite us to compare what they have to what we have in terms of a whole context. In creating integrated displays, designers also think in terms of the direction in which the eye travels and what it is likely to focus upon; arrangements are therefore created to highlight certain key items. Designers call these contextual displays "vignettes," and usually use them in high-exposure areas of stores such as the windows and entry ways. Some of the modern European stores, such as Den Permanente in Copenhagen, are quite sophisticated in the use of integrated or contextual displays: their showrooms consist of a variety of activity settings. Dishes are not stacked on shelves or displayed against the wall; rather, they are set on tables with compatible chairs, serving carts, and with complete place settings. Furniture is arranged in groupings that one would encounter in the home, and is combined with pieces of sculpture, paintings, stereo systems, or whatever, in colors and designs that harmonize with the furniture displayed. In short, merchandise is shown in a setting which beautifully exemplifies its use.

Of course, such vignettes rarely challenge the customer to develop ideas and coherent designs of his own and tend to appeal to those who simply want to buy a beautifully designed and integrated unit. These customers are willing to pay an expert for ideas rather than rely on their own.

In fact, most of us probably feel unqualified to make certain types of purchases and select stores on the basis of our knowledge and competence vis-à-vis different classes of items. Usually, there is anxiety when one lacks the knowledge to judge merchandise. One is anxious because he wonders if he will be buying something that is worth the money it cost (arousal), or if he will find himself stuck with something that nobody else likes (possible displeasure). Such anxiety, when combined with the high arousal resulting from a disorganized store, makes the store especially unappealing, and explains why people prefer to shop with friends: getting a second opinion helps reduce uncertainty or arousal and therefore anxiety. It is quite possible, then, that someone who seeks a well-organized store and expert help to buy clothes may not mind disarray in buying household items, used books, or antiques. He may feel anxious about his ability to judge the quality of clothing or to select an attractive ensemble and consequently shop in a more exclusive (pleasant and moderately loaded) clothing store where he can assume that he will get quality merchandise, good advice, and attention. On the other hand, he may feel more competent and more knowledgeable about books or antiques and enjoy shopping and hunting for them himself; the internal source of uncertainty and arousal is absent, and he can thrive on the occasional thrill provided by a disorganized, complex, bargain-basement environment.

In closing, we can ask why people shop for things they don't need or cannot afford. Our analyses of the various types of shops suggest that the single common element of the shopping experience is arousal. Bargain stores, shopping centers, exclusive shops, and small, privately owned middle-class establishments have respectively decreasing loads, although all tend to be relatively high-load environments. Bargain stores and shopping centers, the kind of establishments most often patronized by the bulk of the population, are the most loaded. This, plus the fact that housewives are represented disproportionately among shoppers, suggests that people shop to increase their arousal and pleasure levels. It follows that shopping should be most reinforcing to those who are confined to boring home and work environments, and that such persons are most likely to shop for the sake of shopping per se and not because they need something. Shopping can also enhance a dominant feeling in the shopper. Exclusive stores specifically seem to aim for moderate arousal in combination with highly pleasant and dominant feelings. This, as we have suggested, leads to pleasant social exchanges among the clientele, but even more so among the shoppers and the tradespeople. So, one might say that for the wealthy, increasing one's arousal is subservient to the dominance and social aspects associated with shopping.

Suggested Readings

For the arousing effect of other people and crowds see D'Atri (1975), McBride, King, and James (1965), Nichols and Champness (1971), and Wheeler (1966). In studying persuasion, Mehrabian and Williams (1969) discovered that a communicator's arousing quality was the most important determinant of his persuasiveness—more so than his positiveness toward the person he was attempting to persuade. Positiveness, however, was the second most important aspect of effective persuasion. These findings show that people are most susceptible to influence when they are highly aroused and feeling pleasant. Stores can be readily designed to elicit this combination of feelings from their customers, thereby increasing customer suggestibility and purchasing. (Russell & Mehrabian, 1976f).

PART SEVEN

COMMUNAL

ENVIRONMENTS

CHAPTER

27

Dormitories

COLLEGE DORMITORIES are specialized apartment complexes, and much of what has already been said about residential environments also applies to them. But dormitories are also work environments. Students are expected to do at least some of their studying in their rooms, and this expectation is explicitly reinforced by standard dormitory furnishings, which generally consist of a bed, a desk, a chair, and a small bookcase. Dormitories are also supposed to be communal environments. They are supposed to foster or at least reflect a shared community of interests, to encourage solidarity and camaraderie among the residents, to familiarize students with the ways of their institution, and to cause them to adopt a positive if not affectionate attitude toward its larger purposes and traditions. They are also designed to give incoming young adults, who must begin to rely on their own resources, the social support they may lack as a result of their separation from the supportive nuclear family. It is primarily the communal aspect of dormitory life that I would like to touch upon here.

You can't begin to get anything like a community unless people get to know one another—socialize. As we have seen, frequency of contact is an important element in developing a network of social relations within an environment. Studies have shown, for example, that people who live close to the main entrance of an apartment building know more neighbors and have more friends, simply because they are more likely to come into contact with others. People's paths must cross frequently to give them a chance to get to know and like each other. But that is not enough. There must also be places that will attract people and keep them there, places that contain some interesting or compelling stimulus—even coffee-making equipment will serve this purpose. Such common socializing areas do not conflict with the need for privacy, if visits to such areas are strictly a matter of choice.

Dormitories built in quasi-imitation of high-rise apartment dwellings tend to isolate individuals from one another. The standard floor plan of such dorms looks like this:

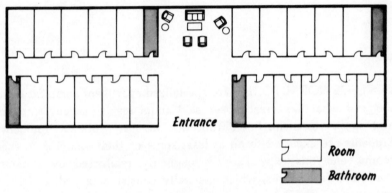

Entrance

Room
Bathroom

FIGURE 19

There may be several of these floors stacked one upon the other, and although theoretically they provide a good deal of privacy, in practice usually they do not. Since these dorms often represent the cheapest kind of student housing, they tend to be poorly insulated. The sounds of doors slamming, people walking or talking in the halls, and noise from the adjacent rooms can produce heightened arousal when it is not wanted. The large lounges, although designed to be socializing areas, are seldom used except for studying, which is of course an individual activity. One reason is that such lounges are furnished with long couches along the walls and hence do not encourage socializing. Or they may be quite blandly decorated and lack stimulating or pleasant views of the campus. A source of music, either a piano or a stereo, is usually lacking, and in freshman dorms TVs are sometimes excluded on the grounds that freshmen lack discipline and may be distracted by the tube's temptations. Sometimes the lounges are located at the far end of the corridors, so that their serious environmental handicaps are augmented by their physical inaccessibility or remoteness from the more central and frequently traversed areas.

Commonly shared bathroom facilities tend of course to increase the possibility of contact among the residents on a particular floor. Nevertheless, the environment of a washroom is hardly as conducive to pleasant social interaction as is a properly designed lounge or recreational facility, and pleasant areas are more likely to lead to positive social exchanges than somewhat unpleasant and uncomfortable ones.

Corridor-type dorms also have another unfortunate environmental spinoff. As a result of their uniform, ordered, regularized, and cost-efficient designs, they tend to encourage a bureaucratic approach to various administrative responsibilities on the part of resident counselors, monitors, and the university administration in general. Rigid rules tend to proliferate, if for no other reason than that they are relatively easy to enforce in the cell-like or modular environment. These include picayune regulations about curfews, proper corridor dress, and what students may or may not have in their rooms—appliances, alcoholic drinks, or certain types of high-load decorations like wall hangings. As a result, students feel submissive. The unpleasant environment, when combined with submissiveness and heightened arousal caused by the pressures of study or noise, will of course result in anxiety or tension. And extensive use of an environmental design conducive to sustained anxiety is hardly wise.

A more generous and effective design is sometimes found in the venerable dorms on older campuses. But, these are unfortunately often reserved for the upperclassmen instead of being made available to entering freshmen who could profit most from their use. The floor plan of such dorms usually groups suites around small, irregularly shaped corridors similar to Figure 20.

That is, two or more individual rooms are grouped around a small lounge shared by those who occupy the suite. Students are thus assured of the privacy or low load needed for sleeping or studying, yet they can also meet in the lounge over coffee or drinks when they choose to socialize. One member of the suite can entertain friends in the lounge without greatly disturbing the others. The lounges can also serve as party areas for a number of residents on the same floor, in this way helping to form a network of social relationships. Since all the members of a suite can contribute something to the lounges in the way of additional decoration, these tend to be interesting and stimulating environments.

Those who have lived in both the suite-type and corridor-type

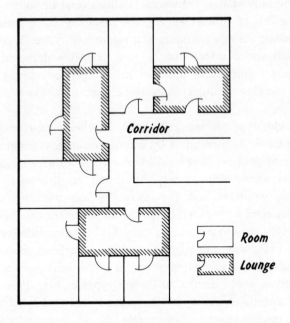

FIGURE 20

dorms know that there is a striking difference between the two in terms of the quality of social life. In the suite dorm there tends to be a good deal of social cohesiveness and friendliness among residents on each floor. There are usually several voluntary organizations or high-level rap sessions in which people help and learn from each other. Close friendships develop that sometimes last a lifetime. The administration of the dorm as a whole also tends to be more relaxed and informal, since it is harder for monitors to snoop around and note deviations from the rules. Moreover, picky regulations are seldom necessary since those who share a suite are far more likely to feel responsible for their living quarters and to work out mutually satisfactory routines to take care of their daily needs.

At the University of Hong Kong, two alternative dormitories are available to female students. These two dormitories are markedly different in character: one is considered a place for serious study and the other is known for being fun, but possibly too distracting. Dormitory A, selected by the more scholarly students, is a seven-story building. It is coeducational, with girls housed on the fifth, sixth, and seventh floors. The only areas shared by male and female students are a lounge on the second floor and a dining room on the first. Because these areas are not readily accessible, students often retire to their rooms after dinner and don't come out again.

Dormitory B, on the other hand, is a four-story structure housing females only. In addition to a lounge and dining room on the ground floor, there is also a penthouse containing hair dryers, beverage machines, and even a co-op store. This dorm is characterized by a sense of belonging, cohesiveness, and generally high spirits. The ground level is cheerful and comfortable, with a fireplace, stereo sets, and a TV. It is pleasant in appearance and overlooks a courtyard on one side and the front lawn on the other. In contrast, dormitory A has a less pleasant and less stimulating common room containing a few card tables. There is no TV, although a stereo system is available. Since the card tables are often occupied by bridge players, however, loud music is pretty much taboo.

Another interesting aspect, and one that greatly affects the general atmosphere, is that dormitory A schedules flexible mealtimes —for example, lunch is served between 12 and 1:30 P.M. Dormitory B, on the other hand, has rigid mealtimes, with the exception of breakfast. Lunch and dinner are announced by a gong, a distinctive feature of this particular dormitory. This effectively encourages the residents to gather together, enjoy a meal, and extend their table conversation to other activities in the lounge area. Since the lounge adjoins the dining room and represents the only access to it, this also encourages its use. In dormitory A the lounge is located on a different floor.

Some student housing in Sweden provides an interesting example of balance between privacy and the opportunity for social exchange. Dormitories are equipped with single rooms, each with its own adjoining bathroom. Privacy in the rooms is strictly enforced by the students themselves. It is very rare for persons whose rooms are along the same corridor to visit each other. Social exchanges take place in a kitchen which is shared by six to fifteen people. This kitchen area serves both as a cooking facility and as a common area fostering contact among the residents. The kitchen usually contains a single table to eat at, and possibly a television set. This makes quite a pleasant dining room, with an often lively atmosphere. Such a combined lounge-kitchen represents an economical use of space and at the same time provides an environment for people to meet and enjoy each other's company.

Effectively designed socializing areas not only provide stimulation and pleasure but also tend to elicit responsible and considerate behavior which in turn reinforces a communal feeling. A pleasant kitchen which is used by several people on a regular basis is less likely to be vandalized or allowed to become a pig sty than is a sterile end-of-corridor room containing only vending machines and no tables or chairs. People tend to assume responsibility for what they truly share, and in the process of sharing they are less likely to be careless or hostile toward their surroundings.

Suggested Readings

For one of the first environmental analyses of dormitories, see Van der Ryn and Silverstein (1967). Also see Heilweil (1973) who devoted an entire issue of journal articles to the environmental psychology of dormitories. For a discussion of how the spatial arrangements of persons affect friendship patterns, see the suggested readings for chapter ten.

28

Retirement Communities

HARDWORKING people who look forward to the day when they can retire and take it easy are often gravely disappointed when the time comes. What happens in most cases is that people who've worked in fairly high-load environments experience sharp and sustained drops in arousal through forced exposure to seemingly endless low-load settings. No matter how resourceful an individual may be, such drastic environmental load changes are difficult to combat and may possibly bring arousal down to levels associated with boredom and depression.

When a person who leads an extremely active life takes a lazy, restful vacation for two or three weeks, there is of course a similar decline in his arousal level. But he welcomes the change because it is relaxing and restorative and usually takes place in an environment that has been selected for its pleasantness. The vacationer also knows that the change in activity level is temporary; he knows that he will soon return to a hectic, highly loaded life. The retired person cannot have this perspective on his retirement. For him, retirement ceases to be a period of rest and recuperation and becomes instead a permanent and frequently unpreferred state of low arousal. These are the people who, after six months of retirement, are out looking for another job. Often they will take jobs for which they are vastly overqualified, since work in their own field is not available to them. It is not unusual to find, for example, formerly successful salesmen or other businessmen who simply cannot bear the low activity and load levels in their homes working as office temporaries, parking lot attendants, or ushers.*

Most corporations today have fixed retirement ages. A far better way of dealing with the problem of retirement would be to consider individual differences and to base the retirement age more flexibly upon these differences. Some people who reach the age of sixty-five or another mandatory retirement age are really ready to retire: they are not as productive as they used to be, or they have Peter-principled their way into positions in which they do not function adequately. Or, they may be nonscreeners who've been working at highly stressful jobs for much too long and welcome the prospect of less stress and more peaceful activities and environments. On the other hand, there are others for whom work has been a major source of excitement and fulfillment throughout their adult lives and who have derived the bulk of their identity from their association with certain tasks or positions. Such individuals tend to remain highly productive as a result of their strong motivation; for them, the retirement age could easily be extended. The company would continue to benefit from these workers' large reserves of experience and knowledge, their good work habits, and their considerable aggressiveness and motivation.

There are many advantages in having a mandatory retirement age, not the least of which is the convenience for those who would otherwise have to decide when each person must retire. And of course there are all those young turks who want a shot at positions that might otherwise remain out of their grasp for an additional decade or more. Nevertheless, such pressures can be accommodated by means of more imaginative and flexible retirement programs.

For example, one of the most severe blows retired persons have to deal with is a loss of dominance. If they were once highly placed executives with real decision-making power—including the power to hire and fire—their views or even their whims or eccentricities had something like the force of law. If they were big executives in a major industry, their opinions, influence, and money were sought by the community at large. Retired, they are just old people and

---

* I am not unmindful of the fact that many retired persons also work because they have to or feel that it is prudent to do so. For some, especially those who've been denied their pensions by unscrupulous or incompetent firms, Social Security benefits are not sufficient to meet their minimal needs. Others who retired at age fifty-five or sixty and have seen the rate at which inflation has eaten up their assets feel that it would be foolish not to supplement their fixed incomes as long as they are able to do so.

nobody cares what they do or think anymore. But for every high-powered executive with the retirement blues there are thousands upon thousands of senior departmental people, shop foremen, machinists, and other skilled or semi-skilled workers who, by virtue of long experience, expertise, and usefulness to their fellow workers, achieved positions of Mr. Chips-like respect and power (dominance) in their own bailiwicks. For them, the problems of retirement are just as acute, if not more so, as for a retiring VP or board chairman. There is no reason why some retirement-age senior or junior people might not be kept on with flexible working hours or on a part-time basis. They might be encouraged to take extended vacations and to be available in an advisory capacity at a reduced salary—perhaps at a rate that is equivalent to their pensions. The training period for new employees is always costly, partly because full-time employees must take time out from their tasks to instruct, correct, or otherwise shoulder additional burdens in relation to the trainees. Retired personnel could readily take over these training functions or otherwise consult and advise. Freed from other previous responsibilities, they would be valuable because of their ability to devote themselves to the communication of skills and knowledge acquired in the course of decades of experience. This in itself would be an arousing, if not downright novel, experience for certain senior people. They could legitimately feel useful, share in the generally more arousing work environment, and participate at will. If they would rather go fishing, they could. There would be a self-selection process at work, with no significant cost increases for the corporation and many potential benefits.

In a somewhat different context, the retired may be engaged to teach and train children and adolescents. In some programs, retired persons are invited to schools to teach crafts, to discuss their hobbies, or to teach subjects in which they have considerable expertise. Other programs enlist the retired to provide friendship or companionship to children, as in the case of a "foster grandparents" program for children from broken homes.

A retired person who is bored or depressed is usually unable to get himself moving in the direction of activities which could raise pleasure and arousal levels. The problem here is that he is not likely to be aware of the relationship between arousal and environmental load, or how arousal relates to emotions such as happiness or excitement. He may instead attribute his "low" periods to old age, the fact that he has effectively been cast out, or that he has fewer friends and has drastically reduced contact with his children. He may not as easily recognize the reduction in his daily environmental load. He may not realize that an environment which is full of people, uncertainties, decision making, and variation is arousing, whereas a home which is monotonous, unchanging, and lacking in interpersonal contacts is extremely low in arousing quality and is therefore conducive to boredom and depression.

Even more importantly, the retired person may not know that arousal must rise to a certain level before any projects will be undertaken, and certainly before socializing can take place. A depressed person—one whose arousal, pleasure, and dominance levels are quite low—is unlikely to leap up suddenly and play a round of tennis. Instead, his arousal must be raised step-by-step until it is somewhat commensurate with the level of arousal associated with a given activity. For example, a greatly bored or depressed person might take a mild stimulant—perhaps a nice cup of coffee or tea— and listen to a favorite piece of somewhat loaded music. Then he might do a little puttering around the house, perhaps effecting a minor household repair. The physical activity involved will be mildly arousing, and the act of fixing something will increase feelings of usefulness and mastery (dominance). Then he might call up a friend and chat awhile. Next he might bestir himself to actually visit this friend. They might then go off somewhere together and play a game of bocci, tennis, or whatever.

Learning to develop leisure-time activities is becoming an increasingly important task for almost everyone in technologically advanced societies. As the amount of nonworking time increases for most people, they must somehow manage to find ways to fill their leisure hours with enjoyable, stimulating activity, or else these hours will become a boring if not unbearable burden.

Most people have the ability, however strapped or enfeebled they may be, to participate in some form of sports or entertainment and to appreciate or even create music, crafts, or art. Sports, for example, have a tremendous capacity to heighten a person's arousal through concentration. Since most sports tend to be competitive, there is uncertainty as to outcomes. Then there are all the diverse bodily sensations associated with movement and exertion. Settings in which a person engages in most sports are usually very different from his home or work environments; the visual, auditory, and other sensory inputs are quite varied and hence stimulating. Interactions with people in a sporting situation also tend to be different in quality—they can be more openly aggressive, competitive, and informal than is normally acceptable.

The person who retires is generally an older man or woman, and certain very strenuous or dangerous sports or recreational activities might have to be relinquished. But there are many games and sports which do not create undue strain and stress yet provide pleasant, moderate activity. Golf, bocci, darts, pool, card games (especially those which traditionally contain a gambling element), and swimming are just a few examples. Most reputable gyms offer carefully planned and supervised programs of calisthenics. Walking or hiking in pleasant environments is another possibility. Traveling, especially in organized tours, can provide variety, company, and much stimulation.

Another way to modify the amount of environmental stimulation is through the careful selection of books, recorded music, TV programs, concerts, or movies. In all these cases, people have certain characteristic preferences. For example, some might prefer to read detective or spy stories containing a lot of excitement, aggression, and exotic settings. These people reveal a desire (probably un-verbalized) to increase their arousal levels. Indeed, most retired persons can probably benefit from reading high-load selections, even if the contents might be considered trashy or somewhat lacking in maturity. The same is true of movies, which are of course stimulating in several sense modalities. By some cultural quirk, entertainment which is considered too arousing for young children is also considered unseemly or inappropriate for the aged. It is time to see such views for what they are: traditional and inappropriate at best, or prejudicial and harmful at worst.

All in all, it is important to recognize that people tend to lose the intellectual, professional, social, and physical-manual skills which they do not use. Some rather effective ways in which the retired can maintain and even enhance such skills are through continuing education in city and community colleges, participation in discussion groups sponsored by local libraries, membership in arts and crafts centers, and volunteer work for organizations such as the Red Cross.

The practice in most modern urban societies of isolating the relatively old and relegating them to boring, lonely, and useless existences is not common in rural cultures or among the less developed nations. In these more integrated cultures the elderly usually live with their families and are not tossed out to fend for themselves, except perhaps in times of extreme cultural crisis. Nor do they lose their usefulness in the eyes of society or their immediate community. They have knowledge to impart, they perform very useful functions vis-à-vis young children, and they are in return respected and looked after. The problems facing the elderly today are to a certain extent new and complex, requiring solutions geared to modern conditions.

For the retired, particularly for those who get old and are unable to transport themselves, the problem is an extremely serious one. Only a small percentage of these people are lucky enough or rich enough to live in a pleasant area where there is a large concentration of people like themselves with whom they can readily interact and develop a sense of community. They don't make the big move to a community of similar people because the benefits are not apparent to them, because they can't afford to, or else because such a community doesn't exist nearby but instead entails a move halfway across the country. For the most part, the elderly are scattered throughout the cities, and spend their later years in the same homes or apartments which they selected many years ago for the privacy these afforded them. This privacy may no longer be preferable to stimulation, or the environment may have changed in such a way as to become dangerous or unpleasant. Also, the fact that they must rely on poor quality public transportation in order to get around, to visit friends, relatives, or clubs, and to participate in recreational activities discourages and isolates them. It forces them into an extremely drab and lonely existence in empty houses or apartments where their primary recourse is the secondhand association with life provided by TV.

In fact, a great deal of the senility attributed to the aged can be explained in terms of insufficient social stimulation. If you take any person and isolate him socially for prolonged periods of time, you will find that his mental abilities begin to deteriorate. Our discussion of the relatively low levels of stimulation experienced by patients in mental hospitals is relevant here. We have seen how slow but progressively serious aberrations in thought were induced in hospitalized patients even with partial deprivation of stimulation (as distinct from the more complete deprivation of subjects in sensory isolation experiments). A person must constantly interact with others to maintain his skills, whether these are manual, social, or intellectual.

If you isolate someone and deprive him not only of adequate sensory stimulation but also of attention, acceptance, approval, and affection, he will become socially less adequate and may begin to manifest aberrant behavior.

It is noteworthy that an isolated and depressed older person who is for some reason suddenly exposed to extensive contacts with friends and relatives begins to make a comeback. He regains his old charm, humor, and intellectual sharpness; he sees things vividly, comments on them vigorously, and generally becomes more alert. If he is once again isolated and forced to return to his lonely and unstimulating home, he reverts to the lack of alertness and progressive deterioration of his mental state.

In certain beach areas of Los Angeles, there is a concentration of older people who seem alert and active. They are fortunate enough to be living in a small community with adequate resources where it is possible to walk or take buses to friends' homes or apartments. There are many pleasant walkways lined with benches where friends or strangers can meet and pass the time together. Some of these public places even have tables with checkerboard patterns on them so that people can come with their chess or checker pieces and find someone to play a game with. Since these beaches are not isolated from the rest of the city, people from different walks of life visit them, and this results in continued activity and varied stimulation rather than the stagnant feeling typical of so many isolated communities for the retired.

There certainly aren't enough of these natural enclaves to accommodate all those who could benefit from some sort of organized or special community. Therefore, planned communities (I don't mean nursing homes) are needed which would be attractive to elderly persons who are unable to benefit from all the opportunities which individual housing offers to younger and middle-aged couples. The planned community can be helpful also to the elderly who are self-reliant and have considerable mobility, but who prefer greater stability in their immediate environment, accessible recreational facilities, and some form of supervision so that help, if needed, would be readily available.

This explains the recent popularity of condominiums among the well-to-do elderly. In condominiums as opposed to apartments, there is an added pride of ownership and a feeling of permanence and community among the residents. There are responsibilities for keeping up the public areas which must be shared and paid for by the whole community. While getting involved in such matters of mutual interest, the residents also meet and make friends with each other. The problem of dealing with the responsibility of ownership is more than offset by the opportunities it provides in bringing people closer together and giving them a sense of community. In addition, being the owner of one's residence produces a more dominant feeling and allows one to effect changes that suit one's needs—extensive redecoration or possibly structural changes that would not be permitted in an apartment.

Such condominiums or other more extensively planned retirement communities should not be extremely artificial in the sense of simply gathering together a large number of the elderly and isolating them from other segments of society. As we saw, the naturally occurring communities of retired persons in our cities are advantageous because they are visited by people of all ages, traffic goes through them, there is more regular activity, and less of a segregated feeling. Ideally, the planned retirement community should have as much of this openness to its surroundings as possible. At least, it should provide easy access to most of the resources of a city or large town. Residents should be able to walk or otherwise get to places without having to drive or face overcrowded or unpleasant public transportation. One cannot overestimate the importance of this factor, nor can one overestimate the desperate need of people living in poorly planned retirement communities to get out and experience the more varied sights and sounds associated with the larger community.

Easy access to the larger community is only one factor which makes a planned community a success. Planned communities can also be healthful because of the physical facilities they provide and because they can encourage individuals to find a niche for themselves within a larger network of social relationships. Other features of paramount importance include the physical arrangement of the units within the complex of dwellings, recreational facilities suitable for the particular age group, and activities that are likely to encourage numerous contacts and possibly help spark new relationships among the residents. All in all, such communities can do much to fill the void created by retirement, loss of an elderly spouse, progressive isolation from one's children and friends of long duration and, most painfully perhaps, by the progressive and unavoidable diminution of one's physical powers and sense of well-being.

Suggested Readings

Detailed analyses of environmental effects on the elderly and retired are lacking. For some preliminary discussions and data, see Lawton (1972) and Lawton and Cohen (1974). The suggested readings for chapters ten and eleven contain references that are relevant here, since the basic psychological issues involved in the design of communal environments are for the most part the same. See Rahe (1969, 1972) and Ross and Mehrabian (1976) on the adverse effects of large life changes on physical and psychological well-being. Also see the suggested readings for chapter seventeen for references on the detrimental effects of sensory deprivation.

CHAPTER
29

Suburbs

ECOLOGICALLY speaking, most suburbs are not true communities, since all the main activities of life, including one of the most important, food gathering or its equivalent, making a living, do not take place there. For many working suburbanites, the car represents the indispensable link between the environment in which they sleep and the environment in which they earn money. It is interesting and significant that the automobile and the suburb are currently inseparable and interdependent—both providing similar emotional benefits that have proven irresistible to those Americans who can afford them as well to those who can barely afford them.

Unlike members of certain other cultures, Americans tend to react to the negative effects of high population density by emphasizing privacy, sometimes to the point of social isolation. Both the car and the suburb afford a great deal more privacy than public transportation or crowded urban areas.

The middle- or upper-middle-class suburb is characterized by large distances, extensive greenery, lack of noise and crowdedness, and an absence of some of the dangers or other highly arousing aspects of urban life, all of which combine to produce a relatively low environmental load. The suburb also tends to be fairly high on pleasure. The houses are usually large, comfortable, and attractive, with manicured lawns and gardens. Usually there are private recreational resources ranging from family rooms containing pool or ping-pong tables to outdoor swimming pools or tennis courts. Many homes have backyard barbecues and picnic tables so that cooking or eating in a pleasant, gardenlike atmosphere is possible, at least during the summer months. And the suburb also tends to be relatively high on dominance. Most suburbanites own their own homes, whereas most city dwellers do not. Ownership contributes to a feeling of dominance, at least in most societies. The larger homes and grounds, relative to what a city dweller could have for the same money, also contribute to feelings of dominance because they represent a respectable amount of territory that the suburbanite has managed to stake out. And of course there are implications for social dominance as well, particularly in the well-to-do suburbs. Some have rigid though informal rules about what constitutes a "desirable" element or family, and these rules usually express or reflect degrees of socioeconomic dominance.

In a similar vein, compared to other practical modes of transportation currently available, the automobile is also low on arousal, high on pleasure, and high on dominance. Obviously, careening along a crowded freeway at seventy miles an hour is an arousing experience. But at such times it is also an exciting experience, because an automobile which rides well, is comfortable, is air-conditioned, and has a good stereo or tape player is also pleasurable. Even in traffic jams the arousing and unpleasant situation is to some extent offset by the pleasantness of the car interior. And in general, riding in one's own quiet, comfortable car on a decent road in fairly good traffic conditions is far less arousing than riding in a crowded, shabby, noisy, or uncomfortable bus, subway, or train.

The dominance aspect is extremely strong for the driver who is experienced and skilled, or at least believes he is. (Of course, student drivers or those who know they are rotten drivers can feel overwhelmed and submissive.) Most people own their own cars, which also contributes to their feelings of dominance. More importantly, the car functions in such a way as to extend one's limited physical abilities, giving enormous power and speed. Being in direct control of a powerful or agile vehicle greatly enhances feelings of dominance. Passengers are more likely to feel submissive unless they form a closely knit group—for example, a group of teenagers or a festive party of adults out on the town. The dominance aspect for drivers is particularly evident in the unusually aggressive or hostile behavior they sometimes exhibit. A minor inconvenience can lead to shouted or gestured obscenities that probably would not be forthcoming in an ordinary, on-foot social situation. Since cars are available in many makes and models, they not only reflect preferences and personalities but also give fairly reliable cues of the owner's social status. Owning and driving a large, expensive car, or a small, expensive one can cue so intensively that sometimes observers are misled, which of course is why some people buy more car than is congruent with their overall life style or their pocketbook.

Cars, then, as well as suburban homes enhance pleasure and dominance while lowering arousal. Inner cities and old-fashioned public transportation, on the other hand, are designed without due regard for emotional needs and thus tend to produce feelings of displeasure, submissiveness, and arousal—in other words, anxiety. In essence, a suburban way of life with its emphasis on cars helps to reduce feelings of anxiety, and this explains the tremendous exodus in recent years to the suburbs. Urban planners, aesthetes, and others who deplore the sprawling suburbs or the increasing numbers of cars on the road need to consider alternatives which reflect these basic emotional preferences. Realistic designs for future urban environments or various modes of public transportation must be keyed to produce feelings of low arousal, high pleasure, and high dominance.

This is especially true of mass transit. If they are to be preferred over the automobile, efficient mass transit systems—efficient in the sense of moving large numbers of people quickly to large numbers of destinations—must match the automobile in comfort, convenience, and dominance, if not in privacy.* The other alternative is to discourage the use of the automobile, for example by making cars prohibitively expensive to own and operate. This is the case in dense urban areas where the operation of the market (very limited and expensive parking or garage space) is sometimes effective because fairly efficient and far less costly alternative means of transportation exist. But people cannot be penalized arbitrarily for using cars in areas which do not have viable mass transit alternatives. This will result in an even more desperate clinging to cars and may discriminate against the poor.

Don't forget that it is much harder to impose something on, or take something away from, people who feel dominant, and it is especially difficult if what you want to take away is something that

---

* Incidentally, mass transit can provide smoother transitions in arousal between home and work environments. Commuter reading of newspapers is a common example of an activity with an intermediate load. Thus, on the way to work in the morning, the newspaper can help smooth the transition from the lower load at home to the higher one at work. On the other hand, someone leaving a high-load work situation can use a newspaper, or even nap, to reduce his arousal. The point here is that a commuter who does not have to drive has a choice of activities which suit his emotional needs, and a properly designed mass transit system will provide such built-in flexibility.

clearly contributes to a dominant feeling in the first place. The well-known capacity of New Yorkers, for example, to take dislocations and inconveniences in stride derives in part from the fact that power failures or bus and subway strikes create situations which tend to reduce social isolation—people get friendlier in such emergencies. And their so-what-else-is-new attitudes toward bus and subway breakdowns indicate that the resulting feelings of helplessness (submissiveness) are not too novel in that context. Taxi strikes or garbage strikes, on the other hand, tend to hit New Yorkers in those areas in which they do have some feelings of dominance, and hence create far more outrage. The weary cynicism of New Yorkers, as well as of other big city dwellers, probably reflects a lot of submissiveness. There is so very little they can actually control within their everyday environments that they develop the kind of ageless and unshakable patience characteristic of certain peasant communities who've been victimized by everything from Cossacks to hailstones and expect that they will always be.

But suburbs have their problems too and the solutions they offer are costly and only temporary. They are inefficient in the sense that each suburb must duplicate the shopping, recreational, and other resources of the city center to meet the needs of its residents. Since the suburbs fail to fully duplicate all the resources that are available within the larger city, particularly those of the city center, it becomes necessary for people to drive considerable distances to get to work, visit special restaurants, or get to places of recreation or entertainment like theatres, sports arenas, and so on. A tremendous amount of time is spent by suburban residents just driving their cars to where the action is.

As a suburb grows, commuter traffic to and from it increases and so does the congestion. It becomes increasingly unpleasant and difficult to drive to the city center; therefore, it becomes important to build new city centers which are more accessible than the original urban inner core. As these new suburban centers are built, they quickly lose their suburban quality and become congested, noisy, polluted, and expensive to live near; and so, gradually, people build new suburbs farther out. And then the same process is repeated, eventually resulting in a megalopolis.

Interestingly enough, the new suburban city centers are usually planned and built by those who have been heavily influenced, either consciously or unconsciously, by the automobile. A paramount design consideration is thus to provide lots of parking space, resulting in the allotment of one-third of all the available space to streets and parking. But designers who succeed in accommodating vast numbers of automobiles in their plans also tend to forget that people who walk have different needs from people who drive. As a result, newly developed suburban centers often have relatively low loads for the pedestrian. Planners who can justly congratulate themselves on the clever way they've handled the access-parking-egress problem sometimes fail to take into account that a long stretch—say 500 yards—which can be traversed in less than a minute by a driver will not only be a relatively long walk for a pedestrian but will also be a dull walk if all he has to look at is lawn and high-rises. A pedestrian requires a lot of visual and other kinds of stimulation in order to make his perambulation interesting. If he's walking through a fairly loaded environment, the distances go by quickly, almost unnoticed. But if he's walking down seemingly endless stretches of sidewalk containing no people or other fairly intense sources of stimulation, it's going to be a bore, and he will avoid it.

This is why New Yorkers, for example, walk far more than most people in Los Angeles. Manhattan residents think nothing of walking a mile (twenty city blocks) to get to work or for that matter anywhere else. Some of them walk the two or three miles to get home from work whenever the weather permits—and do so as a matter of distinct preference. It's good exercise of course, but more importantly it's fun—there is always something to see, unlimited shop windows to look in, people to watch, and so on. There is also a great variety of stimuli: one city block can be an armpit of the world and the next an extremely high-status showplace.

Within the West Los Angeles area, two suburban city sites, Westwood and Century City, have received considerable attention from real estate developers and investors. A large number of high-rise office buildings, shopping malls, and entertainment areas have recently been constructed in both of these locations. However, the Westwood area has enjoyed more success in attracting people and serving as a center. Even though a concerted effort has been made by the developers of Century City to include a major shopping area and an entertainment complex, it is used primarily by people who work in the office buildings or visit the theatre complex at night for the shows.

Westwood was basically a small university town and had the advantage of a central location with better freeway access. Despite the recent high-rise developments, Westwood remains basically a small town, with small-scale buildings, many sidewalk areas for promenading, and a great diversity of shops, restaurants, and movie theatres. Because of the way it's grown, Westwood does not have adequate parking, so it can be difficult to find a place for your car there, especially if you arrive late for an evening show. But this will ultimately prove to be an additional advantage. When adequate public transportation becomes available, Westwood will remain a walking town, with lots of stimulation from the shops and variegated crowds.

In contrast, Century City, which was designed from an empty (completely torn-down) area, contains high-status high-rise office and apartment buildings, an entertainment complex, and a shopping center. The shopping center has plenty of underground parking, as do the office buildings, apartment high-rises, and the entertainment center. But it's a long dull haul on foot from one complex to the other. Consequently, people drive to one of the complexes for a particular purpose, do whatever they intend to do, and leave. If they work in the office buildings, they drive from there to the shopping center, do their shopping, and then go wherever else they have to. If they drive to the theatre complex at night, they see the show and leave; they don't stay on and stroll around the shopping complex. If they live in the apartment buildings, they don't use the nearby facilities any more than do the other residents of West Los Angeles; they certainly don't walk anywhere, especially not at night. They drive because there is nothing connecting any of these centers but sidewalks that seem immensely long and lonely on account of the extremely low levels of variety and stimulation.

Thus the Century City "community" which was designed to be an integrated and lively unit is really nothing of the sort. Instead, it is a blueprint looking pretty good at a distance or through the front windshield of a car at twenty-five miles per hour, but not to people who have to put one foot in front of the next in order to move forward.

Suggested Readings

See Gans (1961, 1968) and Zehner (1971) for general discussions of suburbs. Also relevant here are the extensive references listed at the end of the next chapter. These include studies of carbon monoxide concentration in city traffic and its physiological and psychological effects, as well as a discussion of noise, crowding, and other stresses associated with urban life.

CHAPTER

30

Cities

THE possibility that by the mid-1990s four out of every ten Americans will be living in cities is alarming to contemplate, especially if we imagine tomorrow's cities to be larger versions of contemporary real cities like New York, Philadelphia, or Chicago rather than semi-real or less densely populated cities like Detroit, Los Angeles, or Denver. Given the problems facing most major American cities, it is inevitable that much of what we say about them will tend to have a negative cast. It might therefore be well to begin with a cheer or two for the great urban centers, of which New York City is certainly one.

Cities may be defined economically as concentrations of wealth in the form of capital or other economic goods. Where there is a concentration of money you will also find a concentration of those people who, through luck, skill, talent, imagination, resourcefulness, courage, or accident of birth have managed to garner, or are compelled to seek, more than their fair share of the available riches. There too you will find a concentration of industries which are dependent upon money or upon the freedom from basic survival concerns that money confers. These include the various arts or crafts which create many of the enduring artifacts or aesthetic forms of human civilization, as well as the institutions which provide the ideas or propositions upon which many technologically complex cultures are based. In practical terms, this means that you'll find the best ballet, opera, theatre, art galleries, orchestras, universities, and conversation in cities. For some people such things are supremely important, and they will choose to live in cities as long as cities continue to be the largest reservoirs of culture and talent. For them, the enormous variety and flexibility of a twenty-four-hour-a-day city, especially when it is combined with great cultural, intellectual, and economic resources, more than offset the negative or unpleasant aspects. But for many others the negative features of urban environments cause extreme avoidance.

What causes many people to leave cities if they can, or results in avoidance behavior if they can't, is the unpleasantness—the lack of greenery, the ugliness, certain kinds of noise, rude interpersonal behavior—combined with environmental conditions that create high levels of arousal.

Urban noise, for example, raises arousal levels and is almost invariably unpleasant. Since heightened arousal plus unpleasantness equals stress, noise is usually tension-producing. High-load noise— noise that is unpredictable, complex, and varies randomly in frequency, intensity, or duration—is the most arousing and unpleasant of all. Thus the steady hum from a busy street some distance from your apartment, or the steady chirping of crickets outside your window, is less arousing and less objectionable than an occasional truck or motorcycle roaring by or the sudden loud barking of a dog. Many machines make far more noise than necessary. In some cases manufacturers have simply not bothered to install noise-control devices, but in many others they are responding to consumer demand because people automatically assume that louder objects are also more powerful.* It would certainly be worthwhile to decondition these innate associations. The Federal Council of Scientists reports that urban noise has been doubling every decade, and it is clear that those who are forced to live with high-load, sustained noise are GASed by it—they suffer from chronic fatigue and develop neurotic symptoms.

Noise, however, is only one unpleasant and arousing aspect of our urban areas; overpopulation is another. The crowds common to urban areas are arousing, and often contribute to feelings of displeasure. People are jammed together in uncomfortable, unpleasant trains, subways, or buses. Streets are crowded, especially during rush

* For example, if a company markets two power lawn mowers with identical horsepower, many people will buy the one that sounds louder. They believe that the noisier one does more work and is more powerful. Size and therefore dominance are closely related in the animal mind to the amount of noise something makes: a full-grown chimp who has learned to bang empty oil drums together during his display will earn a higher status than his size or experience would normally warrant; similarly, we find it incongruous or even amusing if a huge and powerful man has a small, squeaky voice.

319

hours and at midday, when people want to get somewhere fast and the presence of so many others functions as an impediment and an annoyance. Stores and restaurants are usually filled, causing high arousal levels. And this runs counter to people's needs for low-load settings during meals or during decisions involving high levels of uncertainty (Should I buy this or that?).

Nevertheless, crowding is not always overly arousing, nor is it always unpleasant. Let us first consider the arousing aspect of crowds. When we think about the possible undesirable effects of crowding, it is important to remember that the arousal caused by crowded social conditions has two sources: density and the uncertainty or novelty arising from social disorganization. When high population densities are combined with unexpected, irregular, and unpredictable social relationships, arousal levels are maximized. In contrast, crowded conditions which are organized, patterned, and orderly are only moderately arousing. Since Oriental cultures are generally well-organized and extremely stable, they are less arousing than high-density American cities where crowding occurs in combination with general social disintegration.

Imagine an extremely crowded market where things are grouped unconventionally and where there are no signs or assistants to tell you where to find various items. You might find the onions next to the detergent and the household cleaners near the bread. This situation involving high uncertainty would force the individual to search for things by trial and error. When combined with the high load of crowding, the situation would result in excessive levels of arousal. Contrast this with a store which is extremely crowded but well organized. Here, the crowding will raise arousal, but there will be no further increases as a result of the physical arrangement and structuring of the store. In comparing these two stores, you can imagine how the first, which combines high density with high uncertainty, will lead to greater avoidance. People will be less likely to shop there in the first place, but if they must do so, they will be more impolite, less willing to help a stranger who needs assistance, less likely to just stop and answer somebody's question, and more easily provoked into quarrels or possibly even fights.

It may be worthwhile to dwell at greater length on these two very important sources of arousal, crowding and social disorganization, by comparing Oriental and American cultures. Let us note first that high arousal resulting from certain social conditions, when combined with displeasure, will lead to anger and hostility, or fear and anxiety. Hostility occurs when a person feels dominant; fear occurs when he feels submissive. People who characteristically respond with anger and hostility in an urban environment probably have dominant and competitive personalities, whereas those who characteristically get confused, anxious, or neurotic are submissive types.

Oriental societies tend to be highly structured and stable, thus, even though they are crowded, the resulting arousal levels are moderate, provided there are no general population trends toward nonscreening. In comparison, certain American cities are not only crowded but extremely unstable in their social makeup, causing frequent occasions of extreme arousal for their residents. Even if we don't assume that American cities are generally more unpleasant than those in the Orient, this still implies that residents of the former are more likely to be exposed to combinations of high arousal and displeasure, with the resulting manifestations of anger or anxiety.*

It is not surprising then that residents of Hong Kong, the world's most densely populated city, are generally healthier than urbanized Americans, and that Hong Kong has a lower crime rate. In Hong Kong, the close unity of the family, with its well-defined social roles and priorities, forms the basis of a highly structured society which attenuates the high loads of crowding.

Although the population density is also extremely high in Japan, we don't find the very high crime rates or the rude and inconsiderate behavior often associated with certain American cities. Japanese culture is extremely organized from a social standpoint. The rules of conduct and the social expectations are stable. In this way, the uncertainty level which is associated with interpersonal relationships is low, even though the density is very high.

But because the Japanese tend to be nonscreeners, many elements of Japanese culture show a continued striving to reduce arousal levels while increasing pleasure. We have already considered some of these in our discussion of the arts in Japan. More specifically, in reference to crowding, Japanese cities lack public gathering and socializing places where interpersonal cues can be intensified; there is nothing comparable to the Greek tavernas, German weinstubes, Austrian weinkellars, Canadian beer parlors, or English pubs. Mundane

---

* In contrast to some American cities which have only recently and rapidly attained comparable population densities, Oriental societies (or England, for that matter) have had more time to develop well-defined social orders, together with an emphasis on politeness and consideration as alternatives to chaos, violence, and eventual social suicide.

examples of the avoidance of highly arousing situations are noted on crowded buses, trains, or boats. Even on fairly short bus rides, it is not uncommon to find ten to twenty percent of the passengers napping. Sleep is obviously an effective device for shutting off the high load of a hot and crowded situation. A less extreme avoidance reaction to density is reading and is quite common in crowded public transportation systems in Japan, or, for that matter, in the United States. Reading channels the attention to different and more distant stimuli which are less loaded than the immediate ones, especially since people tend not to read highly complex materials on buses or trains, but rather read newspapers or magazines they can skim or assimilate without too much concentration.

Even within industry, the Japanese minimize arousal by having a set of organized relationship hierarchies similar to those governing the extended family. Most employees never consider the possibility of changing jobs to improve their positions or salaries. A man picks the company he wants to work for and spends the rest of his life working there. The company in turn shows a great deal of concern and responsibility toward its employees and their families. There are no unpleasant uncertainties about the possibilities of being fired or laid off during a slack period in business. A job is almost guaranteed for a lifetime; children of employees are expected to seek work within the same company which, as a matter of principle, is expected to make room for them. The mutual dependence between an employee and his company is very strong, possessing many of the elements characteristic of family ties.

However, this tightly organized network of relationships is beginning to erode, since some industries which pay much higher wages tempt workers to job hop. This in turn reduces the industrial leaders' feelings of responsibility toward their employees. If the trend continues, Japan will have some very serious social and economic problems resembling those in the United States but compounded by the extremely high population densities.

To summarize, high population density does not in and of itself necessarily result in cultural values that emphasize low-load environments, or when this is not possible, in social deterioration. Excessive arousal becomes a problem when high density is combined with uncertainties of social life, competitive instead of cooperative values, or a predominant trend toward nonscreening among members of a particular cultural group.

The problem is, of course, accentuated when several of the latter factors are combined with high population density. For example, crowding in American cities is associated with tremendous social mobility and generally high rates of social change (uncertainty), often leading to excessive levels of arousal. When, in addition, poverty, pollution, noise, and general environmental ugliness contribute to displeasure, we find unusually high rates of avoidance behavior. There is less concern for others, evidenced by fewer gestures like smiling, greeting, or general friendliness toward strangers. People are also less inclined to offer help when they see strangers in pain or distress. These phenomena can be understood readily in terms of the attempt to lower arousal. Becoming involved in other people's problems tends to disrupt one's own activities and plans and may often result in incursions on one's privacy. On all these counts, such involvement increases arousal and is unpleasant. Since city dwellers are often over-aroused, they are especially likely to avoid these activities which are unpleasant and which increase arousal further. Also, attending to people, noticing them, or responding to them socially, is arousing. So, in a crowded environment, others are ignored, which amounts to the filtering of high-load stimuli. In more peaceful and quiet settings, on the other hand, people become a welcome source of stimulation and are consequently treated in a more considerate manner even if extra effort is required to help them.

In terms of long-range effects, frequent and unavoidable displeasure and high arousal levels result in psychosomatic illnesses from GAS reactions, psychological problems associated with anxiety, or less frequently, in aggressive and anti-social behavior. In other words, the maladaptive consequences are generally associated with submissive rather than dominant feelings. Most of this submissiveness is conditioned by the highly artificial urban environment. City dwellers are surrounded by and dependent upon technology they haven't mastered and cannot control—subways, elevators, air conditioners, ad infinitum—and when one of these things breaks down, there isn't much they can do about it except be patient and wait till someone comes to fix it. Also, submissiveness probably has some adaptive significance. Victims of robbery or mugging who resist are more likely to be seriously injured or killed than those who do not. People who strike out aggressively are more likely to be eventually and forcefully subdued, whereas those who suffer from neurotic or psychosomatic complaints can rely on available social resources to temporarily ameliorate their conditions.

When combinations of high arousal and frequent unpleasant

experiences caused by relatively ruleless social systems threaten to engulf not only the poor but larger segments of middle-class society, it becomes tempting to rely on sociopolitical systems which minimize freedom. These minimize arousal deriving from social uncertainties, but incidentally minimize pleasure and dominance as well.

I am suggesting, then, that one outcome of crowding plus unpleasant environmental conditions is the creation of technologically sophisticated feudal or authoritarian sociopolitical systems. It is possible, for example, to detect in the recent history of the United States an increasing temptation to rely upon enforcement systems or agencies for the surveillance and control of the lower strata of society, as well as those who choose to identify themselves ideologically or otherwise with these strata. When the environmental conditions become so intolerable as to negate certain basic principles that underlie democratic systems, we may see more of this trend toward salvaging whatever is left with authority and force.*

Less damaging outcomes of the combination of crowding and unstructured social networks include the proliferation of eccentric, simple-minded ideologies and their relatively harmless cliques of sheepish followers. The majority of these ideologies and in-groups provide a simple, readily communicable formula which seems to lighten environmental loads by "explaining everything." Some such groups, many of which start or blossom in dense urban centers, go far beyond dictating values and general guidelines, and also minutely prescribe the proper manner of dress, general appearance, quality of social relationships, and attitudes or positions to be taken vis-à-vis marriage, education, and politics. In other words, these groups are exclusionary, parochial, and dogmatic. Some examples are the early peace-and-love hippy movement in the mid-1960s; the early LSD prophets; some of the smaller native, nonassimilated Buddhist groups; witchcraft cults; various therapy movements involving such esoteric

---

* In one sense, Watergate was as much of a shock to U.S. conservatives as it was to liberals. Conservatives are far more likely than liberals to think in terms of low-load patterns of logic and feeling which emphasize long-term systemic relationships. These conservatives have perceived that some of the Watergate abuses which have come to light are systemic in nature and will ultimately threaten the very ecological "home," or delicate, complex, and unequal cultural structure which they seek to preserve. The predictive model conservatives use in a case like this is simple but sensitive: coercive techniques used against members or strata of society will inevitably be employed against those who can actually mobilize or manipulate significant cultural resources; that is, those who have achieved substantial but not total control will be eliminated by others who wish to exercise their unfettered will.

techniques as massage, nudity, touching, or emotional outpourings; certain businesslike philosophies like scientology; and faddist converts to, as opposed to explorers of, particular diets, astrological traditions, or whatever.

These idiosyncratic groups or theories have tremendous potential for reducing the uncertainties that are associated with modern urban life because they provide an overarching mental construct that dictates daily activities as well as general values and interpretations. Such organizations do perform a useful psychological function for those members who simply cannot face or cope with the complexity and uncertainties of urban life. A second important need is also met by these odd but tightly bonded groups in today's unsettled and high-load urban populations. I've already talked about the many problems of loneliness which tend to result from an insistence upon privacy— the automatic and almost inbred reactions of the urbanite. Many urbanites now lack the channels for meeting and interacting with others in a satisfying way. Eccentric or arcane ideological groups serve as vehicles for bringing people back together and creating a sense of intimacy. Their ritual places counteract social isolation and provide group contacts within which to forge or at least assume an identity. Such cults provide a suitable background against which persons sharing similar attitudes and values can meet strangers, make friends, and find a place in a ready-made network of social relationships.

These strained solutions we have been discussing are not however necessary, and we might as well bring this chapter to a close by speculating briefly on what a nice, pleasant, exciting city of the future might look like. One thing seems clear: the automobile or "self-mover" as we now know it will have to go; it simply costs too much in terms of material, space, and environmental degradation.*

---

* Carbon monoxide is one of the major pollutants produced by automobile exhaust and its effect on animals and humans has been studied extensively. Carbon monoxide has a dulling effect. It lowers arousal level because it uses up the hemoglobin in the blood, and consequently less oxygen is available to the brain—thinking and reaction times are slowed down. It is especially dangerous for individuals with high blood pressure or cardiovascular diseases because the heart has to work even faster to get oxygen to the brain. With animals, it has been shown that fifty parts per million concentrations of carbon monoxide can result in irreversible brain damage. On Los Angeles freeways during rush hours the carbon monoxide concentration is often as high as 120 parts per million. We are no longer simply dealing with the question of how bad things might get in the future.

Its enormous psychological benefits—privacy and comfort, which mean pleasantness, low arousal, and dominance—will have to be duplicated in other modes of transport, perhaps by individual or two-seater modules on conveyor belts, perhaps something like the Monsanto ride in Disneyland or on-demand computerized "bubbles" that scoot hither and yon upon insertion of a program and a payment. Denver has already funded a public transportation system that envisions six- to twelve-passenger vehicles that will function as responsive, semiprivate trolley cars.

Take for example the various car-free zones many American and European cities have created, usually in the face of merchant opposition—until these same merchants began to experience an increase in sales. There is absolutely no technological reason why all of Manhattan could not be made car-free within ten years after the passage of such legislation. With the exception of its most venerable neighborhoods, Manhattan is laid out in a grid pattern, and New Yorkers have long been accustomed to walking several blocks to reach the subway line which fits their particular strategy for getting where they want to go.

Once freed of car traffic, only a small segment of the available street surfaces in Manhattan would be given over to one of the many modern alternatives provided by public transportation. The existing subway system could be used for the delivery of stock to merchandisers (as could helicopters) and for conveyor or pneumatic-type subsystems for the delivery of parcels. Cabbies, transit workers, and other travel-related employees could be absorbed into either the subterranean or aerial delivery systems to reduce economic dislocations.

Such a plan could not begin tomorrow, in a literal sense, because it involves massive economic and social changes. However, it can be approached in a series of successive stages through the development of car-free zones that would encompass increasingly larger segments of the city. The forerunner of today's planned pedestrian (car-free) areas was Stroeget, Copenhagen's main business street. In the early 1960s, vehicles were prohibited from Stroeget, except for a four-hour period each day for loading and unloading, and traffic was allowed to cross only at a few intersections.

Car-free zones work well when good public transportation is readily available. Recognizing this, city planners in Munich developed a very efficient public transportation system just prior to the 1972 Olympics held there. At the same time, the car-free zones which were instituted in the inner city included large squares and promenades. The careful integration of public transportation with such pedestrian zones in Munich ensured a viable and pleasant alternative to car-filled and congested streets in the city center.

Public transportation systems can also be instrumental in shaping and centralizing sprawling, undisciplined cities such as Los Angeles, because areas which acquire ready access to transportation become highly prized locations for shopping centers, residences, and offices. When centralization is combined with the elimination of one of the major sources of urban noise, pollution, and congestion—the automobile—cities can be dramatically reshaped. Areas that are now devoted to freeways, streets, parking lots, gas stations, car dealerships, and so forth can be redesigned into pleasant promenades, gardens, outdoor restaurants, cafes, theatres, and recreational parks, enabling cities to once again become active and humane centers of commercial and social life.

A return to high-load yet pleasant city designs will also resolve the privacy versus social stimulation dilemma. We know that much greater environmental loads are sought and can be tolerated in pleasant than in unpleasant places. Today's high-load and unpleasant settings only accentuate the insistence by many on territoriality and privacy, thus aggravating the problems of social isolation and loneliness. One way in which the unpleasantness and discomforts of city life can be significantly reduced is by minimizing the need for wasteful, time-consuming, and frustrating transportation. Residential, work, shopping, and recreational areas can be shaped so that a great diversity of facilities are within easy access, even within walking distance. This means the integration of work, play, and residential environments so that local neighborhoods become communities in the classical ecological sense, that is, locations where all the significant activities of life (getting born, working, eating, sleeping, socializing, mating) take place.

One possible plan that is economically feasible as well as psychologically and socially useful is to pattern cities after the Indian Pueblo-type dwellings, thereby creating high-density but low-rise building areas. Such areas would be structured so that heavy industry and conduits for the transfer of large masses of raw materials would be situated at the lowest level. The second level of this area would be occupied by light industry, such as clothing manufacturing, carpentry, or other kinds of industry which do not require massive amounts of hardware, transportation of bulky goods, or involve major pollution problems. Finally, the third and highest level of such high-density regions would consist of living, work, and recreation spaces; ideally, people could live and work in the same areas. The incorporation of the lowest level of heavy industry within high-density areas of the city would be most difficult to accomplish in that it would be at greatest variance with present-day city designs. However, the second and third levels of this high-density city proposal seem more feasible.

Many other plans can accomplish the same goals, but an important prerequisite for such a city in the Western world is the inclusion of personalized spaces, namely, designs allowing each living and work area the potential to express the individuality of the residents, and each community its own distinctive quality. Smaller units, such as smaller schools and buildings with shared areas of recreation, should add to the intimacy of such spaces and would foster community-oriented attitudes. City planners and architects would have to be less concerned with the clean-cut and neat-looking designs of high-rise buildings that are economical from a technological standpoint and shift to more organic-looking arrangements where units have individuality. Such cities might appear more disorderly or possibly even cluttered, but they would counteract the growing sense of social alienation and the "1984" feeling.

A graduated transition toward this goal would rely on currently available structures, rather than idealistically insisting on a discontinuous and economically unfeasible change. Fifty-story office buildings will no longer be mere work environments; and fifty-story apartment buildings will no longer be mere residential hives. Most of the existing high-rise office buildings in mid-town centers could readily be converted into complex living-working-socializing environments. Thus, large corporations would not occupy the same buildings they now do but would instead be scattered throughout a series of many communities. The centralization of certain decision-making and information-gathering processes would no longer be physical—a lot of warm bodies all in one place—but rather would be achieved through the use of cable communication media providing telephone, picturephone, and computer links.* People who have common occupa-

* Many people can work ten years in a high-rise office building without ever seeing or meeting those who are making the relevant corporate decisions. They might never in fact physically set foot on the fiftieth floor or wherever it is that the power is located, even though all they have to do is push a certain button in an elevator they ride many times a day.

tional interests and responsibilities would tend to live in the same buildings or building clusters in which they work. Shared entertainment, strolling, and socializing areas would be within easy reach of each mini-neighborhood. Such integrated work-live-play mini-communities would in no way eliminate current status distinctions or otherwise detract from the individual's right to be upwardly or downwardly mobile. But they would provide something like an ecologically sound home, and home, someone once said, is the dream of all travelers.

Suggested Readings

Overwhelming evidence on the harmful effects of carbon monoxide, particularly as it exists in its current concentration levels in most big-city traffic, was supplied by Beard and Wertheim (1967), Emik and Plata (1969), Goldsmith (1970), and in *Air Quality Criteria for Carbon Monoxide* (1970). Alternative means of transportation for the future are discussed by Helman (1968).

See Berland (1975), Bragdon (1971), Cohen (1968), Glass and Singer (1972), Harris (1957), Kryter (1950), and Mehrabian and Russell (1974a, chap. 6) for reviews of experimental findings on the effects of noise.

The arousing effect of another person was demonstrated in the studies by D'Atri (1975), McBride, King, and James (1965) and by Nichols and Champness (1971). The effects of crowding in animals and humans have been studied extensively. The following sources provide a representative cross-section of such studies: Calhoun (1962a; 1962b) and Christian (1961) for animal studies; Freedman (1975), Freedman, Klevansky, and Ehrlich (1971), Griffitt and Veitch (1971), and Stokols (1973) for specific experimental studies with humans; and Carson (1969), Chombart de Lauwe (1959), Esser (1972), Galle, Gove, and McPherson (1972), Hollingshead and Redlich (1958), and Winsborough (1965) for population density in relation to crime and psychopathology. Schmitt (1957, 1963) specifically provided data on the effects of crowding on crime and psychopathology in Honolulu and Hong Kong.

See, also, Dubos (1971) for an analysis of how humans deal with crowding by depersonalizing others; Latané and Darley (1970) on experimental studies that relate to ignoring strangers in distress; Berkowitz (1962, 1973) for a general analysis of, and data on, aggression; Mehrabian and Russell (1974a, chap. 7) on how environments affect hostility and aggression; Jacobs (1969) for an analysis of the function of commonly shared areas such as sidewalks in the life of city dwellers; and Cox (1965) on the diversity provided by city life. Finally, see the following sources for more general studies of stress and how it may be induced by crowding: Appley and Trumbull (1967) and Selye (1956).

Epilogue

OUR ANALYSIS of environmental psychology has been based on a few simple though general ideas. One of these is that human emotions can be described and measured along the dimensions of arousal, pleasure, and dominance. Another is that individuals vary in predispositions (possibly innate) to be more or less arousable, more or less dominant, and so on. Also, that widely disparate environments can be described using the concept of environmental load. The final set of ideas deals with relationships between preferences for, and desire to work or socialize in, places, and the emotions induced by those places. These relationships are documented and have strong predictive value.

In this brief overview, I would like to point out how this approach fits into the broader context of the social sciences and to speculate a bit about the value of environmental psychology.

Experimental psychologists, by and large, have limited themselves to the study of physiological responses (like heart rate, palm sweating, or EEG) and have failed to provide an adequate description of emotions. Other researchers or clinicians who have recognized the importance of emotions in humans have either lacked highly developed experimental methods or simply have not cared to approach the subject systematically. As a result of these and other historical factors, emotions—one of the most central aspects of human functioning—

have not been studied to a degree that is commensurate with their importance.

Emotions are the lowest common denominator of response to places, people, and events. They are an ever-present part of existence; that is, a person is always in some emotional state. Stating in general terms which kinds of emotional states are preferred and which are unpreferred allows us to predict the *direction of movement* an individual's emotions are likely to take. The basis for this prediction is that people try to compensate for situations, events, tasks, social exchanges, or temperamental and transitory bodily (hunger, fatigue) conditions that are emotionally unsatisfactory. So, we can predict what kinds of environments an individual is likely to approach or avoid—what kinds of situations, activities, social interactions, drugs, and so on he will choose.

One important by-product of keying in on emotions is that they provide us with a set of basic dimensions of personality—the temperamental dimensions of pleasure-displeasure, arousal-nonarousal, and dominance-submissiveness. These basic dimensions can in turn be used to derive other personality descriptors such as anxiety, neuroticism, extroversion, hostility, sociability, depression, and so forth. In addition to its contribution to the study of personality, our framework also bears in a useful way on the area of social psychology and provides some insights into human development and physiology. In short, there are broad implications here for a general theory of psychology. Emotions, a very important though neglected area of human functioning, can now be studied using methods that are part of the repertoire of experimental psychologists.

We've dealt in this book with three main levels of analysis: the person, the person interacting with small groups or with readily manipulated or semiprivate environments, and the person as a barely traceable mote in environments large enough to be considered macrocosms. Let us look briefly at each of these three levels.

The usefulness of certain kinds of information about yourself is more or less beyond question. Knowing your blood type, your reactions to certain allergens, or the limits to which your heart or liver can be stressed are all fair examples. Other forms of self-knowledge clearly have two cutting edges and may be abused both by the individual possessing the knowledge or by social groups who know what the individual knows. Assuming that the temperamental dimensions are used widely to give each person a description of his or her basic emotional "map" or constitution, the question is, would such information be largely beneficial, or would it invite self-abuse or shameless manipulation by others?

My personal belief, a belief which motivated me to write this book (and which for that matter underlies any systematic study and exposition of a field of knowledge), is that the results will be largely beneficial and will not be subject to extensive individual or social abuse. But doubts about this cannot be willed out of existence, and possible dangers should be recognized.

Many of the high-technology environments—objects of the second level of our analysis—are already standardized. They are created by industrial processes deriving from cost-benefit analyses, the technologically possible, and the often idiosyncratic or even perverse personal tastes, preferences, and talents of the relatively few who function as influential creators or designers. Assume that these now-standardized environments—off-the-rack clothing, furnished apartments, mobile homes, hotel rooms, automobiles, classrooms, mass transit, city streets or plazas—could be analyzed in terms of our framework to highlight their possibly narrow emotional foci and generally to provide the public with information describing their environmental load and other emotion-inducing qualities. Examples might be a movie-rating system that describes a film's emotional impact instead of (or in addition to) the current G to X system, or similar classifications of hotel and motel rooms that would serve to emphasize a client's choice of a variety of environmental moods. To what extent would the manufacturers and purveyors of standardized environments benefit from such a system? To what extent could they abuse or manipulate it? Again, my belief is that the countless commercial spinoffs will be successful not because they allow for unilateral rip-offs but because they prove beneficial to producers and consumers alike.

At the third level of analysis, what I find exciting about a theory of environmental psychology is its potential use as a tool for exploring the macrocosm. Many of the disciplines uneasily clustered together under the heading of "the social sciences" have tremendous theoretical problems in getting from the small to the large—from the individual to the population, from small-group interactions to societal institutions and processes—or vice versa. Our framework cuts across these distinctions and can provide some of the tools to follow and identify individuals even as they "disappear" in the crowd represented by communities, mass audiences, or any other kind of polity. That is, it is theoretically possible not only to identify individual emotional responses to macro-processes or institutions, but also to quantify mass responses and hence to predict large-scale changes in social phenomena—for example, recall our discussion of cultural preferences for art forms.

So, at each of the three levels of analysis—the personal, the micro-environment, and the macro-environment—a common theme of analysis is developed in terms of emotional phenomena; we have only glimpsed a few of its numerous theoretical and practical implications.

References

Agron, G. Behavior in institutional settings. In R. H. Moos & P. M. Insel (Eds.), *Issues in social ecology*. Palo Alto, Calif.: National Press Books, 1974. Pp. 238–247.

Air quality criteria for carbon monoxide. (U.S. Public Health Service Publication). Washington, D.C.: U.S. Government Printing Office, 1970.

Alexander, C., Hirshen, S., Ishikawa, S., Coffin, C., & Angel, S. *Houses generated by patterns.* Berkeley, Calif.: Center for Environmental Structure, 1969.

Alexander, C., Ishikawa, S., & Silverstein, M. *A pattern language which generates multi-service centers.* Berkeley, Calif.: Center for Environmental Structure, 1968.

Allen, E. C., & Guilford, J. P. Factors determining the affective values of color combinations. *American Journal of Psychology*, 1936, *48*, 643–648.

Altered states of awareness: Readings from Scientific American. San Francisco: Freeman, 1972.

Anastasi, A. *Differential psychology.* New York: Macmillan, 1958.

Ankele, C., & Sommer, R. The cheapest apartments in town. *Environment and Behavior*, 1973, *4*, 505–513.

Appley, M. H., & Trumbull, R. (Eds.). *Psychological stress.* New York: Appleton-Century-Crofts, 1967.

Ardrey, R. *The territorial imperative.* New York: Atheneum, 1966.

Attneave, F. *Applications of information theory to psychology: A summary of basic concepts, methods, and results.* New York: Holt, 1959.

Aviado, D. M. *Krantz and Carr's pharmacologic principles of medical practice.* Baltimore: Williams and Wilkins, 1972.

Ayres, L. P. The influence of music on speed in the Six Day Bicycle Race. *American Physical Education Review*, 1911, *16*, 321–324.

Baer, S. *Dome cookbook.* Corrales, New Mexico: Lama Foundation, 1969.

References

Bandura, A. *Principles of behavior modification.* New York: Holt, Rinehart and Winston, 1969.

Barber, T. X. *LSD, marihuana, yoga and hypnosis.* Chicago: Aldine, 1970.

Barker, R. G. On the nature of the environment. *Journal of Social Issues*, 1963, *19*, 1–14.

Barker, R. G., & Gump, P. V. *Big school, small school.* Stanford, Calif.: Stanford University Press, 1964.

Barker, R. G., & Schoggen, P. *Qualtiies of community life.* San Francisco: Jossey-Bass, 1973.

Beard, R. R., & Wertheim, G. A. Behavioral impairment associated with small doses of carbon monoxide. *American Journal of Public Health and the Nation's Health*, 1967, *57*, 2012–2022.

Bedford, T. Researches on thermal comfort. *Ergonomics*, 1961, *4*, 289–310.

Bellugi, U., & Brown, R. The acquisition of language. *Monographs of the Society for Research in Child Development*, 1964, *29* (1, Serial No. 92).

Berkowitz, L. *Aggression: A social psychological analysis.* New York: McGraw-Hill, 1962.

Berkowitz, L. Control of aggression. In B. M. Caldwell & H. N. Ricciuti (Eds.), *Review of child development research* (Vol. 3). Chicago: University of Chicago Press, 1973. Pp. 95–140.

Berland, T. Silence for society's sake. *Humanitas*, 1975, *11*, 133–146.

Berlyne, D. E. *Conflict, arousal, and curiosity.* New York: McGraw-Hill, 1960.

Berlyne, D. E. Arousal and reinforcement. In D. Levine (Ed.), *Nebraska Symposium on Motivation* (Vol. 15). Lincoln: University of Nebraska Press, 1967. Pp. 1–110.

Berlyne, D. E. *Aesthetics and psychobiology.* New York: Appleton-Century-Crofts. 1972.

Berscheid, E., & Walster, E. H. *Interpersonal attraction.* Reading, Mass.: Addison-Wesley, 1969.

Bexton, W. H., Heron, W., & Scott, T. H. Effects of decreased variation in the sensory environment. *Canadian Journal of Psychology*, 1954, *8*, 70–76.

Bliss, E. L., & Branch, C. H. *Anorexia nervosa.* New York: Hoeber-Harper, 1960.

Bourne, P. G. *Men, stress and Vietnam.* Boston: Little, Brown, 1970.

Braddock, J. C. The effect of prior residence upon dominance in the fish *Platypoecilus maculatus. Physiological Zoology*, 1949, *22*, 161–169.

Bragdon, C. R. *Noise pollution: The unquiet crisis.* Philadelphia: University of Pennsylvania Press, 1971.

Brand, S. (Ed.). *The whole earth catalogue.* Menlo Park, Calif.: Point, 1970.

Broadbent, D. E. *Decision and stress.* New York: Academic Press, 1971.

Broen, W. E., Jr. *Schizophrenia research and theory.* New York: Academic Press, 1968.

Buehler, R. E., Patterson, G. R., & Furniss, J. M. The reinforcement of behavior in institutional settings. *Behavior Research and Therapy*, 1966, *5*, 157–167.

Burney, C. *Solitary confinement*. New York: St. Martin's Press, 1961.

Bush, L. E., II. Individual differences multidimensional scaling of adjectives denoting feelings. *Journal of Personality and Social Psychology*, 1973, 25, 50–57.

Buss, A. H. *Psychopathology*. New York: Wiley, 1966.

Byrne, D. *The attraction paradigm*. New York: Academic Press, 1971.

Calhoun, J. B. Population density and social pathology. *Scientific American*, 1962, 206(2), 139–148. (a)

Calhoun, J. B. *The ecology and sociology of the Norway rat*. (U.S. Public Health Service Publication No. 1008). Washington, D.C.: U.S. Government Printing Office, 1962. (b)

Carpenter, C. R. Territoriality: A review of concepts and problems. In A. Roe & G. G. Simpson (Eds.), *Behavior and evolution*. New Haven: Yale University Press, 1958. Pp. 224–250.

Carson, D. H. Population concentration and human stress. In B. P. Rourke (Ed.), *Explorations in the psychology of stress and anxiety*. Don Mills, Canada: Longmans Canada, 1969. Pp. 27–42.

Chapin, F. S. The effects of slum clearance and rehousing on family and community relationships in Minneapolis. *American Journal of Sociology*, 1938, 43, 744–763.

Cherry, C. *On human communication: A review, a survey, and a criticism*. Cambridge, Mass.: M.I.T. Press, 1966.

Child, I. L. Esthetics. In G. Lindzey & E. Aronson (Eds.), *Handbook of social psychology* (Vol. 3). Reading, Mass.: Addison-Wesley, 1968. Pp. 853–916.

Chombart de Lauwe, P. *Famille et habitation*. Paris: Éditions du Centre National de la Récherche Scientifique, 1959.

Christian, J. J. Phenomena associated with population density. *Proceedings of the National Academy of Science*, 1961, 47, 428–449.

Clark, W. G., & del Giudice, J. (Eds.). *Principles of psychopharmacology*. New York: Academic Press, 1970.

Cohen, A. Noise effects on health, productivity, and well-being. *Transactions of the New York Academy of Sciences*, Series 2, 1968, 30, 910–918.

Cohen, M.D. Recycling elementary schools . . . people, program, facilities. *Childhood Education*, 1973, 49, 302–306.

Cohen, S. I. Central nervous system functioning in altered sensory environments. In M. H. Appley & R. Trumbull (Eds.), *Psychological stress: Issues in research*. New York: Appleton-Century-Crofts, 1967. Pp. 77–112.

Cox, H. *The secular city*. New York: Macmillan, 1965.

Craik, K. H. Environmental psychology. In K. H. Craik, B. Kleinmuntz, R. L. Rosnow, R. Rosenthal, J. A. Cheyne, & R. H. Walters (Eds.), *New directions in psychology 4*. New York: Holt, Rinehart and Winston, 1970. Pp. 1–121.

D'Atri, D. A. Psychophysiological responses to crowding. *Environment and Behavior*, 1975, 7, 237–252.

References

Davis, L. E., & Trist, E. L. Improving the quality of work life: Sociotechnical case studies. In J. O'Toole (Ed.), *Work and the quality of life*. Prepared under the auspices of the W. E. Upjohn Institute of Employment Research, 1974. Pp. 246–280.

Dember, W. N., & Earl, R. W. Analysis of exploratory, manipulatory and curiosity behaviors. *Psychological Review*, 1957, *64*, 91–96.

Dement, W. C. The effect of dream deprivation. *Science*, 1960, *131*, 1705–1707.

Deutsch, M., & Collins, M. E. *Interracial housing: A psychological evaluation of a social experiment*. Minneapolis: University of Minnesota Press, 1951.

Doll, R. C., & Fleming, R. S. (Eds.). *Children under pressure*. Columbus, Ohio: Charles E. Merrill, 1966.

Dubos, R. Man overadapting to the environment. *Psychology Today*, 1971, *4*, 50–53.

Duffy, E. The psychological significance of the concept of "arousal" or "activation." *Psychological Review*, 1957, *64*, 265–275.

Duffy, E. *Activation and behavior*. New York: Wiley, 1962.

Dupuy, T. N. *Ferment in college libraries—The impact of information technology*. Washington, D.C.: Communication Service Corporation, 1968.

Ellinwood, E. H., & Cohen, S. *Current concepts on amphetamine abuse*. (National Institute of Mental Health Publication No. HSM 72-9085). Washington, D.C.: U.S. Government Printing Office, 1972.

Ellis, D. S., & Brighouse, G. Effects of music on respiration- and heart-rate. *American Journal of Psychology*, 1952, *65*, 39–47.

Emery, F. E., & Trist, E. L. Socio-technical systems. In C. W. Churchman & M. Verhulst (Eds.), *Management science, models and techniques* (Vol. 2). Oxford, Eng.: Pergamon, 1960. Pp. 83–97.

Emik, L. O., & Plata, R. L. Depression of running activity in mice by exposure to polluted air. *Archives of Environmental Health*, 1969, *18*, 574–579.

Enright, B. J. *New media and the library in education*. Hamden, Conn.: Linnet, 1972.

Esser, A. H. A biosocial perspective on crowding. In J. F. Wohlwill & D. H. Carson (Eds.), *Environment and the social sciences: Perspectives and applications*. Washington, D.C.: American Psychological Association, 1972. Pp. 15–28.

Falender, C., & Mehrabian, A. Environmental effects on parent-infant interaction. *Genetic Psychology Monographs*, 1977.

Featherstone, J. *Schools where children learn*. New York: Liveright, 1971.

Feshbach, S., & Singer, R. D. *Television and aggression: An experimental field study*. San Francisco: Jossey-Bass, 1971.

Festinger, L., Schachter, S., & Back, K. *Social pressures in informal groups: A study of human factors in housing*. Stanford, Calif.: Stanford University Press, 1963.

Fiske, D. W., & Maddi, S. R. *Functions of varied experience*. Homewood, Ill.: Dorsey, 1961.

Fitch, J. M. Experimental bases for aesthetic decision. *Annals of the New York Academy of Sciences*, 1965, *128*, 706–714.

Fitch, J. M. *American building 2: The environmental forces that shape it.* Boston: Houghton Mifflin, 1972.

Ford, C. S., Prothro, E. T., & Child, I. L. Some transcultural comparisons of esthetic judgment. *Journal of Social Psychology*, 1966, *68*, 19–26.

Freedman, J. L. *Crowding and Behavior.* New York: Viking, 1975.

Freedman, J. L., Klevansky, S., & Ehrlich, P. R. The effect of crowding on human task performance. *Journal of Applied Social Psychology*, 1971, *1*, 7–25.

Fried, M. Grieving for a lost home. In L. J. Duhl (Ed.), *The urban condition: People and policy in the metropolis.* New York: Basic Books, 1963. Pp. 151–171.

Fried, M., & Gleicher, P. Some sources of residential satisfaction in an urban slum. *Journal of the American Institute of Planners*, 1961, *27*, 305–315.

Friedman, S., & Juhasz, J. B. (Eds.). *Environments: Notes and selections on objects, spaces, and behavior.* Monterey, Calif.: Brooks/Cole, 1974.

Galle, O. R., Gove, W. R., & McPherson, J. M. Population density and pathology: What are the relations for man? *Science*, 1972, *176*, 23–30.

Gans, H. J. Planning and social life: Friendship and neighbor relations in suburban communities. *Journal of the American Institute of Planners*, 1961, *27*, 134–140.

Gans, H. J. *People and plans: Essays on urban problems and solutions.* New York: Basic Books, 1968.

Garner, W. R. *Uncertainty and structure as psychological concepts.* New York: Wiley, 1962.

Glaser, D. *The effectiveness of a prison and parole system.* Indianapolis: Bobbs-Merrill, 1964.

Glass, D., & Singer, J. *Urban stress: Experiments on noise and social stressors.* New York: Academic Press, 1972.

Goffman, E. *Asylums: Essays on the social situation of mental patients and other inmates.* Chicago: Aldine, 1961.

Goldsmith, J. R. Carbon monoxide research—Recent and remote. *Archives of Environmental Health*, 1970, *21*, 118–120.

Gordon, J. J. *Synectics.* New York: Harper, 1961.

Green, R. The behaviorally feminine male child. In R. C. Freedman, R. M. Richart, & R. L. Van de Wiele (Eds.), *Sex differences in behavior.* New York: Wiley, 1974. Pp. 301–314.

Griffitt, W., & Veitch, R. Hot and crowded: Influences of population density and temperature on interpersonal affective behavior. *Journal of Personality and Social Psychology*, 1971, *17*, 92–98.

Guilford, J. P. The affective value of color as a function of hue, tint, and chroma. *Journal of Experimental Psychology*, 1934, *17*, 342–370.

Guilford, J. P., & Smith, P. C. A system of color preferences. *American Journal of Psychology*, 1959, *72*, 487–502.

References

Gunderson, E. K. E. Emotional symptoms in extremely isolated groups. *Archives of General Psychiatry*, 1963, 9, 362–368.

Gunderson, E. K. E. Mental health problems in Antarctica. *Archives of Environmental Health*, 1968, 17, 558–564.

Hall, E. T. *The hidden dimension*. Garden City, N.Y.: Doubleday, 1966.

Handel, L. A. *Hollywood looks at its audience*. Urbana: University of Illinois Press, 1950.

Haney, C., Banks, C., & Zimbardo, P. G. Interpersonal dynamics in a simulated prison. *International Journal of Criminology and Penology*, 1973, 1, 69–97.

Harmon, D. B. Lighting and child development. *Illuminating engineering*, 1945, 40, 199–228.

Harris, C. M. (Ed.). *Handbook of noise control*. New York: McGraw-Hill, 1957.

Heber, R., Garber, H., Harrington, S., Hoffman, C., & Falender, C. *Rehabilitation of families at risk for mental retardation*. Progress report of the Rehabilitation Research and Training Center in Mental Retardation. Madison: University of Wisconsin, 1972.

Heilweil, M. (Ed.). Student housing, architecture, and social behavior. *Environment and Behavior*, 1973, 5, entire issue.

Hellman, H. *Transportation in the world of the future*. Philadelphia: Lippincott, 1968.

Higgins, J. The concept of process-reactive schizophrenia: Criteria and related research. *Journal of Nervous and Mental Disease*, 1964, 1, 9–25.

Higgins, J. Process-reactive schizophrenia: Recent developments. *Journal of Nervous and Mental Disease*, 1969, 6, 450–472.

Hogg, J. (Ed.). *Psychology and the visual arts*. Baltimore: Penguin, 1969.

Hollingshead, A. B., & Redlich, F. C. *Social class and mental illness: A community study*. New York: Wiley, 1958.

Holmes, T. H., & Masuda, M. Life change and illness susceptibility. In *Separation and depression: Clinical and research aspects*. Symposium presented at the Annual Meeting of the American Association for the Advancement of Science, Chicago, 1970.

Horowitz, F. D., & Paden, L. Y. The effectiveness of environmental intervention programs. In B. M. Caldwell and H. N. Ricciuti (Eds.), *Review of child development research* (Vol. 3). Chicago: University of Chicago Press, 1973. Pp. 331–402.

Illich, I. *Celebration of awareness*. Garden City, N.Y.: Doubleday, 1970.

Illich, I. *Deschooling society*. New York: Harper & Row, 1971.

Ittelson, W. H., Proshansky, H. M., & Rivlin, L. G. The environmental psychology of the psychiatric ward. In H. M. Proshansky, W. H. Ittelson, & L. G. Rivlin (Eds.), *Environmental psychology: Man and his physical setting*. New York: Holt, Rinehart and Winston, 1970. Pp. 419–439.

Ittelson, W. H., Proshansky, H. M., & Rivlin, L. G. Bedroom size and social interaction of the psychiatric ward. In J. F. Wohlwill & D. H. Carson (Eds.), *Environment and the social sciences: Perspectives and applica-*

tions. Washington, D.C.: American Psychological Association, 1972. Pp. 95–104.

Iwao, S., & Child, I. L. Comparison of esthetic judgments by American experts and by Japanese potters. *Journal of Social Psychology*, 1966, *68*, 27–33.

Jackson, P. W. *Life in classrooms*. New York: Holt, Rinehart and Winston, 1968.

Jacobs, J. *Death and life of great American cities*. New York: Random House, 1969.

Jacobson, E. *Progressive relaxation*. Chicago: University of Chicago Press, 1938.

Jaffe, Y., Malamuth, N., Feingold, J., & Feshbach, S. Sexual arousal and behavioral aggression. *Journal of Personality and Social Psychology*, 1974, *30*, 759–764.

Jahoda, M., & West, P. S. Race relations in public housing. *Journal of Social Issues*, 1951, *7*, 132–139.

Jarvik, M. E. Drugs and arousal. In B. P. Rourke (Ed.), *Explorations in the psychology of stress and anxiety*. Don Mills, Canada: Longmans Canada, 1969. Pp. 43–48.

Kryter, K. D. The effects of noise on man. *Journal of Speech Disturbance*, 1950. (Monograph Supplement 1).

Kuper, L. (Ed.). *Living in towns*. London: Cresset, 1953.

Laing, R. D. *Politics of experience*. New York: Ballantine, 1968.

Laing, R. D., & Esterson, A. *Sanity, madness and the family* (Vol. 1, *Families of schizophrenics*). London: Tavistock, 1964.

Latané, B., & Darley, J. M. *The unresponsive bystander: Why doesn't he help?* New York: Appleton-Century-Crofts, 1970.

Lawton, M. P. Some beginnings of an ecological psychology of old age. In J. F. Wohlwill & D. H. Carson (Eds.), *Environment and the social sciences: Perspectives and applications*. Washington, D.C.: American Psychological Association, 1972. Pp. 114–122.

Lawton, M. P., & Cohen, J. Environments and the well-being of elderly inner-city residents. *Environment and Behavior*, 1974, *6*, 194–211.

Lemkau, P. *Mental hygiene in public health*. (2nd ed.). New York: McGraw-Hill, 1955.

Leonard, G. B. *Education and ecstasy*. New York: Delacorte, 1968.

Levine, S., & Scotch, N. A. (Eds.). *Social stress*. Chicago: Aldine, 1970.

Lindsley, D. B. Psychophysiology and motivation. In M. R. Jones (Ed.), *Nebraska Symposium on Motivation* (Vol. 5). Lincoln: University of Nebraska Press, 1957. Pp. 44–105.

Lorentz, K. Z. *On aggression*. New York: Harcourt, Brace and World, 1966.

Manning, P. *Office design: A study of environment*. Liverpool, England: The Pilkington Research Unit, 1965.

Marans, R. W. Outdoor recreation behavior in residential environments. In J. F. Wohlwill & D. H. Carson (Eds.), *Environment and the social sciences: Perspectives and applications*. Washington, D.C.: American Psychological Association, 1972. Pp. 217–232.

Marijuana commission second report on marijuana and drug abuse (Vol. 1). Washington, D.C.: U.S. Government Printing Office, 1973.

Marks, L. E. On colored-hearing synesthesia: Cross-modal translations of sensory dimensions. *Psychological Bulletin,* 1975, *82,* 303–331.

Masters, W. H., & Johnson, V. E. *Human sexual response.* Boston: Little, Brown, 1966.

May, R. Sex differences in fantasy patterns. *Journal of Projective Techniques and Personality Assessment,* 1966, *30,* 576–586.

McBride, G., King, M. G., & James, J. W. Social proximity effects on galvanic skin responses in adult humans. *Journal of Psychology,* 1965, *61,* 153–157.

McClelland, D. C., Atkinson, J. W., Clark, R. A., & Lowell, E. L. *The achievement motive.* New York: Appleton-Century-Crofts, 1953.

McClelland, D. C., Davis, W. N., Kalin, R., & Wanner, E. *The drinking man.* New York: Free Press, 1972.

McGrath, J. E. (Ed.). *Social and psychological factors in stress.* New York: Holt, Rinehart and Winston, 1970.

McLuhan, M. *Understanding media: The extensions of man.* New York: McGraw-Hill, 1964.

McReynolds, P., Acker, M., & Pietila, C. Relation of object curiosity to psychological adjustment in children. *Child Development,* 1961, *32,* 393–400.

Mehrabian, A. *Tactics of social influence.* Englewood Cliffs, N.J.: Prentice-Hall, 1970.

Mehrabian, A. *Silent messages.* Belmont, Calif.: Wadsworth, 1971.

Mehrabian, A. *Nonverbal communication.* Chicago: Aldine-Atherton, 1972. (a)

Mehrabian, A. Nonverbal communication. In J. K. Cole (Ed.), *Nebraska Symposium on Motivation, 1971* (Vol. 19). Lincoln: University of Nebraska Press, 1972. Pp. 107–161. (b)

Mehrabian, A. A questionnaire measure of individual differences in stimulus screening and associated differences in arousability. *Environmental Psychology & Nonverbal Behavior,* 1976.

Mehrabian, A. Individual differences in stimulus screening and arousability. Unpublished manuscript, UCLA, 1976. (b)

Mehrabian, A., & Diamond, S. G. Seating arrangement and conversation. *Sociometry,* 1971, *34,* 281–289. (a)

Mehrabian, A., & Diamond, S. G. The effects of furniture arrangement, props, and personality on social interaction. *Journal of Personality and Social Psychology,* 1971, *20,* 18–30. (b)

Mehrabian, A., & Epstein, N. A measure of emotional empathy. *Journal of Personality,* 1972, *40,* 525–543.

Mehrabian, A., & Ksionzky, S. *A theory of affiliation.* Lexington, Mass.: D.C. Heath, 1974.

Mehrabian, A., & Russell, J. A. A measure of arousal seeking tendency. *Environment and Behavior,* 1973, *5,* 315–333.

Mehrabian, A., & Russell, J. A. *An approach to environmental psychology.* Cambridge, Mass.: M.I.T. Press, 1974. (a)

Mehrabian, A., & Russell, J. A. A verbal measure of information rate for studies in environmental psychology. *Environment and Behavior*, 1974, *6*, 233–252. (b)

Mehrabian, A., & Russell, J. A. The basic emotional impact of environments. *Perceptual and Motor Skills*, 1974, *38*, 283–301. (c)

Mehrabian, A., & Russell, J. A. Environmental effects on affiliation among strangers. *Humanitas*, 1975, *11*, 219–230. (a)

Mehrabian, A., & Russell, J. A. The mediating role of emotions in environmental psychology. In C. S. Richards (Chair), *Psychology and the environment in the 1980s*. Symposium presented at the University of Missouri, Columbia, Missouri, 1975. (b)

Mehrabian, A., & Williams, M. Nonverbal concomitants of perceived and intended persuasiveness. *Journal of Personality and Social Psychology*, 1969, *13*, 37–58.

Mendelson, J. H. Alcohol. In W. G. Clark & J. del Giudice (Eds.), *Principles of psychopharmacology*. New York: Academic Press, 1970. Pp. 505–516.

Moore, O. K. The responsive environments laboratory. In B. Gross & R. Gross (Eds.), *Radical school reform*. New York: Simon & Schuster, 1969.

Moos, R. H., & Insel, P. M. (Eds.). *Issues in social ecology*. Palo Alto, Calif.: National Press Books, 1974.

Morehouse, L. E., & Gross, L. *Total fitness in 30 minutes a week*. New York: Simon & Schuster, 1975.

Moriarty, B. M. Socioeconomic status and residential location choice. *Environment and Behavior*, 1974, *6*, 448–469.

Munsinger, H., & Kessen, W. Uncertainty, structure, and preference. *Psychological Monographs*, 1964, *78*(9, Whole No. 586).

Murdock, B. B., Jr. The serial position effect in free recall. *Journal of Experimental Psychology*, 1962, *64*, 482–488.

Nebylitsyn, V. D. *Fundamental properties of the human nervous system*. New York: Plenum, 1972.

Nebylitsyn, V. D., & Gray, J. A. (Eds.). *Biological bases of individual behavior*. New York: Academic Press, 1972.

Nesbitt, P. D. Smoking, physiological arousal, and emotional response. *Journal of Personality and Social Psychology*, 1973, *25*, 137–144.

Newcomb, T. M. *The acquaintance process*. New York: Holt, Rinehart and Winston, 1961.

Newman, O. *Defensible space*. New York: Macmillan, 1972.

Nichols, K. A., & Champness, B. G. Eye gaze and the GSR. *Journal of Experimental Social Psychology*, 1971, *7*, 623–626.

Opler, M. K. Cultural induction of stress. In M. H. Appley & R. Trumbull (Eds.), *Psychological stress*. New York: Appleton-Century-Crofts, 1967. Pp. 209–241.

Osgood, C. E. The cross-cultural generality of visual-verbal synesthetic tendencies. *Behavioral Science*, 1960, *5*, 146–169.

Osgood, C. E., Suci, G. J., & Tannenbaum, P. H. *The measurement of meaning*. Urbana: University of Illinois Press, 1957.

Osmond, H. Function as the basis of psychiatric ward design. *Mental Hospitals*, 1957, *8*, 23–32.

Osmond, H. The relationship between architect and psychiatrist. In C. Goshen (Ed.), *Psychiatric architecture*. Washington, D.C.: American Psychiatric Association, 1959.

Postman, L., & Phillips, L. W. Short term temporal changes in free recall. *Quarterly Journal of Experimental Psychology*, 1965, *17*, 132–138.

Proshansky, H. M., Ittelson, W. H., & Rivlin, L. G. (Eds.). *Environmental psychology: Man and his physical setting*. New York: Holt, Rinehart and Winston, 1970.

Provins, K. A. Environmental heat, body temperature and behavior: An hypothesis. *Australian Journal of Psychology*, 1966, *18*, 118–129.

Rahe, R. H. Life crisis and health change. In P. R. May & J. R. Wittenborn (Eds.), *Psychotropic drug response*. Springfield, Ill.: Charles C. Thomas, 1969. Pp. 92–125.

Rahe, R. H. Subjects' recent life changes and their near future illness reports. *Annals of Clinical Research*, 1972, *4*, 1–16.

Reich, W. *Character analysis*. New York: Orgone Institute Press, 1945.

Rheingold, H. L. The modification of social responsiveness in institutional babies. *Monographs of the Society for Research in Child Development*, 1956, *21*(2, Serial No. 63).

Rieber, M. The effect of music on the activity level of children. *Psychonomic Science*, 1965, *3*, 325–326.

Robinson, D. E. Style changes: cyclical, inexorable, and foreseeable. *Harvard Business Review*, 1975, *53*, 121–131.

Roethlisberger, F. J., & Dickson, W. J. *Management and the worker*. Cambridge, Mass.: Harvard University Press, 1939.

Ross, M., & Mehrabian, A. Quality of life change and individual differences in stimulus screening in relation to illness incidence. Unpublished manuscript, UCLA, 1976.

Russell, J. A., & Mehrabian, A. Distinguishing anger and anxiety in terms of emotional response factors. *Journal of Consulting and Clinical Psychology*, 1974, *42*, 79–83.

Russell, J. A., and Mehrabian, A. Task, setting, and personality variables affecting the desire to work. *Journal of Applied Psychology*, 1975, *60*, 518–520. (a)

Russell, J. A., & Mehrabian, A. The mediating role of emotions in alcohol use. *Journal of Studies on Alcohol*, 1975, *36*, 1508–1536. (b)

Russell, J. A., & Mehrabian, A. Some behavioral effects of the physical environment. In S. Wapner, S. Cohen, & B. Kaplan (Eds.), *Experiencing the environment*. New York: Plenum, 1976, pp. 5–18. (a)

Russell, J. A., & Mehrabian, A. Approach-avoidance and affiliation as functions of the emotion-eliciting quality of an environment. *Environment and Behavior*, 1976. (b)

Russell, J. A., & Mehrabian, A. Environmental effects on drug use. Unpublished manuscript, UCLA, 1976. (c)

Russell, J. A., & Mehrabian, A. Evidence for a three-factor theory of emotions. *Journal of Research in Personality*. 1976. (d)

Russell, J. A., & Mehrabian, A. Environmental, task, and temperamental effects on work performance. Unpublished manuscript, UCLA, 1976. (e)

Russell, J. A., & Mehrabian, A. Environmental variables in consumer research. *Journal of Consumer Research*, 1976. (f)

Schachter, S., & Rodin, J. *Obese humans and rats.* New York: Halsted, 1974.

Schmitt, R. C. Density, delinquency and crime in Honolulu. *Sociology and Social Research*, 1957, *41*, 274–276.

Schmitt, R. C. Implications of density in Hong Kong. *Journal of the American Institute of Planners*, 1963, *29*, 210–217.

Selye, H. *The stress of life.* New York: McGraw-Hill, 1956.

Shostrom, E. L. Group therapy. Let the buyer beware. *Psychology Today*, 1969, *2*, 39–40.

Siddle, D. A. T., & Mangan, G. L. Arousability and individual differences in resistance to distraction. *Journal of Experimental Research in Personality*, 1971, *5*, 295–303.

Siegel, R. K. Studies of hallucinogens in fish, birds, mice and men. In O. Vinar, Z. Votava, & P. B. Bradley (Eds.), *Advances in neuropsychopharmacology.* Amsterdam: North Holland Publishing Company, 1971.

Smith, P. C., & Curnow, R. "Arousal hypothesis" and the effects of music on purchasing behavior. *Journal of Applied Psychology*, 1966, *50*, 255–256.

Snider, J. G., & Osgood, C. E. (Eds.). *Semantic differential technique.* Chicago: Aldine, 1969.

Snyder, F. The physiology of dreaming. *Behavioral Science*, 1971, *16*, 31–44.

Soleri, P. *Arcology: The city in the image of man.* Cambridge, Mass.: M.I.T. Press, 1969.

Solomon, P., Leiderman, P. H., Mendelson, J., & Wexler, D. Sensory deprivation: A review. *American Journal of Psychiatry*, 1957, *114*, 357–363.

Sommer, R. *Personal space.* Englewood Cliffs, N.J.: Prentice-Hall, 1969.

Sommer, R. *Design awareness.* San Francisco: Rinehart, 1972.

Srivastava, R. K., & Good, L. R. *St. Margaret's Park public housing project, an environmental and behavioral profile.* Topeka, Kan.: Environmental Research Foundation, 1969.

Srivastava, R. K., & Peel, T. S. *Human movement as a function of color stimulation.* Topeka, Kan.: Environmental Research Foundation, 1968.

Stokols, D., Rall, M., Pinner, B., & Schopler, J. Physical, social, and personal determinants of the perception of crowding. *Environment and Behavior*, 1973, *5*, 87–115.

Taylor, F. W. *Principles of scientific management.* New York: Harper, 1911.

The University of Chicago School Review, 1974, *82*(4), entire issue.

Toffler, A. *Future shock.* New York: Random House, 1970.

Valentine, C. W. *The experimental psychology of beauty.* New York: Barnes & Noble, 1968.

Van der Ryn, S., & Silverstein, M. *Dorms at Berkeley: An environmental analysis*. Berkeley, Calif.: Center for Planning and Development Research, 1967.

Wells, B. W. P. The psycho-social influence of building environment. Socio-metric findings in large and small office spaces. *Building Science*, 1965, 1, 153–165.

Wells, B. W. P. Psychological concepts of office design. In C. W. Taylor, R. Bailey, & C. H. H. Branch (Eds.), *Second national conference on architectural psychology*. Salt Lake City: University of Utah, 1967, Pp. 1–27.

Wheeler, L. Toward a theory of behavioral contagion. *Psychological Review*, 1966, 73, 179–192.

White, B. L., & Held, R. Plasticity of sensorimotor development in the human infant. In J. F. Rosenblith & W. Allinsmith (Eds.), *Causes of behavior II*. Boston: Allyn & Bacon, 1966.

Wicker, T. *A time to die*. New York: New York Times Book Co., 1975.

Wilner, D. M., Walkley, R. P., & Cook, S. W. *Human relations in interracial housing*. Minneapolis: University of Minnesota Press, 1955.

Wilner, D. M., Walkley, R. P., Pinkerton, T. C., & Tayback, M. *The housing environment and family life: A longitudinal study of the effects of housing on morbidity and mental health*. Baltimore: Johns Hopkins Press, 1962.

Winsborough, H. H. The social consequences of high population density. *Law and Contemporary Problems*, 1965, 30, 120–126.

Wohlwill, J. F., & Carson, D. H. (Eds.). *Environment and the social sciences: Perspectives and applications*. Washington, D.C.: American Psychological Association, 1972.

Woods, J. H., & Downs, D. A. The psychopharmacology of cocaine. In the *Marijuana commission second report on marijuana and drug abuse* (Vol. 1). Washington, D.C.: U.S. Government Printing Office, 1973. Pp. 116–139.

Zajonc, R. B. Social facilitation. *Science*, 1965, 149, 269–274.

Zajonc, R. B. Attitudinal effects of mere exposure. *Journal of Personality and Social Psychology Monograph*, 1968, 9(2, Pt. 1).

Zehner, R. B. Neighborhood and community satisfaction in new towns and less planned suburbs. *Journal of the American Institute of Planners*, 1971, 37, 379–385.

Zigler, C., & Phillips, L. Social competence and the process-reactive distinction in schizophrenia. *Journal of Abnormal and Social Psychology*, 1962, 65, 215–222.

Zimbardo, P. The human choice: Individuation, reason and order versus deindividuation, impulse and chaos. In W. J. Arnold & D. Levine (Eds.), *Nebraska Symposium on Motivation* (Vol. 17). Lincoln: University of Nebraska Press, 1969.

Zimny, G. H., & Weidenfeller, E. W. Effects of music upon GSR of children. *Child Development*, 1962, 33, 891–896.

Zubek, J. P. Effects of prolonged sensory and perceptual deprivation. *British Medical Bulletin*, 1964, 20, 38–42.

INDEX

Index